Grazie Sisla

Which European Union?

Sergio Fabbrini explains that the European Union (EU) is made up of member states pursuing different aims, rather than simply moving in the same direction at different speeds. He describes the alternative perspectives on the EU (an economic community, an intergovernmental union and a parliamentary union) that led to multiple compromises in its structure and shows how the euro crisis has called them into question. The book argues that a new European political order is necessary to deal with the consequences of the crisis. It should be based on an institutional differentiation between member states interested only in market cooperation and those advancing towards a genuine economic and monetary union. Such a differentiation would allow the latter group to recompose their (intergovernmental and parliamentary) perspectives into an original model of political union, here conceptualized as a compound union of states and citizens. At the same time, a revised framework of the single market, where all European states can participate, should be agreed.

SERGIO FABBRINI is Director of the School of Government and Professor of Political Science and International Relations at the LUISS Guido Carli University of Rome, where he holds the Jean Monnet Chair. He is also Recurrent Visiting Professor of Comparative Politics at the Department of Political Science and Institute of Governmental Studies, University of California at Berkeley. He has published fourteen books, two co-authored books and fourteen edited or co-edited books. His most recent publications in English include *Compound Democracies: Why the United States and Europe Are Becoming Similar*, 2nd edn (2010) and *America and Its Critics: Vices and Virtues of the Democratic Hyperpower* (2008).

Which European Union?

Europe after the Euro Crisis

SERGIO FABBRINI

CAMBRIDGE
UNIVERSITY PRESS

CAMBRIDGE
UNIVERSITY PRESS

University Printing House, Cambridge CB2 8BS, United Kingdom

Cambridge University Press is part of the University of Cambridge.

It furthers the University's mission by disseminating knowledge in the pursuit of education, learning and research at the highest international levels of excellence.

www.cambridge.org
Information on this title: www.cambridge.org/9781107503977

© Sergio Fabbrini 2015

First published 2015

A catalogue record for this publication is available from the British Library

Library of Congress Cataloguing in Publication data
Fabbrini, Sergio.
Which European Union? : Europe after the Euro crisis / Sergio Fabbrini.
    pages   cm
Includes bibliographical references and index.
ISBN 978-1-107-10394-8 (hardback)
1. European Union.   I. Title.
JN30.F32 2015
341.242′2–dc23
2014043723

ISBN 978-1-107-10394-8 Hardback
ISBN 978-1-107-50397-7 Paperback

Contents

Boxes

Figures

Tables

Abbreviations

ABAC	APEC Business Advisory Committee
ALDE	Alliance of Liberals and Democrats for Europe
APEC	Asia-Pacific Economic Cooperation
ARF	ASEAN Regional Forum
ASEAN	Association of Southeast Asian Nations
Benelux	Belgium, the Netherlands and Luxembourg
BRD	Bundesrepublik Deutschland
BRRD	Bank Recovery and Resolution Directive
BVerfG	Bundesverfassungsgericht
CDU	Christian Democratic Union (Germany)
CENTO	Central Treaty Organization
CFSP	Common Foreign and Security Policy
CMC	Common Market Council (MERCOSUR)
CMG	Common Market Group (MERCOSUR)
COMECON	Council for Mutual Economic Assistance
COREPER	Committees of Permanent Representatives of the Member States
CP	comparative politics (approach)
CSU	Christian Social Union (Germany)
CT	Constitutional Treaty
CVP	Christian Democrats (Switzerland)
DDR	Deutsche Demokratische Republik
DGM	Deposit Guarantee Mechanism
EC	European Community
ECB	European Central Bank
ECJ	European Court of Justice
ECOFIN	The Council of the Economic and Financial Ministers
ECSC	European Coal and Steel Community
EDC	European Defence Community
EDP	Excessive Deficit Procedure
EEAS	European External Action Service

EEC	European Economic Community
EFSF	European Financial Stability Facility
EFSM	European Financial Stability Mechanism
EFTA	European Free Trade Association
EMS	European Monetary System
EMU	Economic and Monetary Union
EP	European Parliament
EPP	European People's Party
ESDP	European Security and Defence Policy
ESM	European Stability Mechanism
EU	European Union
EURATOM	European Atomic Energy Community
FDP	Free Democratic Party (Germany) or Free Democratic Party (Switzerland)
FTA	Free Trade Area
FTAA	Free Trade Area of the Americas
GDP	Gross Domestic Product
HR	High Representative of the Union for Foreign Affairs and Security Policy
IGA	intergovernmental agreement
IGC	intergovernmental conference
IR	international relations (approach)
JHA	Justice and Home Affairs
LAFTA/ALALC	Latin American Free Trade Association
LDP	Liberal Democratic Party (Japan)
MEPs	Members of the European Parliament
MERCOSUR	Mercado Común del Sur
MFF	Multiannual Financial Framework
NAFTA	North American Free Trade Agreement
NATO	North Atlantic Treaty Organization
NEG	Non Euro Group
PJCC	Police and Judicial Co-operation in Criminal Matters
PP	People's Party (Spain)
PS	Socialist Party (Portugal)
PSD	Social Democratic Party (Portugal)
PSOE	Socialist Party (Spain)
PR	proportional representation

PSC	Political and Security Committee
QMV	qualified majority voting
RQMV	reverse qualified majority voting
S&D	European Socialists and Democrats
SEA	Single European Act
SEATO	South-East Asia Treaty Organization
SGP	Stability and Growth Pact
SPD	Social Democratic Party (Germany)
SPS	Social Democrats (Switzerland)
SRF	Single Resolution Fund
SRM	Single Resolution Mechanism
SSM	Single Supervisory Mechanism
SVP	People's Party (Switzerland)
TEC	Treaty Establishing the European Community
TEU	Treaty on European Union
TFEU	Treaty on the Functioning of the European Union
UK	United Kingdom
UKIP	UK Independence Party
UN	United Nations
USA	United States of America
WTO	World Trade Organization

Preface – How many unions?

The book

Which European Union (EU)[1] is emerging from the euro crisis? The euro crisis has been a litmus test in terms of bringing the institutional properties of the EU to the surface. Those properties are the outcome of several compromises upon which the EU has been built. Those compromises reflected the different perspectives on the Union that have accompanied the latter's institutionalization as a political system. The EU has harbored more than one union within its legal and institutional order. The euro crisis has made the coexistence of those perspectives highly problematic, raising the necessity of thinking of a new political order in Europe.

The book is organized as follows. Part I identifies the institutional structure of the EU that has emerged from its multilinear institutionalization, showing how that structure reflects the interstate and political cleavages that have accompanied the formation of the EU as a political system. Part II discusses the different perspectives on the EU that have led to the numerous compromises upon which the EU has been built. I have defined them as the perspectives of *economic community*, *intergovernmental union* and *parliamentary union*. The euro crisis has shown their inadequacy both as descriptive and prescriptive interpretations of what the EU is and should become. Part III elaborates an alternative view on the EU's future through a comparative analysis of

---

[1] Even though the organization of the integration process has gone by different names over the years, as is customary in the international scientific debate, I use the terms European Union (EU) or Union to refer to its entire history, and not only to the period after the Treaty of Maastricht, which officially adopted the name. I use the lower case for "union" with reference to a given perspective. I have tried to make parsimonious use of capital letters, adopting them only for specific institutions and not for both their generic term or for the power holders exercising a specific role. I use the lower case also for "member state," contrary to EU official documents, and capitalize the names of political parties.

the models of democracy of nation states (both unitary and federal) and unions of states (such as the United States of America [USA] and Switzerland). I define as compound democracy (S. Fabbrini 2010) the democratic model of unions of states, in order to distinguish it from the models of competitive democracy and consensus democracy that characterize the democratic functioning of nation states (both unitary and federal). I argue (through the comparison of the USA and Switzerland) that the model of compound democracy, organized in a system of separate institutions sharing decision-making power, is the only suitable model for those federations constituted through the aggregation of previously independent states and politically characterized by inter-state cleavages. On these comparative bases, I identify the factors that have obstructed the EU from being a coherent compound union, concluding with the delineation of a strategy for promoting such a union in a European context of multiple unions. That strategy aims to create a political union around the euro-area member states, but keeping the single market as the inclusive framework for all the European states (both currently inside or outside the EU). In conclusion, the euro crisis has made dramatically manifest the paralyzing coexistence of the multiple perspectives within the same legal and institutional framework of the EU. To delineate a new political order for the multiplicity of perspectives on integration constitutes the historical challenge for European elites and citizens. The *Which European Union?* of the book's title alludes thus to both the plurality of perspectives that have accompanied the institutionalization of the EU and the challenge of finding a different institutional setting for organizing their relations in the post-euro crisis era.

The approach

The aims of the book will be pursued through a comparative institutional approach. I consider the EU a political system in its own right (Hix 2011; Hix and Hoyland 2011), comparable with established democratic political systems. The book adopts a comparative politics (CP) approach to the EU, rather than one of the mainstream approaches (neo-functionalism, liberal intergovernmentalism and constructivism: Leuffen, Rittberger and Schimmelfennig 2013) derived from the theories of international relations (IR). My research aims are not to explain the logic of integration, or to assess the role of national or supranational actors in driving the process of integration, or to evaluate the impact of ideational projects in constructing the strategies of those actors. Where necessary, I will rely on one or other of the mainstream IR approaches to describe aspects of the process of institutionalization of the EU, combining them in a pluralist manner. To conceptualize the EU as a political system raises, in fact, different research questions and implies the application of different tools and methods, in my case those elaborated by the historical-institutionalist school of comparative politics (for an overview, see Mahoney and Villegas 2007). This is why my comparative approach will focus on institutions (considered as both independent and dependent variables), on political cleavages underpinning those institutions and on critical junctures when the power relations within a given institutional structure are or might be redefined. The EU is a political system whose institutional structure generates regular decisions (authoritatively allocates values: Easton 1971) on the basis of power relations reflecting the political development of its constitutive cleavages (Rokkan 1999).

If the EU is a political system, then what kind of political system is it? I will argue that the EU that emerged from a long process of institutionalization belongs to the genus of federal political systems, representing, however, a specific species of the latter. My approach is based on the analytical distinction between federal states and federal unions, as the two main species of the genus of democratic federal political systems. I will conceptualize the EU as a *union of states and citizens* in order to stress its properties as a federal union, rather than as a federal state. Unions of states display basic properties that distinguish them from federal states: (1) they aggregate states that were previously independent for a sufficient period of time to develop distinct cultural attitudes, economic patterns and institutional settings; (2) they aggregate states that are asymmetrically correlated, where asymmetry concerns population size and material capability, but also culturally differentiated, where differentiation concerns a distinction of values, attitudes or languages; (3) they aggregate states that shared an experience of insecurity or a perception of an external or internal threat; (4) the aggregation implies the setting up of a center with delimited and controlled powers, to which significant decision-making autonomy recognized by each of the aggregated states corresponds. The USA and Switzerland are the only cases, within established democratic political systems, that were formed through the aggregation of previously independent states or cantons, respecting those properties and functioning (for a long time, in the case of the former) as federal unions.

These properties are foreign to federal states. In fact: (1) such states derive from the disaggregation of a previously unitary unit and tend to share a common political experience; (2) they are designed by a central political authority that tried to keep asymmetry and differentiation under control; (3) they result from the need to decentralize the exercise of power and not from the necessity to face an external or internal threat; (4) they retain significant decision-making resources in the center, since the latter is the institutional level where decentralization is negotiated and promoted. Once institutionalized, federal unions are driven by a political logic based on interstate, and not only partisan, cleavages, whereas federal states are mainly characterized by relations between established political parties representing economic or cultural cleavages. Both species of federal political system have required the existence of a constitution or fundamental law as a formal document for regulating the relations between the center and the units of the federal compact and between them and citizens. If the EU has structural similarities with federal unions (Nicolaidis and Howse 2001), its lack of such a document has given rise to important dissimilarities, however.

Assuming the EU to be a federal union makes it possible to innovate the comparative analytical framework elaborated by several scholars (from Hans Daalder to Arendt Lijphart) for classifying established political systems. That typology is based on analytical units corresponding to nation states. It must therefore be redefined in order to also classify the democratic model of unions of states. Finally, this comparative approach necessarily calls into question the *sui generis* interpretation or perception of the EU, as an idea of some kind of European exceptionalism, shared by functionaries and politicians operating in Brussels. In a speech given at the Humboldt University of Berlin on May 9, 2011, Michel Barnier, then European commissioner for the internal market and services, echoed this view, asserting that the EU "is unique in history and in the world." The view that the EU is an exceptional political system, unprecedented due to "its unique institutional nature" (Orbie 2009: 2), "different to pre-existing political forms (because of) its historical context, hybrid polity and political-legal constitution" (Manners 2002: 240–2), is also shared by scholars and not only practitioners. The EU model "is acknowledged to be *sui generis*, a product of the historical, political, and social conditions of a time and a place" (Farrell 2007: 305). It is certainly true that there are no other experiences of deep-rooted nation states deciding to aggregate around a common project, as happens in post-Second World War Europe (Weiler 2000). Analytically, however, the aggregation of previously independent territorial units is not only an EU experience. In short, considering the EU as a political system, with properties of a federal union, makes it not only possible to understand its structure and logic of functioning, but also to identify testable hypotheses on its future.

The concept

In the EU experience, the very concept of *union* was formally used for the first time in the preamble of the 1957 Rome Treaty establishing the European Economic Community (EEC), when the signatory states expressed their determination "to lay the foundations of an ever-closer union among the peoples of Europe." This concept was then strengthened in the 1992 Maastricht Treaty or Treaty on European Union (TEU), when the signatory states reaffirmed in the Treaty's preamble their resolution "to continue the process of creating an ever closer union among the peoples of Europe." Since then, union is the term used to conceptualize the organizational form assumed by the changing outcome of the European integration process.

The union concept derives from a well-established theoretical tradition. According to the classic definition by Forsyth (1981:1), a union of states might be considered a genus to which belong or belonged different species of relationships that states establish or established among themselves, such as: "confederacy, confederation, union, federal union, federal government, system of states, community, perpetual league, *république fédérative, Staatenbund Bund, Eidgenossenschaft*"(Forsyth 1981:1, original emphasis). These species have in common two properties. First, they fall "short of a complete fusion or incorporation in which one or all the members lose their identity as states." Second, they represent "a union which is specifically 'federal' in nature. This means that it is based on a *foedus* or treaty between states and not on a purely one-sided assertion of will." For Elazar (1987), the union of states is instead a species of a genus conceptualized as a federal political system. The latter is a form of political organization encompassing a variety of species, such as

unions, constitutionally decentralized unions, federations, confederations, federacies, associated states, condominiums, leagues and joint
functional authorities. However, in the European context, where federalism has been traditionally associated with stateness, the distinctive types of organization connected to the concept of federal political
system are missing. If federalism is a territorial system for organizing public authority combining "shared government (for specified
common purposes) with autonomous action by constituent units of
government that maintain their identity and distinctiveness" (Watts
1998: 118), that is a system combining shared rule and self-rule, then
not only can that combination take on different vertical arrangements
that are not necessarily coherent with the idea of stateness (as argued
by the above literature), but it also says nothing regarding the specific governmental organization of the horizontal level of the federal
system. Those differences have to do with the genesis of the federal
political system and the consequential path-dependence logic that has
come to be institutionalized.

This is why, simplifying the typologies elaborated by the scholars
of federalism, one can conceptualize two basic species of *democratic*
federal political system: federal political systems formed through the
aggregation of previously independent states and federal political systems formed through the disaggregation of a previously unitary or
centralized state. The former started as *federal unions* and the latter
as *federal states*. Although the historical process has made them somehow convergent, in federal unions the institutional arrangements for
self-rule (confederacy) are as significant as those for shared rule (fed-
eracy), whereas in federal states the latter are much stronger than the
former (McKay 2001). This means that in federal unions, at the vertical level, territorial units enjoy much more autonomy from the center
than in federal states. At the same time, at the horizontal level federal
unions, contrary to federal states, have tried to prevent the centralization of power by adopting a governmental model that disperses
decision-making resources.

As the comparative analysis indicates, two different arrangements
for organizing the governmental level of the federal center have been
pursued in democracies, one based on the *fusion of powers* and the
other on their *separation*. Interestingly enough, the former has been
adopted by all the federal states, that is federations formed through
the disaggregation of a previously unitary or centralized state, besides

the other unitary states, whereas the latter has been adopted by the two empirical federal unions in the democratic world, the USA and Switzerland, that is federations formed through the aggregation of previously independent states or cantons (Sbragia 1992). Thus federations as federal unions have not only preserved powerful confederal properties at the vertical level, they have also separated the governmental power at the horizontal level in order to prevent the formation of a powerful or unchecked federal center. The opposite has happened in federations as federal states: here the confederal properties are weak at the vertical level, and a fused structure supports the decision-making power at the horizontal level. If what Habermas (2012a: 32, author's emphasis) argued is true, namely that "today all federations have adapted themselves *more or less* to the nation state model; the United States, too, has become a federal state at the latest since the end of the Second World War," it is also true that such adaptation has varied significantly ("more or less"). Since federalism concerns the distribution of powers between the center and the units of the system, and within each of them, then the logic of forming the federation has had an inevitable impact on the distribution of those decision-making powers or policy competences.

The main impact has been at the horizontal level. If federal states *have a government as* a *single institution* monopolizing the ultimate decision-making power, federal unions *do not have a government as a single institution*, but take decisions through separate institutions sharing power, each one having a voice in the decision-making process. The latter's very complex system is the outcome of a systemic need unknown to the federal states that emerge from the disaggregation of previously unitary nation states (as is the case of all other democratic federalisms), namely to keep on board or to aggregate states of different sizes, with different cultural identities and distinct democratic expectations. This is why federal unions combine federal and confederal relations at the territorial (vertical) level and separation of powers at the governmental (horizontal) level. They are open systems based (institutionally) on multiple (horizontal and vertical) separations of powers and (politically) by interstate cleavages and rivalries (although intertwined with partisan divisions). It is thus analytically necessary not to confuse the two types of federal political systems.

The concept of union of states and citizens seems appropriate for the conceptualization of the EU because, being the outcome of the aggregation of previously separated states, it is closer to a federal union than to a federal state. The concept of a union of states not only corresponds to the self-definition of the EU, but it also captures the latter's unresolved nature. The EU is a union because it has the basic properties of a federation formed through the aggregation of previously independent states, but at the same time it differs from the other federal unions because it operates according to a plurality of different decision-making regimes that would be unlikely in those federal unions. In fact, if the latter has a formal constitution that gives order to the functioning of their political system, in the EU, on the contrary, the aggregation has been empirically constitutionalized by the decisions of the European Court of Justice (ECJ). To be sure, the process of constitutionalization has transformed European nation states (with a few exceptions among established democracies, such as Norway and Switzerland) into *member states* of the EU (Sbragia 1994). However, that process of constitutionalization has not led those member states to share a common sense of the finality of the Union. Under the shadow of the process of material constitutionalization, deep constitutional divisions between member states and their citizens have continued to emerge.

Indeed, I conceptualize those divisions in terms of alternative perspectives on the EU, each one based on a reading of *what the EU is* and/or reflecting a view of *what the EU should become*. By perspective I mean a general outlook, utilized by groups of member states and citizens, on the current functioning or future development (*finalité*) of the union, a view that necessarily combines description and prescription. The process of integration has been based on *more than one union*, rather than on *more than one speed*. This book shows that different perspectives on the EU have accompanied the latter's process of institutionalization, a coexistence then destabilized by the euro crisis. The crisis of the euro has indeed become the crisis of the Union. After all, comparative analysis indicates that unions of states can deal with internal or external threats only by relying on a formal constitutional document congealing shared preferences on how to regulate relations between states and citizens – a possibility excluded in the case of the EU. Having defined the structure, the approach and the concept, let us now consider the book's organization in more detail.

The political system

Part I starts from the reconstruction of the process of institutionalization that transformed the European Economic Community (EEC) set
up by the 1957 Rome Treaty into a European Union through the 1992
Maastricht Treaty (Chapter 1). Although the story is known, the conceptualization is not. I look at the institutional outcomes of the institutionalization process, not at its logic. And I interpret those outcomes
as compromises through which the political system of the EU has been
institutionalized. At the origins of the integration process there was the
critical juncture that started with the post-Second World War radical
redefinition of power relations between nation states on the European
continent. A critical juncture is a historical moment when actors with
decision-making power can pursue potentially alternative courses
of action because of the de-structuring of the previous context. The
post-war critical juncture was initially used by the governmental leaders of the main European continental countries (France and Germany
in particular) to promote a federal project through the setting up of
two highly supranational organizations, the European Coal and Steel
Community or ECSC and the European Defence Community or EDC.
Both Treaties were signed in Paris, the first in 1951 (thus approved
in 1952 by the signatory states' legislatures) and the second in 1952,
by the six states that were at the origin of the process of integration
(France, Germany, Italy, Belgium, the Netherlands and Luxembourg).

The failure of the EDC to be approved by the French legislature
in 1954 led the governmental leaders of those states to pursue the
integration of the continent through economic means – the formation of a common market, of which the EEC Treaty was the epitome.
That decision closed the long post-war reassessment of power between
European states, inaugurating a new institutional path. The long process of institutionalization from 1957 to 1992 led to the formation of
a supranational organization dealing with common and then (with the
Single European Act or SEA of 1986) single market policies. The ECJ
gradually constitutionalized the common market, creating a de facto
supranational constitution out of the EEC and SEA Treaties, defining
the powers of member states' governments and the Union's institutions and their reciprocal relations. The supranational evolution of
the Union has been the outcome of the combination of both intergovernmental decisions (as conceptualized by the intergovernmental

school: Moravcsik 1998) and the behavior of the Union's actors in
dealing with the contradictions and spillovers of collective action (as
conceptualized by the neo-functional school: Borzel 2006; Haas 1958),
under the impulse of specific actors and their ideas (as conceptualized
by the constructivist school: Parsons 2003). In Maastricht, however,
this process was substantially altered.

The Maastricht Treaty of 1992 constitutes a crucial turning point
in the institutional trajectory of the integration process. With the
end of the Cold War and the reunification of Germany between
1989 and 1991, the project of integration faced a second critical
juncture, because of the formation of a new scenario that raised
unexpected challenges. In the Union's case, those challenges consisted in the necessity to also extend the integration process to policies that were traditionally at the core of national sovereignty, such
as (inter alia) foreign and security policies and economic and monetary policies. The new critical juncture opened up the possibility, for
national government leaders participating in the debate and draft-
ing the new Treaty, to bring those policies either within the supranational framework that had emerged since the Rome Treaty or to
devise a brand new framework to Europeanize them. At the end,
the latter institutional path was taken, with the formalization of an
intergovernmental constitution, alongside the supranational one, to
deal with nationally sensitive policies. In particular, in Maastricht it
was decided to set up the Economic and Monetary Union (EMU –
see Chapter 1).

In the Treaty's preamble, the signatory states assert their resolution "to achieve the strengthening and the convergence of their
economies and to establish an economic and monetary union
including, in accordance with the provisions of this Treaty, a single and stable currency." The EMU was based on the combination
of a supranational institution (the European Central Bank or ECB)
exclusively in charge of monetary policy and intergovernmental
institutions (the Council of the Economic and Financial Ministers
or ECOFIN and the informal European Council of the heads of
state and government of the member states) coordinating nationally
decentralized economic policies. At the same time, the policies of the
common and then single market continued to be managed through
the supranational framework (inclusive of both supranational institutions such as the Commission and the European Parliament or EP

and intergovernmental institutions such as the Council of Ministers). This was the main Maastricht compromise, which was confirmed through the Lisbon Treaty. The latter has thus formalized that compromise, creating a dual constitution, one intergovernmental and the other supranational.

When the euro crisis exploded, therefore, there was already in place an intergovernmental constitution to frame the policies for dealing with it. Although the euro crisis opened a third critical juncture where it was possible to redefine the institutional and policy features of the EU, its dramatic and accelerated impact has ended up reinforcing the path-dependence logic generated by the previous constitutional settlement. Indeed, the Lisbon Treaty's allocation of economic policy responsibility favored institutional and policy answers to the crisis that have increased the decision-making power of national governments coordinating within the intergovernmental institutions (of the European Council and the Council of Ministers), to the detriment of the Union's actors operating in the supranational institutions (such as the Commission and the EP). Chapter 2 shows the dramatic institutional transformation of the EU induced by the euro crisis. During the crisis the supranational constitution has not been marginalized. Important legislative measures have been taken through the co-decision of the Council and the European Parliament, with an important role played by the Commission. However, the crisis has led to a strengthening of the intergovernmental institutions, in particular through the approval of new intergovernmental treaties and interstate pacts. This has led to an alteration of the constitutional equilibrium formalized in the Lisbon Treaty.

The euro crisis has called into question the multiple compromises that have tried to accommodate the various perspectives on the Union within the same legal and institutional framework. It has not only increased the distance, as in the past, between euro-area member states and those outside it, but it has also deepened the differences of perspective among the euro-area member states. In short, the euro crisis has brought to the surface the divisions that emerged during the process of institutionalizing the EU, and that exploded in the constitutional decade of the 2000s (as discussed in Chapter 3) concerning what the EU *has become* and/or *should become*. Those divisions can be conceptualized in competing perspectives on the EU that have come to clash during the euro crisis.

The perspectives

Part II reconstructs and then critically discusses the main perspectives on the EU. Chapter 4 deals with the view held by a small number of member states (such as the United Kingdom or UK in particular) that interpret the EU as an *economic community*. Although the concept of the EU as a *political union* started to be formally used only at the end of the 1980s, the promise of pursuing an "ever-closer union" is at the origins of the integration process.

The view of the EU as an *economic community* has, nevertheless, accompanied the process of integration, in particular since the first enlargement of 1973. Indeed, the supporters of the economic community perspective have managed to carve out their view within the various treaties, through effective devices such as opt-outs from basic policy frameworks and institutional regimes. Chapter 4 critically tests the interpretation of the EU as an economic community through a comparison with the main regional economic organizations operating on the global market (Asia-Pacific Economic Cooperation or APEC, Association of Southeast Asian Nations or ASEAN, Mercado Común del Sur or MERCOSUR, North American Free Trade Agreement or NAFTA). The comparison shows, first, that the EU, also as a single market, has reached a level of integration that makes it qualitatively different from the other regional economic organizations; and, second, that the EU, also in its intergovernmental aspect, cannot be equated to any of those regional economic organizations. Concerning both its nature and its structure, therefore, the EU cannot be considered part of a continuum with those regional organizations of economic cooperation. Whatever aspect is considered, the EU is at odds with the economic community perspective entertained by some member states and citizens. But if the EU is more than an economic community, what kind of union is it or might it become?

Two other alternative perspectives have continued to emerge from the debate. Both claim to have a political view on the EU, although of a significantly different nature. Since the negotiations that led to the 1992 Maastricht Treaty, those two perspectives have contrasted each other. One is the perspective of *intergovernmental union* and the other of *parliamentary union*. As discussed in Chapter 5, for the supporters of intergovernmental union, the EU is not simply an organization constituted by several single national governments and functioning according to their will, but it is an organization structured around the intergovernmental institutions (of the European Council and the Council) representing national governments as a collective. It is these intergovernmental institutions, not the single national governments, that constitute the engine and the rudder of the integration process. This perspective on the EU was first officialized in the 1992 Maastricht Treaty and became politically important after the failure of the Constitutional Treaty (CT) in popular referenda in France and the Netherlands in 2005, to then become predominant during the post-2009 euro crisis. The intergovernmental union should not be confused with the economic community perspective. Whereas the latter's supporters have called for national control of policies traditionally at the core of member states' sovereignty (such as foreign and defense policies or economic and financial policies), the former's supporters have accepted bringing coordination on those policies to Brussels, on the condition, however, that they remain under their collective control as exercised through the intergovernmental institutions of the EU. Indeed, they have even agreed to give control of monetary policy over the common currency to a supranational (although technocratic) institution such as the ECB. It is certainly true that occasionally supporters of the economic community have come to coalesce with those promoting the intergovernmental union, thus presenting a common front against the backers of an EU that should become a parliamentary federation. However, it would be best not to confuse the two perspectives, because they differ on the finality of the Union and on the institutional arrangements for achieving it. Contrary to the supporters of the EU as a market regime based on *interstate cooperation*, the intergovernmental union is a political project based on *institutionalized coordination* of national governments. Having a common enemy does not mean they are friends.

The supporters of intergovernmental union, contrary to those favoring the economic community perspective, have thus recognized the necessity to increase the coordination of (and not just cooperation on) crucial policies in Brussels. In the case of the EU, the conceptual distinction between cooperation and coordination is crucial for understanding the two different perspectives. Cooperation represents a loose, flexible and unconstrained form of collective action, as aimed at by the supporters of the economic community view, in order to deal with selected problems. Coordination, on the contrary, implies an institutionalized form of interaction between governments in order to decide collectively on a growing range of policies. Indeed, institutionalized coordination constitutes the organizational form of the constitutional principle implicit in the intergovernmental union view, namely the *pooling of national sovereignties* (as a distinct principle from the *sharing of national sovereignties* inspiring the common market policies of the supranational constitution). Chapter 5 reconstructs the response to the euro crisis provided by the intergovernmental union. When the crisis exploded, the EU had just put the Lisbon Treaty into force with its dual constitution. The dual constitution provided the intergovernmental union with the rationale and institutions to handle economic policy. Although the EU has had to deal with financial turmoil of unprecedented magnitude that might have justified new institutional directions, the intergovernmental constitution has been reinforced, notwithstanding its unsatisfactory performance. The euro crisis, in fact, has falsified the intergovernmental decision-making regime in economic policy, showing its systemic difficulty in solving basic problems of collective action (a difficulty not experienced by the supranational but technocratic ECB in monetary policy) and to meet basic criteria of democratic legitimacy (that the ECB is not required to respect). Over the course of the crisis, the intergovernmental union has been transformed so deeply that a highly centralized, intrusive and convoluted organization has grown up in the euro-area, with no counterpart in other federal unions. The basic vulnerability of the intergovernmental union has been in the assumption that the EU can do without a distinction between institutions and functions, so as to make the process of government comply with the basic democratic criteria, as at the national level. The euro crisis has unmasked the idea of an intergovernmental union legitimized mainly by its policy capabilities.

Chapter 6 addresses the alternative political view, the *parliamentary union* perspective. The latter's supporters aim to transform the EU into a coherent parliamentary federation, an organization centered on the decision-making role of the EP and the Commission. As in national parliamentary systems, here the effectiveness and legitimacy of the union are ensured through the activation of a political relationship between the executive and the popular legislature. Chapter 6 discusses this perspective critically. Politically, the euro crisis has shown the persistence and importance of the interstate cleavages

(Northern vs. Southern member states), whereas the EP–Commission relationship can manage mainly partisan cleavages (left vs. right). Systemically, the EU would find it difficult to become a parliamentary federation because of the deep demographic asymmetries and cultural differences among its member states. The European Council and the Council cannot be relegated to a redundant role in the EU. The EP–Commission relationship cannot accommodate the necessary decision-making role of the national governments, if the EU must remain a union of states and not only citizens. Whereas the intergovernmental union relies on the predominant decision-making role of the European Council and Council, allowing legitimacy to be mainly institutionalized at the national level, the parliamentary union stresses the predominant decision-making role of the EP and the Commission, thus bringing legitimacy at the level where decisions are taken. Each perspective misses a crucial point: the former underestimates the role of the EP (and downsizes the role of the Commission and the ECJ); the latter underestimates the role of national governments operating within the intergovernmental institutions of the European Council and Council.

The future

Part III is devoted to constructing an analytical framework to develop an alternative perspective on the EU. Chapter 7 starts by developing a comparative analysis of established democracies, in order to highlight the institutional and political differences between the democracy of (unitary and federal) nation states and the democracy of unions of states. This comparative reconceptualization of established political systems allows the distinguishing, on one side, of the competitive or consensual democratic models organizing the functioning of nation states and, on the other side, the specific compound democratic model presiding over the functioning of unions of states (such as the USA and Switzerland).

Chapter 8 then develops a comparative analysis of the US and Swiss compound unions and the EU in order to delineate similarities and differences between them. This analytical exercise permits a better definition of the empirical concept of compound union. A compound union is a federal union formed through the aggregation of previously independent states that functions according to a democratic logic based on interstate more than partisan cleavages. The supranational EU can be properly considered in that comparative context, although its intergovernmental side contradicts its functioning according to the model of a compound democracy. If the USA and Switzerland are compound unions functioning according to a democratic model based on negotiations and conflicts between separate institutions rather or more than on competition or consociation between political parties as in the established (unitary or federal) nation states, the same cannot be fully said of the EU. The tension between the intergovernmental and supranational sides of the EU, hardened by the euro crisis, has obfuscated the democratic model of the EU. Chapter 8 identifies the crucial dilemmas of inter-institutional relations that, if solved, would recompose the intergovernmental and parliamentary unions in the comprehensive model of an original European compound union. Chapter 9 then builds on the analytical insights of the comparison developed in the two previous chapters to identify the conditions of a compound union. The institutional architecture of a compound union should be based on the principle of (vertical and horizontal) separation of powers as the only institutional principle that can accommodate the demographic asymmetry and cultural difference between member states. Through separation of powers between governmental levels and institutions, a union of states is able both to take decisions without setting up centralized arrangements and to legitimize those decisions without implying the pre-existence of a homogeneous European demos. I would argue that Jacques Delors' proposal of a "European federation of nation states"[2] (Ricard-Nihoul 2012) reflects the same necessity of recomposing the two unions, although Delors' formula does not deal with the constitutional and institutional conditions that might make that "federation" possible.

Chapter 9 finally discusses how the compound union proposal can be implemented in the European context of multiple union projects. If it is true that the multiple divisions that emerged during the integration process, and deepened during the course of the euro crisis, have prevented the various perspectives from developing coherently, then the

[2] This proposal was recalled by the then President of the Commission Manuel Barroso in his "State of the Union address" given on September 12, 2012 ("Let's not be afraid of the word: we will need to move towards a federation of nation states ... A democratic federation of nation states that can tackle our common problems, through the sharing of sovereignty").

time has come to revise the predominant view of the unitary project of integration. A new project should be pursued, based on the recognition of the plurality of unions that already exists within the EU. In this regard, it is necessary, first, to recognize the (institutional and legal) distinction that has already taken place between the non-euro-area and the euro-area member states under the impact of the post-2009 financial crisis. It is thus necessary, second, to recognize that the intergovernmental and the parliamentary unions are both insufficient to grant effective and legitimate governance of the euro-area. This recognition is at the heart of the perspective of the European compound union as the model able to recompose the interests and arguments of the two unions. The latter should be a political union based on the constitutional principle of shared sovereignty with respect to all its policies. The European compound union should be an open project, but it has to start necessarily from a constitutional commitment of the euro-area member states alone.

The compound union should be founded on a formal and essential agreement, a basic or political compact treaty, celebrating the reasons of the union, the principle of the separation of powers that regulates its functioning and that guarantees its member states (in particular the smaller ones), the rights and duties of its citizens and the judicial safeguard of its democratic nature. Third and finally, it would be necessary to connect the member states of the compound union and the other European states that do not belong to it through an agreement, a simplified version of the Lisbon Treaty, redefining rules and conditions for participation in a single market. In short: *separate, recompose, connect*. These are the historical challenges that Europeans and their political leaders must face in the near future.

Acknowledgments

I started to work on this book when the financial crisis reached Europe in 2009. A first draft of the book came into being during the 2012 Spring term I spent at the University of California at Berkeley, where I was invited as Distinguished Professor to lecture on the euro crisis by Jack Citrin, Director of the Institute of Governmental Studies (IGS). As usual, the IGS provided a stimulating environment for thinking about and discussing issues with colleagues. I benefited also from the discussions I had with several American friends: with Jim Caporaso who invited me to lecture on European politics at the Center for Western European Studies, European Union Center for Excellence, University of Washington, Seattle; with Bruce Cain who invited me as Residential Fellow to the University of California Washington DC Center and with David Calleo who asked me to lecture on EU foreign policy at the School of Advanced International Studies, European Program, Johns Hopkins University, Washington DC; with Amie Kreppel who invited me as Jean Monnet Chair Professor in European Politics, University of Florida, Gainesville. I greatly benefited also from discussions and conversations I had with my European friends and colleagues: with Michael Cox who invited me to talk at the London School of Economics; with Stelios Stavridis who invited me to speak at the Greek Institute of Economic International Relations in Athens; with Miguel Maduro who invited me to join a group on the financial crisis at the Global Governance Program and Alexander Trechsel for asking me to participate in a conference organized by the European Union Democracy Observatory, Robert Schuman Centre for Advanced Studies, both at the European University Institute; with Catherine Moury and Andrés Malamud who invited me to lecture at the Centre for Research and Studies in Sociology (CIES), Lisbon University Institute, Lisbon, Portugal; with Renaud Dehousee who invited me to give a seminar at Sciences-Po in Paris; with Daniel Innerarity and Carlos Closa who invited me to give a talk at the Globernance Conference in Bilbao;

with Ulrike Liebert who asked me to participate in a seminar at the Jean Monnet Centre for European Studies at the University of Bremen; with Christian Joerges who involved me in a research seminar on the euro crisis at the Hertie School of Governance in Berlin; and with Erik Erikson and John Fossum who invited me to lecture at ARENA in Oslo. Last, but not least, let me mention the colleagues with whom I discussed the issues raised in this book in various seminars held in my and other universities, such as Marco Brunazzo, Maurizio Ferrera, Jolyon Howorth, Christopher Lord, Nicola Lupo, Augustine Menéndez, Yves Mény, Leonardo Morlino, Kalypso Nicolaidis, Simona Piattoni and Vivien Schmidt. Finally, I benefited from the intense conversations on the European Union I had at the Europeos think tank in Rome, with civil servants, top officials, colleagues and journalists such as (among many) Giuliano Amato, Carlo Bastasin, Sabino Cassese, Marcello Messori, Stefano Micossi, Ferdinando Nelli Feroci and Gian Luigi Tosato. I also wish to acknowledge the support of the Jean Monnet Chair I received from the European Commission, and the technical and editorial help of Gaia Di Martino, Paul Garwood, Lorenzo Valeri and the research assistance of Mariagiulia Amadio.

The work for this book would have been much more difficult without the warmth and joy I constantly found in my wife and my sons (in spite of the latter's geographical distance). However, Manuela, Federico and Sebastiano know that I owe them a much larger world than this tiny book. I was working on this book when my mother Sisla passed away. Notwithstanding the difficulties of her life, she always maintained a grateful attitude towards everybody. She always thanked. It is now I who have to thank her. I dedicate the book to her exemplary life.

Institutionalization of multiple unions

1 | *From Rome to the Lisbon Treaty*

1.1 Introduction

The EU is the result of the evolution and transformation of a historic agreement among, first, Western European nation states and then the Western and Eastern plus the Southern parts of Europe, aimed above all at bringing to a close a long sequence of hot and cold wars. This aim was entrusted to the formation of a common and then single market able to bring economic and social security to European states. European integration has been the response to the trauma and demons of the two halves of the twentieth century. The moral source of European integration resided in the need to avoid further wars and ideological divisions on the continent. After the 1954 failure of the more ambitious project of setting up a European Defence Community (EDC), its success has been dependent, on the military side, on the protection of the North Atlantic Treaty Association or NATO, while, on the economic side, it has rested on the formation and enlargement of a common and then single market. The EU is the outcome of choices made by national elites and supranational actors for peacefully aggregating nation states of different demographic size, historical identity and political cultures. The crucial choices were made at critical junctures, as in the first half of the 1950s, in the first years of the 1990s and then at the start of the 2010s.

Monnet (1978: 46) wrote in his *Memoirs* that "I have always believed that Europe would be built through crises and that it would be the sum of their solutions." This means that the EU is the sum of the choices taken by actors with decision-making power in those crisis periods conceptualized as critical junctures. Critical junctures are windows of opportunity for pursuing new aims (Pierson and Skocpol 2002). In those moments, the path-dependent logic is suspended and different options potentially become available. However, after the founding critical juncture, within which an institutional setting is created, rarely does a new course of action start from scratch. It generally consists in pursuing a new target through a different combination of existing institutional and policy components, or through the strengthening of one or more components and the weakening of others, a combination at times inspired by a new emerging political paradigm. Once a path is taken, however, then the dependency logic starts again, constraining the range of choices available in the following period. The options not pursued during the critical juncture are generally lost and it is unlikely that they will come back later onto the decision-makers' agenda (Pierson 2004). Nevertheless, another critical juncture arises again, placing the previous institutional equilibrium under strain. The new critical juncture will require the consideration of new options, not just the recovery of those abandoned previously. Between one critical juncture and the next, in fact, the context inevitably changes. I assume the institutional structure of the EU is the result of the choices taken at the critical junctures by national and European political elites (Goetz and Meyer-Sahling 2009). However, contrary to Monnet's assumption, I will show that those choices have not necessarily gone in a supranational direction.

This chapter reconstructs the process of institutionalization of the original peace pact, setting out its multilinear development. First, it will discuss the formation of a uniform supranational framework for dealing with the construction of a common and then single market. Once the explicit political view of the integration process was defeated, the latter has in fact been based on the formation of a market regime through the interaction of the institutions representing national and European interests. Second, it will discuss the change introduced in this trajectory by the end of the Cold War and its institutional implications. In the critical juncture of 1989–1991, the EU inaugurated different models of integration in order to make possible the compromises between different views on its nature and future. Third, it will discuss the nature of the multiple compromises reached and their impact on the several treaty rounds that led to the 2009 Lisbon Treaty. The aim of the chapter is to show the multiple and differentiated nature of the process of integration.

1.2 The institutionalization of the single market

An elite-driven peace pact

The EU is a *pact* for promoting peace through prosperity among warring states traditionally jealous of their own national identity. The end of the Second World War left a dramatically disrupted Europe. That disruption imposed the necessity of defining new relations between the main European nation states, France and West Germany in particular. The growing confrontation between the two global superpowers that emerged victorious from the war (the USA and the Soviet Union) created the conditions for relaunching the project of integrating the West European nation states into a new, unspecified federation. The explosion of the conflict between North and South Korea between 1950 and 1953 turned the confrontation between the two superpowers into a proper Cold War. The Cold War required West Germany to be rearmed to better guarantee the political stability and military security of Western Europe. It was in that context that the French foreign minister, Robert Schuman, made public on May 9, 1950 a Declaration of his government for promoting a coal and steel community with Germany, "opened to the participation of other countries of Europe." The crucial point of the Declaration is the following: "The pooling of coal and steel production should immediately provide for the setting up of common foundations for economic development as a first step in the federation of Europe." The following year the European Coal and Steel Community or ECSC Treaty was signed in Paris. Indeed, it was the struggle for control of those primary resources that had led to tensions between France and Germany for nearly a century. While there were other signatories to the agreement (the Treaty was signed by France, West Germany, Italy, Belgium, the Netherlands and Luxembourg), it made abundantly clear that European integration, in whatever form, was not possible without France and Germany's reconciliation. The Franco-German axis was the engine of integration from the very beginning (Hendriks and Morgan 2001). In 1952 a new Treaty, the European Defence Community or EDC, was signed in the same city by the same six European countries.

According to Burgess (2014), the Schuman Declaration of 1950 epitomized the attempt to use the post-war critical juncture to start the project of integration. For institutional analysis,

critical junctures are characterized by a situation in which the structural
(that is, economic, cultural, ideological, organizational) influences on political action are significantly relaxed for a relatively short period, with
two main consequences: the range of plausible choices open to powerful
political actors expands substantially and the consequences of their decisions for the outcome of interests are potentially much more momentous.
Contingency, in other words, becomes paramount (Capoccia and Kelemen
2007: 343).

The two Paris Treaties that emerged from the Schuman Declaration
tried to fill the critical juncture with the launch of the economic and
military pillars of a future (unspecified) European federation, whose
aim was to wrap the nation states signing the Treaties within a supranational framework. This project came to a partial (although traumatic)
halt in 1954, when the French Assemblée Nationale voted down the
EDC Treaty.[1] The military security of Western Europe was thus allocated to NATO (instituted in 1949 in Brussels), controlled and led by
the USA, whereas the integration of Western Europe was reformulated
as the economic project of building a common market. The post-war
critical juncture came to a close with the signing of the Rome Treaties
in 1957, the European Atomic Energy Community (EURATOM) and
the European Economic Community (EEC). By necessity, Jean Monnet
(1978: 93), the main architect of the EEC, wrote in his *Memoirs*, "we
believed in starting with limited achievements, establishing a de facto
solidarity, from which a federation would gradually emerge." Keeping
the security side out of the integration process had, however, contradictory effects. On one side, it helped European states to maximize
their resources for the economic reconstruction of the continent, apart

[1] The EDC was originally proposed in 1950 by René Pleven, the then French
Prime Minister, in response to US pressure to reintegrate West Germany into the
European system of defense. The intention was to form a pan-European force
as an alternative to West Germany's proposed accession to NATO, which was
meant to harness its military potential in the case of conflict with the Soviet
bloc. The EDC was to include West Germany, France, Italy and the Benelux
countries and provided for centralized/supranational military procurement. The
EDC would have had a common budget, armies, command and institutions.
The EDC plan went for ratification to the French National Assembly on August
30, 1954 and failed by a vote of 319 to 264. The Gaullists, who feared that
the EDC threatened France's national sovereignty in military policy, and the
Communists, who opposed a plan set up against the Communist bloc, formed a
successful parliamentary coalition against the government's proposal.

from reassuring each of them that further interstate conflict would be prevented by the tutoring role of the USA. On the other side, however, "the American security blanket obviated the need for greater integration" (Parent 2011: 139).

With the 1957 EEC and EURATOM, signed in Rome, the EU came to be based on interstate treaties intended to create a supra-state polity, able to close the long era of European civil wars (which started with the Prussian invasion of France in 1871, going through the First World War and then ending dramatically in the Second World War: Judt 2005) by fostering the growth of a common market on a continental scale. Since then, a sequence of Treaties has periodically structured what we have come to call the EU (see Appendix Table A.1). Moreover, the EU, which arose out of an agreement between six states in 1957, after several enlargements has come to be composed of twenty-eight member states (since July 1, 2013) and more than half a billion inhabitants with the accession of Croatia[2] (see Appendix, Table A.2). The development of the EU since the Treaties of Rome of 1957[3] has led to the progressive institutionalization of a veritable political system, equipped with its own institutional structure and comparable to other established political systems (Hix 2005).

The debate on how to interpret this long process of integration has continued to be lively. As asserted by scholars of the liberal intergovernmental approach (Moravcsik 1998), the EU is the outcome of intergovernmental agreements between national leaders in intergovernmental conferences (IGCs), in their turn expressing the preferences of the main economic interests of their country. However, although national governments have played a crucial role in treaty-making, those national governments have recognized the need to delegate crucial policy functions to institutions independent from their will, as asserted by the scholars of the neo-functional approach (Borzel 2006; Haas 1958). At the same time, the Treaties, even those justified by dramatic historical events such as the founding Treaties, were and have

[2] On December 9, 2011 Croatia signed the EU accession treaty. The EU accession referendum was held in Croatia on January 22, 2012, with the majority voting for Croatia's accession to the EU, with accession formalized in July 2013. Croatia is thus the twenty-eighth member state of the EU.

[3] Although two treaties were signed in Rome, the EEC Treaty aimed to develop an economic community and the EURATOM Treaty aimed to develop a nuclear energy community, it is the first Treaty that is considered as the founding bloc of the EU for its institutional implications. I will refer to it as the Rome Treaty.

been negotiated by politicians with advice from public officials (such as Jean Monnet, for instance) bringing new ideas and awareness of the limits of the traditional logic of the balance of power, as asserted by the scholars of the constructivist approach (Parsons 2003).

Notwithstanding their differences, all approaches to European integration have stressed the strategic role that political elites played in the founding of the EU. It was political elites (national and supranational) that were the crucial actors that made possible the aggregation of Europe. Unions of states are necessarily the outcome of elite-driven choices of institution-building and the EU has not been an exception in this regard (Haller 2011). In the post-war disorder, the European elites recognized that their states had no chance of avoiding the wars generated by the rivalries their own nationalism produced, except by substituting the balance of powers with institutionalized integration. As stated in the first line of the EEC Rome Treaty of 1957, the signatories declared that they were "determined to lay the foundations of an ever-closer union among the peoples of Europe." The same Jean Monnet (1978: 286) wrote in his *Memoirs*, "I thought it wrong to consult the peoples of Europe about the structure of a Community of which they had no practical experience. It was another matter, however, to ensure that in their limited field the new institutions were thoroughly democratic."

However, in Rome 1957, as opposed to Philadelphia in 1787 (Deudney 1995), the constitutional rationale of the new political order was not discussed, after the failure of the highly political project of constituting an EDC. The founding fathers of the European integration project were aware that the traditional Westphalian system of states, with its balance-of-power logic, was the source of permanent interstate insecurity, thus triggering periodic attempts by one state or another to impose an imperial order on the others. Indeed, the "historic transition ... marked by the settlement of Westphalia in 1648, which ended the Thirty Years' War and opened the quest ... to find a way for independent states, each enjoying sovereignty over a given territory, to pursue their interests without destroying each other or the international system of which each is part" (Lyons and Mastanduno 1995: 5), brought the European Westphalian states to reciprocal destruction in two world wars. The leaders of those Westphalian states were obliged to look for post-Westphalian solutions to the dilemma of reconciling autonomy and peace. They had to go beyond diplomacy in order to guarantee peace on the European continent, launching a process of institutionalized integration. As Eriksen (2014: 30) argued, the EU represents "a move beyond the Westphalian order, that is the international order founded on the principles of co-existence and non-interference among sovereign states with the concomitant self-help principles." However, after 1954 the constitutional rationale of the European post-Westphalian project remained necessarily under-elaborated. The EU is the outcome of the attempt by the European elites to go only de facto beyond the Westphalian solution to interstate rivalries.

The institutional foundations

The 1957 Rome Treaty inaugurated the project to transform the inter-national relations of the European nation states into the internal features of a new supranational polity. The peace pact could not have been guaranteed solely by an interstate (or intergovernmental) agree-ment (as previous experience had amply shown). The interstate (or intergovernmental) agreement needed to be protected and constrained by supra-state (or supranational) institutions and actors. Without supra-state authorities (that is, authorities institutionally separated from the states that had created them in the first place), the Treaty's founders assumed that there was no guarantee that the partners of the interstate (or intergovernmental) agreement would abide by their own rules or would respect their own decisions. In the founding of the EU, thus, supranational features were considered necessary in order to protect the *pact* from interstate rivalries and instability.

The following support for the peace pact came from transnational cooperation on a growing number of common economic matters (Lindberg 1963). This cooperation led to the progressive institution-alization of the close network of institutions envisaged by the Rome Treaty – the intergovernmental Council of Ministers (then called the Council of the Union, now simply the Council, strengthened, since 1974, by the informal meetings of the European Council of heads of state and government: Naurin and Wallace 2008) and the supra-national Commission and European Parliament or EP (originally called the Assembly) – under the supervision of a supranational judicial insti-tution (the European Court of Justice or ECJ) (Dinan 2006: Part III). If the intergovernmental side of the EU stressed the role of the states as masters of the Treaty, the supranational side was necessary in order to embed those masters into a larger institutional context that they could not control individually. For the first time in European history, the leaders of European nation states tried to build a supra-state, and not only interstate, order through peaceful means (basically through negotiation over common economic issues).

The founding Treaties thus established an institutional model that combined two different interests: the national interests as represented by the intergovernmental Council (the decision-making body) and the European interest as represented by the Commission (epitomized by its formal monopoly of legislative initiative). The interaction between the two interests, however, very soon came to be adversarial, as became evident during the 1960s when the then French president, General Charles De Gaulle, ordered his government not to participate in the Council's meetings (the "empty chair" strategy) in protest against the Commission's assertion of its independent role. The conflict between the two institutions led to a vertical policy-making model, with the Council (under the leadership of the French and German governments) acting as the main decision-making actor. The Commission and the ECJ were marked as the institutions with the most committed European vocation; and certainly they had the most to gain in terms of power and influence with the institutionalization of a supranational system.

The EP played a limited role in the founding period because of its indirectly elected nature. It started merely as a parliamentary assembly that became a parliament in 1962 (Rittberger 2005). Within the original institutional architecture of the EEC, the Parliament had a simple consultative role in the Union's decision-making process. Until 1979 its members were nominated by the national parliaments according to their own specific rules. Its nature as a second-tier institution did not inspire its members to claim a larger role in the Union's decision-making process. In 1964 its right to be involved in the signing of trade agreements with non-EEC countries was recognised and in 1975 a procedure that required its opinion for resolving inter-institutional disagreements was introduced. In the first three decades of its existence, although the parliamentary assembly and then the Parliament had important political leaders as president, the institution's role continued to be marginal or secondary.

At the same time, the Rome Treaty served to provide a juridical basis to the EU (Sandholtz and Stone Sweet 1998). The ECJ, profiting from the institutional impasse between the Council and the Commission during the "empty chair" conflict, assumed an increasingly important role in adjudicating disputes between Union institutions and the member states. Two ECJ decisions were particularly important in the 1960s: *van Gend en Loos* in 1962, which established that European law has a direct effect on individuals and firms, and *Costa* v. *Enel* in 1964, which celebrated the principle that European law is superior to national law. This interpretation was a response to the needs of economic actors, especially firms, to operate in a continental economy that had to be regulated in relatively uniform fashion (Stone Sweet, Sandholtz and Fligstein 2001). The direct effect and supremacy of Union law allowed the Commission to deregulate national legal regimes, while defining a supranational regulatory structure. Two other judicial decisions of the 1970s, introducing the principle of mutual recognition, contributed to further constitutionalizing the common market. The mutual recognition principle, "formulated in the *Dassonville* (1974) and *Cassis de Dijon* (1979) rulings, has played a major role in (preventing) a member state from discriminating against foreign goods that have been produced in accordance with the standards of another member state" (Leuffen, Rittberger and Schimmelfennig 2013: 115).

The establishment of the ECJ's constitutional role was the result of a complex web of alliances with national judiciaries, rather than with their national constitutional courts, and with the major national interest groups. On the basis of Article 177 of the Rome Treaty, national judges were able to seek recourse to the ECJ to resolve disputes arising over interpretations of Union law (Stone Sweet 2000). Although the ECJ cannot directly review the legality of member states' laws, its judgments have become binding and national courts have taken them as the legal basis on which to review the compatibility between national and Union law. The national courts thus bypassed constitutional courts and acted as a sort of decentralized mechanism of judicial review of national legislation. This called into question the established principle that review should be carried out only through special constitutional courts. In any case, supranational institutions such as the Commission and the ECJ proved to be necessary to guarantee respect for the agreements formally reached by the member state governments within the Council. Without such a mixed institutional model, it would have been difficult to support economic cooperation as a condition for deepening regional integration. Notwithstanding such a mixed institutional model, policy-making was largely determined by the Council and, within it, by the French and German ministers.

From a common to a single market

With the 1986 Single European Act (SEA), the project moved from a common to a single market to be completed by the end of 1992. The SEA celebrated the four freedoms that define the single market: freedom of movement for goods, services, capital and people. The 1970s rulings of the ECJ on mutual recognition triggered the process that led to the SEA. Indeed, "the SEA announces a paradigmatic shift from harmonizing member states' national legislation towards liberalization based on the principle of mutual recognition" (Leuffen, Rittberger and Schimmelfennig 2013: 116). In order to achieve the objective of a single market, the SEA introduced new institutional provisions. Decision-making rules (within the Council) were changed from unanimity to qualified majority voting (QMV), thus departing from the gentlemen's agreement known as "Luxembourg compromise" that helped to solve the empty chair crisis of the 1960s (and consisting in the privilege recognized to a member state to ask to continue a negotiation, regarding an issue deemed of national interest, until unanimity can be reached). At the same time, the SEA recognized new powers for the directly elected (as from 1979) EP. The EP was granted the right to veto enlargements and international agreements and its consent was required (due to a new cooperation procedure) for passing legislation related to the completion of the single market. Through the cooperation procedure a legislative dialogue between the EP and the Council was introduced. It should be recalled that the EP achieved significant budgetary authority as early as 1970–75, although the budget resources at the disposal of EU institutions continued to remain at extremely low levels. The direct election of the EP was instrumental in accelerating the process of institutionalization of the EU. Since then, the powers of the EP have increased enormously, transforming it into an influential legislative institution (Steuenberg and Thomassen 2002).

Once directly elected, the Members of the EP (MEPs) claimed the right to be involved in the Union's decision-making process in order to meet the expectations of their constituencies or parties (Farrell and Scully 2007). With the creation of the single market, many issues related to the proper functioning of modern capitalism gradually became Europeanized. Policy areas that were traditionally within the national domain shifted to the European level. It was not just the Commission and the EP (and the ECJ) that had an institutional interest in widening the range of EU competencies; the intergovernmental institutions representing national interests (the Council and the then informal European Council of heads of state and government) did not limit themselves to defending the status quo ante. They also benefited from the institutionalization of a supranational system in that it allowed states to solve problems they could not address on their own (Milward 2000). Once French ostracism ended in the late 1960s, with General de Gaulle's resignation in 1968 from his role as president of the Republic, the member states became increasingly active participants in the EU through *their own* intergovernmental institutions.

The institutionalization of a supranational system can be differently interpreted. Certainly the single market project was motivated as much by the changes in the international economic system induced by the crisis of the mid 1970s and the decline of the dollar as an international currency, as it was the result of the interaction between European and national institutions (and the actors operating within them).[4] The neo-liberal agenda of the Conservative British government of the 1980s headed by Margaret Thatcher that generated consensus around privatization and liberalization as the foundations of the single market (and the future common currency) was also important. That agenda met the interests of powerful economic actors that were calling for an open continental market as a condition for relaunching growth in Europe. At the same time, the Commission and its president (the French socialist Jacques Delors) were crucial for justifying the need for a strengthened supranational system in order to support the single market. In short, Margaret Thatcher and Jacques Delors helped each other,[5] notwithstanding their radical ideological differences (S. Fabbrini 2005a).

However, what matters, from my institutional analysis, is the outcome of institutionalization that took place between 1957 and 1986: namely,

[4] For a theoretically dense interpretation of the EU process of institutionalization, see Heritier (2007).
[5] The Conservative leader Margaret Thatcher was UK Prime Minister from 1979 to 1990, while the Socialist leader Jacques Delors was President of the Commission from 1985 to 1994.

the formation of a trilateral institutional decision-making system, definable as a supranational system, with the Commission as the driving force (because of its monopoly over legislative initiative celebrated by the Treaties) and the Council and the EP as a sort of bicameral legislature (although the former had much more power than the latter for approving the Commission's proposals). This supranational system was then supervised by the ECJ, which contributed to further establishing the principle of *integration through law* (as famously conceptualized by Cappelletti, Seccombe and Weiler 1986).

1.3 Maastricht and the new critical juncture

If the SEA consolidated the process of institutionalization that started with the Rome Treaty, the Treaty on European Union (TEU), also known as the Maastricht Treaty and signed on February 7, 1992, introduced a structural discontinuity in the institutional evolution of the EU. Organized after the end of the Cold War (epitomized by the fall of the Berlin Wall in 1989 and the implosion of the Soviet Union in 1991), the intergovernmental conference (IGC) held in Maastricht in 1991 took place at a critical juncture of post-war European history. If the post-Second World War critical juncture opened the possibility of establishing a new institutional equilibrium between Western European nation states, the post-Cold War critical juncture created an unexpected scenario challenging the previous established institutional or political balance of forces.

The new scenario facing political leaders (at the national and European level) consisted in the geopolitical opening up of the European system. The EU had inevitably to deal with issues (such as foreign and security policy or home and justice affairs) unconnected with the single market policies pursued in the previous period (Baun 1995). Already in the 1970s a loose form of political cooperation between national governments on foreign policy had started at the fringe of the Union system. National governments, however, retained their full sovereignty over foreign policy, limiting themselves only to exchanging information on individual practices, also because the security side continued to be delegated to NATO, that is to the US leadership within that organization. This loose cooperation was untenable after the end of the Cold War. The EU member states had to acknowledge the radical change of the context that had justified the choice of cooperation. Although military policy had to remain inevitably in US hands, the Union had to face the necessity of setting up a common foreign and security policy. At the same time, the end of the Cold War made possible, for the very first time since the trauma of 1945, the reunification of Germany that eventually took place in 1990. The reunification of Germany was not welcomed by many national governmental leaders of EU member states. However, once reunification was a fact, those national leaders had to find a way to embrace the reunified and larger Germany within a tighter institutional framework. This framework was decided to be an economic and monetary union based on a new currency (what then came to be called Economic and Monetary Union or EMU). The surrender by Germany of its powerful national currency the Deutsche Mark, a symbol of its post-war economic resurgence, was considered the condition for also making possible its political resurgence as a reunified state.

The IGC negotiating the TEU had thus to deal with unprecedented policies. Once those policies entered the EU agenda, they could have been framed within the supranational Union that organized single market policies. Or better, they could have been managed through that successful approach, called the "Community method," used for supranationalizing the single market. According to this method:

the European Commission alone makes legislative and policy proposals. Its independence strengthens its ability to execute policy, act as the guardian of the Treaty and represent the Community in international negotiations. Legislative and budgetary acts are adopted by the Council of Ministers ... and the European Parliament ... The use of qualified majority voting in the Council is an essential element in ensuring the effectiveness of this method. Execution of policy is entrusted to the Commission and national authority. The European Court of Justice guarantees respect for the rule of law (Dehousse 2011: 4).

Indeed, in the Maastricht Treaty this method was strengthened with regard to single market policies through the introduction of the co-decision legislative procedure (which was then extended with the Amsterdam Treaty of 1997). With the new legislative procedure, the EP was recognized fully as the popular branch of a bicameral legislature (with the Council representing the member state branch). The increasing decision-making role of the EP was, however, contained within single market policies.

The supranational approach, based on the idea that decision-making power has to be shared between supranational institutions (such as the Commission and the EP) and intergovernmental institutions (represented by the Council and the informal European Council of the heads of state and government – with the role of defining the strategies of the Union), was not, however, adopted for dealing with the new policies. A different path was taken. In the debate that accompanied and followed those events (Laursen 2012), the national governmental leaders constituting the IGC decided to bring those issues within the integration process, but on the condition that they could strictly control them. The TEU introduced an institutional differentiation that promoted different decision-making regimes for dealing with different policy problems. These regimes came to be called "pillars." Single market policies came to be organized by the supranational first pillar, through amendment to the EEC of the 1957 Rome Treaty, now renamed the Treaty Establishing the European Community (TEC), and became a distinct part of the TEU, whereas foreign and home affairs policies, traditionally close to the sovereignty of member states, were to be managed by two distinct intergovernmental pillars. At the same time, "the first pillar contained the plans for EMU, including the introduction of a single currency" (Laursen 2012: 121), although it had to be organized through a specific regime combining supranationalization in monetary policy with powerful intergovernmental features in economic policy. The unitary character of the supranational entity that had emerged from the previous decades was thus internally differentiated through the formation of different decision-making regimes.

The first pillar, regulating single market policies, was the only pillar with a legal personality, consisting not only of the amended 1957 Rome Treaty instituting the EEC (now TEC), but also of the 1951 ECSC Treaty (which expired in 2002) and the EURATOM Treaty. The second pillar, the Common Foreign and Security Policy (CFSP), had to take care of foreign policy and security matters. The third pillar, Police and Judicial Co-operation in Criminal Matters (PJCC), had to bring together cooperation in the fight against crime. This pillar was originally named Justice and Home Affairs (JHA). In these last two pillars, the decision-making process was exclusively controlled by the governments of the member states through their intergovernmental institutions. The policies of the first pillar were decided through the mixed institutional model, which, recognizing a decision-making role of the Commission and the EP along with the Council, created the conditions for a balanced policy-making model. The second and third pillars, on the other hand, were organized as an intergovernmental model with a policy-making process centered around the institutions representing primarily national governments. In the latter pillars, the member state governments (in the Councils of Foreign Affairs and Justice and Home Affairs) had the last word on any decision. At the same time, all the Council's formations continued to be coordinated by the rotating presidency (every six months) of one of the member state governments.

Meanwhile, under the pressure of the then Commission president Jacques Delors, the national leaders declared in the TEU's Preamble to be "resolved ... to establish an economic and monetary union including ... a single and stable currency," a resolution that eventually led to the launching of a new sub-institutional system within the EU, the EMU. EMU, and monetary integration specifically, had been in the Union's pipeline since the 1970s. With the dissolution between 1968 and 1972 of the Bretton Woods system (established by the Allied authorities, under US leadership, after the end of the Second World War) of the US dollar's fixed value against gold, projects and proposals for promoting a European monetary system were advanced and discussed in European capitals. In 1972 a Currency Snake Regime was created. Following an initiative by France and West Germany, in 1979 a European Monetary System (EMS) was set up. The SEA accelerated the discussion on monetary union. In 1988 an ad hoc committee, chaired by the then president of the Commission Jacques Delors and consisting of the governors of the central banks of the then twelve member states, was set up to define the blueprint of a monetary union, subsequently made public as the Delors Report in 1989 (Issing 2008). The Delors Report was, however, a solution in search of a problem. The problem arrived finally with the necessity to enfold a reunified Germany into a stronger European monetary framework. It seems implausible to assume, as a few political economists did (see the discussion in Alesina and Giavazzi 2010), that the EMU would have been inaugurated in any case because of the internal logic of the single market or the transformation of the international currency system. As argued instead by political historians (Calleo 2001), those economic factors represented the necessary but not the sufficient condition for setting up the EMU. The EMU was the political answer to German reunification. Through the launch of the common currency project, it was indeed expected that a reunified Germany would continue to remain a European Germany (Jabko 2006).

On the basis of the Delors Report, in Maastricht a plan was set out to introduce the EMU in three stages. On January 1, 1994 a European Monetary Institute was established as the forerunner of a new banking institution for controlling monetary policy. On June 1, 1998 this new institution, the European Central Bank (ECB), was created, tailored on the model of the institutionally and politically independent Deutsche Bundesbank. On December 31, 1998 the conversion rates between the eleven participating national currencies and the euro were established. On January 1, 2002 the euro notes and coins started to circulate (Martin and Ross 2004). The decision was also taken to bring the set of policies connected to the common currency within a special regime, combining the control of monetary policy by a supranational but technocratic institution such as the ECB and of economic policies by the intergovernmental institution of the Council of Economic and Financial Ministers (or ECOFIN Council), operating under the supervision of the European Council. In terms of institutional analysis, the political logic of the EMU is determined by the ECOFIN Council, not the ECB, since the primary objective of the ECB is only "to maintain price stability" (as its Statute states) and its behavior is strictly constrained by its internal statutory rules. In short (Majone 2014: 52), "the ECB is not a politically independent institution operating in the context of a democratic government (but) rather ... a 'disembedded' non-majoritarian institution" operating in the intergovernmental context of the EMU.

It seems thus questionable to consider, within the EMU, monetary policy and economic policy as two distinct policy regimes (as argued, inter alia, by Leuffen, Rittberger and Schimmelfennig 2013: chapter 6). The existence of a supranational ECB is not sufficient to make the EMU a supranational regime. Political supranationalism implies a decision-making role for the Commission and the EP, although in interaction with the intergovernmental Council. The ECB is not a political institution, but a technocratic institution that has to operate within pre-established rules (that it can certainly interpret differently according to the different economic contexts within which it has to operate). This is why the EMU is an intergovernmental decision-making regime, notwithstanding the existence of the ECB within it. Also in this regard, rather than extending the supranational approach into the new economic policy, governmental leaders decided, in Maastricht, to design a new regime for it. Since foreign and security policies as well as economic and financial policies were traditionally at the core of national sovereignty, a decision-making regime was devised that is characterized by the predominance of intergovernmental institutions. It is understandable that national governments tried to keep those policies under their own scrutiny. However, nothing prevented the possibility of confirming the policy path followed from Rome through to the SEA. The Maastricht Treaty instead established that different policies should be regulated by different institutional regimes.

In the first pillar, the Council and the EP gradually came to share the legislative power through the co-decision procedure (legislation must pass through approval by the EP and the Council), while the Commission kept its monopoly over policy initiatives. In the other two pillars, however, the Commission and the EP were kept at the margins, although the pillarization of the EU did not prevent MEPs from being involved in EU foreign and justice affairs, claiming in particular their competence over crucial international issues such as human rights. At the same time, it was established that the economic and monetary policy of the EU would be defined and regulated in another separate institutional regime within the first pillar, which was intergovernmental in nature. Moreover, although not formalized in the TEU, it was agreed that the European Council of the heads of state and government of the member states "shall meet at least twice a year, under the chairmanship of the Heads of State or Government of the Member State which holds the Presidency of the Council" (Article D, second paragraph) in order to define the strategic orientation of the Union. Although preserving the informal status of the European Council, in Maastricht the governmental leaders started to promote it as the main institutional check on the growing role acquired by the EP.

This differentiation can be considered as the outcome of the political choices made by national and European elites to deal with the new context of a reunified continent. The critical juncture of 1989–1991 obliged them to think of the EU as more than an economic community, or better as a *political union* facing the unexpected challenge of unifying the entire continent. "The shock of 1989 forced the member states to change their stance. They turned their association into a Union and admitted new members. The borders of institutional Europe crept towards those of geographical Europe" (Van Middelaar 2013: 182). Although the expression of *political union* was now and again recalled in the first decades of the integration process (Dullien and Torreblanca 2012), the term came to be used officially only after the 1989 fall of the Berlin Wall (de Schoutheete and Micossi 2013). The European Council held in Dublin on June 25–26, 1990 confirmed "its commitment to Political Union and decided that Foreign Ministers should carry out a detailed examination of the need for possible treaty changes," adding that "Political Union will need to strengthen in a global and balanced manner the capacity of the Community and its Member States to act in the areas of their common interests," thus recognizing that "the transformation of the Community from an entity mainly based on economic integration and political cooperation into a union of a political nature … raises a number of general questions" (Annex I.1 and 2 to the EC resolution). The European Council held in Rome on December 13–14, 1990 insisted on the need "to define the stages in the process of transforming the Community into a Political Union" (EC resolution, p. 2), noting "with satisfaction all the preparatory work which is to serve as basis for the Intergovernmental Conference on Political Union" (p. 3). The following European Council held in Luxembourg on June 28–29, 1991 stated that "the final decision on the text of the Treaty on Political Union and on Economic and Monetary Union will be taken by the Maastricht European Council" (EC resolution, p. 2). The European Council held in Maastricht on December 9–10, 1991 "reached an agreement on the Draft Treaty on the European Union based on the text concerning Political Union and … Economic and Monetary Union" (EC resolution, p. 2).

However, the expression of political union did not appear in the 1992 Maastricht Treaty, but only in the Final Act that concluded the intergovernmental negotiations that led to the Treaty (where the "common accord (on) the amendments to be made … with a view to the achievement of political union" is acknowledged). With the Maastricht Treaty, the concept of political union has become the container of different institutional regimes. At the same time, the Maastricht Treaty introduced the notion of a common European citizenship as distinct from national citizenship in that it connoted particular rights. In Title I on Common Provisions, Article B declares that the Union aims "to strengthen the protection of the rights and interests of the nationals of its Member States through the introduction of a citizenship of the Union." It was the Maastricht Treaty that for the first time celebrated the EU as a Union of both states and their citizens. As Article A of the Common Provisions stresses: "The task [of the Treaty] shall be to organize … relations between the Member States and between *their* people" (author's emphasis).

1.4 Maastricht's multiple compromises

The Maastricht Treaty was the outcome of multiple compromises between national governments and European actors. Those compromises had institutional, political and economic features. The critical juncture of 1989–1991, increasing the options available on the IGC table, sharpened the differences of views between the actors negotiating the Treaty. The compromise nature of the Treaty was thus inevitable.

The first compromise was institutional. It consisted in balancing the pressure for extending the integration process to new sensitive policies and the need for preserving, if not strengthening, the role of national governments in collectively deciding such policies. The Treaty introduced an institutional differentiation that promoted different decision-making regimes for dealing with different policy areas. Behind the compromise there were in action different member states with their alternative agendas and interests. The outcome of the compromise was, however, unprecedented. The answer to the crisis did not lead to more supranationality. The supranational union, in fact, was not considered by all the member states (and France in particular) as the solution to the problems emerging with the end of the Cold War. In the end, the agreement was to introduce an alternative constitutional model of integration to govern policies that were traditionally linked to national sovereignty.

Those policies were Europeanized but kept under the control of the collectivity of national governments (as represented by the Council and the European Council, without the involvement of the supranational institutions of the Commission and the EP). It was also established that, in those policies, integration would have to proceed through voluntary non-legal acts negotiated by national governments within their intergovernmental institutions. Since in those policies integration could not take place through the ordinary legislative procedure derived from the "Community method," then the role of the ECJ (whose power was and has continued to be crucial in the supranational constitution) would have been curtailed. The supranational model was based on the principle of sharing decision-making power between institutions representing European and national interests, according to various forms of majority voting. The intergovernmental model was instead based on the principle of pooling decision-making power within the intergovernmental institutions alone, where decisions have to be taken through the consensual coordination of national preferences. It should be stressed that the intergovernmentalism institutionalized in Maastricht recognized the necessity of deepening integration; it was not just the formula for preventing the latter's development. Supranationalism and intergovernmentalism reflected alternative approaches to integration, but both aimed to advance it (Laursen and Vanhoonacker 1992).

The political compromise concerned instead the composition of the EMU. The EMU was not merely a policy project. Since its inception it had a political and not only economic rationale (Dyson and Quaglia 2010). That political rationale was, however, unacceptable for a small number of EU member states (the UK in particular). The launching of the EMU thus required the search for a political solution to the latter's objections. It was necessary to find a political compromise between the UK, on the one side, and the other member states, on the other. Although the EMU was celebrated as the economic and monetary regime for all the EU member states, the UK was allowed to formally opt out from the obligation to convert its national currency into the new common currency, regardless of its macroeconomic conditions. Indeed, Denmark, after having rejected the Maastricht Treaty in a popular referendum held in 1992, finally came to accept it through a new referendum held in 1993 because of the so-called Edinburgh Agreement of December 1992 that allowed the country to opt out from the need to adopt the future common currency. De facto, a third member state, Sweden, has also been allowed to keep its own national currency, thanks to calculations regularly showing its inability to fulfill the required macroeconomic criteria. These three countries, it should be remembered, contributed with others in the 1960s to developing a project of economic coordination, the European Free Trade Association (EFTA),[6] in its turn the heir of the Free Trade Area (FTA), an alternative to the project started with the 1952 Paris Treaties and the 1957 Rome Treaties.

Above all, the Maastricht Treaty was also a turning point symbolically. The semantic change from the European Economic Community of the Rome Treaty to the European Union, although inclusive of a pillar called the European Community (EC), signaled the deepening of the integration process. To accept this qualitative leap, the member states supporting the vision of a merely *economic community* were allowed to opt out from the most integrationist policies. The opt-out clause reflected the compromise to prevent some of the ex-EFTA countries from obstructing the extension of the integration process to policies traditionally linked to national sovereignty. The opting out from undesired legislation or Treaty provisions gave those member states the right both not to participate in specific policy areas and not to be subject to a general jurisdiction within it. The opting out compromise has accompanied the process of integration from Maastricht onward.

Finally, in Maastricht an economic compromise was also set up, this time concerning the functioning of the EMU. This compromise emerged from the need to accommodate the unequivocal request of Germany to establish a politically independent European Central Bank to manage monetary policy and the unequivocal request of France to keep the control of the correlated economic policies at the national level. According to Tuori and Tuori (2014: 26–7):

EMU was established as a part of the Maastricht package, whose aim was to further political not only economic integration. France held a strong negotiating position as one of the Four Powers and could decisively influence not

---

[6] The European Free Trade Association (EFTA) was created in 1960 by seven countries as a looser alternative to the then EEC. It was the heir to the Free Trade Area (FTA), a project pursued by the UK between 1956 and 1958. The EFTA as a trade bloc was established by the Stockholm Convention held on January 4, 1960 in the Swedish capital. The founding members of EFTA were Austria, Denmark, Norway, Portugal, Sweden, Switzerland and the UK. During the 1960s these countries were often referred to as the Outer Seven, as opposed to the Inner Six of the then EEC. Most of its membership has since joined the EEC, and then the EU. At the end of 2012, EFTA consisted of four countries: Iceland, Norway, Switzerland and Liechtenstein.

only the establishment of EMU, but even the shape it received. Thus, the combination of centralised monetary policy with mainly national fiscal and economic policy was largely due to French misgivings, while Germany had pushed for more extensive centralisation of fiscal and economic policy as a precondition for successful common monetary policy.

If the solution was found in combining centralization (of monetary policy) with decentralization (of the economic, budgetary and fiscal policies connected to the common currency), that combination had, however, to operate within predefined economic parameters endowed with a legal status. Indeed, the "Protocol on the excessive deficit procedure," recalled by TEC Article 104.2, makes explicit that economic policy decentralization should respect the following measures: "3% for the ratio to the planned or actual governmental deficit to gross domestic product at market prices; 60% for the ratio of government debt to gross domestic product at market prices."

In order to promote the respect of those parameters, or better to prevent the externalization of domestic moral hazard, a Stability and Growth Pact or SGP (Heipertz and Verdun 2010) was later introduced to institutionalize the coordination and control of domestic budgets. It consisted in a resolution and two Council regulations approved in 1998. The first regulation "on the strengthening of the surveillance of budgetary positions and the surveillance and coordination of economic policies," known as the preventive arm, came into force on July 1, 1998, and the second regulation "on speeding up and clarifying the implementation of the excessive deficit procedure," known as the dissuasive arm, came into force on January 1, 1999. The SGP was based on Article 104.14 of the TEC, part of the Maastricht Treaty, which "set out in the Protocol on the excessive deficit procedure" the conditions for ordering the coordination of national economic policies. The SGP and the Excessive Deficit Procedure (EDP) Protocol epitomized the German ordo-liberal idea of an economic constitution structured around pre-established (and non-negotiable) legal rules – an idea elaborated since the 1930s by the so-called Freiburg School (Young 2012). As Joerges (forthcoming 2015: 9) stresses, "EMU was understood as a political project, albeit one that was to be shielded strictly from the influence of daily politics, and entrusted to the medium of law instead, and a strictly politically independent institution," then adding that this "economic constitution with the material and institutional substitution of legal rules for politics was … nothing less than a *sine qua non* for German participation within EMU."

Although it was decided that coordination of national economic policies should take place within specific macroeconomic and legal parameters, at the same time it was also established that only national governments through their intergovernmental institutions could decide how to deal with those that did not respect the established parameters. No direct supranational imposition on national government behavior was envisaged by any of the supranational institutions (the Commission in particular). The implications of this legal arrangement became evident in 2003, when Germany and France did not keep their budgetary parameters (in particular that regarding the deficit) within the prescribed limits. TEC Article 104.5 prescribed that "If the Commission considers that an excessive deficit in a Member State exists or may occur, the Commission shall address an opinion to the Council." The Commission submitted a report to the ECOFIN Council, proposing the start of the EDP for Germany and France. TEC Article 104.6 added, however, that "The Council shall, acting by a qualified majority on a recommendation from the Commission, and having considered any observations which the Member State concerned may wish to make, decide after an overall assessment whether an excessive deficit exists." The Council, in fact, did not embrace the Commission's proposal. Under pressure from small member states, the Commission then appealed to the ECJ against the Council's decision. In July 2004 the ECJ declared that the ECOFIN Council was authorized by the TEC to hold the EDP in abeyance for not adopting a Commission recommendation to start an EDP against a member state (if it decides to do that). It thus became clear that the SGP, although it appeared to have celebrated the economic parameters as statutory rules, could not challenge national discretion, in particular that of the larger member states. Yet the ECJ decision did not settle the problem. Immediately afterwards, the Commission urged revision of the legal texts of the SGP. This process was concluded in March 2005 through a reform of the SGP procedural rules that paradoxically strengthened the discretion of national governments. In short, "the legal nature of the Pact was not substantially altered" (Heipertz and Verdun 2010: 2). The economic constitution of the EMU continued to be based on voluntary coordination between governments, even though the coordination had to be regulated by macroeconomic and judicial rules established by the same national governments through their intergovernmental institutions and monitored by the Commission "for examining compliance with budgetary discipline" (TEC, Article 104.2).

1.5 Maastricht to the Lisbon Treaty

The Maastricht Treaty represented a crucial turning point in the integration process. To include the EEC (enlarged and renamed as the European Community or EC) within a larger EU also constituted of common foreign, security, justice and home affairs policies had more than a semantic significance (Dinan 2006: Part IV). It signaled a willingness to enlarge the scope of the Union and thus to make its political nature more evident. The change was resented by those member states, such as the UK, that had joined a project of building an EEC (Gifford 2008: chapter 6). In particular, the project of creating a single currency was "seen by its detractors as a significant additional step towards the creation of a unified system of government … [It promised] to completely change the way the Europeans do business with each other" (McCormick 1999: 223). In France it was barely accepted in a popular referendum and criticism of it was widespread in the UK (and within the Conservative Party then in government). In the event, the Treaty survived probably because of its compromise nature. The supporters of the economic community perspective (the ex-EFTA group) came to accept it because it strengthened the single market, without obliging them to participate in the project of the future single currency (thanks to the opt-out clause). France saw recognition of the role of intergovernmental institutions in controlling policy-making in sensitive areas, whereas Germany could assuage its fears of becoming the paymaster of the EMU thanks to the ordo-liberal principles embedded within it.

There was also a general expectation that the further development of the process of integration would reduce the distinction between the pillars. The EU experience showed cases when a policy started in an intergovernmental way, which then gradually became managed by the "Community method." Indeed, the growing interaction between the various policy fields called into question the neat distinction of policies and institutions designed at Maastricht. A process of cross-pillarization led the third intergovernmental pillar to be affected by the logic of the first pillar (Stetter 2007). In particular, after the terrorist attacks on September 11, 2001, the EU had to strengthen cooperation in the areas of the third pillar, in order to deal with the threat of the migration of terrorist groups into EU member states. That threat led to closer cooperation between member state governments under the supervision of the Commission, making the pillar more and more supranational. A similar process, although much more limited in scope, concerned the second pillar, through the interaction between trade policy, formally under the first pillar with the Commission playing a prominent role, and foreign and security policy, formally under the second pillar with the Commission constrained to play a secondary role (Howorth 2007). Nevertheless, the distinction between supranational and inter-governmental decision-making regimes agreed in Maastricht came to be institutionalized as a basic structure of the EU.

Once it had taken the multilinear and internally differentiated path, the 1997 Amsterdam Treaty consolidated this institutional development, strengthening in particular the legislative role of the EP through the extension of the co-decision procedure to new policy realms in the area of the single market (Bogdandy 2000). So as to bring some order to the growing complexity of the EU, an Intergovernmental Conference (IGC) was organized in Nice in December 2000, whose resultant Treaty was signed in 2001. The 2001 Nice Treaty is important for having recognized (but not included) a Charter of Fundamental Rights (a proper constitutional document), but its institutional outcomes were considered largely unsatisfactory. Given the unsatisfactory outcome of the Nice Treaty, the European Council held in Laeken (Belgium) on December 15, 2001 adopted a "Declaration on the Future of Europe" that committed the EU to defining its constitutional basis. Indeed, the Laeken Council convened a constitutional convention in Brussels, bringing together the representatives of both the member state governments and parliaments and Union institutions with the task of preparing a draft treaty establishing "a Constitution for Europe" for the 2004 IGC. The Brussels constitutional convention lasted from February 2002 to June 2003, concluding its activities with a unanimous agreement on the proposed Constitutional Treaty or CT (Crum 2010; De Witte 2003; Norman 2003). On June 18, 2004 the heads of state and government of the member states reached a compromise on a slightly revised form, then signed it in Rome in 2004. Since the CT was the closest approximation to a formal constitution ever agreed by member state governments, it was said that the out-come of the Brussels constitutional convention transformed the EU from a *constitutional project* (Walker 2004) into a *constitutional pro-cess* (Shaw 2005), the so-called "Laeken process."

The CT seemed to confirm the supranational predisposition of the Union. The main aims of the CT were to replace the overlapping set of existing treaties that composed the EU, to codify human rights throughout the EU and to streamline decision-making in what was becoming an organization with twenty-seven member states (with the accession of Eastern and Southern European states in 2004 and 2007). Although the CT preserved the double constitution of the Maastricht Treaty, it nevertheless created the momentum that would have plausibly led to the supranational overhauling of the EU.[7] After being signed, it was subjected to ratification. Most member states did so by parliamentary ratification or by referenda, but France and the Netherlands rejected it in two popular referenda held respectively on May 29 and June 1, 2005. This outcome interrupted the supranational narrative, legitimizing, on the contrary, the compromise between the two views of the Union. Had it been ratified by all member states, the Treaty would have come into force on November 1, 2006. By that date, eighteen member states (that is two-thirds of the member states) had ratified the text.

Although it has been argued that failure is inevitable when com-plex constitutional treaties must be approved by popular referendum (among many, see Hierlemann 2008), one also has to consider cases, such as Spain, Luxembourg and Romania, where popular referenda brought approval, and not rejection, of the CT. Thus the contestation was not due to the instrument (the referendum) used to resolve the dispute on the constitutional nature of the EU, but rather that contest-ation was enflamed by the unanimity criterion required to adopt the CT, a criterion that precluded the formation of even a super-majority coalition supporting change. Although the EU was no longer an international organization, it kept an amendment procedure gener-ally adopted by international organizations.[8] The failure of the CT

[7] This was also my interpretation when I was working on the first edition of S. Fabbrini (2010).

[8] It should be noted that the United Nations (UN) Charter can be amended by a super-majority, although with the consent of the five permanent members of the Security Council.

to win popular support in those two member states caused the other seven remaining member states to postpone their ratification procedures and the European Council to call for a period of reflection. The Lisbon Treaty is the outcome of the period of reflection. Negotiated between the two largely expected enlargements of 2004 and 2007, it includes most of the content of the abandoned CT, without the constitutional symbols attached to it (such as the flag, the anthem and the preamble).

The EU emerging from this long process is a highly differentiated and flexible organization. From a comparative perspective, institutional and policy flexibility is certainly the defining property of federal political systems (both states and unions). Indeed, even unitary political systems have been pressured, by the growing complexity of policy-making, to adopt flexible regimes of taking and implementing decisions (Torfing *et al.* 2012). In federal political systems, however, flexibility is recognized and practiced within the boundaries of the constitutional distinction between shared rule and self-rule (Elazar 1987). In federal unions (the USA and Switzerland), variable configurations of states or cantons can set up specific policy compacts between themselves for dealing with problems of sectional interests. But those compacts have to remain within the competences of self-rule, without spilling over into the area of shared rule, as has been the case of the opt-out from the EMU. Although the border between self-rule and shared rule is permanently moving, policies pertaining to the latter are managed by the same decision-making regime and have an impact on all the members of the union.

For a state doing otherwise would mean unilaterally nullifying a legitimate federal decision: as, for instance, the South Carolina legislature did in 1828 by nullifying the effects of a federal tariff within the boundaries of its state. That decision, however, led to a deep conflict between the state and the federal center, then resolved in 1833 with South Carolina obliged to repeal, through a special convention, its previous Nullification Ordinance. The outcome of the Civil War of 1861–65 settled not only the issue of whether a group of states can leave the federation if they disagree with the latter's legislative decisions or constitutional principles, but it excluded for ever the feasibility of the nullification option (Elazar 1988). Flexibility is also recognized and largely utilized by a federal state such as Canada (Fossum and Menéndez 2011: chapter 6), in order to deal with the multinational

nature of the federation. However, flexibility has been used for extending the area of self-rule, in particular with regard to the province of
Quebec, not for introducing differentiation within the area of shared
rule. In short, in both federal unions and federal states flexibility is
managed with care because, if it exceeds a given threshold, it may call
into question the very sustainability of the federal political system. It
has been the existence of a formal constitutional document, accepted
by all the members of the federal political system, that has furnished
the criteria for patrolling the boundary between self-rule and shared
rule. The lack of such a document in the EU, on the contrary, has left
the latter without reliable criteria for ordering its institutional and
policy differentiation.

1.6 Conclusion

This chapter has reconstructed the multilinear character of the process of institutionalization of the EU. Although starting as a common
market project, the EU has developed as a proper political system
endowed with the authority of taking decisions on a growing number
of policies. Precisely because it aims to produce an "ever closer union",
the EU has grown in quantity and quality, leaving, however, its military side to the tutoring of NATO. An increasing number of policies
have been added to the original agricultural, trade and competition
policies of the 1950s. Market competition has become central, as has
anti-trust policy since the approval of the SEA. The critical juncture
of 1989–1991 also led to a deepening of integration in policies that
were traditionally at the core of the national sovereignty of its member
states. In those crucial years, the division between Western and Eastern
Europe suddenly disappeared, bringing a German question back to the
European agenda. The 1990 reunification of Germany solicited the
formation of an economic and monetary union based on a common
currency. Germany had to give up the symbol of its post-war economic
resurgence (the Deutsche Mark) in order to be allowed to move in the
direction of its political resurgence. At the same time, the geopolitical
opening of the continent to the east required the Union to redefine its
foreign policy responsibility in order to promote collective security in
the region. Indeed, in 1994 the EMU was put into place and in 2002
a new common currency (the euro) started to circulate, shared first
by twelve and then nineteen member states (out of twenty-eight) as

of January 1, 2015.[9] And finally foreign and security policies came to be considered policies of common interest. However, the new sensitive policies have come to be organized outside of the supranational regime inaugurated by the 1957 Rome Treaty.

Starting with the 1992 Maastricht Treaty, the EU has thus institutionalized different institutional regimes for deciding or managing different policies. This differentiation has been the outcome of several compromises between member states and EU actors. An institutional compromise led to the formation of two distinct decision-making regimes, supranational for single market policies and intergovernmental for the new sensitive policies. At the same time, with the launch of the EMU, a political compromise was made between the member states adopting or willing to adopt the common currency and those member states (such as the UK and Denmark) unwilling to take part in monetary integration and thus allowed to opt out from the new currency regime. Finally, an economic compromise was negotiated within the EMU between those member states (France in particular) claiming the necessity to guarantee a decision-making role to national governments in economic policy and those member states (Germany in particular) pressing to set up an independent central bank (ECB) and introduce formal parameters within which coordination of national policies would have to take place.

The panoply of constitutional compromises negotiated in Maastricht, which were then preserved by the following treaty rounds, was necessary in order to maintain a balance among different institutional, political and economic views on the EU, thus preserving the *unitary* character of the integration project. The role of the various compromises was to accommodate different needs and perspectives, on the assumption that they would not become reciprocally incompatible. The systemic condition for the success of these multiple constitutional balancing acts was the respective equilibrium between the

---

[9] The euro-area consisted, as of January 1, 2015, of nineteen member states: Austria, Belgium, Cyprus, Estonia, Finland, France, Germany, Greece, Ireland, Italy, Latvia, Lithuania, Luxembourg, Malta, the Netherlands, Portugal, Slovakia, Slovenia, and Spain. The currency is also used in a further four very small European countries (Andorra, Monaco, San Marino, Vatican City) and consequently used daily by some 335 million Europeans. Additionally, more than 175 million people worldwide, including 150 million people in Africa, used currencies pegged to the euro.

interests and the views supporting the two sides of the forces making the compromise. In short, from the 1992 Maastricht Treaty to the 2009 Lisbon Treaty, the EU developed as an internally highly differentiated political system (Leuffen, Rittberger and Schimmelfennig 2013; Dyson and Sepos 2010), in order to accommodate member states interpreting the integration process differently, but still expressing an inclusive project of integration. Within the same legal order, the EU has been allowed to differentiate both vertically (through different policy regimes) and horizontally (aggregating different clusters of member states in the various policy regimes), emphasizing its flexible nature: a flexibility finally magnified by the Lisbon Treaty, TEU Article 50.1, declaring that "any Member State may decide to withdraw from the Union in accordance with its own constitutional requirements." That differentiation, however, has developed in the vacuum of agreed constitutional criteria for ordering the relations between the member states and the Union.

2 | *The Lisbon Treaty and the euro crisis*

2.1 Introduction

The Lisbon Treaty came into force on December 1, 2009. The last member state to endorse it, Ireland, which first rejected it in a popular referendum held on June 12, 2008, finally approved the new Treaty in a second popular referendum held on October 2, 2009. The Lisbon Treaty consists of a series of amendments to the Treaty on European Union (TEU, Maastricht 1992) and the Treaty Establishing the European Community (TEC, Rome 1957), the latter being renamed the Treaty on the Functioning of the European Union (TFEU) in the process. The Charter of Fundamental Rights, elaborated for the Nice Treaty of 2001, has been given legal value as a third treaty included in the Lisbon Treaty. The two consolidated Treaties and the Charter form the legal basis of the Union. The Lisbon Treaty has tried to impose order on the institutional complexity acquired by the EU, giving a legal personality to the latter when acting in international affairs and abolishing the three pillar structure (Devuyst 2012). Notwithstanding the formal suppression of the pillar structure, the Lisbon Treaty did, however, recognize the existence of two different decision-making regimes (one supranational and the other intergovernmental).

This chapter is organized as follows. First, it will discuss the differentiation between the two decision-making regimes, here conceptualized as the dual constitution of the Lisbon Treaty. After analysis of the supranational constitution, it puts forward a detailed analysis of the intergovernmental constitution, regarding both foreign policy and economic policy decision-making regimes. Here I use the concept of "constitution" in a "material" sense (see Chapter 3) as a decision-making regime supported or justified by a distinct principle of power distribution. If the supranational constitution sustains and justifies a system of government characterized by the *sharing* of decision-making power among four institutions (the dual executive

constituted by the European Council – recognized as a formal institution of the Union for the first time – and the Commission and the
bicameral legislative branch constituted by the EP and the Council),
the intergovernmental constitution instead sustains and justifies a system of governance, characterized by the *pooling* of decision-making
power in two institutions, the European Council and the Council,
representing the national governments of the Union's member states.
Second, this chapter will analyse the institutional and policy impact
of the euro crisis on the intergovernmental constitution (considering the period 2010–2014). In fact, when the financial crisis reached
Europe, shortly before the coming into force of the Lisbon Treaty, not
only was there in place an intergovernmental constitution for framing the answer to it, but there was also a general consensus that only
national governments could find solutions for the financial turmoil.
Third, having reconstructed in detail the impact of the euro crisis on
the intergovernmental Union, this chapter will show the contradictory features assumed by the latter to manage the financial turmoil and
prevent it in the future.

2.2 The supranational Lisbon Treaty

Although the Treaty of Lisbon scrapped any constitutional symbolism,
it has defined (in terms of roles and functions) the EU's institutional
structure (Craig 2010; Foster 2010; Piris 2010). For a vast majority of
single market policies, the Treaty establishes that integration proceeds
through formal acts (*integration through law*). The legal activity of the
EU is based on:

(a) *regulations*, which are laws binding in all their elements and dir-
     ectly applicable in all member states. A regulation establishes
     direct rights and imposes duties on private parties without inter-
     ference of national law. It is immediately enforceable in all mem-
     ber states simultaneously;
(b) *directives*, which bind each member state to achieve a given result
     but leave the means and methods to the individual member state's
     control. Directives have to be transposed into national law and
     may concern a subgroup of member states;
(c) *decisions*, which are binding too, but they are of an individual
     nature.

One should also add (d) *recommendations and opinions*, which are not binding but consist of orientation documents to implement and to interpret legislation.

In order to manage those policies, the Lisbon Treaty has set up a system of government (that is, using David Easton's (1971) classic formulation, a formal structure of institutions endowed with the power of allocating values authoritatively). As in all established democracies, government and governance are also intertwined in the EU (Borzel 2010), that is, formal decision-making by distinct institutions (typical of government) interacts with informal relations between public officials, social groups and epistemic communities of experts (typical of governance).[1] In single market policies, the Lisbon Treaty has institutionalized a supranational system of government, cementing a long process of distinction between the executive and the legislative branches. Regarding the latter, the Treaty institutionalized a bicameral legislative branch, consisting of a lower chamber representing the European electorate (the EP) and an upper chamber representing the governments of the member states (the Council). The Council is constituted by functional configurations of member states' ministers, plus the General Affairs Council that coordinates them (see Appendix, Table A.3). According to TFEU Article 289, "the ordinary legislative procedure shall consist in the joint adoption by the EP and the Council of a regulation, directive or decision on a proposal from the Commission."

The Treaty thus celebrates the growing role acquired by the EP since its direct election in 1979. Starting with the elections of May 2014, the EP consists of 751 members (MEPs). The parliamentary seats are not apportioned according to the criterion of the population of member

---

[1] Although the two terms are frequently used interchangeably, institutionally they do not overlap at all. *Government* refers to an organization, with a clear distinction of roles and responsibilities, whose office holders operate according to some majority's criterion and are held to account according to formalized procedures. In contrast, *governance* refers to a practice of relations, involving public and private actors and organizations, with an unclear distinction of roles and responsibilities, where accountability is an unresolved issue (Piattoni 2010). In the EU case, however, governance is generally used with regard to the intergovernmental constitution (i.e., the "economic governance of EMU"). But, as I will show, that constitution is based on distinct institutions (European Council and Council) that take authoritative decisions, rather than on informal practices.

states, but in accordance with the criterion of *degressive proportion-ality*. This means: (1) a minimum of 6 EP seats is assigned to each member state (162 seats); (2) the remaining 589 seats are assigned to member states in proportion to their population; (3) the largest member state (Germany) can obtain a maximum of 96 seats. The EP has finally become an institution of equal standing with the Council representing (in its various ministerial formations) the ministers of member states' governments. At the same time, within the Council decisions are taken on a QMV basis, which is: "as from 1 November 2014 a qualified majority shall be defined as at least 55% of the members of the Council, comprising at least fifteen of them and representing Member States comprising at least 65% of the population of the Union" (TEU, Article 16.4). The EP and the Council not only support the process of integration through law, but give legitimacy to the law-making process through the representation of both voters and member states.

Celebrating the ordinary legislative procedure for the approval of legal acts, the Lisbon Treaty institutionalized a bicameral legislature. In fact, "where reference is made in the Treaties to the ordinary legislative procedure for the adoption of an act," the above procedure shall apply (TFEU, Article 294): the Commission has a monopoly over legislative proposals (although its proposals increasingly reflect European Council guidance) that might take the form of a directive, regulation or decision; before submitting its proposal, the Commission will have to consult the various Committees of Permanent Representatives of the member states (or COREPER) supporting the activities of the Council (Kreppel 2006), the parliamentary committees and interested or influential social and functional private organizations; once submitted, the Commission's proposal will have to be discussed, amended and approved by both legislative branches (the EP and the Council). It is interesting to note that, in the first years after the Lisbon Treaty came into force, when a Commission proposal was finally submitted to one or other legislative chamber, it was generally approved by them at first reading, avoiding passage through the time-consuming procedure of reconciling their different views on the proposal, thus de facto reducing the influence of the same Commission (Costa, Dehousse and Trakalova 2011). Moreover, contrary to what happens in parliamentary bicameral legislatures, that "voting unity is ... caused ... by an overarching intra- and inter-institutional consensus," not by parties connecting those institutions. In the EU, in fact, "parties are not able to co-ordinate voting behaviour of their own ministers and MEPs" (Muhlbock 2013: 583–4).

At the same time, regarding the executive, by formally recognizing for the first time the European Council as a Union institution, chaired by a president elected "by a qualified majority" of its members "for a term of two and half years, renewable once" (TEU, Article 15.5) and no longer chaired by the rotating presidency as in the past, thus requiring (TEU, Article 15.6) that "the President of the European Council shall not hold a national office," the Treaty has given the European Council a permanent political head (Closa 2012). In fact, the president of the European Council should "ensure the external representation of the Union on issues concerning its common foreign and security policy" (TEU, Article 15.6). Moreover, because the Treaty explicitly states (TEU, Article 15.1) that the European Council "shall not exercise legislative functions," the distinction with the Council (and its various formations) is now formalized. No longer can they be considered as components of the same institution (having both executive and legislative functions) as in the past (Hayes-Renshaw and Wallace 2006; Naurin and Wallace 2008), because now the Council exercises legislative functions, while the European Council exercises only executive functions (Kreppel 2011). The rotating presidency has remained for chairing the Council's formations on a semester basis, but its role has been significantly downsized.

Since its formation as an *informal* institution in 1974, the European Council has played a crucial role in deciding the most controversial issues raised by the integration process. As Kreppel (2006: 267) observed, "the broad policy agenda [was] determined in the European Council, which serve[d] as the political executive, and the Commission [the more bureaucratic arm of the executive] then formalize[d] the agenda into specific proposals". It has been argued that it was "the weak political leadership [of the Commission which] constituted a prominent reason for creating the European Council" (Tallberg 2006:54), with the exception represented by the Delors presidency of the Commission in the period 1985–1994. The European Council has behaved as the decision-maker of last resort, the institution where strategic decisions have been negotiated. Its informal nature protected the European Council from being absorbed by the supranational logic, allowing it to play a supervisory role on the functioning of the "trilogue," that is, on the interaction between the Commission, the Council and the EP.

This informality led many observers to underestimate the role of the European Council as a proper Union institution.

The Lisbon Treaty has thus formalized a longstanding practice, recognizing the European Council as the only institution able to bridge member states within the Union's decision-making process. To use the words of Van Middelaar (2013: 12), between the outermost sphere deriving from Europe's geography and history and the innermost sphere created by the founding treaties, there emerged an intermediate sphere. "This in-between world went unnoticed for years and cannot be fully captured in legal terms. Perhaps, for that reason, it has not been given a name. Yet it is crucial. This is the sphere of Europe's member states ... When the member states act together, as a single entity, they are the motor of 'Europe.'" This in-between sphere (representing the union of the states) has been gradually institutionalized in the European Council in order to balance the "inner sphere" (representing the union of the citizens) of the integration process. It should be added that Jean Monnet was also in favor of the institutionalization of the summits of the heads of state and government, perceiving that their involvement in Union affairs was essential for deciding the most controversial issues and dealing with difficult disputes between member states (Duchene 1994).

Formally recognizing the European Council as an institution with no legislative functions and confirming the Commission as the institution in charge of promoting "the general interest of the Union," the Lisbon Treaty has delineated a dual executive. According to the TEU Article 17.1, the Commission "shall oversee the application of Union laws under the control of the Court of Justice ... It shall execute the budget and manage programmes. It shall exercise coordinating, executive and management functions." At the same time, stating that the European Council should "define the general political directions and priorities" of the Union (TEU, Article 15.1), the Treaty has created a dual or Janus-like executive: a development that had already been discussed in the post-Laeken process (Hoffman 2003; Lassalle and Levrat 2004).

The institutional architecture of the executive power designed by the Lisbon Treaty has affected the traditional distinction between an intergovernmental European Council and a supranational Commission (De Scoutheete 2011). The European Council, with its permanent presidency, has become more than the mere institution representing the heads of state and government. The permanent president has

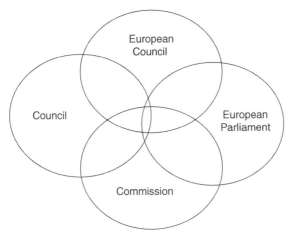

Figure 2.1 The supranational constitution: decision-making structure

contributed to make the European Council a core institution of the Union, although the president has not been recognized the formal power to vote on that institution's deliberations. The first new President (Herman Van Rompuy) was quick to set up his permanent office in Brussels (at the Justus Lipsius building), which also symbolized that the European Council's presidency is now based in the Union's capital and no longer in the capital of the member state holding the rotating presidency. In its turn, the Commission, which will continue "to consist of a number of members equal to the number of Member States" (EUCO 2013), "including its President and the High Representative of the Union for Foreign Affairs and Security Policy who shall be one of its Vice Presidents" (TEU, Article 17.4), has become less than a purely supranational institution. The decision to maintain a commissioner for each member state in the Commission has had the effect of diluting its traditional supranational character. The Lisbon Treaty has therefore built a four-sided institutional framework for governing EU policies (in the single market), with a bicameral legislature and a dual executive branch (see Figure 2.1).

Where integration takes place through legal acts, the EU thus decides through the complex interplay of institutions each operationally independent from the others. The European Council and the Council are expressions of member state governments, and their composition depends on the outcomes of periodical and temporarily differentiated national elections in the member states. The EP depends on the outcome of the elections organized in districts within member states every five years. The Commission's president is nominated by the European Council, but should then receive the EP's vote of approval. The commissioners are nominated by the European Council, in cooperation with the Commission's president, but they too have to pass through a process of approval by the EP.

One might argue (Curtin 2009) that the governmental system of the supranational EU has tried to deal with the trade-off between effectiveness and legitimacy: in order to achieve the former, it provides an incentive for competitive cooperation between the European Council and the Commission; in order to achieve the latter, it establishes the legislative co-decision of the EP and the Council and the supervisory role of the ECJ. It should also be noted that the institutionalization of a quadrilateral decision-making system has had contradictory effects on the "Community method" that helped the EU's transformation into a supranational organization. This method of integration does not recognize a decision-making role to the European Council, although it has always been an institution of strategic importance for the EU and it has formally entered into the institutional core of the EU decision-making system (De Scoutheete 2012). How can we reconcile the European Council's decision-making role with the decision-making independence of the Commission (which is the fulcrum of the "Community method") given that both institutions exercise executive functions? Remaining within a strict "Community method" framework, it would be difficult to find an answer.[2] Since the European Council is here to stay, the supranational method would also require a broader interpretation than the traditional one.

At the same time, the governmental (horizontal) separation of powers of the supranational EU intertwines with the separation of powers at the territorial (vertical) level. Following a federal criterion, but never celebrated as such, TEU Article 4.1 states that "competences not conferred upon the Union in the Treaties remain with

---

[2] In fact, in the most detailed study on the Community method (Dehousse 2011), there are no references to the role acquired by the European Council in the supranational EU. The in-depth study of the European executive order by Trondal (2010) also does not consider the role of the European Council. For a discussion on the erosion of the Commission's power of initiative, see Ponzano, Hermanin and Corona (2012).

the Member States": thus specifying (in TEU, Article 5.1) that "the limits of Union competences are governed by the principle of conferral," which means that the Union has to act within the limits of the competences conferred upon it by the member states in the Treaties. This principle restricts the power of the Union's institutions because it prevents the latter from intervening on issues not assigned to the competence of the Union. At the same time, any competence not formally conferred to the Union should remain with the member states. Moreover (TEU, Article 5.1), "the use of Union competences is governed by the principle of subsidiarity and proportionality." The subsidiarity principle requires that the Union, in areas that do not fall within its exclusive competence, "shall act only if and in so far as the objectives of the proposed action cannot be sufficiently achieved by the Member States, either at the central level or regional and local level" (TEU, Article 5.3). In its turn, the proportionality principle implies (TEU, Article 5.4) that "the content and form of Union action shall not exceed what is necessary to achieve the objectives of the Treaties." This federalizing approach is thus specified in TFEU Articles 2, 3 and 4. In particular, TFEU Article 3 defines the exclusive competence of the Union, whereas TFEU Article 4 identifies the competences that the Union has to share with the member states. Since the EU is the outcome of a process of aggregation of previously independent states, it seems inevitable that the latter have tried to promote a federalizing model that preserves as much power (or competence) as possible to themselves. In this regard, the EU is no different from the other federal unions.

2.3 The intergovernmental Lisbon Treaty: foreign policy

Integration through legislative acts does not represent the only idea celebrated by the Lisbon Treaty. With the extension of the integration process to policy realms traditionally considered sensitive in terms of the national sovereignty of the member states, such as welfare and employment policies, foreign and security policy (CFSP), defense and security policy (European Security and Defence Policy or ESDP) and economic and monetary policies (the EMU), the EU has looked to organize the decision-making process through an intergovernmental constitution. The Lisbon Treaty inherited the 1992 Maastricht Treaty's multiple compromises, starting with the compromise between supranational and intergovernmental decision-making regimes. The intergovernmental decision-making regime is based on the assumption that integration should proceed through *voluntary or consensual policy coordination* between member state governments.

The boundary between the supranational and intergovernmental Union has not been fixed and is not insurmountable, as shown by the justice and home affairs pillar that was gradually transformed from an intergovernmental to a supranational policy. Nonetheless, the Lisbon Treaty formally entrenched the intergovernmental method of policy- and decision-making, thus celebrating an alternative model of integration characterized by Allerkamp (2009: 14): (a) the "policy entrepreneurship (coming) from some national capitals and the active involvement of the European Council in setting the overall direction of policy"; (b) "the predominance of the Council of Ministers in consolidating cooperation"; (c) "the limited or marginal role of the Commission"; (d) "the exclusion of the EP and the ECJ from the circle of involvement"; (e) "the involvement of a distinct circle of key national policy-makers"; (f) "the adoption of special arrangements for managing cooperation, in particular the Council Secretariat"; (g) "the opaqueness of the process to national Parliaments and citizens"; (h) "the capacity on occasion to deliver substantial joint policy." What we have here is a system of governance (Tsebelis and Garrett 2001), as the same Treaty calls it, yet functionally equivalent to a governmental system. It is a system where there is neither a distinction between (executive and legislative) functions and institutions, nor between national government and intergovernmental institutions.

Regarding the CFSP and EMU in particular, the intergovernmental Lisbon Treaty formally confirmed the principle that integration should *not* proceed through legislative acts that are directly binding for all the subjects involved. These policies are based on *soft law*, not *hard law*. As TEU Article 24.1 states expressly, in CFSP "the adoption of legislative acts shall be excluded" and decisions are implemented through actions and positions (TEU, Article 25). Thus not only is the EP ruled out of the decision-making process, but, as TEU Article 24 clarifies, "the Court of Justice of the European Union shall not have jurisdiction with respect to these provisions," unless the foreign policy decisions infringe upon fundamental principles and rights the EU should respect, as stated in TEU Article 2 ("The Union is founded on the values of respect for human dignity") and TEU Article 3 ("The Union's

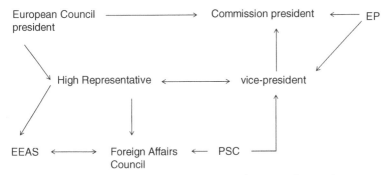

Figure 2.2 The intergovernmental constitution: foreign policy-making structure

aim is to promote peace"). Moreover, the Lisbon Treaty recognizes a special status to the Foreign Affairs Council. The latter is the only Council configuration, among the other permanent configurations plus the General Affairs Council, chaired for five years by the High Representative of the Union for Foreign Affairs and Security Policy (HR), while the other Council formations are chaired by the corresponding minister of the half-yearly rotating presidency of the EU.

The HR role was initially introduced in the 1997 Amsterdam Treaty with the aim of giving technical support to the Foreign Affairs Council. Through the HR, the latter did not need to rely solely on the work of the General Affairs Council secretariat, thus giving the Foreign Affairs Council an autonomous functional structure. The Lisbon Treaty not only makes the HR the permanent chairperson of the Foreign Affairs Council, but it also gives him/her the role of vice-president of the Commission. Moreover, the Foreign Affairs Council and the HR are supported in their activity by a Political and Security Committee (PSC) that, according to TEU Article 38, has to "contribute to the definitions of policies by delivering opinions" and by controlling the "strategic direction of the crisis management operation." According to the Treaty (TEU, Article 18.2), the HR must thus wear two hats, that of vice president of the Commission and that of permanent chairperson of the Foreign Affairs Council. He or she must be appointed by the European Council in agreement with the president of the Commission – an appointment that must then be approved by the EP (see Figure 2.2).

Moreover, the Lisbon Treaty (TEU, Article. 27.3) envisages the formation of a European External Action Service (EEAS) as a distinct organization at the disposal of the HR that will allow the implementation of the Union's foreign policy (Carta 2012). The EEAS "shall comprise officials from relevant departments of the General Secretariat of the Council and of the Commission as well as staff seconded from national diplomatic services of the Member States." The HR was thus expected to fulfill a rather difficult (if not schizophrenic) job, being a member at the same time of both a supranational institution (in his/her capacity as vice-president of the Commission) and an intergovernmental institution (because s/he permanently presides over the Foreign Affairs Council). Reformation of the role of the HR has been considered by many scholars (Allen 2012; Missiroli 2010) to be one of the main innovations introduced by the Lisbon Treaty for bringing foreign and security policy as close as possible to the supranational institutions.

The design of the ambiguous role for the HR reflected the expectation that s/he might bridge the supranational culture represented by the Commission and the intergovernmental interests protected by the Foreign Affairs Council. The Lisbon Treaty left unanswered the question of whether the HR should be a policy entrepreneur promoting a common foreign policy position, thus reframing the interests of the member states in a more integrated perspective, or a mere policy coordinator of the ministers of foreign affairs who make up the Council. The institutional solution has not resolved the puzzle of who speaks on behalf of the Union in international relations, given also the important role that the president of the European Council, the president of the Commission and the Trade Commissioner are allowed or expected to play in the external relations of the Union. Notwithstanding the Lisbon Treaty's effort, the CFSP has continued to function in accordance with the model of "intensive trans-governmentalism" as it was defined by Wallace and Wallace (2007): a model that expresses an intergovernmental logic, although it fosters a process of socialization between national civil servants and ministers engaged in this policy realm at the Union level. Nevertheless, the Lisbon Treaty clearly recognizes the Foreign Affairs Council as the only institution able to decide "actions" and "positions" (Thym 2011), which are the operational instruments of EU foreign policy, making it at the same time a legislative and executive institution. Although it is plausible to argue that the EP may have an influence in foreign and security policy through its role in approving the HR, nevertheless that influence is institutionally constrained by the decision-making model adopted in this policy.

2.4 The intergovernmental Lisbon Treaty: economic policy

A similar logic governs the functioning of the economic policy of the EU organized within the EMU (Heipertz and Verdun 2010). If monetary policy has been assigned to exclusive control by the ECB, all the policies connected to the management of a sound common currency (such as economic, financial, fiscal and budgetary policies) have remained under the control of each national government, coordinating with the other national governments in the intergovernmental institutions set up in Brussels. The Lisbon Treaty has thus taken on the Maastricht Treaty's design of the EMU: monetary policy's centralization and economic policy's decentralization.

As stated by TFEU Article 5.1, "The Member States shall coordinate their economic policies within the Union" and thus by TFEU Article 119, "the adoption of an economic policy … is based on the close coordination of Member States' economic policies." Economic and financial policy is controlled by the Council (in its formation as the ECOFIN Council). The ECOFIN Council monopolizes decision-making in economic policy, although decisions are generally based on reports or recommendations by and from the Commission. As stated in TFEU Article 126.14, "the Council shall, acting unanimously in accordance with a special legislative procedure and after consulting the European Parliament and the European Central Bank, adopt the appropriate provisions" for implementing agreed-upon economic guidelines. According to the special legislative procedure, the Council, acting either unanimously or by a qualified majority depending on the issue concerned, can adopt legislation based on a proposal by the Commission after consulting the EP. However, while being required to consult the EP on legislative proposals concerning economic and financial policy, the Council is not bound by the latter's position. Indeed, the Council has frequently taken decisions without waiting for the EP's opinion. The ECOFIN Council is supported in its activities by an Economic and Financial Committee whose task (TFEU, Article. 134) is to supervise the economic and financial situations of the member states. It is an advisory body to the ECOFIN Council, to which "the Member States, the Commission and the European Central Bank shall each appoint no more than two members" (TFEU, Article 134.2). It has been argued (Puetter 2012) that the EMU functions according to a variant of the intergovernmental method, a variant defined as "deliberative intergovernmentalism." However, either through recommendations or special legislative procedures, the ECOFIN Council is the institution with the power to take and execute decisions concerning the economic and financial policies of the Union.

The Lisbon Treaty also formalized the economic compromise represented by the post-Maastricht SGP. As stated by TFEU Article 126.1, member states "shall avoid excessive government deficits" and shall respect (TFEU, Article 126.2) the reference values (with regard to the ratio of deficit and debt to GDP) already defined in the Maastricht Treaty (TEC, Article 104.2 and now celebrated in Protocol No. 12 annexed to the Lisbon Treaty on the EDP). Also in this case, the logic remains strictly intergovernmental, notwithstanding the spectacular failure of the SGP in 2003 (upheld by the subsequent reform of 2005). The Commission has seen its power of recommendation recognized, but its role is still subordinate to the Council. TFEU Article 121.2 states that "The Council shall, on recommendation from the Commission, formulate a draft for the broad guidelines of the economic policies of the Member States and of the Union." And TFEU Article 126.2 clarifies that "The Commission shall monitor the development of the budgetary situation and of the stock of Government debt in the Member States," in order to evaluate whether the latter respect the criteria set up in the EDP annexed to the Treaty. Article 126.5 also recognizes to the Commission the power to "address an opinion to the Member State concerned and … [to] inform the Council" that an excessive deficit in that member state "exists or may occur." However, a following paragraph of TFEU Article 126.6 makes it again clear that only "the Council shall … decide after an overall assessment whether an excessive deficit exists." If a deficit exists, says TFEU Article 126.7, the Council "shall adopt … on a recommendation from the Commission, recommendations addressed to the Member State concerned with a view to bringing that situation to an end within a given period." If the member state concerned fails to comply with the decision taken, adds TFEU Article 126.11, "the Council may decide to apply … one or more of [several] measures … [until] to impose fines of an appropriate size."

Thus, although it is recognized that the Commission has the possibility to initiate a procedure against a member state running an excessive budget deficit, nonetheless the Commission's recommendation has the status of a proposal, because only the ECOFIN Council can take the appropriate measures (that may range from requests for information addressed to the non-compliant member state to fines imposed on it). In economic and financial policy, it is up to the ECOFIN Council to decide whether or not to proceed along the lines of the Commission's proposal. The Commission certainly matters in this process, but it can only play a technical role (the role of monitoring the economic performance of member states), not a decision-making one. This is why, for the Lisbon Treaty, economic and financial policy is based on voluntary coordination. The sanctions for excessive deficits and debt are always subject to the will of member state governments (or their finance ministers in the ECOFIN Council).

This is even truer for euro-area member states, whose main deliberations take place in the informal Euro Group constituted by the economic and financial ministers of the governments of the euro-area ("The Ministers of the Member States whose currency is the euro shall meet *informally*," as declared by Protocol No. 14, Article 1, annexed to the Lisbon Treaty, author's emphasis), chaired by a president elected "for two and a half years by a majority of those Member States" (Protocol No. 14, Article 2), with the technical support of the Commission. The Euro Group embodies a specific approach to policy-making defined as "informal governance" (Puetter 2006). Protocol No. 14 does not even mention the EP, at least as the institution that requires information about the decisions to be taken. And, as in the CFSP, no supervisory role is recognized or assigned to the ECJ. This is because, by establishing a common currency (the euro), the EU has centralized monetary policy (assigning its management to a genuine supranational institution, the ECB, that "shall be invited to take part in ... [the] meetings" of the Euro Group: Protocol No. 14, Article 1) and at the same time, by introducing the coordination framework it has allowed for the decentralization of those fiscal and budgetary policies that are structurally connected to monetary policy (see Figure 2.3).

The Lisbon Treaty also recognized the political compromise negotiated in Maastricht and formalized in the EMU that granted the option to opt out of adopting the euro to the UK and Denmark.

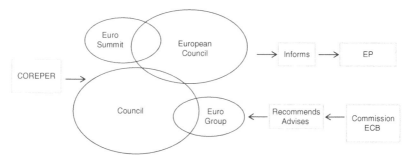

Figure 2.3 The intergovernmental constitution: economic policy-making structure

Protocol No. 15, Article 1 states that "unless the United Kingdom notifies the Council that it intends to adopt the euro, it shall be under no obligation to do so" and Protocol No. 16, Article 1 recognizes that "in view of the notice given to the Council by the Danish Government on 3 November 1993, Denmark shall have an exemption" from adopting the euro. The opting out from adoption of the euro had a special character: it formalized the existence of different economic and monetary regimes within the EU. Notwithstanding what the Lisbon Treaty (TEU, Article 3.4) reasserted, namely that "the Union shall establish an economic and monetary union whose currency is the euro," and thus that the adoption of the euro is not an option but a requirement for EU membership, the UK and Denmark were left free to keep their national currencies. Formally, the Lisbon Treaty (TFEU, Article 139.1) recognizes this possibility only to those member states that do not "fulfil the necessary conditions for the adoption of the euro [and for this reason they] shall hereinafter be referred to as 'Member States with derogation,'" or "pre-ins" member states. This has never been the case for Denmark and the UK. Thus, within the single market area different economic and monetary regimes have come to coexist: within the EMU, the regime of the euro-area member states (the "ins") and the regimes of those member states not yet fulfilling the macroeconomic criteria but committed to meeting them (the "pre-ins"); outside the EMU, the monetary and economic regime of the member states self-excluded from the common currency (the "outs"). The Lisbon Treaty has thus institutionalized in the same legal framework diverging economic and monetary interests, through the compromise between Continental member states and the UK and some ex-EFTA countries, on the assumption that they would converge towards a shared goal of economic growth and monetary stability.

In short, once the Union started to deal with policies traditionally at the core of member states' sovereignty (e.g. foreign, security, economic and fiscal policy, or electorally sensitive policies such as employment or welfare), it decided to promote, in those policies, an integrative model based on voluntary coordination by member state governments, a model free from supranational constraints. This was the compromise made in Maastricht and then inherited by the CT and the Lisbon Treaty. In the management of public policies linked to the internal single market, the Lisbon Treaty institutionalized a supranational constitution with characteristics that are similar to those of other democratic unions of states or federal unions. Such a constitution sustains and justifies a system of government characterized by a form of sharing powers among the four institutions that participate in the decision-making process (a dual executive constituted by the European Council and the Commission and a bicameral legislative branch consisting of the EP and the Council). At the same time, for policies that have traditionally been sensitive to national sovereignty, the Lisbon Treaty institutionalized an intergovernmental constitution. Such a constitution sustains a decision-making system where power is pooled in the two institutions (the European Council and the Council) that represent the governments of the Union, to be used consensually by the latter through voluntary coordination, without distinction between legislative and executive functions. This system of governance indeed consists in a confusion of powers that prevents any significant check on the choices of the intergovernmental institutions by the EP and the ECJ.

2.5 The euro crisis and the European Council

When the financial crisis started to hit Greece, there was therefore in place a decision-making regime for structuring the institutional and policy answers to financial turmoil. As established by the intergovernmental constitution, the European Council and the ECOFIN Council immediately took center stage in the policy-making process, while the Commission was marginalized and the EP left dormant. One

might speculate that stronger leadership by the Commission and the
EP would have claimed a decision-making role for their institutions.
The financial crisis opened a critical juncture that might have been
used for altering the existing institutional path. However, the governmental leaders within the European Council seized the initiative,
using the new critical juncture to advance their collective leadership
of the Union in facing the economic crisis. Continual meetings of the
European Council and the ECOFIN Council were organized between
2010 and 2014,[3] although none of them proved decisive (Bastasin
2014). In that period there were different rounds of crucial decisions
concerning the new economic governance of the EU aimed at both
crisis management and prevention (S. Fabbrini 2013). For economy
of discourse, I will reconstruct the yearly sequence of those decisions
to highlight not only the formidable array of measures taken to deal
with the crisis, but also to show the unquestionable decision-making
role played by the European Council, which became the true executive of the Union although in constant interaction with the ECOFIN
Council.

The first round of deliberations took place in 2010. At the ECOFIN
Council of May 9–10, 2010, it was first decided to adopt a regulation
creating the European Financial Stability Mechanism (or EFSM) as a
new EU instrument of law. Then, on the margins of that meeting, "the
members of the Council from the 17 euro-area countries 'switched
hats' and transformed themselves into representatives of their states
at an intergovernmental conference; in that capacity, they adopted
a decision by which they committed themselves to establishing the
European Financial Stability Facility (or EFSF) outside the EU legal
framework" (De Witte 2012: 2). The EFSF consisted of an executive
agreement (not a new formal treaty), establishing a private company

[3] It is interesting to note that, while the Lisbon Treaty (TEU, Article 15.3) states
that "the European Council shall meet twice every six months," in 2010 it
met six times (including one meeting of the euro-area member states' heads
of state and government); in 2011 it met nine times (including three meetings
of the euro-area member states' heads of state and government); in 2012 it
met six times (including one meeting of the euro-area member states' heads of
state and government); in 2013 it met six times (including one meeting of the
euro-area member states' heads of state and government); in 2014 it met six
times (including one meeting of the euro-area member states' heads of state and
government, plus an informal meeting after the EP elections in May).

under Luxembourg law, authorized to negotiate with its seventeen shareholders. Moreover, in the ECOFIN Council of September 7, 2010, the European Semester was approved as an instrument for enhancing temporal consistency in EU economic policy coordination. The European Semester came into force in January 2011. If the former (the EFSF) was an instrument of crisis management (to help Greece, Ireland and Portugal face the sovereign debt crisis), the latter (the European Semester) was rather a framework for promoting crisis prevention because it aimed to coordinate *ex ante* the budgetary and economic policies of the EU member states, in line with both the SGP and the Europe 2010 strategy (see Hallerberg, Marzinotto and Wolff 2012).

The second round of deliberations took place in 2011 when the financial crisis started to hit home dramatically. Between the European Council of March 24–25 and the European Council of June 23–24, several measures were decided. First of all, the so-called Six Pack (see Table 2.1), consisting of a package of legislative proposals finalized to further tighten the policy coordination required by both the European Semester and the SGP, was proposed and thus adopted through the ordinary legislative procedure. These measures came into force on December 13, 2011. To these measures one should add the Euro Plus Pact, consisting of a political commitment between the euro-area member states, but also open to non-euro-area member states (Denmark, Poland, Latvia, Lithuania, Bulgaria and Romania) aimed at fostering stronger economic policy coordination. The signatories of the Pact made concrete commitments to a list of political reforms to be adopted domestically that were intended to improve the fiscal strength and competitiveness of each country. The Pact aimed to strengthen the SGP, although it was still based on the intergovernmental open method of coordination. It was finally adopted in March 2011.

In the second half of 2011 the work of the European Council concerned the speeding up of the approval of an intergovernmental treaty called the European Stability Mechanism (ESM). On December 16, 2010 the European Council agreed an amendment to TFEU Article 136 that states that "the Member States whose currency is the euro may establish a stability mechanism to be activated if indispensable to safeguard the stability of the euro area as a whole." Thanks to this amendment, the ESM was established as a new treaty among

Table 2.1 *The Six Pack*

Legal acts	Policy aims
Regulation (EU) No. 1173/2011: it concerns the enforcement of budgetary surveillance in the euro-area by imposing sanctions in the form of interest-bearing deposits or non-interest-bearing deposits for significant divergences in the budgetary position.	Introduction of new sanctions on both the preventive and corrective sides of the SGP. Approved through the ordinary legislative procedure.
Regulation (EU) No. 1174/2011: it confers new powers on the ECOFIN Council to preserve the effective correction of excessive macroeconomic imbalances in the euro-area.	Reinforced correction mechanism for excessive macroeconomic imbalances. Approved through the ordinary legislative procedure.
Regulation (EU) No. 1175/2011: it strengthens the multilateral surveillance of budgetary positions and economic policies in order to prevent the occurrence of excessive deficits.	*Ex-ante* and *ex-post* surveillance on convergence programs or stability laws: medium-term objectives. Approved through the ordinary legislative procedure.
Regulation (EU) No. 1176/2011: it sets up an alert mechanism in order to facilitate the pre-emptive identification and monitoring of imbalances. Corrective action plans of member states, for which an excessive imbalance procedure is opened, are under the control of the Commission.	Macroeconomic surveillance and alert mechanism. Approved through the ordinary legislative procedure.

Table 2.1 (*cont.*)

Legal acts	Policy aims
Council Regulation (EU) No. 1177/2011: it speeds up the implementation of the excessive deficit procedure. It establishes new rules for sanctions in the preventive and in the corrective parts of the SGP, i.e. the reverse qualified majority voting (RQMV) procedure.	Stricter voting procedures for excessive deficits. Approved through the special legislative procedure.
Council Directive 2011/85/EU: it provides detailed rules concerning the characteristics of the budgetary frameworks of member states.	Requirements for budgetary frameworks of the member states. Approved through a non-legislative procedure.

Key: The first two regulations concern only the euro-area member states, whereas the last three plus the directive concern all the EU member states.

the euro-area member states, endowed with its own institutions,[4] by a European Council decision of March 25, 2011. It was signed by all of the then twenty-seven EU member states on March 2, 2012, although it could come into force only as of September 27, 2012, having to await the decision of the German Constitutional Court regarding its constitutional congruence with the German Basic Law, a decision finally and positively expressed on September 12, 2012. Its legal nature was the object of several negotiations. Finally, it was established as an

---

[4] The Conclusions of the European Council of March 24–25, 2011 state: "The ESM will have a Board of Governors consisting of the Ministers of Finance of the euro-area Member States (as voting members), with the European Commissioner for Economic and Monetary Affairs and the President of the ECB as observers. The Board of Directors will elect a Chairperson from among its voting members ... The ESM will have a Board of Directors which will carry out specific tasks as delegated by the Board of Governors ... All decisions by the Board of Directors will be taken by qualified majority ... A qualified majority is defined as 80 percent of the votes," (EUCO 2011: 21–3).

international organization, under public international law, located in Luxembourg, which provides financial assistance to member states of the euro-area in financial difficulty. It functions as a permanent firewall for the euro-area with a maximum lending capacity of €500 billion. It replaces the two existing temporary EU funding programs: the EFSF and the EFSM. All new bailout applications and deals for any euro-area member state with a financial stability issue will in principle be covered by the ESM, while the EFSF and EFSM continue to handle the transfer and monitoring of the previously approved bailout loans for Ireland, Portugal and Greece.

In the same period, other crucial decisions were made, particularly during the European Council's meeting of December 8–9, 2011. Under the irresistible leadership of German Chancellor Angela Merkel, followed by French President Nicolas Sarkozy, a proposal to amend the Lisbon Treaty in order to integrate the fiscal policies of the member states was advanced. This time automatic mechanisms of sanctions on member states that did not respect more stringent criteria for the deficit–GDP ratio (0.5 percent a year) and debt–GDP ratio (60 percent, with the reduction of 1/20 of the excess stock every year) were advanced, with the request that each member state introduce the rule (frequently defined as the "golden rule") of a mandatory balanced budget domestically at the constitutional or equivalent level. The UK's opposition to pursuing fiscal integration within the Lisbon Treaty's legal framework, motivated by the need to protect the London financial district from possibly restrictive fiscal regulations, made it necessary to move outside of the Lisbon Treaty, an outcome that the French president, given his mistrust if not distrust of the supranational features present in the Lisbon Treaty, aimed for.

Indeed, it may have been possible to use the procedure of enhanced cooperation (TEU, Article 20), on the basis of which a group of member states is allowed to advance towards deeper integration in policy fields that are not in the exclusive competence of the Union or that do not concern the CFSP (F. Fabbrini 2012). However, this institutional strategy was not considered viable for several reasons: probably because of German domestic considerations (Chancellor Merkel had to appease her electoral constituencies by displaying her capacity to impose stricter rules on the euro-area member states), but also because the activation of the enhanced cooperation procedure would have required (TFEU, Articles 326–334) the approval and support of the supranational institutions. In fact, for the enhanced cooperation to take place, according to TFEU Article 329.1, "the Commission may submit a proposal to the Council to that effect ... Authorization to proceed ... shall be granted by the Council, on a proposal from the Commission and after obtaining the consent of the European Parliament." Thus, although it would have been constitutionally questionable to manage a complex set of policies through enhanced cooperation, the latter would have required the support of the EP and the Commission, a condition that the larger euro-area member states clearly disliked. For these reasons, it was decided that a new intergovernmental treaty, the Fiscal Compact Treaty (see Box 2.1) with its own governance structure and aimed at making the SGP's parameters more rigid, would be set up outside the Lisbon Treaty and signed by all of the then seventeen euro-area member states plus those non-euro-area member states (all of them, apart from the UK and the Czech Republic) interested in participating in the Treaty.

Box 2.1 – Fiscal Compact Treaty

The Fiscal Compact Treaty, formally the Treaty on Stability, Coordination and Governance in the Economic and Monetary Union, is an intergovernmental treaty that was signed on March 2, 2012 by all member states of the EU, except the Czech Republic (that finally signed it in March 2014) and the UK. The Treaty requires its ratifying member states to enact laws (preferably in the form of constitutional amendments or of equivalent status) guaranteeing national budgets to be in balance or in surplus. These laws must provide for a self-correcting mechanism to prevent breach of them in the form of a domestic legal requirement. The Treaty defines a balanced budget as one that has a general budget deficit of less than 3% of GDP and a structural deficit of less than either 0.5% or 1%, depending on a country's debt-to-GDP ratio. In particular, the Treaty is concerned with the need to reduce public debt. For the first time, a procedure is legalized for reducing it automatically. Article 4 states that: "When the ratio of a Contracting Party's general government debt to gross domestic product exceeds the 60% reference value referred to in

Article 1 of the Protocol [No. 12] on the excessive deficit procedure, annexed to the European Union Treaties, that Contracting Party shall reduce it at an average rate of one twentieth per year as a benchmark." If the structural deficit for the annual account is found to exceed those limits, or the contracting party does not respect the timeline for re-entering within the 60% parameter for public debt, the country will have to correct the accounts under strict Commission supervision. The Treaty also places compliance with its budgetary and other requirements under the jurisdiction of the ECJ. A member state found in breach of its obligations can ultimately be fined up to 0.1% of its GDP. On the constitutionalization of budgetary constraints, see Adams, F. Fabbrini and Larouche (2014).

The two new intergovernmental treaties (the ESM and the Fiscal Compact), established outside the legal order of the Lisbon Treaty between 2010 and 2011, introduced important innovations in the intergovernmental logic, however. Indeed, in order to prevent future veto threats, the new intergovernmental treaties set up new organizations where unanimity is no longer needed for decision-taking. The Fiscal Compact has established (Title VI, Article 14.2) that, to enter into force, it requires the approval of twelve out of the then seventeen euro-area member states (and out of the then twenty-five member states) signing it. Moreover, the Commission's intervention with a contracting party that disrespects the agreement is now quasi-automatic, an automaticity that can be neutralized only by a reversed qualified majority of the financial ministers of the signatory member states (Fiscal Compact, Article 17), already introduced in the Six Pack. However, the governing body of those organizations consists of representatives of national governments and ministers. Indeed, the Fiscal Compact formalizes the informal Euro Summit as the center of the governance system. As Article 12.1 states:

The Heads of State or Government of the Contracting Parties whose currency is the euro shall meet informally in Euro Summit meetings, together with the President of the European Commission ... The President of the Euro Summit shall be appointed by the Heads of State or Government of the Contracting Parties whose currency is the euro by simple majority at the same time as the European Council elects its President and for the same term of office.

Article 12.4 then adds: "The President of the Euro Summit shall ensure the preparation and continuity of Euro Summit meetings, in close cooperation with the President of the European Commission. The body charged with the preparation of and follow up to the Euro Summit meetings shall be the Euro Group and its President may be invited to attend such meetings for that purpose." Article 12.5 finally points out that the EP should only be informed of the activities of the executive body: "The President of the European Parliament may be invited to be heard. The President of the Euro Summit shall present a report to the European Parliament after each Euro Summit meeting."

A third round of deliberations developed in the second half of 2012, between the European Council of June 28–29 and December 13–14, 2012. In that period it became clear that fiscal consolidation was not enough to deal with the crisis and indeed the June European Council approved the guidelines of a growth pact. However, not only was it considered necessary to relaunch economic growth on a continental scale, but also the new intergovernmental treaties and legislative measures would have to be reframed within a reformed EMU. The same June European Council thus invited its president "to develop in close collaboration with the President of the Commission, the President of the Euro Group and the President of the ECB, a specific and time-bound road map for the achievement of a genuine Economic Monetary Union." A Report with the same title was presented by the president of the European Council to the December meeting of the latter (EUCO 2012). It draws a road map that started with defining the guidelines for setting up an integrated financial framework (a banking union), then an integrated budgetary framework (a budgetary union), then an integrated economic policy framework (an economic union) and finally a system of democratic legitimacy and accountability (a political union). This Report constitutes the most comprehensive and strategic attempt by the European Council to identify the contours of a de facto euro-political union based on intergovernmental logic. Although the EP was excluded in the elaboration of the Report, the latter had to admit that "one of the guiding principles is that democratic control and accountability should occur at the level at which the decisions are taken … This implies the involvement of the European

Parliament as regards accountability taken at the European level," then adding: "while maintaining the pivotal role of national parliaments, as appropriate." In short, the intergovernmental constitution has to rely on national parliaments in order to guarantee the accountability of its decision-making process. Intergovernmentalism requires interparliamentarism as its main check.

A fourth round of deliberations developed throughout 2013 and 2014 to start implementation of the initial stage of the four presidents Report's road map, that is banking union. The aim was to prevent the intermingling of national banks and sovereign debt in order to create the condition of a stable currency area (Barucci, Bassanini and Messori 2014). According to the Report, a banking union should consist of a Single Supervisory Mechanism (SSM), a Single Resolution Mechanism (SRM) and a Deposit Guarantee Mechanism (DGM). Although there was an agreement on the general aim of the banking union, conflicts immediately emerged on how to set the scope of the SSM. The majority of the European Council proposed to extend it to the entire banking system of the Union, while the German government had a preference for supervising only the most important national banks, the so-called systemic banks. In the end, it was agreed to set up, under ECB monitoring, an SSM for the main systemic banks, that was also authorized to intervene in the other banks should national supervisory authorities prove unable to exercise their role. The SSM entered into force in November 2013. Following that, a discussion took place within the European Council on how to set up the second pillar of a banking union, the SRM. This discussion arrived at a general draft agreement on the SRM in the December European Council.

The SRM, which applies to all banks in the euro-area and other member states that decide to participate, was enacted through a regulation and an intergovernmental agreement (IGA), on the basis of a Bank Recovery and Resolution Directive (BRRD), approved in April 2014 after an understanding reached between the Council and the EP in December 2013. The regulation (approved by the EP in April 2014 and by the Council in July 2014) establishes uniform rules and a uniform procedure for the resolution of credit institutions and certain investment firms. The regulation provides for a single resolution board with broad powers in cases of banking disputes. The board consists of an executive director, four full-time appointed members and the representatives of the national resolution authorities of all the participating states. The board can take decisions, unless the Council objects and calls for change. However, any decision involving "liquidity support exceeding 20% of the capital paid into the fund, or other forms of support, such as bank recapitalisation, exceeding 10% of the funds" will have to be taken by the plenary session of the board, and not only by the appointed officials. Finally, in order to guarantee the budgetary sovereignty of the member states, "decisions that would require a member state to provide extraordinary public support without its prior approval under national budgetary procedures" were prohibited. Germany made clear that its financial resources were not available for the indebted banks of other member states.

In its turn, the IGA instituted a Single Resolution Fund (SRF), located outside the EU legal order, as a new intergovernmental treaty. Although the IGA was part of the compromise reached by the ECOFIN Council and the EP on the SRM, its formation was considered by many as unnecessary. Indeed, member states do not need intergovernmental treaties to transfer funds to the EU budget (F. Fabbrini 2014a), as they normally do so through the procedure of the Multiannual Financial Framework (MFF). Again the EP reacted forcefully to the national governments' decision. In a letter sent in February 2014 to the Commission president, Manuel Barroso, the EP president, Martin Schulz, wrote: "The Commission should make use of all available means to defend the Treaties and to stop the Council from setting a disastrous precedent through the adoption of an intergovernmental agreement to regulate matters that were part of a Commission proposal and on which the European Parliament as co-legislators has voted in committee and in plenary." Nevertheless, the IGA was not stopped. At the end of 2014, twenty-six member states signed it, whereas the UK and Sweden did not. The SRF includes the transfer and mutualization of funds from national authorities to a distinct (from the EU) and centralized organization. It will enter into force following the deposit of instruments of ratification by states representing at least 90% of the weighted vote of states participating in the SSM and SRM. The SRF ensures the availability of medium-term funding to enable the bank to continue operating and it can borrow from the markets if so decided by its governing body, the Single Resolution Board. It will reach the target level over eight years, starting in 2016. The SRF and the decision-making on its use is regulated by the SRM regulation. The IGA will also regulate the progressive mutualization of the

Table 2.2 *The Two Pack*

Legal acts	Policy aims
Regulation No. 473/2013: it introduces common provisions for monitoring and assessing draft budgetary plans and ensuring the correction of excessive deficits of member states in the euro-area. It completes the European Semester with a common budgetary timeline (see below).	Common budgetary timeline and *ex-ante* examination of draft budgets by the Commission. Crisis prevention mechanism. Approved through ordinary legislative procedure.
Regulation No. 472/2013: it strengthens economic and budgetary surveillance of member states in the euro-area experiencing or threatened with serious difficulties with respect to their financial stability. A member state subject to enhanced surveillance shall adopt measures aimed at addressing the sources or potential sources of difficulties.	Enhanced surveillance. Crisis management mechanism. Approved through ordinary legislative procedure.

national compartments during the transitional period. The resources accumulated will be progressively mutualized, starting with 40% of these resources in the first year. With these measures, the governance of the banking sector in the EU has come to be based on a "dual system" (Tosato 2014): the first (the system of financial supervision) applies to all member states; the second (the banking union) only to the euro-area member states (and those non-euro-area member states willing to be part of it).

Eventually, in May 2013 two new regulations were approved through the co-decision procedure (the so-called Two Pack), applicable to the euro-area member states only, on the basis of TFEU Article 136, aimed at further strengthening crisis prevention and crisis management mechanisms in the euro-area (see Table 2.2). The two regulations are based on the SGP and the European Semester and require the euro-area member states to submit their budgetary plans for the following year to the Commission and the Euro Group before October 15 along with the independent macroeconomic forecasts on

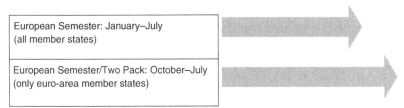

European Semester: January–July
(all member states)

European Semester/Two Pack: October–July
(only euro-area member states)

Figure 2.4 Budgetary policy-making cycle

which they are based. The Autumn exercise introduced by the Two Pack would allow the monitoring and sharing of information on the member states' budgetary policies before their adoption. Owing to the Two Pack, the euro-area member states are subject to a reinforced European Semester that is extended to a ten-month cycle:

(a) by October 15, euro-area member states must publish their draft budgets for the following year;
(b) by November 30 at the latest, the Commission will examine and give an opinion on each draft budget;
(c) by December 31, euro-area member states must adopt their budgets for the following year.

The Two Pack ensures consistency between budgetary and other economic policy processes and decisions. It integrates some of the elements of the Fiscal Compact Treaty into EU law, including the requirements for member states in the EDP to prepare economic partnership programs and the requirement for *ex-ante* coordination of member states' debt issuance plans. The Two Pack is a further and more stringent contribution to the crisis prevention regime of the euro-area member states (see Figure 2.4).

Considering the set of measures adopted in the crucial years of the euro crisis, one has to acknowledge their policy magnitude and institutional complexity (Adams, Fabbrini and Larouche 2014). Although the critical juncture of the onset of the euro crisis potentially opened the possibility of adopting the supranational method for dealing with it, the deepening of the crisis put the intergovernmental leaders in the driving seat. Certainly crucial legislative measures (as was the case with the European Semester, the Six Pack and the Two Pack) were taken through the supranational constitution of the ordinary legislative procedure. However, in the course of the crisis, national leaders coordinating within the European Council chose to resort to international treaties (such as the ESM, the Fiscal Compact and the SRF) that further increased their decision-making autonomy from the EU supranational institutions. Moreover, during the crisis the political inputs and the corresponding policy decisions came from the European Council, not the Commission. Even regarding directives and regulations, the Commission was crucial in technically translating the political input of the European Council, but not in autonomously elaborating and deciding their content. It has been observed that those decisions have put "the EU system … in the throes of a revolution [although] like all revolutions, this one [also] displays numerous evolutionary features" (Ludlow 2011a: 5). In short, with the deepening of the euro crisis, the EU has increasingly shifted in an intergovernmental direction.

2.6 Conclusion

This chapter has described how the multiple compromises realized since the Maastricht Treaty have been formalized by the Lisbon Treaty and how they have been affected by the euro crisis. It started by reconstructing the institutional features of the supranational constitution and then moved on to consider the institutional features of the intergovernmental constitution, both in foreign policy and in economic policy. I used the concept of constitution (which will be further developed in the following chapter) in empirical terms, interpreting it as the institutional order, backed by Treaty norms and expression of a principle of distribution of powers, which presides over the decision-making process. In this sense, a decision-making regime can be considered functionally equivalent to a constitutional regime.

After the analytical reconstruction of the two constitutional or decision-making regimes, the chapter then discussed in detail the sequence of decisions taken during the crucial years of the euro crisis, which I assumed to be a (third) critical juncture for the EU, showing that the logic of the intergovernmental constitution has become predominant over the alternative logic of the supranational constitution. National governmental leaders, now operating within an institutionalized European Council chaired by a permanent president, decided to use the decision-making advantage recognized to the intergovernmental institutions by the Lisbon Treaty to increase their influence. Theoretically, a different course of action might have been taken, bringing the economic policy decisions back to the supranational constitution. Indeed, crucial measures (such as the European Semester, the Six Pack, the Two Pack, the banking union directive and regulations) were taken through the ordinary legislative procedure. However, the predominant logic of the answer to the crisis has been increasingly intergovernmental. The European Council has emerged as the most powerful institution of the EMU decision-making system. Even when it recognized an important role to the Commission (for instance, in sanctioning member states breaching budgetary rules, sanctions that can be neutralized only by the RQMV of the ECOFIN Council), the European Council maintained control over agenda-setting, elaboration of and decision on the measures adopted. For a different course of action to be taken, a powerful initiative of the Commission and the EP would have been necessary, but both institutions were (at least in the first years of the crisis) faltering.

In particular through the new intergovernmental treaties, the institutional equilibrium nested within the Lisbon Treaty has been substantially altered. The distance between the two constitutional regimes has deepened, with the intergovernmental institutions of the European Council and Council emerging as the indisputable decision-makers. At the same time, the necessity to stem the common currency's crisis led to the approval of measures that have also increased the distinction between the euro-area and the non-euro-area member states. The intergovernmental framework, facing the difficulty of generating effective and legitimate answers to the crisis, has pushed the European Council and the Council to harden the ordo-liberal approach to the coordination of national economic policies, through the approval of an increasing family of judicial and technocratic devices for managing the growing interdependence between the euro-area member states. If it is true that the EU has been built through the solutions to a crisis, it is also true that those solutions have not resulted in the strengthening of the supranational constitution. The euro crisis has brought to the surface the different perspectives on the Union, deepening their differences. The EU that has emerged from the euro crisis is an organization internally divided more than differentiated. Those divisions, however, have deeper roots in the project and experience of the EU's institutionalization.

3 | Institutionalization and constitutional divisions

3.1 Introduction

If it is true that the euro crisis has deepened the divisions within the EU, it is also true that those divisions have constituted a permanent feature of its process of institutionalization. With the progressive deepening of European integration (i.e. the proliferation of public policies decided in Brussels) and its periodical widening, the institutionalization of the EU has grown increasingly more political and less economic (Maduro 2003; Walker 2007), and thus more contentious (Glencross 2014a). The euro crisis has ended up bringing in through the back door the very issue that was not allowed to enter through the front door at the foundation of the EU (after the rejection by the French Assemblée Nationale in 1954 of the EDC project), namely the issue of what the Union should be. In the 1990s, with the end of the Cold War and the prospect of the political reunification of the continent, the dispute on the constitutional identity of the EU came to the fore. The necessity to give a constitutional identity to the EU accompanied the constitutional decade of the 2000s. That necessity was then frozen by the French and Dutch referenda on the CT in 2005. It seemed that the 2009 Lisbon Treaty had finally settled the problem, institutionalizing a truce between the alternative views of the Union. But events have not followed expectations. The euro crisis entered like a tornado against the apparent lethargy that led to the signing of the Treaty, reopening and deepening the old constitutional divisions between member states and bringing to the surface tensions among EU institutions (such as the European Council, on one side, and the EP, on the other). With approval of new intergovernmental treaties, the issue of what the EU is and should be has re-emerged.

As with all established political systems, the EU is also structured around cleavages. But being a union of demographically asymmetrical and culturally differentiated states, those cleavages reflect the different interests and views of the states and citizens aggregating in the union (S. Fabbrini 2008a; Snyder 2003). It is the aim of this chapter to conceptualize the structural divisions that emerged in the EU as a union of states that have different historical identities, are demographically asymmetrical and whose citizens entertain divergent political views on the union, lacking, however, a formal document delimiting the perimeter and the terms of the divisions (S. Fabbrini 2008b). In fact, if it is the role of a formal constitution to furnish the language and the procedure for running and regulating the conflicts of a given political system, that role is magnified in a union of states. The absence of a formal document, establishing what the EU is and should be, has nurtured the reproduction of incompatible views on the Union, allowing them to coexist but also preventing any project of recomposing them in an agreed formal framework. This is why the EU has had to opt for an alternative and empirical road of constitutionalization.

This chapter is organized as follows. First, it will offer a discussion on the EU as a constitutional regime without a formal constitution. It is the constitutionalized nature of the Union, as it came to develop through the ECJ's decisions and the political IGC deliberations, that has fomented and justified the different views on the EU. Second, it will reconstruct and discuss the cleavages underpinning those divisions. Those cleavages relate to different member state views on national sovereignty, on democratic legitimacy and on the proper relations that should be set up between member states. Third, and finally, the chapter will analyse the political implications of these structural cleavages in the context of the euro crisis, showing how the latter has made them deeper.

3.2 A constitutional regime without a constitution

The concept of constitution is not as unequivocal as it might seem (Menéndez 2004). From the perspective of comparative analysis (Bellamy 2007; Finer, Bogdanor and Rudden 1995; Pennock and Chapman 1979), we can distinguish, at least, between a formal and a material constitution. A *formal* constitution is a single written document that is regarded (by the governed and governors alike) as the supreme text of the legal order. It regulates matters that are more fundamental than others and it may be changed only through stringent amendment procedures (Elster 1997). It is a document that symbolically connects the citizens with the polity and not only with its political authorities. Although all formal constitutions establish the set of fundamental rights, institutional arrangements and functional procedures that must regulate the workings of a given political community (which constitutes itself through this founding document), one might argue (with Elazar 1985) that important differences are detectable among them. In fact, some formal constitutions (for example, the US constitution) are first a *frame of government* and then a protector of rights (indeed, the Bill of Rights is a set of ten amendments added to the formal document two years after its approval), while other formal constitutions (such as the ones approved in post-Second World War Europe) have the features of a *state code*, the expression of a declared democratic ideology (indeed, the French and Italian constitutions start with a definition of fundamental rights and end with a specification of the distribution of powers and institutional procedures to preserve them) (S. Fabbrini 2004).

On the other hand, a *material* constitution consists of the social practices, derived from political conventions, historical traditions, specific judiciary regulations or ad hoc fundamental laws (considered of an equivalent status to a constitution) recognized as the basic norms of a given society. It is the case in democratic countries like the UK, Germany or Israel: in the UK the material constitution is constituted by a historical accumulation of ordinary laws and judicial sentences considered of fundamental importance for the polity, in the other two countries by ad hoc fundamental laws (called *Grundgesetz* in post-Second World War Germany and Basic Law in Israel).[1] It is not expected that material constitutions generate symbolic identification of the citizens with the polity because that identification predates the polity itself, being the outcome of a meta-constitutional tradition (the Jewish people do not need to have a constitution to recognize themselves, German identity predates the 1871 unitary state and the same

---

[1] Both in (West) Germany and in Israel it was an explicit choice of the post-Second World War ruling political elite to approve a fundamental or basic law but not a constitution. Through that choice, the political elite wanted to underline the "transitory" nature of the political regime, because of the continuing Jewish diaspora (in the Israeli case) and the division between West and East Germany (in the German case). It is interesting to note that the 1990 *Deutsche Einheit* or "German unity" was not based on a new formal constitution. In fact it coincided with the inclusion of the five Eastern *Länder* into the West German federal state (see Appendix, A.4).

has long been considered true for British "subjects," whose identity was based on the historical tradition of the 1215 Magna Carta freedoms). The EU does not have a formal constitution, but it is indisputable that it has acquired a material constitution consisting of both the juridical expression of high-order principles (such as supremacy of Union law or the direct effect of Union law on individual citizens) established by the ECJ on the basis of the treaties interpreted as quasi-constitutions. The Charter of Fundamental Rights included in the Lisbon Treaty has further increased the constitutional predisposition of the ECJ. In its turn, the ECJ has moved within the political specification of the powers allocated to the various institutions by the deliberations of national governments in their periodic IGCs (Amato and Ziller 2007; Griller and Ziller 2008). Functionalism and intergovernmentalism have supported each other.

One might argue that the process of constitutionalization of the EU was promoted and supported by both Union judges and domestic government decisions, decisions then integrated into the ordinary business of politics and policy. The ECJ has interpreted the founding treaties as constitutional documents and its rulings have been gradually integrated into the constitutional orders of the member states (Craig and De Bursa 1999; De Witte 1999; Everson and Eisner 2007; Mancini 1998). Contrary to other international treaties, the EU treaties have thus given rise to a legal order that not only binds the governments that signed them (as is typical of international treaties) but that is also of direct influence on the citizens of its member states (Curtin and Kellerman 2006; Weiler 1999). The normative activity of the ECJ arose from the need to deal with the functional problems emerging from increasing levels of transnational exchange and cross-border cooperation, as argued by the neo-functional school (Stone Sweet 2005; Stone Sweet, Sandholtz and Fligstein 2001). Increasing transnational economic activity exacerbated legal disputes among economic actors operating in different national jurisdictions, and this in turn required the Union's judicial organ, the ECJ, to play an active role in settling them. The ECJ used the opportunities afforded by the treaties to construct a new legal order for a supranational market, transforming those treaties into sources of law superior to those of the EU member states. At the same time, as shown by the intergovernmental school (Moravcsik 2005), the various IGCs have periodically fine-tuned the distribution of powers between the Union institutions and between the latter and member state institutions, frequently rationalizing empirical processes that have created new functional practices (Christiansen and Reh 2009). The fine-tuning of the institutions by the IGCs arose from the necessity to deal with the growing complexity of the EU decision-making process, complexity that emerged from the widening and deepening of the integration process. These processes have sustained a process of constitutionalization where the latter has to be interpreted as "an exclusively descriptive concept [indicating] the recollection of constitutional norms, rules and decisions as outcomes of a process" (Wiener 2008: 26) that empirically regulates relations between institutions and member states.

The traditional European nation states have differently redefined their sovereignty within the context of the EU's constitutionalization. Domestic elites elaborated or used different ideational frames to make sense of the integration project, as argued by the constructivist school (Risse 2010). The national redefinition of identity has been uneven, due to the differing perseverance of the national narrative in each member state. Identity is tied to sovereignty or better sovereignty is the knot that identity can strengthen or unravel. One might argue that the two constitutions finally formalized in the Lisbon Treaty reflected the ambiguities or difficulties of unraveling the knot of sovereignty in crucial member states (such as France). In the supranational constitution, member states agreed to *share* their ultimate decision-making power on several policies regulating the functioning of the single market with Union actors politically connected to them but also institutionally independent from them. At the same time, member states claimed to *pool* their sovereignty on policies strategically important to them (such as economic and foreign policies) in an intergovernmental framework at the Union level. *Sharing* and *pooling* imply different decision-making regimes: in the former, the participants cannot be guaranteed to be on the majority side; in the latter, that guarantee is celebrated by the criterion of unanimity. Those two constitutions reflected different ways of dealing with national sovereignty, accepting its dilution in the former case but not in the latter case. If the coexistence of those two organizational *principles* of the Union represented the main constitutional compromise celebrated by the treaties, and if the transfer of the opt-out clause from one treaty to the other tried to accommodate the less integrationist view on the EU, those multiple compromises had their bases in the different relations between identity and sovereignty in each member state.

Stressing the empirical quality of the process of constitutionalization that has taken place within the EU, intended as the creation of both a functional integrated legal order and an institutionally defined political order on the European continent (Rittberger and Schimmelfennig 2007), cannot mean underestimating its constitutional ambiguity and weakness (Longo 2006; O'Neil 2008). On the contrary, not only does the material constitution of the EU continue to have none of the symbolic implications and shared meanings that are part of a formal constitution, but a material constitution also cannot be sufficient to settle conflicts between the states of a union, if they result from different identities (regarding national sovereignty and democratic legitimacy) and asymmetries that are not easily bridgeable. Comparative analysis shows that constitutionalization based on interstate treaties, as in the EU, is significantly different from constitutionalization based on a constitutional document, in particular in comparable federal unions such as the USA and Switzerland (Ackerman 1991; Avbij and Komàrek 2012; Ziller 2009). Indeed, the lack of a formal document, able to crystallize a common political will and to furnish a common normative language for framing the divisions on the nature of the constitutional order, has made the constitutional debate in the EU particularly sour. The unanimity criterion for approving a new treaty or emending old ones has further increased the drama of the constitutional dispute (Closa 2013). In a union of several member states this criterion has been a recipe for stalemate.

This constitutional and procedural context has made the structural cleavages an unresolved feature of the EU political system. The structural cleavages, which laid dormant during the passive consensus of the long period of the material constitutionalization of the EU, emerged vociferously during the tortuous journey that led to the CT. The constitutional process, developed between the 1990s and the first half of the 2000s, was characterized by deep divisions concerning the nature of the EU, the institutional structure the EU should assume, its powers and competences vis-à-vis the member states, but also the guarantees that should be introduced to promote individual rights and to protect social rights (Sbragia *et al.* 2006). After the 2005 French and Dutch referenda, those divisions were silenced by the transformation of the CT into two treaty amendments and an annexed Charter of Fundamental Rights that constitute the Lisbon Treaty. It seemed that the negotiations that led to the amended treaties (TEU and TFEU) had finally silenced the discussion on the EU and its future. Instead, the opposite has happened. With the explosion of the euro crisis, those divisions have emerged again in a more acute manner. The nature of those permanent constitutional divisions now deserves to be identified.

3.3 Divisions on national sovereignty

The basic structural cleavage that has accompanied the process of integration concerns the very interpretation of state sovereignty in a union of states. It has its origin in the traditional division between the countries of Continental Western Europe and the island and peninsular states of Northern Europe (S. Fabbrini 2010: 254–8). This cleavage emerged during the empty seat crisis of the 1960s because of the Gaullist distrust of any federalizing project, but it has become permanent since 1973 when the UK, Denmark and Ireland entered the EU (Gilbert 2003). It is a cleavage that reflects the different historical experiences of the islands and the Continent in the formation of the nation state and its international extensions. Indeed, since its accession to the EU, the UK has come to head a coalition of member states that view integration primarily as a process of strengthening a common market. At issue for these member states has been the formation of a market regime, of an *economic community*, not of a political union, however defined. These member states regarded the deepening of the integration process, which has taken place from the Maastricht Treaty onwards, as a threat to their national sovereignty that needed to be countered by pressing for further enlargement in order to increase the patchy nature of the Union (Geddes 2013).

These member states, with others, were those that contributed in the 1960s to developing a project of economic cooperation, the EFTA, in its turn the heir of the FTA, separate from, and competitive with, the project started with the 1951 Paris Treaties and the 1957 Rome Treaties. According to Warlouzet (2011: 433–4):

the UK and the Scandinavian countries shared a cultural preference for a loose form of co-operation, which was less supranational than the EEC and more free-market in scope. The FTA was thus a forerunner not only of the

EFTA but also of the concept of European integration that was later to be defended by several member states [within the EU]. Both the UK and Denmark, for example, belonged to the "Luxembourg Compromise Club," which made extensive use of the veto in the early 1980s.

The UK entered the EU for contradictory reasons. It decided to do so because of the economic weakness of the alternative project of the EFTA, but also because of the necessity to sit at the EU table, which at that point in time seemed to matter most, in order to influence or neutralize any plausible undesired development (Growland, Turner and Wright 2010). However, the deepening of the process of integration, from the 1986 SEA and the 1992 Maastricht Treaty to the 2001 adoption of the euro (and its circulation the following year) and the 2009 Lisbon Treaty, has transformed the original ambiguity of the political elites of both main British parties into an increased uneasiness towards the EU, uneasiness shared by the larger public (as made evident by the spectacular success of the anti-European UK Independence Party, UKIP, in the EP elections of May 2014, when it became the first party of the country). What the British Prime Minister said on January 23, 2013 in his celebrated speech on Europe made official a widespread view in his country (and not only in his Conservative Party). David Cameron said: "The European Treaty commits the member states to lay the foundation of an ever closer union among the peoples of Europe ... We understand and respect the rights of others to maintain their commitment to this goal. But for Britain – and perhaps for others – it is not the objective."

The British defense of sovereignty springs from the distinct historical phenomenon of the democratic nationalism of the country (Garton Ash 2001, 2006): it was nationalism that enabled the UK to preserve democracy (MacCormick 1996) and democratic nationalism is the cultural basis of the country's identity. In addition to opting out from adopting the euro (with Denmark and Sweden), the UK and Poland, in exchange for signing the Lisbon Treaty, obtained the possibility of opting out from the Charter of Fundamental Rights. Protocol No. 30 of the Lisbon Treaty asserts (Article 1) that the Charter of Fundamental Rights "does not extend the ability of the Court of Justice of the European Union ... to find that the laws, regulations or administrative provisions, practices or action of Poland or of the United Kingdom are inconsistent with the fundamental rights, freedoms and principles that it reaffirms." The Czech Republic has joined the two member states in opting out from the Charter with the 2013 Treaty on the accession of Croatia. UK, Ireland and Denmark have also opted out from legislation adopted through qualified majority voting (QMV) in the field of police and judicial cooperation in criminal matters. Ireland and the UK have opted out from the Schengen Agreement on the free circulation of persons within the Union.[2] Denmark has opted out from foreign and security policies. The UK, Ireland, Denmark and Sweden (and later also the Czech Republic) have asked and obtained regular opt-outs from parts of the Treaties or from recognizing the jurisdiction of the ECJ concerning specific social and economic rights. And, as we have seen, the UK has not signed the Fiscal Compact Treaty (the only member state not to do so, given that the Czech Republic finally signed it on March 2014) and neither UK nor Sweden have signed the SRF. At the end of 2014, five member states had such opt-outs: Denmark and the UK (four opt-outs), Ireland (two), Poland (one), Sweden (one, but only de facto) and the Czech Republic (one, ratified with the 2013 accession treaty of Croatia).

That notwithstanding, these concessions have not reduced the above countries' fears of seeing their national prerogatives challenged by Brussels-based institutions and officials. Indeed, in 2011 the British Parliament approved a European Union Act that calls into question the very constitutionalization of the EU brought about by the ECJ's decisions of the 1960s on the direct effect and supremacy of Union law.[3]

---

[2] The Schengen Agreement was an intergovernmental treaty signed on June 14, 1985 in the town of Schengen in Luxembourg, by five of the then nine member states of the EU (then called the EEC). It was supplemented by the Convention implementing the Schengen Agreement five years later. The Agreement, Convention and rules were implemented in March 1995. Together these treaties created Europe's borderless Schengen area, which operates as a single area for international travel with external border controls for those travelling in and out of it, but with no or minimal internal border controls. The Schengen Agreements and the rules adopted under it were, for the EU members of the Agreement, entirely separate from the EU legal order until the 1997 Amsterdam Treaty, which incorporated them into the EU law. The borderless area created by the Schengen Agreements, at the end of 2013, consisted of twenty-five states, including four non-EU member states (Iceland, Liechtenstein, Norway, and Switzerland). Three European micro-states (Monaco, San Marino, and the Vatican City) do not have any immigration controls with the Schengen countries.

[3] The European Union Act was enacted in UK on July 19, 2011. On the UK's growing distance from the EU, see Schnapper (2012).

The Act states that "there are no circumstances in which the jurisprudence of the Court of Justice can elevate Community Law to a status within the corpus of English domestic law to which it could not aspire by any route of English law itself ... The conditions of Parliament's legislative supremacy in the UK necessarily remain in the UK's hands." The Act exacts any UK government to organize a popular referendum in the case of a further transfer of competences from the member states to the Union (Craig 2011).

This group of traditional guardians of national prerogatives was joined by some of the new East European member states, even before the enlargements of the 2000s (Lequesne 2012). One has to think of the Czech Republic when Vaclav Klaus was first prime minister from 1992 to 1997 and then head of state from 2003 to 2013; or the Polish government of the period 2005–2007, and Hungary when Viktor Orban was prime minister from 1998 to 2002 and after his re-election in 2010. In some of the new Eastern European member states the spread of EU rules was perceived as an imperial policy pursued by the West (Zielonka 2006). The nationalistic governments of new member states have engaged powerfully in defending their regained national sovereignty after almost half a century of enforced Soviet domination. For these member states also, the EU should be (or should return to be) mainly an economic community, a common market regime, through which they can remedy their economic backwardness without constraints on their regained political sovereignty. Certainly, the sovereignist coalition has not been homogeneous. Some member states, like the UK, have largely accepted the European regulatory framework of the single market, while others, such as Orban's Hungary, have plainly distrusted it. One might argue that the enlargement to Eastern and Southern European states has reinforced the sovereignist coalition. This is why enlargement has been the battle cry of the UK. These member states have constituted a modern form of a state rights group acting to protect national sovereignty (Dehousse 2005). Their objective has been to promote a common market, not an ever closer union, because the former, contrary to the latter, has been considered compatible with the preservation of national sovereignty (or a large part of it). For them, in short, the EU should be an *economic community*.

The other side of the cleavage was represented by the large majority of Western European Continental member states. Indeed, their historical experience was very different from that of the Northern islands or peninsula and Eastern European member states. In the case of many Western Continental states, nationalism was historically the force that erased democracy, owing to a set of cultural and ecological factors. The development of the democratic state encountered much more unfavorable conditions in the land-bound European countries than it had in the sea-bound ones (Tilly 1975). In the former, nationalism was frequently anti-democratic (Smith 1991), bending to (or sustaining) the centralist ambitions of dominant authoritarian groups. Inevitably, for the member states inheriting this historical experience and memory, integration represents the antidote to the virus of authoritarian nationalism, while those inheriting the island or peninsula experience view integration as a threat to their democratic sovereignty. After all, this is the core of countries that needed to sign the peace pact to end the long era of European wars.

For this reason, many Western countries in Continental Europe tended to interpret integration as a political rather than a market process, although what should be understood by "political" was left to the future development of the integration process (Hendricks and Morgan 2001). Even though these countries recognized the process of integration as a political necessity, they came to interpret it in different terms in different historical periods (Lacroix and Nicolaidis 2010). This is the case, in particular, of France, which displayed rather ambivalent and oscillating sentiments towards an integrated Europe. At the beginning of the integration process a federal Europe was considered, by statesmen such as Robert Schuman and public officials such as Jean Monnet, as the only solution to rivalry with Germany and particularly in relation to the threat represented by the reconstruction of the latter; in the 1960s the Gaullist component of the French political elite moved the country in the opposite direction, aggressively contrasting any significant transfer of sovereignty from the national to the European level. French ambivalence towards the form of the political project of the union has been the cause of the cyclical stop-and-go in the process of integration. Such ambivalence probably reflects the peculiar development of nationalism in France, which was the condition for promoting the rights of "the man and the citizen," having thus both a universal and a national character.

In France, a continuous divide between those supporting and those opposing European integration has cut across the main parties or poles of the right and left (Guyomarch, Machin and Richtie 1998). From the parliamentary rejection of the EDC in 1954 to the empty chair strategy of Charles de Gaulle in the 1960s (Vanke 2006), from the difficult referendum that barely approved the Maastricht Treaty in 1992 to the fatal blow to the CT in the referendum of 2005, it has been in France that the process of integration has been periodically halted. The unprecedented success of the highly nationalistic party the National Front in the EP elections of May 22–25, 2014, when it became the first party of the country with 24.85 percent of the popular vote, is the expression of a sovereignist mood that is quite widespread in the country. At the same time, sectors of the French political and administrative elites have regularly come to the rescue of the integration process, identifying plausible exit options from the stalemate caused to the process by French choices. It was Jean Monnet who promoted a neo-functional approach to overcome the 1954 crisis; it was Jacques Delors who talked of a federation of nation states to accommodate the growing decision-making role of national governments after the critical juncture of 1989–1991. The situation changed substantially, however, with the 1989 fall of the Berlin Wall and the 1990 reunification of Germany, which Francois Mitterrand, then President of the Republic, initially opposed because of its inevitable structural implications for upsetting the balance of power between his country and Germany (a balance that made possible the very process of integration: Calleo 2001). The new power context opened up a dramatic dilemma for the French political elite, that is, how to prevent Germany from transforming its demographic and economic superiority into political influence.

In the discussion that led to the Maastricht Treaty, it was the French political elite that put forward a model of integration based on the pooling (not the sharing) at the European level of national sovereignties on the sensitive policies of foreign and economic integration. After all, it was the then President of the French Republic, Valéry Giscard D'Estaing, who in 1974 inaugurated the (twice yearly) meetings of the heads of state and government of the members of the then EEC as an informal intergovernmental institution, subsequently called the European Council, where strategic negotiations were undertaken. In advancing the intergovernmental model in Maastricht, the French political elite assumed that it could still use its political power to balance the growing economic power of Germany, thanks to the consensual rule underpinning the intergovernmental decision-making logic. Although other French (Christian Democratic or Socialist) politicians and officials have continued to operate, in Paris as in Brussels, in coherence with the teaching of Robert Schuman, supporting the sharing of national sovereignties in sensitive policies through the extension of the supranational logic, political intergovernmentalism has become the mainstream perspective of the French political elite, in particular after the popular rejection of the CT in the 2005 referendum (Grossman 2008). The heirs of the Gaullist movement have moved their battle cry from a Europe of nation states (Calleo 2011) to an integrated Europe based on intergovernmental institutions. The euro crisis and its institutional implications have removed any plausibility from the old Gaullist view of a Union as a diplomatic forum of cooperation and information exchange between sovereign states. With the new treaties and measures approved for dealing with the crisis, however, the consensual logic has not prevented the formation of hierarchical relations within the intergovernmental institutions to the advantage of Germany.

Although French and British politicians have frequently seen eye to eye on slowing down the process of integration (Ludlow 2012), the post-Maastricht French elite cannot be included among the supporters of the economic community perspective on the EU. France and the UK certainly have in common a preference for preserving the power of national governments, but that power should be collectively exercised in Brussels (for the French) and individually in each of the national capitals (for the British). Also before the Maastricht turning point, France and the UK displayed different cultural attitudes towards Europe. British political culture has continued to be insular, justifying intervention on the Continent mainly on the basis of the rationale of the balance of powers. French political culture has continued to be hegemonic, justifying support of the integration of the Continent on the basis of the country's leadership role. The rivalry between the two countries has never stopped. After all, they are the only two European countries with strong democratic credentials, with their own military strength, with a tradition of international power (which for a long time assumed the form of colonialism and imperialism), with a permanent seat on the United Nations Security Council and with a ruling elite aware of the role to be played in global affairs. Their competition has also been based on two different interpretations of Europe's role in the Western military alliance. After the Second World War, the UK has traditionally been in favor of a neo-Churchillian perspective, that is, of a Europe firmly allied with the USA, with the UK playing the crucial role of bridging the two shores of the Atlantic, whereas France has pursued a neo-Gaullist perspective, based on the idea that Europe should be independent from the USA (Garton Ash 2004). This French predisposition started to change with the post-Gaullist presidency of Nicolas Sarkozy of 2007–2012. In fact, President Sarkozy brought France back to full membership of NATO in 2009, forty-three years after the former president and general Charles de Gaulle withdrew France from the military command of the Atlantic alliance.

Ambivalence towards the EU has traditionally been less significant in the other Western Continental member states. In Germany, Italy, the Netherlands, Spain and Austria, there has been a widespread (although not always majoritarian) acceptance of a federal project for the EU. However, this federal predisposition has been restrained by the euro crisis and its economic effects. In Germany, however, with the 1990 reunification, powerful sectors of the financial and legal establishment opposed the start-up of the EMU and more generally the giving up of the country's monetary sovereignty in the name of a less providential view of integration. The institutional and economic compromises realized with and after the Maastricht Treaty have ended up strengthening the critical position of those financial and legal circles. Once the intergovernmental road was taken (a road that the German government would not have taken in Maastricht), the interests and culture of the largest EMU member state have become inevitably predominant. Although Germany had not (or could not have) entertained an intergovernmental predisposition before its reunification, once reunified, it started to make explicit its request of being considered a member just like the others in the Union, with its own legitimate national interests to pursue. The intergovernmental decision-making regime institutionalized by the Lisbon Treaty has proved to be a happy hunting ground for highlighting and promoting those national interests. It has fitted well with the post-unification German ruling elite's relationship with the EU.

In short, national sovereignty (and its correlated national identity) has (and have) continuously played a dividing role in Europe, first between those supporting a view of the Union as a merely economic community and those accepting the project of an ever-closer Union, and thus, within the latter group, between supranational and intergovernmental views. The contrast between different perspectives on national sovereignty has represented a centrifugal force in the debate on the constitutional identity of the EU, a feature that the euro crisis has dramatically exacerbated. One has only to think of the deeper separation, induced by the crisis, between euro-area and non-euro-area member states.

3.4 Divisions on democratic legitimacy

The previous cleavage has been reinforced by a cleavage of a political kind, regarding the democratic legitimacy of the Union, that has accompanied the latter's process of institutionalization, then exploding during the 2005 French and Dutch referenda on the CT (Schmidt 2012; Taggart 2006). Even regarding democratic legitimacy, different interpretations emerged and overlapped during the heated discussions on the constitutional identity of the EU. These interpretations, at times expressions of national moods, became less emotional with the approval of the Lisbon Treaty, only to re-emerge during the euro crisis.

A fault line has continued to divide EU member states on democracy, considered by some as a form of government that is viable only by remaining at the national level and by others as a political regime that should be adapted to new historical needs. The former position has been largely shared in the Northern islands and peninsula in Europe (from the UK to Scandinavian countries), as well as in some of its Eastern member states. Frequently, this position has been motivated by criticism of the Brussels bureaucracy, although such criticism has served to celebrate the virtues of homeland democracy in the name of popular sovereignty. No serious elaboration of this position has ever emerged comparable to the Anti-Federalist papers of the post-Philadelphia convention debate. This position has stressed the impossibility for the EU to enjoy democratic legitimacy, because legitimacy can be claimed only at the national level where it is implemented through domestic parliaments keeping their domestic governments accountable. For the sovereignists, whose expectation of the EU was that of an economic community, national parliaments are the only institutions legitimated to represent the citizenry. Keeping the EU within the limits of an economic community would preserve the democratic role of national parliaments.

The political criticism of the EU as an elitist experiment has also been raised by fringe groups in European politics, such as the National

Front in France or the Northern League in Italy. The euro crisis and the growing role of unelected technocracies in managing it (starting with the ECB, the Commission and the multitude of regulatory agencies) has given further ammunition to the opponents of the integration process (particularly of the EMU project). These groups and media actors have ventilated popular unease against some of the crudest side effects of a crisis dealt with through austerity policies, but also of an integration process that has facilitated the circulation of immigrants from poor to rich member states or areas, or that has increased difficulties in combating the trans-nationalization of criminal organizations. The narrative has continued to refer to the need to repatriate many of the policies that have emigrated to Brussels, due to the virtues of national (if not sub-national) communities where democracy has been preserved by the active participation of citizens (Lacroix and Nicolaidis 2010). Such participation is considered unfeasible at the EU level, whose logic is necessarily technocratic and elitist. The criticism of the Brussels bureaucracy has continued to be very common in the British press, although the Brussels bureaucracy is smaller than that administering the larger European cities (such as London). From this group came headstrong resistance to any federal development of the EU during the various treaty rounds. During the 2002–2003 Brussels constitutional convention, for example, spokespeople for this position opposed even semantic references to "federalism" or its variants. In fact, the word "federalism" was removed from the final version of the CT at the request of the British representatives.

The other side of the cleavage has been much more spurious. It has been traditionally represented by those groups and public intellectuals advocating a federal state with parliamentary features in order to deal with the memories of the past and the challenges of the future. This was the position of the German and Italian political elites that drove the reconstruction of their countries in the long post-war period. According to this position, shared also by the Spanish and Portuguese political elites that have led the process of democratization in their countries since the 1970s, democracy can survive only by extending it at the supranational level, thus purging its identity from the waste of nationalism. For the supporters of supranational democracy, only a fully integrated Europe can keep national evils under control and at the same time play a role in the global system, necessary to preserve civilization's values. The euro crisis has also made evident, according to this view, that only a politically integrated Europe may effectively protect the social welfare model that characterizes many of the EU member states (Habermas 2009, 2012a). The assertion is that, on their own, each of the EU member states, including the larger ones, have no prospect of protecting their own way of life. However, it was also from within this rank of supranationalists that criticism of the CT emerged for not doing enough to protect the European social model. In France (Schmidt 2008), some of them voted against the CT, in the company of fierce defenders of national sovereignty and democracy. The fear of the incompatibility between European integration and national welfare states has been dramatized by the euro crisis. Sectors of the anti-nationalistic left, even in countries such as Germany, have come to criticize the very process of monetary integration because of its effects in dismantling national programs of social protection, effects made dramatically real by the domestic adjustments imposed by the euro crisis on Southern member states (Scharpf 2013).

The criticism of the democratic deficit of the EU, which was leveled for a long time against the EU by the more radical sections of public opinion (Offe and Preuss 2006), has produced contradictory outcomes: some supporters of the criticism have joined the supranational democracy camp, claiming the necessity to adopt a parliamentary-federal model in Brussels; others have filled the ranks of the intergovernmentalists, arguing that the democratic deficit can be solved only by bringing national parliaments into the Union's decision-making system. Once the coordination between national governments was assumed in Brussels as the condition for promoting the process of integration, then it became inevitable that a stronger role would be claimed for national parliaments in checking national governments at both domestic and Union level (Lindseth 2014). The role of national parliaments has been considered crucial not only by the sovereignists, but also by those supporting an intergovernmental evolution of the EU. The intergovernmental Union is not hospitable towards the EP, because the logic of that Union, stressing the role of national governments, implies that legitimacy can come primarily from national electorates represented in and by national parliaments. The two camps (sovereignists and intergovernmentalists) were crucial for the approval, in the 2002–2003 Brussels constitutional convention, of what has become Protocol No. 1 of the Lisbon Treaty, according to which, not only "Draft legislative acts to the European Parliament and to the Council shall be forwarded to national Parliaments" (Article 2), but also the latter "may send to the Presidents of the European Parliament, the Council and the Commission a reasoned opinion on whether a draft legislative act complies with the principle of subsidiarity" (Article 3). Protocol No. 2 thus specifies in Article 7.2 that "where reasoned opinions on a draft legislative act's non-compliance with the principle of subsidiarity represent at least one third of all the votes allocated to national parliaments ... the draft must be reviewed."

The claim to strengthen the role of national parliaments has received a powerful boost from the German Constitutional Court, which has insisted on maintaining a powerful role for the Bundestag (the lower chamber of the legislature) in the integration process as the condition for recognizing the legitimacy of the treaties. Given the lack of a European demos, and because of the degressive proportionality criterion regulating the formation of the EP, according to the German Constitutional Court, only national parliaments (and the Bundestag, in their case) can lend legitimacy to the choices of national governments coordinating in Brussels.[4] The short circuit is manifest. Since, as Nicolaidis (2003: 98) wrote, "Europeans cannot hold their politicians accountable for what the EU does," then, according to the German Constitutional Court, it is imperative that those politicians be accountable to their electorate, as represented by national parliaments. However, the decisions for which those politicians should be accountable are taken in a different institutional context than the national one, they have effects on a larger electorate than the national one, and they result from a negotiation between governments that national parliaments cannot anticipate.

If the basic fault line between sovereignists and those supporting the need for an ever-closer union has been always evident, the division within the latter group (between those recognizing integration as a necessity, as for the intergovernmentalists, and those celebrating it as a virtue, as for the supranationalists) has not been always clear-cut. If

---

[4] In the judgment approving the Lisbon Treaty (*BVerfG, 2BvE 2/08* of June 30, 2009), the German Constitutional Court stated that the degressive proportionality criterion does not comply with the standards of democratic representation that "one person one vote" implies. It is for this reason, as Leonardy (2010: 5) critically stressed, that the Court considers it "impossible for Germany to belong to a European Federation with such an institution at its center, because that would be a violation of democracy."

the sovereignist coalition is mainly based in the Northern islands and peninsula, backed by a few Eastern European member states, inter-governmentalists and supranationalists are in all the main Continental member states. The euro crisis has increased the basic fault line, but it has also deepened the division between intergovernmentalists and supranationalists, inducing an unexpected re-elaboration of national identity. During the post-2009 financial crisis, for instance, a country such as Germany, traditionally in favor of a supranational Europe understood as a parliamentary federation (Bulmer, Jefferey and Padgett 2010), discovered the virtues of an intergovernmental union, whereas a country such as France, traditionally the main supporter of intergovernmental union, came to realize the many defects of the latter. Nevertheless, the cleavage on democratic legitimacy has become a stable constitutional division in the EU political system. The Lisbon Treaty has tried to mediate between those conflicting views, but the compromises formalized have been called into question by the tsunami of the euro crisis.

3.5 Divisions on interstate relations

A third kind of cleavage has accompanied the process of integration and has been particularly damaging during the euro crisis. This is the structural cleavage setting the minority of large and medium member states against the majority of small member states (Bunse and Nicolaidis 2012). This cleavage is an effect of the asymmetry between member states within the EU. It emerged regularly during the development of the EU, which started as a pact between two large countries (France and West Germany), mediated by another quasi-large country (Italy) and three small countries (Belgium, the Netherlands and Luxembourg, the so-called Benelux group). During the process of institutionalization of the EU, the smaller member states have entertained opposing moods towards integration. On one hand, they feared being swallowed up by the larger states. For this reason, they represented a blocking group towards an excessive majoritarian direction to the EU decision-making process. On the other hand, they considered institutionalization as a better alternative to the traditional interstate balance of power for protecting their role. In this sense, "for the smaller countries, the European ideal of a Community represented a higher form of national interest, in that it offered them protection against larger nations … the Community was more than a legal order based on a treaty. It was a political association that also involved a balance of power based on national interest" (Van Middelaar 2013: 169). Or at least, this is what many small states expected.

The enlargements of the 1990s and 2000s have made this cleavage more central. One has only to think of the Nice Treaty of 2001, when medium-sized member states (such as Spain) were able to obtain very favorable conditions concerning the weighting of votes within the Council (thus also benefiting the then candidate states of equivalent size, such as Poland). This advantage provoked a negative reaction in large member states such as France and (especially) Germany, which (also on the basis of other considerations) pushed for a revision of the Nice Treaty through the Laeken Declaration. Inevitably, this division emerged during the works of the Brussels Constitutional Convention of 2002–2003, with the small and medium member states asking for over-representation in the voting system within the Council and the larger member states asking (in compensation) for parliamentary representation proportional to population (which would strengthen them in relation to the small/medium states in the EP).

The compromise found at the Rome European Council of October 2004, and then preserved in the Lisbon Treaty, that a decision of the Council will be effective if supported by a majority of 55 percent of the member states representing at least 65 percent of the population, was subsequently challenged by the Polish government at the Berlin European Council of June 2007. In the Lisbon European Council, which formally agreed on a new treaty and retained a large part of the CT as amendments to the two existing treaties, the Polish government successfully imposed the deferral of the introduction of this rule to November 2014 (with an extra transition period until March 2017, during which a member state can ask for a qualified majority on a specific issue if considered of national importance). If the majoritarian twist was successful regarding decision-making within the Council, the smaller member states were able to reduce the advantage of larger member states in the allocation of the EP seats by imposing the criterion of *degressive proportionality* that over-represents the smaller member states.

This cleavage also emerged on the issue of the Commission's composition during and after the 2002–2003 Brussels Constitutional Convention (Magnette and Nicolaidis 2004). The small/medium member states asked for the number of commissioners to be equivalent to the number of the member states (that is one commissioner for each member state), whereas the large member states supported the idea of downsizing the Commission (setting the number of commissioners at two-thirds of the number of member states). The compromise reached envisaged that the number of commissioners would be reduced, in the sense that only two out of three member states would have the right to representation (on a rotating basis). The introduction of this reform was postponed to 2014 in order to appease Irish voters required to vote on the Lisbon Treaty for a second time (in October 2009), after having rejected it in a previous referendum (in June 2008). Indeed, the Lisbon Treaty, TEU Article 17.5, states that each member state has a right to propose a national as commissioner until November 1, 2014, adding that after that date the Commission will be composed of "two thirds of the number of the Member States, unless the European Council, acting unanimously, decides to alter this number." As expected, the small member states (which then represented 19 out of 27 member states[5]) exerted pressure to preserve the status quo, exactly because they also wanted to guarantee the equally weighted geographical composition within the Commission regardless of what the Treaty states. On May 22, 2013 the European Council unanimously adopted a decision providing "that the Commission will continue to consist of a number of members equal to the number of Member States. This number also includes the Commission President and the High Representative of the European Union for Foreign Affairs and Security Policy/Vice President of the Commission. The decision, which in effect maintains the current practice, will apply from 1 November 2014" (EUCO 2013).

An interstate division is inevitable in a union of demographically asymmetrical states. It represents a clash between the legitimate interests of small, medium and large member states. If properly represented, and adopting the necessary and pragmatic compromises, it may produce a centripetal pressure within the Union. Indeed, in order

[5] That is: Austria, Belgium, Cyprus, Czech Republic, Estonia, Finland, Denmark, Greece, Hungary, Ireland, Latvia, Lithuania, Luxembourg, Malta, the Netherlands, Portugal, Slovakia, Slovenia, Sweden. Croatia joined the group in July 2013, bringing the ratio to 20 out of 28 member states. Spain, Poland, Romania and Bulgaria are considered medium-sized member states. Germany, France, the UK and Italy are the large member states.

to solicit such centripetal pressure, US constitution-makers meeting at Philadelphia in 1787 were prone to introduce those institutional devices that, although they were at odds with democratic criteria (Dahl 2001), could keep such divisions of interests under control. One only has to think of the compromise of assigning two senators to each state regardless of its demographic size and of electing the president through states' electoral colleges that over-represent the small states (see Chapter 8). In the case of the EU, the cleavage between small, medium and large member states was, and is, more complex also because of its economic implications. The large states (such as Germany, France and the UK) are more developed and richer than the small ones (Schelkle 2012), especially those that entered the EU with the enlargements of the 2000s. Through the structural fund policy, introduced to compensate the economically weak states for the costs they have to pay for operating within a single market, this cleavage has been restrained by a significant redistribution of resources from the larger and richer member states to the smaller and poorer ones. This policy was also important for attracting the small/medium size states of Eastern and Southern Europe to the EU in the 1990s and the early 2000s (Leonardi 2005).

However, with the explosion of the euro crisis, this cleavage has started to spawn centrifugal, not centripetal, forces. First of all, the financial crisis has reduced the resources available for policies of territorial redistribution at the European level. The Multiannual Financial Framework (MFF) for the period 2014–20, eventually agreed by the Council and the EP between October and November 2013, was, for the first time in EU history, 3.5 percent lower than the MFF for the previous period (2007–2013). Some of the large member states, Germany in particular, have called into question their traditional paymaster role within the EU. Greece, Portugal, Ireland, Spain, Cyprus and Slovenia received various forms of financial support from the crisis management programs activated during the crisis; however, the economic distance between them and Germany has dramatically increased. The euro crisis has shown the economic dependence of the smaller member states on the larger ones (Germany in particular), an economic status that has gradually shifted in the direction of political subordination. This outcome has incited old fears on the part of the small member states of being colonized by the large member states. The small member states' fear of being dominated by larger member states, in the past as during the euro crisis, fostered and continues to foster a sovereignist mood in countries such as Ireland, Denmark, the Czech Republic, Greece and Portugal. Size matters, although it is not the only factor for establishing how a member state relates to the integration process. In the sovereignist coalition there are member states with memories of having been dominated by external powers in the past, having thus developed an unfavorable attitude to integration. Some small member states are also in the opposing camp on the assumption that the formation of a supranational framework is the condition for preventing the hegemonic orders of large member states.

Although this cleavage should be taken into serious consideration in a union of asymmetrical states, it can find a proper institutional solution if the parties involved share a common perspective on the nature of the union. In the case of the EU, a pragmatic compromise was found between the need of the small member states not to be overruled in the decision-making process and the request of the large member states to preserve a correlation with the democratic principle of "one person, one vote." The over-representation of the small member states in the EP thanks to the adoption of the principle of *degressive proportionality* (see Chapter 2), the qualified majority voting (QMV) adopted for deliberation in the Council and the decision to recognize for each member state the right to have a national commissioner are pieces of a pragmatic compromise between large and small member states. Nevertheless, this pragmatic compromise was questioned by the larger member states, in particular by the German Constitutional Court, which disavowed the democratic nature of the EP exactly because of the criterion of degressive proportionality adopted for allocating its seats among the member states. As we have seen, this criterion, according to the judgment of June 30, 2009 that approved the Lisbon Treaty, does not comply with the normative standards of democratic representation that imply "one person one vote."[6] In a union of asymmetrical states, however, any compromise

---

[6] In several decisions the German Constitutional Court has continued to equate the democratic legitimacy of a union of states with that of a nation state. Consequently, it could not take into consideration the constraints on popular representation that are typical of federal unions. Those constraints concern not only the higher chamber but also the lower chamber. In the USA, for example, the principle of "one person one vote" was obviously contradicted by the compromise made for the composition of the Senate (two senators for each federated state regardless of its demographic size), but it was contradicted also by the 1929 Permanent Apportionment Act fixing the number of members

between the interests of small and large member states will never satisfy a view of democracy coherent with Rousseau's idea of a political regime based *exclusively* on individual citizens. A union of asymmetrical states, in fact, will have also to recognize the territoriality of its units as a source of equal political subjectivity: states and individuals alike constitute the foundation of the union (Lord and Pollack 2013).

3.6 Conclusion

This chapter has reconstructed the recurrent divisions on the constitutional nature of the EU that have developed since the negotiations that led to the Maastricht Treaty. EU member states and their citizens have periodically divided on how to frame national sovereignty in the integration process, how to promote the democratic legitimacy of the decision-making process and how to guarantee a balance between small and large member states within the latter. What was swept under the carpet in Rome in 1957, as an effect of the 1954 failure of the EDC project, has come to the surface after decades of passive consensus on the integration process. The Lisbon Treaty was the attempt to find a point of balance between contrasting perspectives on the Union. It achieved that through the formalization of several compromises wrapped up by the rigid rule of unanimity for any future amendment of the Treaty (as TEU Article 48.4 asserts: "The amendments shall enter into force after being ratified by all the Member States in accordance with their respective constitutional requirements"). However, with the explosion of the euro crisis, the Lisbon Treaty's structure of compromises has not endured. If it was thought that the Lisbon Treaty would finally settle the constitutional divisions that emerged during the previous two decades, the euro crisis has reopened those divisions in dramatic fashion.

In considering the structural and not the contingent divisions related to specific policies that have been adopted or pursued, this

of the House of Representatives at 435 (a practice already started after the 1910 census). Since the constitution says that no state may have fewer than one House member, this means that small states (Wyoming, Vermont, North Dakota) are also over-represented in the popular chamber, whereas other states (California above all) are under-represented, notwithstanding that the principle of "one person one vote" was also celebrated by the 1964 ruling of the Supreme Court in the *Reynolds* v. *Sims* case.

chapter has shown how the euro crisis has increased the distance between the sovereignist coalition and the other member states. The political compromise inaugurated in Maastricht, and based on the idea of letting a small number of member states opt out from crucial policy regimes such as the EMU, has been shaken by the financial turmoil that has started a genuine conflict of interests between euro-area and non-euro-area member states. At the same time, the euro crisis has dramatized the dispute on the democratic legitimacy of the EU's decisions, also because the latter have been taken through an intergovernmental decision-making regime that is an alternative to the supranational regime. In this regard, too, the euro crisis has called into question the institutional compromise between the supranational and the intergovernmental constitutions inaugurated in Maastricht and then confirmed in the following treaties. Finally, the euro crisis has exacerbated the uneven relations between member states of different size and economic capability. The more the financial crisis has advanced, the more the divisions between North and South, creditors and debtors, large and small member states have increased.

This chapter has shown that, although never coherently elaborated and defined, three main and different perspectives have regularly emerged from the divisions that have accompanied the EU's institutionalization and its response to the euro crisis. The first is the perspective of the EU as an *economic community*, advanced by the defenders of national sovereignty, interested in protecting domestic democracy and in utilizing the Union as a means for creating and maintaining a common market. The second is the perspective of the EU as an *intergovernmental union*, advanced by those politicians and public servants who have recognized the need to institutionalize coordination between national governments also in crucial policies such as economic issues and foreign affairs, keeping on the margins, however, the supranational institutions of the Union. From this perspective, national sovereignty should be pooled at the European level of intergovernmental institutions, democratic legitimacy should be guaranteed by the strengthening of the relations between national governments and national parliaments both in Brussels and at the domestic level, and the division between member states of different size should be restrained by a politics of reciprocal trade-offs and adaptations within the intergovernmental institutions. The third is the perspective of the *parliamentary union*, advanced by those politicians and public servants who considered themselves to be the heirs of the founders' project of building a European federation. Here, national sovereignty should be shared with supranational institutions, democratic legitimacy should be promoted by the strengthening of the EP as the legislative institution that controls the Commission, and the divisions between small and large member states should be restrained through transnational party competition.

In the context of the euro crisis, while the economic community perspective has heightened the call for repatriating policy competences previously assumed by the EU, the other two perspectives have instead increased their federal drive. Given the deep integration induced by the crisis in the euro-area member states and given the request to strengthen relations between the EP and the Commission in managing the post-euro crisis, some scholars (Crum 2012) have labeled the two perspectives as different forms of federalism: "executive federalism" (which I would rather call "federalism of governments," see Chapter 5) and "parliamentary federalism" (see Chapter 6). Rather than a multi-speed EU, that is, an EU constituted by member states moving at different speeds towards a common goal, what has emerged in the euro crisis is a Union constituted by member states and citizens with different perspectives on it. Rather than a division between vanguards and rearguards (Piris 2012), the divisions have focused on what the EU is and should become. It is time to investigate those different perspectives, elaborating their rationale, in order to test both their descriptive and prescriptive power.

PART II

Main perspectives on the European Union

4 | *The perspective of the economic community*

At the core of the European Union must be, as it is now, the single market ... the EU must be able to act with the speed and flexibility of a network.

David Cameron, British Prime Minister, January 23, 2013

4.1 Introduction

Notwithstanding the extraordinary institutional development of the EU and the formidable complexity of its decision-making systems constitutionalized by the Lisbon Treaty and made even more complex by the need to deal with the euro crisis, the claim that the EU is and should be an economic community similar to other regional economic organizations has continued to be heard in the European debate. In his speech on Europe, given on January 23, 2013, the British Prime Minister David Cameron said that "at the core of the European Union must be, as it is now, the single market," adding that "the EU must be able to act with the speed and flexibility of a network." Cameron reclaimed the concept of an EU as the organization of an economic community that was subsumed into a larger Union with the 1992 Maastricht Treaty. Indeed, the Northern core of the ex-EFTA countries has persistently interpreted the EU as an economic confederation, a forum where national governments meet to find solutions to common economic problems (Berrington and Hague 2001). As Cameron stressed on that occasion, if some member states "are contemplating much closer economic and political integration ... many others, including Britain, would never embrace that goal."

Politically, the economic community perspective has been interpreted by their supporters as the one that both allows for cooperation between states and preserves the sovereignty (or crucial parts of it) of each of them. In this sense, this has been and continues to be the perspective of the *sovereignist coalition*. Although the economic community perspective has never been coherently elaborated, it might be assumed that

it is based on cooperation rather than coordination between states
regarding the promotion of common policies, a cooperation that is
much looser than the one envisioned in the intergovernmental constitution of the Lisbon Treaty. The EU is considered an economic community because the national governments have preserved crucial veto
powers to block any undesired evolution of their cooperation. For the
sovereignist coalition, the control of the Union should be in the hands
of *each* member state's government rather than in those of the intergovernmental institutions (such as the European Council and the various Council formations). If the EU must be a flexible network, then it
might be counterproductive to strengthen its intergovernmental institutions. Excessive institutionalization might make the system too rigid.
The intergovernmental institutions should be semi-removed from the
EU institutional core, should be based on the recognition of the indisputable veto power of each national government, and should resemble
a diplomatic more than a policy arena. Moreover, other arenas are
expected to be used, as is the case with bilateral and multilateral meetings at the sub-regional level, organized externally to the Union's legal
and institutional structure, where neighboring countries with strong
cultural affinities share information and transfer good practice (one
has to think of the Nordic Council's meetings aggregating ministers of
member states of the EU such as Denmark, Sweden and Finland with
non-EU countries such as Norway and Iceland). According to Majone
(2014: 17–18), "James Buchanan's economic theory of clubs may be
used to provide a robust conceptual basis for … integration à la carte
and … other forms of functional integration. [After all] the view of
Europe as a 'club of clubs,' rather than as a would-be federation, has
deep roots in the history of the Old Continent." In this perspective,
one might assume the single market as one of the clubs, a functional
aggregation of states for reaching a specific target.

The member states' leaders and politicians interpreting the EU as
an economic community have nevertheless had to face the fact that
its institutional structure has become so dense that it could not fit a
traditional confederal model (with its very light institutional coordination). As Heywood (2004: 148–9) put it, "in strict terms, [the
EU] is no longer a confederation of independent states operating on
the basis of intergovernmentalism," supposing that it has ever been
so. The common and then single market (a transformation largely
induced by the British promotion of the 1986 SEA) would have

been inconceivable without the operation of institutions (such as the Commission and the ECJ) independent from the member states' will and preferences. Nevertheless, the functional activity of those supranational institutions has traditionally been resented. The Commission, in particular, has been the constant target of criticism because of its presumed attempt to enlarge its organization and functions. Cameron asked rhetorically in the abovementioned speech: "Can we justify a Commission that gets ever larger?" Notwithstanding this criticism, it should be remembered that the UK has been one of the most compliant member states in terms of EU laws and ECJ decisions. As noted by Grant (2008: 1), "the British have a good record of implementing EU directives and of respecting the decisions of the European Court of Justice, while a supposedly pro-EU country such as France has a poor record on those counts."

It is essential to clarify that the expression *economic community* cannot be confused with that of economic union. In the EU's history, the concept of economic union has been connected to monetary union, thus becoming a specific system of governance with the EMU. In the history of the EU, by economic community one has to understand the organization of the common market. Although the expression economic community is at the origin of the integration process (as we have seen, the 1957 Rome Treaty set up the European Economic Community, EEC, which became the first pillar of the European Community, EC, with the 1992 Maastricht Treaty), that expression has come to be interpreted by the sovereignist coalition as a light and à la carte common market. This is why the concept of economic union cannot be equated to the concept of economic community.

This chapter will critically discuss the assessment that the EU is an economic community not qualitatively different from other regional economic organizations. It is organized as follows. First, it will consider the basic literature on the growth of a new world order based on organized economic regions. Second, it will analyze the most significant experiences, at the global level, of regional organizations such as the Association of Southeast Asian Nations (ASEAN), the Asia-Pacific Economic Cooperation (APEC), the Mercado Común del Sur (MERCOSUR) and the North American Free Trade Agreement (NAFTA). Third, it will develop an institutional and policy comparison between the latter regional economic organizations and the EU. Such comparison makes it possible to show both the substantial

differences between the EU and the other regional economic organizations and the scarce plausibility of the economic community perspective on the EU.

4.2 Regional economic organizations

The interpretation of the EU as a regional economic organization,
structured around a network of institutions not affecting the national
sovereignty of its members, has been supported by influential international relations (IR) literature on the formation of a new world order.
For Slaughter (2004: 264–5), "the European Union is pioneering governance through government networks in its international affairs ...
[It is a] distinctive form of government by network exportable to other
regions and to the world at large." For Katzenstein (2005), the EU
has become, in particular after the Maastricht Treaty, a successful and
attractive example of regional economic organizations. For Gamble
(2007), the EU epitomizes the formation of an international system of
overlapping authorities, forerunner of a new medievalism at the global
level. Since the EU has been the first and most prominent experience
of regional cooperation (Roy and Dominguez 2005; Telò 2009), and
since it has played a pivotal role in promoting world regionalism (De
Lombaerde and Schulz 2009), it has been common to locate it in a
continuum with other regional organizations (Slaughter 2004). The
difference between the EU and other regional organizations is considered to be a difference of degree and not of kind.

Thus, although the perspective of the EU as an economic community has accompanied the process of integration, in particular after the
first enlargement of 1973, the political salience of that perspective has,
however, increased with the diffusion of forms of regional economic
cooperation after the end of the Cold War. This is why several scholars
have assumed the EU as a pioneer of a larger movement of regional
organizations aimed at dealing with the challenges of globalization
(Hettne, Inotai and Sunkel 2002; Lawson 2009). The global experience of regional economic organizations seems to confirm the possibility of combining interstate cooperation, necessary for facing policy
challenges that nation states are too small to handle, with the preservation of the latter's prerogatives. Indeed, any attempt at deepening
European integration was considered *unnecessary* by the supporters
of this perspective, while instead any attempt at its enlargement was

considered *necessary* in order to increase the economic capability of the European region in facing those policy challenges. As Slaughter (2004: 5 and 6) argued forcefully, "stop imagining the international system as a system of states – unitary entities like billiard balls or black boxes – subject to rules created by international institutions that are apart from, 'above' these states. Start thinking about a world of governments," that is, a world of transnational institutions, with "government officials within these various institutions [participating] in many different types of networks."

Economic regionalism is considered one, if not the predominant, form of intergovernmental cooperation pursued in different areas of the world. Such regionalism reflects important differences regarding the nature, scope, decision-making styles, compliance mechanisms, structures and international status of the different regional organizations. With the end of the Cold War, regional organizations were created in Asia, South and Central America, North America and Africa (Laursen 2010; Telò 2007). Moreover, this regionalism was not limited geographically, as some forms of regional blocs, such as APEC, brought together members from different continents. In some cases, closer interdependence was seen as a way of protecting specific developmental models or specific cultural patterns from the influence of powerful economic and cultural forces (sometimes these two coincided). In other cases, the new regionalism was seen as a way of resolving longstanding rivalries between neighbors. The new regional organizations were also a result of imitation and a means of increasing bargaining power in international negotiations for states in certain areas of the world.

Post-Cold War regionalism is different from Cold War regionalism (Hurrell 1995). The latter (known also as "old" regionalism) consisted of a series of alliances promoted by the USA in Europe, South America and East Asia in order to guarantee regional security.[1] NATO, SEATO (the South-East Asia Treaty Organization instituted in 1954 in Manila) and CENTO (the Central Treaty Organization

---

[1] It should be remembered that during the Cold War a few economic integration projects were promoted, such as the Latin American Free Trade Association (LAFTA/ALALC) created in 1960 between Argentina, Brazil, Chile, Mexico, Paraguay, Peru and Uruguay, without considering the Soviet Union-dominated bloc of socialist countries (COMECON or Council for Mutual Economic Assistance) instituted in 1949.

instituted in 1955 first in Baghdad and then in Ankara and which collapsed in 1979) are the examples of this US-led regionalism (the USA joined CENTO in 1958, while it was the main driver for the establishment of the other two treaties) (Ikenberry 2001). Only in Europe did the regional organization for security come to be complemented by a regional organization for market integration, with the creation of the ECSC in the 1951 Paris Treaty, and thus its development into the EEC and the EURATOM in the 1957 Rome Treaties (see Part I). It was thus the end of the Cold War that reopened the way for regional experiments or for the strengthening and reinterpretation of existing ones. The contemporary concept of regionalism is exclusively based on interstate cooperation on economic and trade issues (Mansfield and Milner 2000).

The new regional organizations are the expression of the new economic consensus that extols promotion of exports rather than import substitution strategies. They are open to globalizing markets and they pursue non-protectionist policies. They represent a "region as a platform" rather than a "region as a fortress." Developed and developing countries have thus come to share the same vision of economic policy, a vision based on the idea that nationalization of economic activities no longer represents the recipe for successful development. Moreover, they are the expression of the necessity to reduce the complexity of multilateral negotiation in liberalized world trade. Negotiations between regions (rather than between countries) have seemed to reduce that complexity, not only through limiting the actors involved but also through simplifying the agenda (focusing on the issues that may be better solved at the regional level). Finally, they are an expression of a need to protect or preserve regional peculiarities (in cultural and social terms) against what is perceived as a homogenizing process of globalization. At the end of 2010 there were more than 80 regional agreements with preferential conditions for associated states, although such agreements are generally open and not antagonistic. Indeed, in 2013 very few of the 159 members and observers at the World Trade Organization (WTO) did not belong to at least one of the existing regional organizations or blocs. Regional economic organizations display important differences on several fronts. They may be the expression of low or high economic integration between the countries of a specific area. They might reflect different degrees of asymmetry between the largest and smallest associated states. They might be open or closed organizations, with different concepts of trade exchange. Some organizations might have low trade barriers internally and high trade barriers with the outside world, while other organizations might leave to the associated states the possibility to pursue bilateral trade relations with the countries of the outside world.

However, looking at the regional economic organizations from a comparative politics (CP) approach leads to a different conclusion, namely that they are not in a continuum with the EU. The main regional economic organizations such as ASEAN, APEC, MERCOSUR and NAFTA do not have the institutional and policy properties of the EU. They are interstate agreements aimed primarily at dismantling national barriers to cross-border trade or investment and (when it is possible) at reducing the national externalities of cross-border economic activity. They are regional organizations pursuing market-supporting, but not market-correcting, strategies. Positive integration has not been the subject of treaty discussion. If one assumes the analytical framework elaborated by Balassa (1961) of the five stages of economic integration, that is, free trade area, custom union, common market, economic union as harmonization of national economic policies and total economic integration, implying unification of monetary, fiscal, social and macroeconomic policies and finally the formation of a political union whose decisions are binding for member states (Laffan, O'Donnell and Smith 2000: 102), it might be argued that the regional economic organizations here discussed have oscillated between the first stage (which implies the removal of tariffs and quotas on imports from members, although members retain national tariffs against third countries) and the second stage (which also implies a common external tariff).

After all, the promotion of a common market stage (as the EU experience has shown) would inevitably have some implications in reducing the decision-making discretion of the associated states. It is necessary to have supra-state/supranational rules, preserved or promoted by institutions and actors not dependent on national governments, in order to have a functioning common market (which implies, in addition to the measures of the other two stages, free movement of labor and capital). Without substituting national rules (negative integration) with supranational ones (positive integration), the common market stage would be unattainable. Moreover, none of those organizations ever considered reaching the fourth stage of economic union (which implies harmonization of national economic policies), nor the fifth of total integration (with its implications of unifying monetary, fiscal, social and macroeconomic policies, controlled by a supranational authority whose decisions are binding for member states). It is the different stages of economic integration reached by those regional economic organizations, on the one hand, and the EU, on the other, that has triggered the formation of radically different institutional and policy-making structures in each of them. Looking at those structures from a CP approach, one may argue that they belong to a different genus, not a different species, of regional organizations. One might notice that, for the EU supporters of the economic community perspective, integration should include the first three stages (free trade area, custom unions and common market), but not the fourth stage (harmonization of national economic policies). Of course, the fifth stage is not even considered.

ASEAN, APEC, MERCOSUR and NAFTA have had a different historical genesis. They are economic pacts aimed at fostering cooperation among different states. MERCOSUR is probably the only regional organization that has tried to inaugurate a new political phase of cooperation between two traditional rival states such as Brazil and Argentina. Although ASEAN came into existence in the second half of the 1960s, the other three regional organizations are the expression of the possibilities of interstate cooperation opened up by the ending of the Cold War (Haggard 1997). All of them are intergovernmental organizations, functioning, however, on a transgovernmental logic (in particular the Asia-Pacific organizations). The institutionalization of the intergovernmental councils is generally weak. Their functional logic is based on horizontal communication between governments, rather than on structured practices of coordination between them within stable intergovernmental institutions. The comparison of these organizations' institutional and policy-making structures with those of the EU calls into question the very idea of a "continuum" between them.

4.3 Economic cooperation in the Asia-Pacific region

Since the beginning, ASEAN (1967)[2] and APEC (1989)[3] have acquired the features of organizations connecting governments and sectors of the

---

[2] The founders were: Indonesia, Malaysia, Philippines, Singapore, Thailand; then joined by Brunei Darussalam (1984), Vietnam (1995), Laos and Myanmar (1997) and Cambodia (1998).

[3] The founders were: Indonesia, Singapore, Brunei, Malaysia, Philippines, Thailand, Australia, Japan, New Zealand, South Korea and Canada; then

business community. Both have transgovernmental and transnational features, in the sense that business groups of different countries have interacted directly with governmental ministers within a loose institutional framework (Aggarwal 1994). Both ASEAN and APEC are customs unions, whose decision-making system is based on consensus unanimity, although in 1996 the former introduced some forms of majority voting regarding very limited issues (Ravenhill 2001). It was the Asian crisis of the second half of the 1990s (and its mismanagement by international financial institutions) that created among Asian countries the perception of the need to cooperate in order to counter outside negative influences (Higgott 1998). Since then the quest for Asian collaboration has remained strategic for many Asian countries, although its development has followed an uncertain path, moving from a general trade liberalization agenda to a more sector-based approach. Since APEC is an organization including developed and developing countries, and democratic and non-democratic countries, it has been characterized by huge asymmetry among them (in terms of economic power, trade capability and political legitimacy). With the adherence of China in 1991 and Russia in 1998, the asymmetrical complexity of the organization increased dramatically (Yamazawa and Hirata 1996). Different needs and contrasting interests have not been easily reconciled. Certainly the experience of the crisis and the fear of being marginalized in a world trade system constrained by powerful regional blocs have fostered the demand for economic collaboration between the states in the Pacific area. Indeed, in the case of APEC, having the USA within the organization has been a way to counterbalance its projection towards Europe.

Given these huge demographic, economic and political asymmetries, both ASEAN and APEC are regional organizations with light horizontal governance structures. They do not have established compliance mechanisms, but use loose resolution practices (ASEAN) or clearly voluntary practices (APEC). Their operation is not based on supra-state institutions and actors. ASEAN is based on a meeting of heads of state and government (Summit) once every three years (see Table 4.1), whereas APEC has more operative continuity thanks to the annual meeting of governmental leaders (Leaders' Meetings; see Table 4.2). The APEC Leaders' Meeting is the main decision-making

joined by China, Hong Kong and Taiwan (1991), Mexico and Papua New Guinea (1993), Chile (1994), Peru, Russia, Vietnam (1998).

Table 4.1 ASEAN institutional structure

Institutional structure		Features	Role	Functions
ASEAN Summit		Intergovernmental body	Decision-making	To agree on the aims of the organization
ASEAN Coordinating Council		Intergovernmental body	Coordination	To transform the Summit's agreements into policies
ASEAN Community Council	Political-Security Community Council Economic Community Council Socio-Cultural Community Council	Sectoral intergovernmental bodies	Sectoral policy implementation	To combine political and technical requirements
Sectoral Ministerial Bodies		Sectoral ministerial-level meetings	Technical role	To provide reports and recommendations to the Community Council
ASEAN Secretariat		Central functional body	Supervisory role	To monitor the implementation of policies
Committee of Permanent Representatives		Permanent inter-bureaucratic body	Mediating role	To smooth the works of Community Councils and Sectoral Ministerial Bodies

Table 4.2 *APEC institutional structure*

Institutional structure	Features	Role	Functions
Leaders' Meeting Joint Ministerial Meeting	Intergovernmental body Ministerial-level body	Decision-making Policy definition	To set the policy agenda To prepare for the Leaders' Meeting
Sectoral Ministerial Meetings	Specialized ministerial-level bodies	Technical support	To give recommendations to the Leaders' Meeting
APEC Business Advisory Council	Advisory body composed of private sector representatives	Political and functional advice	To represent the private sector, annual report to the Leaders' Meeting
Senior Officials' Meeting (Working Groups)	Coordinating body composed of officials from the member economies	Policy coordination	To coordinate the committees and working groups
Committees APEC Secretariat	Specialized technical bodies Administrative permanent body	Technical support Bureaucratic monitoring	To negotiate technicalities To provide information

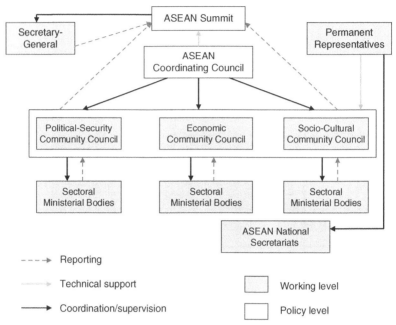

Figure 4.1 ASEAN policy-making structure

forum of the organization. "APEC leaders set goals, publicize them, and provide momentum for the process. This is usually held in November of each year, and is attended by heads of state except for those from Taiwan (Chinese Taipei) and Hong Kong who send other representatives" (Nanto 2002: 5). Many APEC policy options are first considered in the annual ministerial meetings with their functional composition. The largest is the annual Joint Ministerial Meeting, which meets to prepare for the Leaders' Meeting. Finance ministers and heads of central banks are generally the main actors at the Joint Ministerial Meeting.

ASEAN has a Secretariat (in Jakarta) with ministerial status, several (29–30) committees of senior officials (permanent representatives) and more than a hundred (122) working groups on the various policy issues, complemented by a limited number of specialized (but non-independent) agencies. Since the institutional model is fully intergovernmental, the policy-making structure functions according to a horizontal logic: decisions are taken in the ASEAN Summit through unanimous consensus (see Figure 4.1).

APEC has a Secretariat (in Singapore) of a couple of dozen civil servants, supported by a limited number of committees (3) and working groups of experts (10) that deal with economic issues of importance to the region. The committees are: the Committee on Trade and Investment, the Economic Committee and the Budget and Administrative Committee. The working groups are: trade and investment data, trade promotion, industrial science and technology, human resource development, energy cooperation, marine resource conservation, telecommunication, transportation, tourism and fisheries. Each working group is coordinated by a permanent representative of one of the associated members. Regarding their transnational side, apart from the celebratory Eminent Person Groups, instituted in 1992, with the duty of developing a vision for APEC's future, it is the APEC Business Advisory Council (ABAC), instituted in 1995, that has come to play an influential role. ABAC consists of up to three members appointed by each APEC member and makes recommendations to APEC governments on issues related to trade, investment, finance and technology. Here the institutional model is also formally intergovernmental and the policy-making structure follows a horizontal logic: in the Leaders' Meeting decisions are taken through unanimous consensus, transformed into policies after a long technical screening process, and it is then left to each state to implement them (see Figure 4.2). The national governments have not provided the Secretariat with the institutional resources to play the functional role of fostering further integration. No spillover effects have emerged in the two organizations.

Both ASEAN and APEC are careful not to invade areas other than trade and economic cooperation. In particular, "APEC had carefully kept its distance from security matters for fear that such issues would cause divisions within the group, particularly among China, Taiwan, US, Japan and Russia. Such divisions could thwart cooperation in achieving economic goals" (Nanto 2002: 7). Since 1995 the consensus among APEC leaders has been that regional security issues have to be discussed in other fora or in the ASEAN Regional Forum (ARF). The ARF generally meets after the ASEAN Ministerial Conference and includes the ten members of the organization, plus the USA, China, Russia, Japan, South Korea, Australia, New Zealand, Canada and the EU.

In conclusion, both ASEAN and APEC are organizations for creating a free trade area through a loose form of voluntary economic

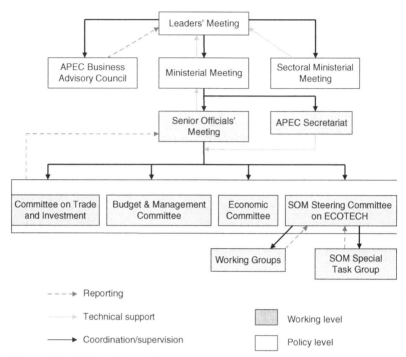

Figure 4.2 APEC policy-making structure

cooperation among states. Both are intergovernmental organizations
that encourage, but do not impose, the voluntarily liberalization of
specific sectors on the national economies of a given area. They do
not have judicial institutions endowed with the power of checking
whether intergovernmental deliberations are respected. Both oscillate
between open and closed regionalism, in the sense that there is no
stable consensus among their members on whether to discriminate
(closed regionalism) or not (open regionalism) against non-members
in trade relations. More generally, the longstanding (political and economic) rivalry between the most powerful Asian countries (such as
Japan and China, both members of APEC that have never dealt pub-
licly with the responsibilities of their own historical past) represents
a permanent hurdle in the path towards a more sustainable Asian
regional cooperation (Hemmer and Katzenstein 2002). Thus Asian
regionalism seems to be squeezed between two opposing forces. On
the one side, there is the necessity to cooperate in order to address the

challenges of globalized markets. On the other, Asian countries have not elaborated a common narrative to construct an Asian project of integration that is sufficiently inclusive of their differences.

4.4 Economic cooperation in the Americas

MERCOSUR[4] and NAFTA[5] are also intergovernmental regional organizations. Both are homogeneous in terms of the political system of their members, but highly asymmetrical in terms of economic power relations between them. The predominance of (respectively) Brazil and the USA is undisputed. MERCOSUR and NAFTA represent a hierarchical model of economic regionalism, contrary to ASEAN and APEC, which function along the lines of a horizontal model.

MERCOSUR was founded in 1991 with the Treaty of Asunción, with the goal of establishing a free trade area by 1994, then a customs union by 1995 and finally a common market and a common external commercial policy (Bulmer-Thomas 2001). Its political aim was to stabilize the new democratic systems of the South Cone, which were emerging from the authoritarian experiences of the previous decades (Hurrell 2001). "The key to the emergence of MERCOSUR ... was the development of closer relations between Argentina and Brazil from the mid-1980s as both returned to democracy and began economic liberalization" (Mechan 2003: 376). Since its inception, however, MERCOSUR has been conditioned by the interests of Brazil. Brazil has a longstanding big country perspective. "From a geo-strategic perspective, Brazil uses MERCOSUR as a political and economic alliance to confront other powers, in particular the US in the FTAA [Free Trade Area of the Americas] and the WTO, and the EU in the EU–MERCOSUR context and in the WTO" (Klom 2003: 352). In fact, to contain the expansive presence of the USA in Latin America, it is much more effective for Brazil to act as the leader of a regional bloc than as a single, although big, country. This is why Brazil has always opposed any institutional model implying some supranational features (desired or proposed by the small members such as Uruguay

---

[4] The founders were: Brazil, Argentina, Paraguay, Uruguay; then joined by Chile (as an associate in 1996), Bolivia (as an associate in 1997), Peru (as an associate in 2003), Colombia (as an associate in 2004), Ecuador (as an associate in 2004) and Venezuela (as full member in 2010).
[5] Still constituted by its founders: the USA, Canada and Mexico.

and Paraguay, but also Argentina), protecting instead the intergovernmental character of MERCOSUR.

The political potential of the organization has thus been kept in check by Brazil, which, however, has accepted that MERCOSUR should move beyond trade liberalization in the direction of a common market program. Indeed, because of the need to institutionalize the cooperation between Brazil and Argentina, once they became stable democratic systems, in 1994 the MERCOSUR countries (through the Ouro Preto Protocol) agreed to give legal personality to the organization. However, MERCOSUR norms are not the equivalent of EU laws, but rather international laws that require translation into the national legislation of all the members of MERCOSUR to be implemented. MERCOSUR's legal system mirrors the ambiguity of Latin American legal systems: "while treaties incorporate far-reaching commitments, implementation lacks discipline and rules are flouted" (Mechan 2003: 386). Influenced by the EU experience, and actively supported by EU institutions (and the Commission in particular), MERCOSUR has unsuccessfully tried to advance along the road of political regionalism (Malamud and Schmitter 2010). Although structured according to an architecture that recalls the founding period of the EU (see Table 4.3), the highly asymmetrical relation between Brazil and the other members has represented an insurmountable hurdle for the creation of a supranational authority that could check the intergovernmental institutions.

This is why progress within MERCOSUR has been uneven, notwithstanding a formal declaration in favor of deeper integration. For instance, MERCOSUR introduced a formal dispute settlement mechanism in 2006, with the implementation of the Protocol of Olivos that established the current rules for the resolution of disputes and created a judicial body, the Permanent Review Tribunal. This was a clear step towards supranationalism. However, as Malamud (2013) efficaciously argued, it was a step only on paper, because the mechanism has continued to function as defectively as in the past (only six rulings in six years, 2006–2012). The lack of an effective supranational dispute resolution mechanism (that is, of an independent judicial body), although envisioned since the Ouro Preto Protocol of 1994, has obstructed the process of reciprocal policy harmonization among its members. Disputes are discussed by ad hoc intergovernmental arbitration panels that do not enjoy any real compliance powers. Their decisions,

Table 4.3 *MERCOSUR institutional structure*

Institutional structure	Features	Role	Functions
Common Market Council (CMC)	Intergovernmental decision-making body	Policy direction	To agree on the objectives defined by the Treaty of Asunción
Common Market Group (CMG)	Intergovernmental executive body	Policy coordination	To propose draft policies to the CMC, to implement the decisions of the CMC
MERCOSUR Trade Commission	Intergovernmental technical body	Technical support	To assist the CMG
Economic and Social Advisory Forum	Consultative body	Policy advice	To give *ex-post* information
MERCOSUR Parliament (*in fieri*)	Consultative body	Symbolic	To represent MERCOSUR's citizens
Permanent Review Tribunal	Judicial body	Judicial role	To resolve disputes and to guarantee uniformity and consistency of MERCOSUR norms
MERCOSUR Secretariat	Permanent administrative body	Supervisory role	To support other MERCOSUR organs
Commission of Permanent Representatives	Auxiliary intergovernmental body	Technical role	To help MERCOSUR *pro tempore* Presidency

although formally mandatory, "were neither immediately applicable nor have direct effect, so members need not necessarily enforce them" (Bouzas and Soltz 2001: 107). Indeed, handling disputes case by case has undermined the legal unity of the organization.

MERCOSUR has paid the price of an institutional deficit. Its institutional underdevelopment is an effect of a lack of political will in promoting the means to achieve the aims proclaimed in the Treaty of Asunción. For instance, the latter established two key intergovernmental bodies: the Common Market Council (consisting of ministers of economic affairs with the role of giving political direction) and the Common Market Group (consisting of officials charged with macroeconomic and policy coordination). However, the two bodies have not worked as expected. Decisions have mostly been taken in the informal twice-a-year presidential summits, organized by the six-month rotating presidency (which has had, however, more of an organizational than an agenda-setting role). Indeed, in its development MERCOSUR has come to adopt a peculiar decision-making procedure based on the meetings of the presidents of the associated countries that has made the organization even more hierarchical. Inter-presidentialism (Malamud 2003, 2005) is the variant assumed by MERCOSUR's intergovernmentalism. The meetings between the presidents of the MERCOSUR countries have become the forum for taking decisions, for resolving disputes, and for soothing contrasts and rivalries. The inter-presidential summit has become the informal institution for MERCOSUR governance. However, once decisions have been taken, implementation has not necessarily followed (Malamud 2013). At the same time, the MERCOSUR Parliament, created in 2005, has been unable to win an autonomous role, even less so to check inter-presidential decisions. As argued by Dri (2009), although the MERCOSUR Parliament (Parlasur) has tried to follow the experience of the European Parliament (EP), it has not reached a level of institutionalization such as to be taken in consideration by the other institutions. Its role has remained symbolic.

The daily operation of the organization is in the hands of a small Secretariat located in Montevideo, supported by working and ad hoc groups. Although originally designed along the lines of the European Commission, the Secretariat has not played an independent role because of a lack of administrative resources and a legal basis. Moreover, Brazil, but also Argentina, has been unwilling to promote horizontal policy-making models to build an effective common

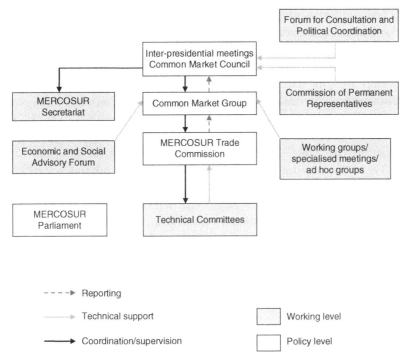

Figure 4.3 MERCOSUR policy-making structure

market. The Common Market Council has continued to be the main policy-making institution (see Figure 4.3). In particular, Brazil has tried to impose its own economic weight on the other partners. In 2010 Brazil covered around 75 percent of total assets (trade, GDP, population) of MERCOSUR, while Germany covers much less in the EU. Moreover, no policies for reallocating resources from richer to poorer states or sub-national regions are in operation in MERCOSUR, making the latter countries largely dependent on the former. Also in this case, no logic of spillover has ever emerged.

The North American Free Trade Agreement (NAFTA), signed by Mexico, Canada and the USA in 1992 and which came into effect on January 1, 1994, aims to stabilize economic relations among those states. It has a very high economic differentiation (one of the most globally dynamic economies alongside a newly industrialized country), profound political asymmetry (the global military power alongside medium-sized powers with limited military capacity) and unusual geographical features (the longest borders shared by states). NAFTA is less ambitious than MERCOSUR, in the sense that its aims are those befitting a trade agreement (Milner 1998), but also more effective than MERCOSUR. Given that tariffs across the three countries' borders (and particularly between Canada and the USA) have largely disappeared, the nature of the agreement was geared mainly at solving disputes on other trade-related items. Although it is a purely intergovernmental organization, and notwithstanding the presence of the USA in that organization, NAFTA has created a regularized institutional structure (see Table 4.4).

The main provisions of NAFTA reflect a concern with trying to place some limits on the application of US trade policy and to subject it to the logic of a regional agreement. The main mechanism for this has been the binding dispute settlement mechanism that resolves disputes between states or between economic actors and states. Article 1904 of NAFTA provides an alternative to the domestic courts for resolving disputes on anti-dumping and countervailing duties. Chapter 20 of the Agreement spells out the procedures and provisions of the settlement mechanism, which begins with a government-to-government meeting. If this does not bring about a resolution, then the matter can be sent to the NAFTA Free Trade Commission, which comprises the trade ministers of the states involved. If the matter is not settled there, a state may request that a five-member panel be formed to settle the dispute. The panelists are chosen from a roster of names, with each country choosing two and the choice of the fifth member alternating with each dispute between the two countries. The fact that the USA has agreed to have a judicial body that is not part of its formal constitutional structure and is formally a transnational institution is not insignificant. Certainly the USA is part of the WTO, but one has also to remember that it has refused to sign on to the Statute establishing the International Criminal Court because it does not accept that an external judicial body can override the US legal system. Mexico and Canada have sought to insulate their commercial relationship from the application of US trade law in US courts. The USA, on the other hand, has been willing to accept the settlement mechanism as it is less cumbersome than the WTO route.

From the point of view of creating a free trade area that provides stable relationships, NAFTA has had clear success. While Mexican–Canadian trade remains marginal, on the whole NAFTA has become central to the commercial policy of all three partners. The

Table 4.4 *NAFTA institutional structure*

Institutional structure		Features	Role	Functions
Free Trade Commission		Intergovernmental body	Policy direction	To agree on dispute resolution
NAFTA Secretariat	US Section Canadian Section Mexican Section	Nation-based Secretariat	Administrative role	To manage the dispute resolution mechanism and to select national panels
Working Groups and Committees		Technical ad hoc bodies	Technical support	To prepare informal resolution of disputes
Side Agreements linked to the NAFTA	Commission for Environmental Cooperation	Intergovernmental permanent body	Policy coordination	To promote the enforcement of environmental law
	Commission for Labor Cooperation	Intergovernmental permanent body	Policy coordination	To promote the enforcement of labor standards

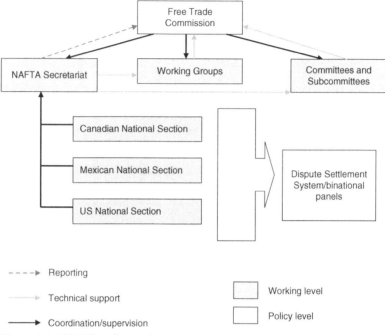

Figure 4.4 NAFTA policy-making structure

dispute settlement mechanism for anti-dumping and countervailing issues has been used extensively by all three governments and has brought a measure of protection to the smaller partners to the agreement. The NAFTA members are not concerned simply with trade. They represent economic interests that go beyond the application of trade law, such as the protection of investor rights. This reflects an important feature of the North American economy, where a great deal of cross-border trade is carried out within the various branches of the same multinational firm. Mexico, and to an even greater extent Canada, have been described as "branch plant" economies because large parts of their industrial base are satellites of US multinationals. This intra-firm international trade is less likely to generate disputes about dumping and government subsidies; but it may lead to questions about the free movement of capital and protection of foreign direct investment. Multinational firms were concerned to ensure that the increasing transnationalization of production across the North American continent would not be subject to constraints on investment, such as employment protection. One mechanism to protect foreign investment was national treatment: that is, foreign firms cannot be treated any differently than domestic actors.

NAFTA is an intergovernmental regional organization. Although it has a limited institutional architecture, the dispute settlement mechanisms do exert a degree of independence and form clear institutional boundaries between the associated states and the implementation of stable and durable rules. Its decisions are binding. The decision-making process is structured and regularized and is based on a once-a-year Cabinet-level representative meeting. There are twenty-five trilateral committees and ad hoc working groups on different economic and trade issues. The policy-making model is centralized in the Free Trade Commission, where the US representatives play a crucial role (see Figure 4.4). Also here, however, the NAFTA Secretariat has not received any delegation of powers from the (three) national governments to be (potentially) used for deepening economic cooperation among them.

4.5 Comparing regional economic organizations

The comparison of both the scope and structure of the main regional economic organizations makes clear the substantial differences between them and the EU. Let us first compare policy scope.

Following Balassa's conceptualization of regional economic integration, one can argue that the regional economic organizations analyzed here have created free trade areas and customs unions but have stopped short from creating a common market (and even less so an economic union). The EU instead has created a common and then single market and an EMU as a sub-set of the organization, based on a common currency adopted by two-thirds of its member states (as of 2015). Under the impact of the euro crisis, the EMU has moved towards the formation of a banking union, which will have to be followed by a fiscal and budgetary union. The single market has required the promotion of significant market-correcting strategies that have curtailed national prerogatives in many policy areas. The EU has introduced autonomous legislation on issues such as health, safety, labor relations and the environment. It has an agricultural welfare state (through the financial support of product prices) and a territorial welfare state (through structural funds allocated to the poorest sub-national regions), although in the EU social and welfare policy continues to be addressed mainly by member state governments and

Table 4.5 *Comparing regional organizations and the EU*

	ASEAN Association of Southern Asian Nations (1967)	APEC Asia-Pacific Economic Cooperation (1989)	MERCOSUR Mercado Común del Sur (1991)	NAFTA North American Free Trade Agreement (1994)	EU European Union (1951–1957)
Founders	Indonesia, Malaysia, Philippines, Singapore, Thailand	Indonesia, Singapore, Brunei, Malaysia, Philippines, Thailand, Australia, Japan, New Zealand, South Korea and Canada	Brazil, Argentina, Paraguay, Uruguay	USA, Canada, Mexico	France, Germany, Italy, Belgium, the Netherlands, Luxembourg
Joiners	1984 – Brunei Darussalam 1995 – Vietnam 1997 – Laos and Myanmar 1999 – Cambodia	1991 – China, Hong Kong, Taiwan 1993 – Mexico and Papua New Guinea 1994 – Chile 1998 – Peru, Russia, Vietnam	1996 – Chile (associate) 1997 – Bolivia (associate) 2003 – Peru (associate) 2004 – Colombia (associate) 2004 – Ecuador (associate) 2010 – Venezuela	Development of a FTA (USA and Canada)	1973 – UK, Denmark, Ireland 1981 – Greece 1986 – Spain and Portugal 1995 – Austria, Finland, Sweden 2004 – Czech Republic, Cyprus, Estonia, Hungary, Latvia, Lithuania, Malta, Poland, Slovakia, Slovenia 2007 – Bulgaria, Romania, 2013 – Croatia

Table 4.5 (*cont.*)

	ASEAN Association of Southern Asian Nations (1967)	APEC Asia-Pacific Economic Cooperation (1989)	MERCOSUR Mercado Común del Sur (1991)	NAFTA North American Free Trade Agreement (1994)	EU European Union (1951–1957)
Member states	10	21	5+5	3	28
Nature	Trans/intergovernmental	Trans/intergovernmental	Inter/transgovernmental	Inter/transgovernmental	Supranational and intergovernmental
Scope	Economic collaboration Free Trade Area	Economic cooperation Customs Union	Customs union	Free Trade Agreement	An ever-closer union
Policy-making pattern	Flexible consensus (horizontal)	Consensus – unanimity (horizontal)	Flexible consensus (vertical)	Structured and regularized (vertical)	Supranational and intergovernmental (dependent on the policies)
Compliance	Loose dispute resolution mechanisms	Voluntary	Ad hoc arbitration panel (chosen by a roster of judges)	Binding dispute resolutions mechanisms	ECJ – Highly binding
Operation	• Three-yearly meeting of Heads of State/and Government • Ministerial Conference	• annual meeting of finance ministers and heads of Central Banks and others • annually rotating chair • annual leaders meeting	• twice a year presidential summits • six month rotating presidency	• once a year Cabinet level representatives meeting	Highly institutionalized

Table 4.5 (*cont.*)

	ASEAN Association of Southern Asian Nations (1967)	APEC Asia-Pacific Economic Cooperation (1989)	MERCOSUR Mercado Común del Sur (1991)	NAFTA North American Free Trade Agreement (1994)	EU European Union (1951–1957)
Structure	• Secretariat (Jakarta) with ministerial status • 29 committees of senior officials • 122 technical working groups • specialized agencies	• Secretariat (Singapore) of 23 civil servants (2001) • 3 committees • 10 working groups	• Secretariat (Montevideo) • Common Market Council • working groups (Common Market Group) • ad hoc groups	• 25 trilateral committees • ad hoc working groups	Dual: 1. intergovernmental: highly institutionalized meetings of the European Council and Council 2. supranational: highly formalized quadrilateral system (Commission, EP, Council and European Council)
International status	None	None	None (de facto)	None	Yes

legislatures. While in the EU the single market is far from being fully achieved, none of the economic regional organizations examined here has ever started to build one.

Second, regarding the institutional structure, in the EU single market the supranational institutions (such as the Commission, the EP and ECJ) are as important as the intergovernmental institutions (the European Council and the Council). If it is true that intergovernmental institutions have played an exclusive decision-making role in strategic policies (such as economic and financial policy in addition to foreign and security policies), it is also true that in those policies national governments have institutionalized their coordination within the Brussels intergovernmental institutions. Moreover, the euro crisis has increased the operative role of the Brussels supranational institutions (such as the ECB, the Commission and the ECJ). To be sure, in the EU the common market project was decided and supported by national governments. However, market integration has also been driven by supranational institutions, such as the ECJ, the Commission and the EP, which are not dependent on the will of national governments. In the case of the ECJ, its independence has also been necessary to solve the contrasts within the intergovernmental treaties adopted for dealing with the euro crisis; in the case of the Commission, it has been crucial for transforming intergovernmental decisions into policy choices or for structuring the agenda of the policy-making process; in the case of the EP, it has been essential for lending legitimacy to the legislative process of single market policies. The EU has institutionalized the operational logic of the single market, recognizing the need to embed it in the larger social system (Caporaso and Tarrow 2009; Ferrera 2005), although other scholars consider this possibility untenable (Scharpf 2009a, 2013). The EMU itself has institutionalized as an organization where deep-rooted intergovernmental institutions coordinate national economic policies, but a supranational central bank (the ECB) monopolizes the control of its monetary side.

As Table 4.5 shows, the dissimilarities, in relation to both scope and structure, between the EU and the other regional economic organizations are much more significant than their similarity regarding the indisputable role that national governments play in each of them and the indisputable fact that the EU is *also* a regional economic organization.

If the other regional economic organizations differ in the interstate pattern (hierarchical in the case of NAFTA and MERCOSUR, because of the overwhelming influence exercised respectively by the USA and Brazil; horizontal instead in the cases of APEC and ASEAN: Higgott 2007; Sbragia 2007; Vasconcelos 2007), nevertheless they share the same institutional model, which is exclusively based on loose cooperation between governments. Indeed, it would be incorrect to define their model as intergovernmental, if one looks at that model from the EU's experience. In the EU, the intergovernmental model constitutes the institutionalization of the coordination (and not just cooperation) among national governments in permanent institutions operating in Brussels, where the whole (the intergovernmental institution) matters more than its parts (the national governments constituting it). On the contrary, the model of the regional economic organizations is more transgovernmental than intergovernmental. The IR literature does not distinguish analytically between cooperation and coordination because it is not interested in analyzing the internal institutional structure that makes those concepts empirically distinct. Moreover, the EU has created a single market through the law-making action of supranational and intergovernmental institutions. The promotion of the single market has been driven by the interaction of a plurality of institutions, those representing intergovernmental and those representing supranational interests and views. And even if on sensitive policies (such as the EMU) the EU has utilized an intergovernmental decision-making regime to manage them, although mitigated by a monetary policy controlled by a supranational institution such as the ECB, the post-2009 euro crisis has driven that intergovernmental regime to foster the formation of a highly centralized policy-making process. This is why EU intergovernmentalism constitutes a form of institutionalized *coordination*, and not of transgovernmental *cooperation*.

Thus, from the CP approach, the difference between the EU and the other regional organizations is of a *qualitative*, not just quantitative, nature. The EU started as a project of building a common and then single market before now reaching (for the majority of its member states) the phase of economic and monetary union. All other regional organizations are the outcome of a project to create either a free trade area or a customs union as answers to the challenges of globalization (Madeira and Caporaso 2011). At the same time, the EU has come to acquire a dense institutional and policy-making structure, with both intergovernmental and supranational features, whereas all the other regional organizations have adopted only a loose transgovernmental model with a light structure of cooperation. There is a qualitative difference between the EU Commission and the ASEAN, APEC, MERCOSUR and NAFTA Secretariats. None of the regional economic organizations has a directly elected parliament as has the EU, and which has become a co-legislator with the Council (acting through QMV) in all single market policies. Nor do those organizations have an accepted and independent judicial body (such as the ECJ) that operates a system of judicial review (although, in the case of NAFTA, an effective mechanism of dispute resolution has been regularized). Nor do any of the other regional economic organizations have a common currency managed by a supranational bank within an economic and monetary union. Also in the EU national governments matter, but they have to operate in a maze of institutions and procedures that cannot be considered a dependent variable of their single will.

Comparative institutional analysis does not lend plausibility to the argument that the EU and the other economic regionalisms represent different species of the same genus, that is, the organization of economic cooperation between governments, or that the EU is in a *continuum* with the other regional organizations (so far as that argument is plausible for IR theory). Comparative institutional analysis also does not lend plausibility to the perspective that the EU is an economic community, organized around a common market. Comparative institutional analysis makes it even harder to claim, as scholars and politicians have, that the EU should operate as a network where each member state can decide the policy it wants to adopt (*l'Europe à la carte*) or should become "a Europe of clubs organized around functional tasks" (Majone 2014: 320). Given the level of institutionalization of single-market policies, their surgical dissection seems highly unlikely. Moreover, the euro crisis has led to a deepening of the distinction between the euro-area and non-euro-area member states. The UK has responded to the financial crisis through its domestic institutions and policy tools, whereas the euro-area member states have deepened their coordination for adopting common institutions and policy tools (to the extent of attracting even the opted-out Denmark and Sweden in their action).

The euro crisis has deepened integration in the EMU, although not in a supranational direction. One might certainly argue (Majone 2014: 234) that, given the economic and institutional heterogeneity of the euro-area member states, "the attempts to solve the crisis of monetary union by centralizing economic, fiscal, and even key aspects of social policy, such as pensions, may turn out to be self-defeating"; nevertheless, the institutional development induced by the euro crisis has emptied the claim of a Union à la carte. The pursuit of the perspective of the EU as a flexible network of governments, constituting variable geometries of member states with regard to the various policy issues or club of clubs organized around specific and differentiated functional tasks, would require a significant institutional change in the EU. The British political elite, for the first time since 1973, has had to face the existential question of whether the country should remain in the EU or should exit from it. As the House of Lords (2014: 67) remarked, "the euro-zone remains on the road towards greater integration. The implications of this for the UK are immense." Will a popular referendum give the answer?

4.6 Conclusion

This chapter has considered the EU from the perspective of those member states asserting that it is (or it should behave as) an economic community, whose purpose should consist in helping its members to deal with common challenges such as those raised by the process of globalization. Indeed, as shown by IR literature, the post-Cold War world has witnessed the formation of a panoply of regional organizations for economic cooperation. Influential representatives of that literature have thus argued that the EU should be located in a continuum with those organizations, together epitomizing a new world order. However, the comparison of the institutional structure and the policy scope of the most important examples of regional economic organizations and the EU does not confirm the continuum hypothesis. Contrary to the EU, those regional economic organizations have pursued limited economic targets (free trade area or customs union), on the basis of a light institutional model of cooperation between national governments. The EU continues to be the only example, among regional organizations, that pursues a project of an ever-closer union, as shown by the decision, taken after the end of the Cold War, to deal with policies not envisioned in the original framework agreed in the 1957 Rome Treaty. Since the Maastricht Treaty, in addition to the promotion of a single market, the EU has pursued the project of the EMU that has ended up, under the impact of the euro crisis, in a highly structured institutional system. Contrary to the other regional organizations, the EU has set up a dense institutional model with supranational and intergovernmental features.

The comparative approach adopted in this chapter does not lend justification to either the scholarly argument that the EU belongs to the family of regional economic organizations or the political argument that the EU "must be able to act … [as] a network," as stated by David Cameron in his speech of January 23, 2013. The EU has reached a degree of institutionalization and constitutionalization that prevents its ad hoc or sectoral utilization. Contrary to the other regional economic organizations, EU member states' sovereignty has been drastically redefined. In the supranational single market policies, each member state has come to share its decision-making power with other member states' governments and supranational institutions; in the intergovernmental EMU, each euro-area member state has come to pool its sovereignty within a dense institutional framework, as no other regional economic organization has done with its associated states. The euro crisis has further deepened integration between the euro-area member states, with unexpected although uneven downsizing of each national government's capacity to control economic, fiscal and budgetary policies. The distance between the euro-area and non-euro-area (the UK in particular) member states has increased. Although the unequal effects generated by the Union's policies to contrast the financial turmoil have invigorated the call for their renationalization, the renegotiation of Union policies and competences in order to bring them "back home" implies an extremely complex process of institutional change. No other existing regional organization has gone so far as the EU in destructuring the Westphalian principle of national sovereignty.

In conclusion, the empirical reality of the EU does not justify the claim of the sovereignist coalition, as expressed by the British prime minister in his speech on January 23, 2013, that the EU should behave as a flexible organization where each member state can pick the policies it prefers. The perspective of the EU as an economic community managed by a network of flexible institutions is at odds even with the reality of the single market. To achieve that perspective would require a substantial restructuring of the EU. A single market requires a form of supranational regulation incompatible with a Europe à la carte, although its functioning does not necessarily imply the existence of an economic and monetary union.

5 | *The perspective of intergovernmental union*

The reform of Europe is not a march towards supra-nationality ... The crisis has pushed the heads of state and government to assume greater responsibility because ultimately they have the democratic legitimacy to take decisions ... The integration of Europe will go the intergovernmental way because Europe needs to make strategic political choices.

Nicolas Sarkozy, President of the French Republic, December 1, 2011

5.1 Introduction

The intergovernmental perspective on the EU emerged during the negotiations that led to the 1992 Maastricht Treaty, to then acquire the form of a specific constitutional model or decision-making regime. The intergovernmental constitution was fully institutionalized by the 2009 Lisbon Treaty. Since financial policy has been assigned, by the latter, to the control of the intergovernmental constitution, the euro crisis has been a formidable test of its capability (Dinan 2011). Indeed, once the EU had to face the failure of the CT in the French and Dutch popular referenda of 2005, the intergovernmental perspective emerged as the predominant view of integration. As *The Economist's* Charlemagne (2012) wrote, after "the French and Dutch voters killed the proposed EU constitution ... intergovernmentalism [became] the new fashion."[1] The view expressed by the then French President Sarkozy in his Toulon speech on December 1, 2011, that "the integration of Europe" will have to go the intergovernmental way if Europe wants "to make strategic political choices," was and continues to be shared by several national governments and groups of citizens.

This intergovernmental perspective is not skeptical of the European integration process, as is the view of the supporters of the economic

---

[1] See Charlemagne, 'Angela the lawgiver', *The Economist*, February 2, 2012, www.economist.com/blogs/Charlemagne.

124

community. Post-Maastricht intergovernmentalism has recognized that integration should proceed without, however, going in the supranational direction. On the contrary, integration should consist in *pooling* national sovereignties within intergovernmental institutions. The decision-making power should not be in the hands of each member state, but in those of the institutions that coordinate the action of the member state governments (the European Council and the Council). As a sympathetic supporter of this perspective, Van Middelaar (2013: 195) observed:

In the Lisbon Treaty, the legal distinction between the Community and the Union was abolished: the Community disappeared, leaving the Union. The institutions remained the same, on the understanding that the European Council of heads of state or government would now make all the strategic decisions, irrespective of the policy field. The gathering of national leaders also chose to give itself a permanent president, who could represent it externally. The existence of such a figure turns the Union into a single political body.

The dramatic events of the financial crisis since 2009 have led the intergovernmental constitution to reduce the national prerogatives of euro-area member states in crucial realms such as economic, fiscal and budgetary policies without, at the same time, rebalancing this reduction with an increased role of supranational institutions, as has continued to happen in single market policies. The reduction of the prerogatives of national governments has been offset by an increased transfer of prerogatives to the institutions coordinating them (such as the European Council and the ECOFIN Council specifically). What was lost at the national level was certainly regained at the Union level, but by the latter's intergovernmental rather than supranational institutions.

This chapter will reconstruct the formation and affirmation of the intergovernmental perspective (as it has come to be institutionalized with the EMU, that is here the empirical backdrop of my intergovernmental union concept). It is organized as follows. First, it will clarify the difference between an International Relations (IR) and a Comparative Politics (CP) approach to intergovernmentalism, thus identifying the institutional logic of the intergovernmental union as a political system. Second, it will consider the political constellation that has made intergovernmentalism, particularly in France and Germany, the predominant perspective after the failure of the CT. Third, it will develop a critical analysis of the intergovernmental constitution in dealing with the euro crisis. Owing to the difficulties in resolving basic problems of collective action, the intergovernmental constitution has proven to be a recipe neither for efficacy nor for legitimacy in the decision-making process. Finally, it will evaluate the institutional contours of the intergovernmental union that has emerged from the euro crisis, that is, a sort of federation of domestic governments that is highly centralized and intrusive in member states' economic policies, something unprecedented in federal political systems. The strengthening of the decision-making role of the European Council and the ECOFIN Council (and the Euro Summit and the Euro Group) has meant transferring policy decisions to an organism within which the larger and richer member states have come to play a dominant role. Celebrated as the perspective able to combine, through the pooling of national sovereignties in intergovernmental institutions, domestic policy prerogatives and political legitimacy with the deepening of the integration process, intergovernmentalism has favored the formation of an EMU based on the power of a few larger member states to the detriment of the others.

5.2 Intergovernmentalism as a political system

The perspective of intergovernmental union is analytically distinct from the political theory of the process of integration that has assumed national governments as the strategic actors in the latter (a political theory defined as the *intergovernmental school*). The intergovernmental interpretation of the European process of integration, which is simultaneously a descriptive and a normative theory, has deep roots in IR scholarship, whereas the conceptualization of the intergovernmental union as a political system derives from a CP approach to the institutional structure of the EMU. IR intergovernmentalism is based on the work of one of its modern founders (Hoffmann 1966), then developed by the sophisticated work of Moravcsik (1998) based on the exogenous preferences formation of national governments negotiating in intergovernmental conferences (IGCs). In Moravcsik's interpretation of the grand bargains between national governments, societal interests play a crucial role in identifying the latter's negotiating positions.

IR intergovernmentalism has become one of the main theories explaining (empirically) why the EU emerged in the first place and how it has continued to integrate, thus assessing (normatively) that it should continue to go along the same road if integration has to proceed. According to the intergovernmental school, the EU dynamic has been controlled by its member states and the integration process will advance as long as the member states wish or decide to do so. National governments define and control the terms and the conditions of the EU's functioning, through their periodical IGCs and through the regular action of formal (the Council) and for a long time informal (the European Council) intergovernmental institutions that, since the beginning of the integration process, have supervised and steered the latter. The Lisbon Treaty celebrated national governments' power in treaty-making by formally recognizing (for the first time) the possibility that they could leave the Union (TEU, Article 50.1, as recalled above). For the intergovernmental school (Moravcsik, 2005; Moravcsik and Schimmelfennig, 2009), supranational actors can be considered the functional agents of principals constituted by national governments. National governments delegate to functional agents the power to frame specific solutions for their common problems. Although these functional agents are necessary to reduce the transaction costs of inter-governmental negotiation, their action is strictly supervised by their principals. They have to behave according to guidelines established by the national governments that created the agencies in the first place and maintain their operations. Indeed, national governments delegate to those supranational institutions the task of transforming the nego-tiating outcome in a regularized and supervised policy pattern. On this basis, a huge number of empirical studies, based on principal–agent theory, have investigated the forms and the possibilities of delegation.

For a CP approach, the research questions raised by intergovern-mentalism as a political system are different. Here what matters is to analyze the institutional logic of the intergovernmental union, thus conceptualizing its limits in dealing with the policy challenges it has to face, in order to then finally identify its critical outcomes, namely, the formation of relations within its decision-making structure that have the features of domination. The intergovernmental union is a subsection of the political system of the EU; in our case it is the institu-tional form of the EMU. It emerged through the critical juncture of the Maastricht Treaty, it was consolidated by a sequence of decisions such as those institutionalizing the SGP, it was legitimized by the failure of the CT and then constitutionalized by the Lisbon Treaty as a distinct decision-making regime based on the predominance of the inter-governmental institutions. The formalization of the decision-making power of the European Council, chaired for the first time by a permanent president, epitomizes the decision-making role finally acquired by the intergovernmental institutions in the EU. The decision to give a permanent president to the European Council is the epitome of the strategy to bring a previously informal institution into the formal decision-making core of the EU. In this approach, the role played by member state governments in treaty-making is not relevant. What is relevant is the formation of permanent decision-making institutions representing the coordinated interests of national governments within the institutional system of the EU. Adopting the CP approach, delegation is not the central theoretical issue, because national governments do not go home after treaty-making, but remain in Brussels through the operation of their intergovernmental institutions. Rather, what is a central issue is the investigation of the forms taken by the relations between permanent intergovernmental and permanent supranational institutions operating in Brussels.

The intergovernmental union can be conceptualized as an organization that on a permanent basis coordinates member state policies in Brussels in sensitive areas (such as economic and foreign policies). This coordination implies the technical support of supranational institutions (such as the Commission and the ECJ) to monitor and implement those policies. The Commission is necessary for neutralizing free-riding, whereas the ECJ is indispensable for resolving intergovernmental disputes. In an intergovernmental union, the EP is a redundant institution, given that the function of legitimacy is performed by the parliaments of its member states. Logically, in an intergovernmental union the national governments should be controlled by their corresponding national parliaments. This means, in the case of the EU, the formation of an inter-parliamentary legislature (a chamber constituted by representatives of the national parliaments), substituting or integrating the EP, as a check on the European Council and Council.[2] The

---

[2] Proposals on the necessity to strengthen the role of national parliaments vary. One of the most radical has been advanced by Chalmers (2013: 9), according to which "unless two thirds of parliaments indicate their support for a measure, a Commission proposal should not go forward to the Council," or "if one third

knowledge of the logic of how the intergovernmental union functions has been enriched by a sophisticated literature on the new modes of governance tried out in several policies, in particular after the crisis of the EU's constitutionalization process in the mid 2000s. The new mode of governance has become both an empirical concept and also a normative theory of *how* the EU might integrate in areas where supranationalism is not accepted by crucial national governments.[3] In this view the new modes of governance have come to be seen as an alternative to the "Community method" in advancing the integration process in those policy realms that are sensitive for member states. New modes of governance include a panoply of policy patterns, such as the open method of coordination, benchmarking, mainstreaming, peer review and other forms of *voluntary coordination* between governments and supranational actors (Caporaso and Wittenbrinck 2006; Heritier and Rhodes 2010; Kohler-Koch and Rittberger 2006; Trubek and Trubek 2007). However, as argued by Idema and Kelemen (2006), the functional efficacy of the new approach has not only been exaggerated (in particular by practitioners), but its rationale has contributed to an indirect disqualification of the view of integration as a legal process. Along the road, this literature has risked justifying the ideology of EU exceptionalism.

In short, from Maastricht to Lisbon, in policy areas traditionally at the core of member state national sovereignty, an intergovernmental union has come to be institutionalized where the institutions aggregating national governments (heads of state and government and ministers) have acquired powers and resources to control a regularized decision-making process. Those institutions have justified themselves, in particular after the failure of the CT, through their capacity to resolve consensually the collective problems arising from the extension of the process of integration to new crucial policies. The supporters of this perspective (the intergovernmentalists) assume that institutions are instrumental to the solution of policy problems and

---

of national parliaments propose either that legislation be reviewed or that new legislation should be proposed, the Commission is obliged to make a proposal to that effect."

[3] I am aware of the fact that the literature on the new modes of governance cannot be considered in its entirety to be coherent with intergovernmentalism. However, it shares with the latter an emphasis on the importance of voluntary coordination and an underestimation of the process of legalization.

that their features are justified mainly on effectiveness criteria. Indeed
for intergovernmentalists, whether the EU is organized according to
the (undemocratic) principle of a confusion of powers rather than in
accordance with the (democratic) principle of formal division of powers is not an issue. As long as the confusion of (executive and legislative) powers concerns the Union level but not its member states, it
will not be a problem for intergovernmentalists. The legitimacy of the
intergovernmental institutions derives from the national legitimacies
of the national governments constituting them. The intergovernmental
institutions also pool the national legitimacy of the governments constituting them. At the same time, the legal distinction of competences
between the center and the territorial units as in all federal unions or
federal states is problematic in the intergovernmental union because
there is no discontinuity between national governments and intergovernmental institutions. Contrary to the perspective of the EU as a network of governments, here the intergovernmental institutions should
be adequately consolidated and endowed with enough institutional
and policy resources in order to exercise their decision-making role.
Those institutions aim to transform a plurality into a singularity. They
are a whole distinct from their parts. This intergovernmental union
has embodied a specific institutional perspective on the EU supported
by several governments and sections of national political elites.

5.3 The political constellation of intergovernmentalism

If the Lisbon Treaty allowed the intergovernmental institutions to
take the lead in facing the financial turmoil, the intergovernmental
approach to the crisis has, however, been supported by a political constellation (in the two main EU member states in particular) favorable
to the decision-making predominance of the intergovernmental institutions. From 2009 to 2012 French and German governments – for
the first time – converged towards the shared view that only national
governments, coordinating in the European Council and the ECOFIN
Council, could face and resolve the euro crisis. President Sarkozy,
elected in 2007 and then defeated in 2012, was the spokesperson
for the vision of a Union based on, and driven by, national governments coordinating in Brussels-based intergovernmental institutions.
In Sarkozy's vision (as indeed in de Gaulle's vision: Calleo 2011) there
was no room for the EP and the Commission in the decision-making

process, not to mention the ECJ. But contrary to de Gaulle's view, for Sarkozy integration was a necessity to be met by strengthening the decision-making and legitimating roles of the intergovernmental institutions (the European Council in particular).

Sarkozy's intergovernmental view went well with the French semi-presidential government based on the decision-making primacy of the president of the Republic (see Glossary); a system, moreover, where the popular legislature (Assemblée Nationale) played a marginal role, at least until the reforms of the 2000s. The 2008 constitutional law on the "Modernization of the Institutions of the Fifth Republic" increased the parliament's prerogatives, but the institutional bias of the governmental system continues to be in favor of the power of the executive (and the president of the Republic). Sarkozy's view stressed the role of the European Council as the new political executive of the Union. During Sarkozy's tenure as president, the intergovernmental perspective became the dominant one for the French government. It still remains to be seen whether the Socialist François Hollande, who succeeded Sarkozy in 2012 as president of the French Republic, will distance himself from that perspective. To affirm, as he did in his talk to the European Parliament on February 6, 2013, that "Europe is a political project" larger than the setting up of a common market, is sufficient in terms of distancing himself from the economic community perspective, but not for clarifying which political union he has in mind. Indeed, what he said subsequently in September 2013 (Hollande 2013) seemed to confirm his being part of the intergovernmental mainstream: "Je ne crois pas aux États-Unis d'Europe. Commençons à faire en sorte que les États soient unis pour l'Europe."

At the same time, it may be surprising that such an intergovernmental vision of the Union also came to be shared by the German government of Angela Merkel, particularly in the period 2009–2013. This marked a significant change for a country that was traditionally the defender of the Commission and the EP (Pederson 1998). However, after Helmut Kohl's chancellorship, a new generation of German politicians, with no personal experience of the Second World War, came into power. This change emerged clearly with the Schroeder government that followed the last Kohl government in 1998, lasting until 2005. Since then, "generational change … allowed (German) political leaders to *normalise* EU policy in the sense of becoming more like other large Member States" (Sloam 2005: 98, original emphasis); in particular,

the new generation was "ready to articulate material German interests" (Sloam 2005: 88). During the first half of the 2000s, the Social
Democratic Party (SPD) and Green governmental elites began questioning the paymaster role that Germany traditionally played within
the process of European integration (for instance, asking for a renegotiation of the EU budget), and they did not refrain from mobilizing
German military force abroad (for instance, participating in the 1999
Kosovo war), and articulated a vision of a German interest distinct
from the general European interest.[4] However, this new German assert-
iveness remained within the federal perspective of an increasingly economically – and politically – integrated Europe. This continuity was
clearly expressed in the famous and influential speech by the Foreign
Affairs Minister Joschka Fischer at Humboldt University in Berlin on
May 12, 2000, a speech not by chance titled "From Confederacy to
Federation: Thoughts on the Finality of European Integration."

When Angela Merkel became chancellor the first time in 2005,[5] the
generational changeover was not only confirmed, but also took the
connotation of a geopolitical redefinition of German politics. Not only
was, and is, Angela Merkel the first chancellor from an Eastern *Land*
of Germany (an aspect that for many[6] explains why she seems to be
a European more in her head than in her heart, although this does
not seem to be a handicap for a politician), but the Eastern *Länder*
have also come to affect the mood of the country with their different
relation to the process of integration. After all, the decision to absorb
the five *Länder* of the Deutsche Demokratische Republik (DDR or
East Germany) into the Bundesrepublik Deutschland (BRD or West
Federal Republic of Germany), although politically necessary, did not
help to raise their European awareness. Contrary to the other (previously pro-Soviet Union) Eastern European countries, that were
required to reach precise standards to enter the EU, the DDR was

---

[4] In a famous 1997 statement, the new leader of the SPD Gerhard Schroeder
said: "Kohl says the Germans have to be tied into Europe or they will stir
up old fears of the 'furor teutonicus.' I say that's not the case. I believe that
Germans have become European not because they have to be, but because they
want to be. That is the difference" (now in Sloam 2005: 89).

[5] She was elected chancellor of a grand coalition government consisting of her
party (the Christian Democratic Union, CDU), the sister party of the latter (the
Christian Social Union, CSU) and the SPD.

[6] See Charlemagne, 'Angela the lawgiver', *The Economist*, February 2, 2012,
www.economist.com/blogs/Charlemagne.

integrated into the Federal Republic of Germany (and consequently into the EU) through a de facto annexation of its five *Länder*, without passing through the complex procedures on (economic, legal and political) conditionality. It is reasonable to assume that this accelerated process of inclusion did not make possible the start of a serious debate among the Eastern German elites and public on their historical responsibilities in the hot and cold wars of Europe, as occurred instead in the Western *Länder* of the country.

Between the result of the September 2009 elections, which led to the formation of a coalition government of the CDU/CSU and the Free Democratic Party (FDP), and the elections of September 2013, which led to a (new) grand coalition government between a stronger CDU/CSU and a weaker SPD, the chancellorship of Angela Merkel assumed an increasingly intergovernmental tone. This tone was also justified by specific factors. The FDP increasingly took a clear euro-realist position, quite unusual for German politics (and also for the party's political traditions). The German Constitutional Court or Bundesverfassungsgericht (BVerfG)[7] kept introducing powerful hurdles to the further transfer of national prerogatives to EU institutions and the Deutsche Bundesbank kept raising vociferous criticisms of the ECB's handling of the euro crisis. The German public seemed increasingly wary of paying taxes to aid countries with high public debts and deficits. It was probably this combination of factors that led Merkel's government to search for intergovernmental solutions to the euro crisis that would not be questioned by the court, the central bank, her coalition partners or her voters.

Merkel's government between 2009 and 2013 moved from a reaffirmation of national interests to a preference for an intergovernmental solution to the financial crisis – a preference certainly at odds with the institutional system of the country. In fact, German parliamentary

---

[7] It is true that the judgment of June 30, 2009 stated that the Statute ratifying the Treaty of Lisbon (Zustimmungsgesetz zum Vertrag von Lissabon) was compatible with the German Basic Law, the judgment of September 6, 2011 upheld the country's participation in bailing out financially ailing euro-area member states such as Greece and the judgment of September 12, 2012 cleared the way for Germany's accession to the ESM and the Fiscal Compact Treaties; however, all of these judgments introduced increased constraints on German participation in the process of integration. In particular, they required that any increase in the prerogatives transferred to the EU should receive the prior authorization of the Bundesrat.

federalism is quite different from the French semi-presidential governmental system operating in the context of a traditionally unitary
and centralized state (although recently a functional autonomy has
been recognized to French regions as an answer to the EU structural
funds policy of territorial readjustment: Leonardi 2005). In Germany
the bicameral legislature (the Bundestag, representing the citizens,
and the Bundesrat, representing the *Länder* executives) plays a crucial
role in the policy-making process (Schmidt 2003), and the judiciary
is the indispensable mediator of any constitutional dispute (Umbach
2002). Thus, if France came to adopt the German economic paradigm,
enshrined in the two new intergovernmental treaties – the 2011 ESM
and the 2012 Fiscal Compact Treaty – Germany came to adopt the
French political paradigm, accepting that decision-making power in
the EU should be in the exclusive hands of the governments meeting
within the European Council and the ECOFIN Council.

Facing the German–French slide towards an intergovernmental logic,
the EP and the Commission started to react, more and more vociferously, to the financial *directoire* and its lack of legitimacy. Particularly
under EP pressure, the two intergovernmental treaties mentioned
above were subjected to several revisions, as the decision to create an
SRF through an intergovernmental agreement (IGA) was subjected to
criticism by the EP. The Fiscal Compact Treaty, which passed through
five different drafts in less than two months (December 8–9, 2011/
January 31, 2012) before a final version was published, was particularly affected (Kreilinger 2012). In the final version, for instance, it
refers to the necessity of applying it (Article 2.1) "in conformity with
the Treaties on which the European Union is founded … and with
European Union law." Moreover, because of the EP's mobilization, the
Treaty declares (Article 16) that:

within five years at most following the entry into force of this Treaty, on the
basis of an assessment of the experience with its implementation, the necessary steps shall be taken, in compliance with the provisions of the Treaty
on the European Union and the Treaty on the Functioning of the European
Union, with the aim of incorporating the substance of this Treaty into the
legal framework of the European Union.

The supranational institutions' criticism of the Fiscal Compact Treaty
pressured the national governmental leaders to recognize that the

operation of the intergovernmental Summit of the heads of state and government should rely on the president of the Commission. As stated in Article 12(4), "the President of the Euro Summit shall ensure the preparation and continuity of Euro Summits meetings, in close cooperation with the President of the European Commission."

The Fiscal Compact Treaty has finally established (Article 10) the possibility for member states whose currency is the euro to have recourse "to enhanced cooperation as provided for in Article 20 of the Treaty on the European Union (TEU) and in Articles 326 to 334 of the Treaty on the function of the European Union (TFEU)," thus making the new Treaty de facto redundant. After long negotiation, the Fiscal Compact Treaty has come to recognize, first, that the Commission's role in monitoring the excessive deficit of member states is indispensable and, second, that the EP cannot be considered an outsider on a par with EU member states whose currency is not the euro (both conditions being absent in the initial announcement of the Fiscal Compact Treaty). However, while the Commission was finally included in the policy-making process, the EP was kept on the margins, also because of the impossibility of distinguishing within it between MEPs elected in euro-area and non-euro-area member states (TEU Article 14.2 states that "the European Parliament shall be composed of representatives of the Union's citizens," without specifying the nationality of its members). Although the intentions of the German and French promoters of the new treaties were originally much more intergovernmental, the reaction from the EP and the Commission restrained them, but only to a certain extent. In fact, the EP's charge that the new treaties posed "a risk to the integrity of the Treaty-based system" of the EU (as the EP had already denounced on the occasion of approval of the ESM)[8] has not had significant impact.

If the decision-making pre-eminence of national governments coordinating in the intergovernmental institutions was justified by the legitimacy accruing to them from their own domestic electorates, as both Sarkozy and Merkel asserted on several occasions, then the control over their actions within those institutions should be assigned to national legislatures, rather than to the EP. This is, in fact, the position expressed by the German Constitutional Court in its numerous

---

[8] Text adopted by the European Parliament at the sitting of Wednesday March 23, 2011, O.7.

judgments. For instance, in the decision of September 12, 2012 on the ESM and Fiscal Compact Treaties, the court states (Article 2.4), that "in matters of the European Stability Mechanism ... the responsibility shall be exercised by the plenary session of the German Bundestag ... [and] in all other matters ... which affect the budgetary responsibility of the German Bundestag ... the budget committee of the German Bundestag shall be involved."[9] Thus the intergovernmental logic has brought with it an inter-parliamentary balancing: national parliaments should coordinate in order to control national governments coordinating in Brussels (Kreilinger 2014). The Lisbon Treaty prefigured this possibility, when (in Protocol No. 1) it encourages "greater involvement of national Parliaments in the activities of the European Union and ... enhance[s] their ability to express their views on draft legislative acts of the European Union as well as on other matters which may be of particular interest to them." In a speech given on January 11, 2012, the then French Minister for European Affairs, Jean Leonetti, proposed the creation of an indirectly formed "Euro-area Parliament," consisting of parliamentarians of the national parliaments of the euro-area, as an institution balancing the Euro Summit of the heads of state and government of the euro-area member states.

It was this French–German political constellation that led to the formidable institutionalization of the European Council immediately after its formal recognition by the Lisbon Treaty, an institutionalization accelerated by the approval of new intergovernmental treaties. These treaties, in addition to the new legislative measures, had the effect of further reducing national sovereignty in the field of financial, budgetary and fiscal policies (F. Fabbrini 2013), to the advantage of the intergovernmental institutions and at the expense of the supranational ones. Chancellor Merkel tried to justify the intergovernmental conversion of her government through a reinterpretation of the integration context created by the Lisbon Treaty. On November 2, 2010, at the opening ceremony of the 61st academic year of the College of Europe in Bruges, she assessed that "the Lisbon Treaty has placed the institutional structure [of the EU] on a new foundation," to the point of rendering outdated the traditional distinctions between "Community and intergovernmental methods." Indeed, she added, the

---

[9] See: Zitierung: BVerfG, 2 BvR 1390/12 vom 12.9.2012, Absatz-Nr. (1–248), www.bverfg.de/entscheidungen/rs20120912_2bvr139012en.html.

EU is already functioning according to a "new Union method," which consists of "coordinated action in a spirit of solidarity."

5.4 Dilemmas of the intergovernmental union

Why has the intergovernmental EU set up an extremely complex system of economic governance that nevertheless has been unable to appease the markets and to convince citizens of indebted countries? It was a common opinion that even the most audacious decisions for dealing with the euro crisis arrived too late to respond to market pressures, were too limited in their scope and were perceived as illegitimate by the affected stakeholders. One might answer that the euro crisis hit the EU so hard as to require the setting up of amazingly complex instruments of both crisis management and crisis prevention. But why have crucial policy instruments been located outside the legal structure of the EU? Such institutional intricacy has to be considered the logical outcome of a decision-making regime based primarily on the voluntary coordination of national governments, although institutionalized within intergovernmental institutions. Voluntary coordination has been insufficient for resolving basic dilemmas of collective action (S. Fabbrini 2013), that is, to generate effective and legitimate solutions to resolve the crisis in a democratic Union.

Let me start by considering the effectiveness side of the intergovernmental decision-making regime. Three basic dilemmas emerged during the euro crisis. The first was the *veto dilemma*: how to neutralize opposition in a decision-making process requiring unanimous consent. This dilemma accompanied the entire evolution of the euro crisis, often bringing the European Council and the ECOFIN Council to respond to the crisis with too little, too late.[10] Although the financial crisis was initially circumscribed only to Greece, it gradually began expanding to other euro-area member states because of the decision-making stalemate produced by divergent strategies for dealing with it. Divergences in the domestic electoral interests of the various incumbent governments (governments with a sound budget did not want to pay for the difficulties of indebted countries whose governments expected instead to be helped in order to survive politically) made the decision-making

---

[10] A useful source of information is represented by the *Eurocomment* reports written by Peter Ludlow.

process inevitably muddled. The opposing financial needs of creditors and debtors caused endless negotiations between governmental leaders despite the crisis requiring immediate answers. Indeed, in order to neutralize the British veto on fiscal coordination, it was necessary to move outside of the Lisbon Treaty, setting up a new treaty. At the same time, the difficulty in speeding up the decision-making process during the crisis increased the importance of the leadership role in driving the EU toward the necessary answers. As the financial crisis deepened, the bilateral leadership of Germany and France, in the period 2009–2011, was transformed into a compelling *directoire* of EU financial policy, before becoming a purely German *directoire* afterwards. To be sure, as Heipertz and Verdun (2010: 20) argued, "when Member States governments bargain with one another, the largest countries have the greater influence." And of course the bilateral leadership of France and Germany has historically represented the engine of the integration process, although the various waves of enlargement, increasing the number of the EU member states, have inevitably reduced its efficacy (Cole 2010). This bilateral leadership was not resented by the other member states as long as the two countries, although sharing a strategic goal, "started from quite diverging points when it came to sketching the road toward this common goal" (Schild 2010: 1380). As Webber (1999: 16) put it, the greater the divergence between French and German preferences on the policy before reaching a common goal, the easier it was for the other member states to "multilateralize" that common goal.

The deepening of the euro crisis, however, prevented this multilateralization for two reasons. First, Merkel's Germany and Sarkozy's France came to share the same ends and means for dealing with the crisis. Although France initially used a different strategy from Germany's, fear of falling victim to market speculation if unprotected by an alliance with Germany brought France closer and closer to Germany's restrictive monetary position. Through the coordination of the Brussels office of President Herman van Rompuy, the financial strategy for dealing with the crisis came to be dictated by Berlin and Paris sharing not only the same strategic goals (financial stability and fiscal integration), but also the policies with which to achieve them (the introduction of a balanced budget clause in the constitutions of member states also through a new treaty, domestic structural reforms, fiscal discipline). Second, Sarkozy and Merkel, in their attempt to solve the veto dilemma of the intergovernmental method, came to "verticalize" the decision-making process. They met regularly (in Berlin or Paris) before the Brussels European Council meetings to identify common or shared positions that were later imposed in the following formal meeting of the heads of state and governments.[11] The epitome of this attitude was probably the meeting between the two leaders in Deauville on December 5, 2011 where they took decisions, and then reported to the following European Council meeting on December 8–9. Indeed, it became common to talk in the press of a "Merkozy" government within the European Council (and then of a Merkel domination of the latter's deliberations).

The second dilemma is the *enforcement dilemma*: how to guarantee the application of a decision taken on a voluntary basis. The enforcement dilemma emerged dramatically with regard to the approval of the new treaties (the ESM and the Fiscal Compact) by their contracting parties. In fact, to avoid jeopardizing the entire project by the possible rejection of one or another intergovernmental treaty by a few of their contracting parties, the Fiscal Compact Treaty (Title VI, Article 14.2) states that it "shall enter to force on 1 January 2013, provided that twelve Contracting Parties whose currency is the euro have deposited their instrument of ratification." Thus the approval of twelve and not of all the (then) seventeen member states of the euro-area was considered sufficient for allowing the Treaty to enter into force (and, indeed, that is what happened). It was the first time (in the European integration experience) that unanimity had been removed as a barrier to activating an intergovernmental treaty (which would logically require the unanimous consent of all the contracting parties). Anticipating a plausible rejection of the Fiscal Compact Treaty, the ESM Treaty also states (Point 5) that "the granting of financial assistance … will be conditional, as of 1 March 2013, on the ratification of the Fiscal Compact Treaty by the ESM Member concerned." This threat was efficacious in cooling down the euro-skeptical mood of Irish voters (in the referendum on the Fiscal Compact Treaty held on May 31, 2012) or the anti-European mood of Greek voters. However, in moving in this

[11] It is worthwhile reading the chronicles of the preparation of the various European Councils held in 2011 by Peter Ludlow with their detailed description of the triangulation between Chancellor Angela Merkel and her staff, President Nicolas Sarkozy and his staff and the office of President Herman Van Rompuy. A good example is Ludlow (2011b).

direction the intergovernmental logic had not only contradicted itself, but it had also introduced explicit threats that were not really congenial with "the spirit of solidarity" celebrated by Angela Merkel in her November 2, 2011 speech.

The third dilemma is the *compliance dilemma*: once an agreement is enforced, how to guarantee respect of its rules when they no longer suit the interests of one or other of the voluntary contracting parties. This dilemma emerged dramatically in the case of non-compliance with the rules of the SGP. It became apparent in 2009 that Greece deceived the other euro-area member states' governments by manipulating its statistical data regarding its public deficit and debt in a way that disrespected the agreed parameters. However, as we know, the same dilemma emerged in 2003, when France and Germany were saved from sanctions by a decision of the ECOFIN Council (and in contrast to a Commission recommendation), notwithstanding their non-compliance with the SGP parameters. The Fiscal Compact Treaty tries to deal with the possibility of non-compliance by providing for binding intervention by the ECJ upon those contracting parties that do not respect the agreed rules. It is stated (Article 8.1) that "where a Contracting Party considers, independently of the Commission's report, that another Contracting Party has failed to comply with Article 3.2, it may also bring the matter before the Court of Justice … the judgment of the Court of Justice shall be binding on the parties in the procedure." This also applies when the Commission issues a report on a contracting party failing to comply with the rules established by the Treaty. In the latter case, if the Commission, after having given the contracting party concerned the opportunity to submit its observations, still confirms non-compliance by the contracting party in question, the matter will be brought before the ECJ. Moreover, Article 17 of the Fiscal Compact Treaty stresses that, in order to neutralize a recommendation of the Commission to intervene against a member state breaching a deficit criterion, "a qualified majority of the Member States [should be] opposed to the decision proposed or recommended."

The clause of the reversed qualified majority is an attempt to make non-compliance less likely. In fact, the discretion of the ECOFIN Council has been reduced (if compared with the rules concerning the SGP institutionalized on the intergovernmental side of the Lisbon Treaty), not only by the Treaty but also by the combination of the Six Pack and the Two Pack, recognizing the need to rely on third actors (the ECJ or the Commission) to keep the contracting parties aligned with the agreed aims of the Treaty. The ESM Treaty also states that, in case of a dispute between an ESM member and the ESM (Article 37.2), "the dispute shall be submitted to the Court of Justice of the European Union. The judgement of the Court of Justice of the European Union shall be binding on the parties in the procedure, which shall take the necessary measures to comply with the judgement within a period to be decided by said Court" (Article 37.3). At the same time, majority voting is also extended in the ESM. In fact, its Board of Directors "shall take decisions by qualified majority, unless otherwise stated in this Treaty" (Article 6.5), whereas "a qualified majority is defined as 80 percent of the votes." Since Germany holds a stake of almost 28 percent (27.1464 of the ESM keys as they are called), it will be impossible to have a qualified majority (QMV) against Germany. In matters of financial stability, there is a German line that no member state, in particular the small ones (Ginter and Narits 2013), can cross.

The various solutions to the non-compliance dilemma seem problematic. It is problematic, in fact, that a new organization (set up by the Fiscal Compact Treaty or ESM Treaty) might use an institution (such as the ECJ) of another organization (the EU of the Lisbon Treaty) to bind its own members (Kocharov 2012). This may also apply to the technical expertise of the Commission or ECB, upon which both Treaties rely. In the ESM Treaty, for instance, it is stated (Article 17.5) that "the Board of Directors shall decide by mutual agreement, on a proposal from the Managing Director and after having received a report from the Commission ... the disbursement of financial assistance to a beneficiary Member State"; or (Article 18.2) that "decisions on interventions ... shall be taken on the basis of an analysis of the ECB recognising the existence of exceptional financial market circumstances," although the Commission and the ECB are not allowed to play an independent role in the decision-making process. Certainly, the intervention of the ECJ is justified by TFEU Article 273, which states: "the Court of Justice shall have jurisdiction in any dispute between Member States which relates to the subject matter of the Treaties if the dispute is submitted to it under a special agreement between the parties." Nevertheless, the ECJ or the Commission or the ECB are institutions operating within a legal structure defined also by the UK and the Czech Republic, which did not agree upon the Fiscal Compact Treaty that utilizes them (although the latter country decided finally to sign it in March 2014, as we have seen). What are the political implications of this discrepancy? As Craig (2014: 28) remarked: "We should think long and hard before according a very broad discretionary power to an EU institution … participating in an agreement made with states outside the EU."

If the above dilemmas constrained the effectiveness of the intergovernmental union (regarding crisis management in the first case and crisis prevention in the other two cases), that union has also encountered difficult hurdles in dealing with the *legitimacy dilemma*: how to guarantee legitimacy to decisions reached by national executives in the European Council or the ECOFIN Council that were never discussed, let alone approved, by the institution representing the European citizens (the EP). Indeed, this dilemma became evident as the crisis deepened and the citizens of the indebted member states had to pay high costs to make the necessary structural adjustments in their countries (Schmidt 2010). Not only did they have to abide by decisions imposed by impersonal financial markets, but above all by the ECOFIN Council and the European Council where the national executives of the larger member states (they never voted) played a predominant role. The problem did not concern only the content of the decision but also the process for reaching it. The highly centralized crisis prevention regime, set up during the euro crisis, operated under the control of the large creditor member states, not the supranational institutions, and they imposed their criteria on the small debtor member states. The effects of intergovernmental centralization have been uneven.

Analyzing the content of quality newspaper articles on the euro crisis in six European countries (Austria, the UK, France, Germany, Sweden and Switzerland) from December 2009 to March 2012, Kriesi and Grande (2012: 19) arrived at the conclusion that "by far the most important individual actor in this [euro crisis] debate was the German Chancellor Angela Merkel … followed by the [then] French President Nicolas Sarkozy." Indeed, the affected citizens have continued to protest against Angela Merkel and not Herman van Rompuy or Manuel Barroso (then presidents of, respectively, the European Council and the Commission). This effect has inevitably increased the public perception of the illegitimacy of the intergovernmental decision-making regime. The intergovernmental framework cannot identify a satisfactory solution to this dilemma because it assumes that the legitimacy of the EU derives from the legitimacy of its member states' governments, as asserted by President Sarkozy in his Toulon speech on December 1, 2011. However, the legitimacy of decisions taken on behalf of the EU cannot derive from the legitimacy enjoyed by the governments of its member states. Decisions made at the EU level would require a legitimizing mechanism at that level, not at the level of its member states. Without proper involvement of the EP in those decisions, the outcome of such decisions inevitably lacks the justification for being considered legitimate by the European citizens affected by those decisions. Indeed, Chancellor Merkel came to recognize, in her speech given to the EP on November 8, 2012, that "legitimacy and oversight are to be found on the level where decisions are made and implemented. That means that if one of the European level competences is strengthened, the role of the European Parliament must also be strengthened," then adding "we should not contemplate – as is sometimes suggested – establishing an additional parliamentary institution. The European Parliament is the bedrock."

However, this statement has not changed the subordinate role of the EP in the intergovernmental union. As seen in Chapter 2, according to the Fiscal Compact Treaty the EP has no sanction powers over the decisions of the Euro Summit. The Treaty only recognizes (Article 12.5) that "the President of the European Parliament may be invited to be heard [by the Euro Summit]" and that "the President of the Euro Summit shall present a report to the European Parliament after each of the meetings of the Euro Summits." Thus the EP has entered the intergovernmental Treaty, but its powers over Euro Summit Reports remain undefined. At the same time, the EP is never mentioned in the ESM Treaty.

5.5 The post-euro crisis intergovernmental union

The euro crisis has upset the complex structure of compromises built within the Lisbon Treaty. In order to manage the euro crisis, the EU has acquired unprecedented institutional features. First, the equilibrium between supranational and intergovernmental constitutions has been radically changed in favor of the latter. Certainly, the Lisbon Treaty empowered the European Council as the true decision-making center for economic and related policies. Since the financial agenda has engulfed EU policy-making, the European Council, led by a permanent president, has become the true decision-maker (De Scoutheete 2011;

Eggermont 2012) or better the new center of EU politics (Puetter 2013), rather than an institution limiting itself to defining the general aims of the integration process. Given the constraints set up in the Lisbon Treaty, in economic policy the Commission has come to play an administrative role, transforming and implementing the policy indications of the European Council. As Curtin (2014: 7) observed: "empirical evidence points to a 'progressive erosion' of the Commission's power of initiative, and the European Council's detailed setting of the legislative agenda is pronounced." The more the crisis has deepened, the more it has required "leadership and decision-making at the highest political level, which has contributed to strengthening of the position of the European Council" (Leino and Salminen 2012: 864). Unsurprisingly, the European Council has also tried to extend its influence to other crucial policies of the EU (Dawson and De Witte 2013). Assuming that the Commission was the exclusive Union executive when the EU policies centered around the single market (Page 1997), this assumption no longer holds true with the shift of policy focus in the direction of euro stability and economic governance. This does not mean that the Commission has become irrelevant. Indeed, because intergovernmental coordination has not been able to overcome the fundamental dilemmas of collective action, the governmental leaders of the European Council have had to resort to the Commission. However, in the executive branch that emerged from the crisis, the Commission has proven to be a technocratic structure in support of the European Council's deliberations, rather than an institution with the capacity to define the political agenda of the EU.

Second, the European Council-based executive has developed without a significant check from the EP. With the euro crisis, the decision-making barycenter has moved towards the relation between the European Council (and the Euro Summit) and the ECOFIN Council (and the Euro Group), with the EP and its co-decisional power shadowed by the intergovernmental logic. It is true that important legislative measures were adopted through either the ordinary or the special legislative procedure that recognize a legislative or consultative role to the EP, but it is also true that the deepening of the euro crisis has led to new treaties that do not recognize the EP as a policy-making actor. The SRF is the last, but probably not the least, crucial institution deriving from an intergovernmental treaty that is protected against the EP's oversight. Of course, it was difficult to identify a role for the EP (once it was required to represent the citizens of the EU) in new organizations set up by only some of the EU member states (Hefftler and Wessels 2013). However, national parliaments also had very limited impact on intergovernmental decision-making. The intergovernmental union is constrained by a basic paradox. If the domestic parliaments are successful in constraining their governments in Brussels, then the latter will not be able to find the necessary adjustments to deal with the issues at stake. If the domestic governments are unconstrained enough to start successful negotiations, then they will operate without the control of domestic parliaments. At the end of the day, the intergovernmental union is based on decision-making institutions that are controlled neither in Brussels nor in the capitals of the member states (Lord 2011a; Sjursen 2011). The confusion between executive and legislative institutions and functions in Brussels has led to unprecedented decision-making independence for the European Council and the Council in economic policy, with the consequence that a crucial policy (such as economic policy) has escaped the basic mechanisms of democratic accountability. As Habermas (2012a: 44) stressed:

there is a strange contrast between the political power concentrated in the European Council and the fact that its decisions lack legal force … The Lisbon Treaty was supposed to confer enhanced decision-making power on the EU by incorporating the European Council into its institutional structure; but it pays a high price for this in the form of the lack of legitimacy of decisions with far-reaching implications.

Third, the euro crisis, by upsetting the compromise between a centralized monetary policy and nationalized economic policies, has led to the hardening of the ordo-liberal principle that rules, not politics, should govern the EMU. If one remains within the intergovernmental framework, then it is inevitable to assume that coordination of national policies should be disciplined by stricter macroeconomic and legal rules to be activated through automatic, that is non-discretionary, mechanisms. With the deepening of the financial crisis, the European Council has allocated increasing disciplinary powers to technocratic institutions, such as the Commission and the ECJ. In the Fiscal Compact Treaty, the Commission's intervention with the contracting party that defaults on the agreement is now quasi-automatic, something that can be neutralized only by a reversed qualified majority of the financial ministers of the signatory member states. The discretionary power of the ECOFIN Council, that led to the controversial decision in 2003 to disregard the Commission's recommendation to subject Germany and France to the EDP, has been drastically curtailed.

Furthermore the Fiscal Compact Treaty has required the contracting parties to introduce at the constitutional level (or equivalent) the balanced-budget rule, thus also limiting within the domestic system the possibilities of political discretion. The new legislative measures (European Semester, Six Pack, Two Pack) have increased both the supervisory role of the Commission in monitoring *ex-ante* member states' behavior regarding their respect of the legal parameters and the sanctioning role of the Commission in activating *ex-post* the EDP. The banking union taking shape through the Single Supervisory Mechanism (SSM) and the Single Resolution Mechanism (SRM) is based on strict legal rules as well. Owing to a lack of reciprocal trust between the member states, which should voluntarily coordinate their economic, budgetary and fiscal policies, the policy-making process has been judicialized and entrusted to the control of non-political institutions. This is why the Commission, weakened as both an agenda-setting and a decision-making institution, has seen an increase in its technical role as a bureaucracy in charge of guaranteeing respect for the EMU rules.

The financial aid to member states unable to respect those rules has been accompanied by conditionality rules that have led to the downsizing of their decision-making autonomy. Notwithstanding the persistence of deep differences between models of national political economy, in particular between Northern and Southern socio-economic patterns (Hall and Soskice 2001; Schmidt 2002), the intergovernmental EMU has tried to force convergence between those political economies through a policy regime constrained by formal judicial rules and technocratic automatism. This approach, in a context of structural differences within euro-area member states, has deepened the cleavage between the latter, with some member states benefiting from the imposed rules and others paying significant costs. The euro crisis has thus sharpened the divisions within the EU between the different political economies of its member states or regional sections (and between groups within each of them: Fligstein 2010). National political discretion has been unevenly restructured, with the debtor member states becoming less autonomous than the creditor member states due to their inability to control the externalities of their policies.

Under the impact of the euro crisis, the intergovernmental EMU has not prevented its transformation into a centralized regime, highly convoluted in technical and legal terms and extremely intrusive in terms of national prerogatives that it was supposed to respect in the first place. The assumption that, through the logic of voluntary policy coordination, it would have been possible to govern the common currency has been dramatically unmasked by the euro crisis. The combination of an intergovernmental decision-making regime with the German ordo-liberal approach has led to an automatic imposition of rules that have undermined the political debate on the policies to pursue.

Fourth, within the European Council (and the Euro Summit) a decision-making hierarchy has emerged in the form of a German–French (and then only German) directorate for the EMU. As Craig (2014: 36 and 37) observed:

The Euro crisis has … impacted on the EU inter-institutional division of political power. It would be tempting to conclude that it has had a predictably Schmittian effect, with power being concentrated to an ever greater extent in the EU executive, the rationale being that only it can respond with sufficient speed to the profound problems generated by the Euro crisis … In terms of process, the lead on measures to address the Euro crisis has been taken by the European Council, and by Germany and France acting partly within the European Council and partly through bilateral discussion.

The Schmittian state of exception has thus pressured the supporters of the intergovernmental institutions to also operate on the borders of them if necessary to reach a decision (Joerges 2012). Indeed, with the deepening of the crisis, the financial strategy for dealing with the latter has come to be more and more dictated by Berlin (supported by its Northern allies), although together with the Brussels office of the European Council president. The growing unilateral German leadership of the euro-area has led to an unprecedented split between Northern and Southern member states. If the euro was adopted in the first place to preserve a European Germany, the crisis of the euro has led to its opposite, that is to the emergence of a German Europe.

The dominant position of Germany is a serious problem for the intergovernmental union, not only because it contradicts the rationale of the integration project, but also because Germany does not have the cultural and political resources to play the role of a constructive hegemon. In international relations, hegemony has been traditionally accepted when the hegemonic state had shown it was able to generate common goods benefiting other states too (although in different degrees). This hardly seems the case with Germany. Germany cannot rely on an historical legitimacy to be accepted as a hegemonic state by the other EMU member states. Moreover, Germany does not have the necessary political culture to accommodate different and divergent national interests within a comprehensive, although hegemonic, strategy. Its rules-based culture prevents Germany from using democratic politics as a pragmatic activity for mediating between opposing interests and for adapting to unforeseen conflicts. Germany has an insufficient democratic self-confidence to be the political leader of the EU, although it has sufficient economic power to be continuously tempted, if not required, to exercise the leadership role in the EU. If it is true (Van Middelaar 2013: 193) that "Germany bears more responsibility than … Luxembourg … the member states of the Union are unequal – large and small, rich and poor, with long or short external borders, with friendly and hostile neighbours inside or outside the Union," it is also true that the legal principle of equality between member states cannot be made redundant if the EU aims to persist as a union of states (Eriksen 2014). The hierarchical relations between creditor and debtor member states is incompatible with the "republican principles" of political constitutionalism (Bellamy 2013).

From a comparative perspective, this outcome would have been unconceivable, for instance in the US federal union (F. Fabbrini 2013). Certainly, in the USA, since the 1840s, each federated state is responsible for its public debt. Since then, the states cannot be bailed out by the federal government if they are in financial default (Sbragia 1996), while balanced budget rules have been gradually introduced in most states (Von Hagen and Eichengreen 1996). The financial accountability of each state represents one of the properties of the US federal system that has remained dual in this regard, although it has evolved towards forms of cooperation in other policies (Schutze 2010). However, since the 1930s the federal government has started to intervene in the various states, through the use of the federal budget for reasons of public investment or other forms of grants-in-aid (Rodden 2006), in several cases triggered by military considerations, to stimulate growth. Debt has continued to remain a state's business, but growth has become a federal preoccupation. To be sure, the use of the federal budget has been decided through various forms of log-rolling and pork-barreling, and at times inter-institutional conflict, between members of Congress and the president. Nevertheless, states have had a supra-state arena (federal institutions) to use, and a supra-state budget to appeal to, to make their needs heard. The EU bicameral legislature, and the EP in particular, has a very limited budget (less than 1 percent of the total GDP of the Union[12]). The budget is financially dependent on transfers from member states, a condition that has inevitably raised tension between member states and between the latter and the supranational institutions. Deprived even of the limited internal custom duties abolished with the SEA of 1986 and of the authority for promoting autonomous policies, the EP has been pushed to the margins in those policies that constitute the core business of federal union legislatures, such as the US Congress (Henning and Kessler 2012) or the Swiss Federal Assembly.

Although the Lisbon Treaty celebrates the "no bail-out clause" (TFEU Article 125.1 states: "the Union shall not be liable for or assume the commitments of central governments, regional, local or other public authorities, other bodies governed by public law, or public undertakings of any Member State"), de facto during the euro crisis the indebted member states were helped by the creditor member states because of the fear of a general collapse of the euro-area. In the absence of a Union budget that can be drawn on by democratically accountable institutions to indirectly support the economy (not the debt) of the indebted states, help has come directly from the richer member states (that gave it out of interest, not only solidarity) aimed at relieving their debt (not to support their growth). One might argue that this was also the pattern used in Germany after the 1990 unification, when the Western *Länder* helped the Eastern *Länder* through ad hoc pacts and constitutional provisions. However, in Germany cooperative federalism was and continues to be regulated primarily

[12] After the negotiation for setting the multiannual financial budget (2014–2020), as we have seen in Chapter 3, the latter has become less than 1 percent of the total GDP of the EU. The size of the budget is defined according to the following procedure, as stated by TFEU Article 312.2: "The Council, acting in accordance with a special legislative procedure, shall adopt a regulation laying down the multiannual financial framework. The Council shall act unanimously after obtaining the consent of the European Parliament, which shall be given by a majority of its component members."

by federal democratic institutions (the Bundesrat representing *Länder* executives and the Bundestag representing individual citizens organized in *Länder* constituencies), not by purely inter-*Länder* arrangements. Any direct financial relations between states harbors the danger of both domination and resentment.

Lacking a federal method and federal resources for preserving the boundary between the member states' and the center's prerogatives and responsibilities, the euro-area has set up a system of economic governance that has allowed the stronger member states to intrude, through the decisions imposed on the intergovernmental institutions (such as the so-called austerity measures of fiscal consolidation enshrined in intergovernmental treaties and legislative packages), into the national prerogatives of the weaker member states. However, this outcome was neither effective during the euro crisis, nor was it perceived as legitimate by the citizens of the member states most affected by the crisis. The electoral affirmation of anti-EU parties in debtor member states, in the EP elections of May 22–25, 2014, made evident the difficulties of the intergovernmental union. In Greece, the radical left Syriza party, running a campaign against German austerity, became the first party of the country with 26.58 percent of the popular vote. In Spain, the two main parties (the People's Party or PP and the Socialist Party or PSOE) that have alternatively supported austerity measures, lost around one-third of their electorate (the former dropping from 42.2 percent in the 2009 EP election to 26.1 percent, and the latter from 38.8 percent to 23 percent). In Italy, the newly created populist anti-European Five Stars Movement became the second party with 21.2 percent of the popular vote. In Portugal, the party that governed the readjustment of the economy under the impact of financial bankruptcy, the Social Democratic Party/People's Party, lost more than one-quarter of the votes it received in the previous EP elections. The same was true in Ireland for the governing party, Fine Gael, which also lost one-quarter of the votes it received in 2009.

5.6 Conclusion

This chapter started by looking at the distinction between IR and CP approaches to intergovernmentalism, thus identifying the institutional bases of the intergovernmental perspective on the EU. At the origin of the intergovernmental perspective, which emerged with the

1992 Maastricht Treaty, there was the assumption that crucial policies (such as economic policy) may be Europeanized only if elaborated and decided by the member state governments coordinating in the European Council and ECOFIN Council. Supranational institutions such as the Commission and the ECJ were considered necessary for supervising respect for the intergovernmental decisions by the "contracting governments," for implementing those decisions in cooperation with national administrations and for resolving disputes between them – but not for elaborating and deciding the policies to adopt. The Lisbon Treaty has thus formalized this intergovernmental union. After the 2005 defeat of the CT, the intergovernmental perspective emerged as the main perspective for relaunching the process of integration, thanks also to the support of a powerful constellation of political actors in France and Germany in particular.

This chapter has thus analyzed how the intergovernmental EU has performed during the euro crisis. Indeed, during the latter, notwithstanding the supranational independence of monetary policy, economic policy was largely determined by the intergovernmental institutions of the European Council and the ECOFIN Council, which controlled the elaboration and decision-making phases of the policy-making process. The role of the Commission in the decision-making phase was curtailed and its contribution to the agenda-setting phase limited, but its power in supervision and implementation increased. At the same time, the EP has become a secondary institution within the EMU, given that the legitimacy of the intergovernmental institutions derives from the domestic legitimacy of their components, national government leaders and ministers. The intergovernmental union has not, however, solved the dilemma of collective action in an effective and legitimate way. The euro crisis has shown that the intergovernmental EU has not only had difficulty in taking timely decisions for crisis management, but it has also had to rely increasingly on the technocratic and judicial intervention of the supranational institutions in order to make credible commitments for crisis prevention.

In facing the danger of the negative externalities from voluntary coordination, the EMU has ended up becoming a centralized, technocratic and judicialized policy regime. The construction of a centralized policy-making regime, regulated by automatic rules, does not fit easily with the intergovernmental assumption that the EU is based on member state governments' will and legitimacy. At the same time,

the euro crisis has also called into question this assumption, showing that indirect legitimacy is insufficient to justify decisions taken
at the level of and on behalf of the Union. Also from a normative
point of view, as Lord (2011b) stated, "indirect legitimacy cannot
justify coercive powers that have not themselves been delegated to
EU institutions by its member states, and nor can it answer the question 'what is the basis of political obligation to the EU?' in any way
that presupposes EU institutions can enjoy inherent, rather than
delegated, democratic authority." President Sarkozy's argument that
the EU either goes down the intergovernmental road or it does not
proceed has been negatively falsified. Under the dramatic impact of
a financial crisis perceived as an existential crisis (Menéndez 2013),
the intergovernmental union has ended up not only in centralizing decision-making in the intergovernmental institutions of the
ECOFIN Council and the European Council, but also in institutionalizing hierarchical relations between national governments within
them. Through the creation of a "euro-zone fiscal colonialism"
(Legrain 2014), domination, rather than consensual coordination,
has become the code of intergovernmental union, an outcome that
Germany (because of its past) should have had the rational interest
to prevent. Indeed, as one might expect, a directoire emerged also in
CFSP, i.e. during the Libyan crisis, although constituted in this case
by France and the UK (Fabbrini 2014).

The unsatisfactory performance of the intergovernmental EU has
bolstered the voice of those claiming the necessity of bringing the
intergovernmental EMU back to the supranational EU, a claim consisting in the reaffirmation of the need to strengthen the role of the EP
in controlling the main policies through its political connection with
the Commission as in parliamentary federations. Can the parliamentary union be considered a viable alternative to the intergovernmental
union perspective?

6 | *The perspective of parliamentary union*

An important means to deepen the pan-European political debate would be the presentation by European political parties of their candidate for the post of Commission President at the European Parliament elections
José Manuel Barroso, President of the European Commission,
September 12, 2012

6.1 Introduction

Having recognized the unsatisfactory performance of intergovernmental union, it is now time to discuss the alternative perspective advanced for promoting a political union. The perspective of parliamentary union continues to be the mainstream alternative to intergovernmental union, advanced by very influential scholarship with roots in the neo-functional school of European integration that promoted the "Community method" of integration. And, of course, it has been the most popular perspective among officials working in the supranational institutions of the EU in Brussels. Its salience has increased with the deepening of the euro crisis and the difficulty experienced by the intergovernmental institutions in taming it. It is based on the assumption that, without becoming a parliamentary federation with the Commission acting as a federal government elected and controlled by the EP or its majority, the EU will never truly resolve the euro crisis. One can even argue (as the Spinelli Group and Bertelsmann Stiftung (2013) did) that the euro crisis has been the dramatic but welcome opportunity for relaunching the federal project frozen after the failure of the CT in 2005.

This perspective consists in "the ambition to establish … a system of government at the European level with a strong priority-setting and policy-planning input for the EP, a system that in a way would resemble *mutatis mutandis* parliamentary democracy in a nation-state"

(Lehmann and Schunz 2005: 10). At its core there is the strengthening of the political relations between the EP and the Commission.
Although there are several definitions of parliamentarism, its crucial
feature resides in the fact that "the head of the government ... and
his or her cabinet are dependent on the confidence of the legislature
and can be dismissed from office by a legislative vote of no confidence
or censure" (Lijphart 1992: 2). Investigating one of the first experiments in parliamentarism, Bagehot (1867: chapter 2) remarked that
"the efficient secret of the English Constitution may be described as
the close union, the nearly complete fusion, of the executive and legislative powers" (see Glossary). The supranational constitution of the
single market, as institutionalized by the Lisbon Treaty, is considered
not only the closest approximation to that system of government,
but also the framework within which a parliamentary government
can fully emerge. The proposal for the parliamentary election of the
Commission president has come to represent the centerpiece of the
strategy for accelerating that emergence.

The debate on how to elect the Commission president started in the
1980s and has continued since then. Some scholars have argued in
favor of the direct election of the Commission president (among them,
Bogdanor 1986; Decker and Sonnicksen 2011; Laver *et al.* 1995),
others instead for the indirect election of the latter by the EP (among
them, Estella 2009; Hix and Lord 1996; Westlake 1998, but also
again Bogdanor 2007). Both proposals were discussed at the Brussels
constitutional convention of 2002–2003, but it was the latter that
received the necessary support to be made part of the CT (Norman
2003) through the mitigated formula of the European Council that
should take into consideration the elections of the EP in nominating
the candidate for the role of Commission president. The two proposals differed regarding the modalities to elect the Commission president
(Decker and Sonnicksen 2009), but converged on the idea of politically connecting the Commission president to the EP. With the EP election of 2014, the proposal of indirect or parliamentary election of the
Commission's president was picked up by EU institutional actors such
as the EP and the Commission. On March 12, 2013 the Commission
made public Communication IP/13/215 recommending "political parties (to) nominate a candidate for European Commission President in
the next European Elections (2014) and [to] display their European
political party affiliation." In its *Blueprint for a Deep and Genuine*

Economic and Monetary Union (EMU) of November 28, 2012, the Commission stressed the necessity, "without this being a point specific to EMU, [of considering] a number of steps ... to foster the emergence of a genuine European political sphere. This includes, in the context of the European elections of 2014, most importantly the nomination of candidates for the office of Commission President by political parties."

In its Resolution of November 22, 2012 on Elections to the European Parliament in 2014, the EP:

urges the European political parties to nominate candidates for the Presidency of the Commission and expects those candidates to play a leading role in the parliamentary electoral campaign in particular by personally presenting their programme in all member states of the Union; stresses the importance of reinforcing the political legitimacy of both Parliament and Commission by connecting their respective elections more directly to the choice of the voters.

In his State of the Union Address on September 12, 2012, the President of the Commission, José Manuel Barroso, formally endorsed the parliamentary union perspective. This proposal was finally picked up by all the main European political parties, first by the Socialists and Democrats (or S&D), then by the Alliance of Liberal and Democrats for Europe (or ALDE), then by the Greens–European Free Alliance (Greens–EFA) and lastly by the European People's Party (or EPP) for the EP elections of May 22–25, 2014, through the indication of the *Spitzenkandidat* of each party for the role of Commission president in case of electoral success.

Indeed, in the European Council held on June 26–27, 2014, taking into consideration the outcome of the EP elections of May 22–25, 2014, the heads of state and government proposed Jean-Claude Juncker as president of the Commission. For the first time, the nomination was not unanimous. The prime ministers of the UK and Hungary voted against the proposal. Assembling on July 15, 2014, the EP approved the European Council's proposal with the majority of 422 MEPs – out of the 729 total cast in the secret ballot and out of 751 MEPs in total. Jean-Claude Juncker was the *Spitzenkandidat* of the EPP, which got the plurality of seats in the EP elections. Contrary to the past, the Commission president was chosen from a popular vote, rather than from negotiation between national leaders within the European

Council. Addressing the EP in his speech on July 15, 2014, Jean-Claude Juncker said: "for the first time, a direct link has thereby been established between the outcome of the European Parliament elections and the proposal of the President of the European Commission ... [This link] has the potential to insert a very necessary additional dose of democratic legitimacy into the European decision-making process, *in line with the rules and practices of parliamentary democracy*" (author's emphasis).

Could the EU move in the direction of a parliamentary government? This chapter will discuss critically the feasibility of the parliamentary government model for the EU. The discussion will be based on a comparative institutional analysis, with the focus on the horizontal inter-institutional relations between legislative and executive institutions at the EU level. Its aim is to show the difficulty, if not impossibility, of transforming the EU into a parliamentary federation, both with an unchanged Lisbon Treaty and with a new Treaty. The chapter proceeds as follows. First, it will reconstruct the process of institutionalization of the EP regarding its external role and internal organization, in order to investigate the relation between institutionalization and parliamentarization. Second, it will discuss the institutional features, supporting and opposing the parliamentarization of the EU, formalized by the institutional framework of the Lisbon Treaty. Third, it will discuss the parliamentary union perspective in the context of a new Treaty, through the critical analysis of a formal proposal (a "Fundamental Law of the European Union" advanced by the Spinelli Group and Bertelsmann Stiftung 2013) that aims to go beyond the Lisbon Treaty. Fourth, it will investigate the structural conditions that have made possible the formation of democratic parliamentary federations in Germany and in Canada, conditions that are lacking in the EU even with a change to the Lisbon Treaty.

6.2 The institutionalization of the EP: role and organization

The EP in the supranational architecture

The Lisbon Treaty has unmistakably recognized the EP as the popular chamber of the EU bicameral legislature. The Treaty set the number of MEPs at 751, allocated to each member state according to the electoral already discussed criterion of degressive proportionality, although that threshold was consolidated with the elections of 2014 (in the elections of 2009 754 MEPs were elected in order to accommodate the new member states). Since 1979 MEPs have been directly elected every five years according to national versions of the proportional representation (PR) system.[1] If compared with the lower chamber of democratic federal systems, the EP is the largest legislative institution in the democratic federal or federalizing world, followed by the Indian House of the People, known as the Lok Sabha, consisting of 545 members, then the Brazilian Chamber of Deputies with 513 members and the US House of Representatives with its 435 members. It serves the largest transnational democratic electorate in the world (approximately 380 million eligible voters in 2014).

The spread of the ordinary legislative procedure to a large majority of EU single market policies constitutes a spectacular success for an institution that, at the beginning of the integration process, was merely an indirectly formed assembly. In establishing itself as a new institutional actor in the system, the EP first tried to consolidate its legislative role. The Commission welcomed this effort as it had an institutional interest in reducing the power of the Council and the latter's capacity to condition its choices. The strengthening of the legislative power of the EP, however, produced contradictory effects on the Commission. On the one hand, the EP has become an effective ally of the Commission in balancing the legislative power of the Council; on the other, the EP has started to negotiate directly with the Council, thus reducing the mediating role of the Commission. In particular with the extension of the co-decisional procedure, the Commission, although it has formally kept the monopoly over legislative initiative, has seen a reduction in its power to affect the legislative process through the threat of withholding a proposal (regulation or directive) if not accepted by the EP or the Council. Once submitted, the fate of the proposal has migrated to the bicameral legislature. The EP and the Council, in fact, have developed procedures to reconcile their different views on the proposals at stake that have seen the approval of many of them at first reading (see

[1] Although British MEPs were elected by a system of simple plurality (majoritarian uninominal electoral rule, better known as first-past-the-post) until 1999, since then the British electoral system for the EP has become proportional.

Chapter 2), thus reducing the Commission's power to control the out-come of the legislative process.

Through its powers of information, investigation and interrogation, and stressing its nature as the only directly elected institution of the EU, the EP has also tried to intervene in the Commission's formation, which is controlled by member state governments. The EP has imposed its right of checking the adequacy of member state candidates for positions in the Commission (such as the president and commissioners) and thus of controlling the Commission's behavior. By asking candidates for the position of Commission president and commissioner to show their credentials for the job to which they have been assigned, the EP has become an important variable in the political calculus of member state governments concerning the choice of the various candidates. Not only has the EP avoided self-restraint in its role of checking the validity of the European Council's choices for the Commission president and commissioners, but in fact it has further expanded that role by becoming the supervisor of the Commission's activities. The scandal that involved the Santer Commission in 1999 allowed the EP to create the political conditions for the resignation of the entire body due to allegations of corruption against a few of its members (who refused to resign individually) (Moury 2007), although formally its power to vote down the Commission was already recognized by the Maastricht Treaty.

Following the Santer affair it has no longer been possible to exclude the EP from intervening in the strategic choices of the Union's institutions. The period following the Santer affair has registered the institutionalization of a competitive relation between, on one side, national governments (organized within the European Council and the Council) and supranational institutions (such as the EP and the Commission). Through various devices (such as inter-institutional agreements, internal statutes or best practices) the EP has institutionalized its role in balancing the European Council's power to both nominate the president and members of the Commission and in checking the latter's behavior. Between the EP and the European Council competition over control of the Commission has gradually emerged. The formation of the European Council outside the Treaty framework in 1974 and thus its development have been interpreted as the national governments' need to keep a check on an increasingly self-assertive EP. Gradually, the political dynamic has focused on the relations between the European Council and the EP. If the political dynamic in the first decade of the EU's development was between the Council (the institution representing member state governments) and the Commission (the institution representing the European interest), since the 1980s and 1990s the European Council has become instrumental to balancing the increasing role of the EP. One should note that the EP and the European Council have continued to grow together, in a sort of competitive relation, with the former epitomizing the parliamentary union and the latter the intergovernmental union.

Utilizing specific windows of opportunity and claiming its status as the only Union institution directly elected by voters, and thus the only one representing European citizens, the EP has gone through a process of transformation and not simple evolution (Kreppel 2002). The EP represents a successful story of a supranational legislature's institutionalization. Internal incentives and external pressures have created a favorable environment to increase the legislative role and powers of the EP (Rittberger 2003). The transformation of the EP is epitomized, from Maastricht to Lisbon, by the radical redefinition of its nature. If the Maastricht Treaty (TEC, Article 137) stated that "The European Parliament … shall consist of representatives of the peoples of the States brought together in the Community," the Lisbon Treaty (TEU, Article 14.2) instead makes clear, as we have seen, that the EP "shall be composed of representatives of the Union's citizens," not of representatives of member state citizens. If in parliamentary *states* the popular legislature has been celebrated, since the 1789 French revolution, as "the representative of the nation" (Pitkin 1972), in the EU parliamentary *state* in the making the EP has come to represent "the European citizenry," if not "Europe" as such. That Article of the Lisbon Treaty symbolizes, more than any other Article of the Treaty, the *statist* view of the supporters of the parliamentary union perspective. The EU should no longer represent states and their citizens, but a European demos in formation.

The internal organization of the EP

The growth of the EP's power has been supported by a constant rationalization of its internal structure, on both institutional and partisan levels. The EP has used any new treaty to rationalize its internal structure and rules of procedure (Kreppel 2003) – a rationalization, it might be added, that has also led the EP to call into question the Byzantine convention of splitting its activities between Strasbourg for plenary sessions, Brussels for semi-plenary sessions and committee and party meetings and, finally, Luxembourg for the activities of the secretariat and technical services. A few federal systems have located their central institutions in newly created places, in order to keep the rivalry and the jealousy between their constituent states under control (one has only to think of the choice of creating brand new cities, such as Washington DC and Brasilia, to house the capitals of the federal USA and Brazil). However, the EU is the only one that splits its activities geographically, with the result being the inevitable increase in the financial and functional costs of its institutional activities.[2]

The EP structure operates according to three criteria (Corbett, Jacobs and Shackleton 2005):

(1) each deliberation is valid if supported by the majority of the votes expressed, although in specific cases a quorum of participants has to be respected;
(2) parliamentary deliberation is directed by a leadership structure based on one president, fourteen vice-presidents, several committees and parliamentary groups;
(3) the decision-making process is organized around parliamentary committees more than parliamentary parties or groups.

The role of the president and his/her vice-presidents is of particular importance. Since 1979 the president has played a leading role in accelerating the full entrance of the EP into the Union policy-making process. After the 1992 Maastricht Treaty, not only has the president's

---

[2] Again, in November 2013 the EP voted by a large majority of its members a motion to end the practice of dividing its works between three headquarters (Strasbourg, Brussels and Luxembourg) and to make the Spinelli building in Brussels the only site for its activities (and where the monthly semi-plenary sessions are now held). Moreover, the EP has also shut down all but its historical archives in Luxembourg. However, all French governments have strenuously objected to this project, insisting on preserving Strasbourg as a meeting place (as established by the Treaties). The bargain struck was that France subsidizes the building of new EP facilities in Strasbourg in exchange for the continuation of meetings in that city. Due to this unsatisfactory bargain, it has been proposed to transform the Strasbourg building into the site for a European School of Administration (Goulard and Monti 2012).

office been recognized as the focal point of the institution, but furthermore the vice-presidents' offices have been strengthened, in part because they have specialized and differentiated their roles and competences. Since 1979 an informal rule has also been adopted to share the presidency for the entire legislature (2.5 years each) between the two main parties of the EP (the EPP and the European Socialist Party, the latter renamed as the Progressive Alliance of Socialists and Democrats or S&D since 2009, with only two concessions to leaders of the Liberal-Democrats[3]). This informal rule reflects the highly consensual politics taking place within the EP, but also the difficulty of the EP in expressing a clear party majority within the institution. Starting with the presidency of Nicole Fontaine, inaugurated in July 1999, EP presidents have established their role of representing the institution in the EU member states, intergovernmental conferences and international institutions and meetings.

Since the 1980s the committees have become the main deliberative structures of the EP, defining themselves in relation to the policy areas dealt with by the Commission and the Council (Bowler and Farrell 1995). In the post-2009 EP, each committee has acquired between a minimum of twenty-four and a maximum of seventy-six members. Each committee has a president, a number of vice-presidents and a secretariat. The party composition of the committees reflects the party percentage in the general assembly and each political group has its own coordinator. The main negotiations for recomposing party positions and member states' interests take place within the committees (Settembri and Neuhold 2009). Also in this regard, the process of institutionalization has been spectacular. Only eight permanent committees existed in 1953; they became twenty (plus two quasi-independent sub-committees) in 2014. Moreover, temporary committees of inquiry have been set up to monitor specific issues. Although EP committees have become much stronger than the equivalent committees in EU member state parliaments, their decision-making role continues to be constrained by the absence of sub-committees and seniority rules for allocating committee chairs. Moreover, committee chairs and

---

[3] First from July 1979 to January 1982 and then from January 2002 to July 2004 two members (respectively Simon Weil and Pat Cox) of the ELDR (the European Liberal Democrat and Reform Party) were nominated as presidents of the EP.

members change every 2.5 years (Kreppel 2006), again to favor consensus within the institution.

Parliamentary groups and European political parties have also come to play an important role in the institutionalization of the EP. The various types of PR electoral formula adopted by all the member states to elect MEPs have guaranteed the formation of a multi-party system within the assembly, although the EPP and the European Socialist Party/S&D have traditionally controlled 3/5 of the seats. The formation of a political group requires (as a minimum) 25 representatives, that is 3.3 percent of the total number of MEPs who have to come from at least one-quarter of the member states. The enlargement to include the Eastern European countries has altered the partisan pattern of the EP. The parties representing Eastern European voters do not fit within the established EP party system, requiring the EP to adapt to different needs and representative cultures (Best, Christiansen and Settembri 2008; Bressanelli 2012), although the European People's Party has been favored by the arrival of new representatives. Moreover, new white-hot issues (immigration, unemployment, public expenditure cuts) have triggered the creation and growth of anti-European parties in many of the core EU member states, bringing them to represent one-quarter of the EP seats after the elections of May 2014 (or 30 percent if the Nordic Green Left is counted as a fringe group). Nevertheless, the party composition of the EP has continued to be characterized by the consolidated European political parties.

Although the EP political parties are mainly federations, if not confederations, of distinct national parties, each parliamentary party (and the main ones in particular) have increased their ideological cohesion, learning to operate in a coordinated manner within the legislature, as shown by the roll call vote. However, this coordination has worked effectively in relation more to low politics or isomorphic issues (issues that mirror national ones) than high politics or constitutive issues (issues concerning the nature and the future of the integration process) (Bartolini 2008). Indeed, according to VoteWatchEU (see Table 6.1), in the constitutional decade of the 2000s the loyalty of MEPs to their member state interests persisted, notwithstanding different partisan allegiances.

With the explosion of the euro crisis, new constitutive issues have entered the legislative agenda. In this context, MEPs tended to coalesce around the institutional interest of the EP, but many of them could not

Table **6.1** *Roll call vote (2004–2009) in the EP*

Loyalty (2004–2009)	High (100%–80%)	Good (79%–60%)	Sufficient (59%–40%)	Low (39%–20%)	Not at all (19%–0%)
to the EP group	90.3%	8.4%	1.1%	0.1%	0%
to the national group	98.30%	1.7%	1.7%	0%	0%
to the member state	55.0%	32.2%	10.8%	1.8%	0%

Source: Elaboration of data provided by VoteWatchEU.

forget the national interest of their countries. On February 15, 2012 the EP had to deliberate on a Resolution in favor of stability bonds (known as Eurobonds) for tackling the sovereign debt crisis of some the euro-area member states (the indebted member states could borrow new funds at better conditions as they are supported by the rating of the non-crisis member states). Germany and its Northern allies and, under their leadership, the intergovernmental institutions opposed the possibility of issuing Eurobonds guaranteed by all the euro-area member states. As Hix (2013: 8) reported, a super grand coalition within the EP (centered on the EPP, S&D and ALDE MEPs) finally approved the Resolution, but "29 EPP MEPs from Germany and Sweden voted against, and 19 ALDE MEPs, also mainly from Germany, abstained." The same logic emerged during the March 13, 2013 vote on the Resolution criticizing the Multiannual Financial Framework (MFF) for 2014–21. The MFF proposal, as recorded above, initially negotiated in the European Council and thus formalized by the Council, was significantly lower than the previous MFF (2007–2014), because of budget cuts introduced under the pressure of the sovereignist coalition (the UK, the Scandinavian and some Eastern member states), with the complicity of Germany. A broad parliamentary coalition (constituted by the larger EP parties) supported the Resolution criticizing those cuts. However:

a significant number of MEPs voted against the group line in the EPP, mainly from Central and Eastern Europe (Poland and Romania) and the Nordic Countries (Denmark, Sweden, and Finland). Also within the S&D, the British, Swedish and Danish delegations rebelled against the group position, and voted against the Resolution. In fact, despite the large majority in the vote, most Danish, Polish, Swedish and British MEPs voted against the Resolution (Hix 2013: 9).

While the EP's powers have increased, the same cannot be said for voters' participation in the elections of its members. In the EU of nine member states of 1979, 61.99 percent of voters went to the polls. Since then, electoral participation has decreased regularly, while the number of member states has been increasing significantly (Schmitt 2010). In the EP elections of May 2014, the average participation was 43.09 percent, a very slight increase relative to the 43 percent of 2009, notwithstanding the social malaise induced by the euro crisis and the personalization of parties' campaigns through their *Spitzenkandidaten.* In short, the popularity of the EP has decreased, while its powers have gone in the opposite direction, with the rec- ognition of its co-decisional power with the Council in the ordinary legislative procedure.

6.3 Features supporting and contradicting parliamentarization

Supporting parliamentarization

Notwithstanding what the EP has become in the supranational con- stitution, however, a critique has continued to be raised since 1979 (Marquand 1979), namely that "the European Parliament is a par- liament but not a very European one" (Lord 2003: 31). According to many authors (Follesdal and Hix 2005; Hix 2008a, 2008b, 2013; Hix, Noury and Roland 2006; Kohler-Koch and Rittberger 2007), the EP is not a *true* parliament because it does not play a decisive role in the for- mation of the Commission (which is assumed to be the European gov- ernment). The EP does not have a party link with the Commission in the sense that the composition of the latter does not reflect the partisan majority of the EP, nor is there a government vs. opposition logic in its functioning (Majone 2009). The election of MEPs is a second-order election because of a lack of a truly trans-European party system (which explains, for those scholars, the low turnout in those elec- tions). During the debate that accompanied the re-elaboration of the failed CT into the Lisbon Treaty, there was the acknowledgement

(Hix 2008a: 38) that the EU "is ... a quasi-parliamentary system of government – where a particular political majority could choose 'its' Commission with a particular policy agenda and so be 'in government' at the EU level for the 5 year legislative mandate, while several Member States and some political parties could find themselves 'in opposition.' " Hix (2008a: 4) admits that "the EU never will be, and never should be, like the Westminster model of government, where a narrow political majority can dictate policy outcomes," but rather "the EU should become more like the German or Scandinavian models," that is more consensus-oriented parliamentary systems. Such consensualism, for Hix (2008a: 4), has not prevented German or Scandinavian parliamentary systems from functioning through the formation of "a broad coalition ... in support of policy changes via an open and vigorous political debate." With the reforms introduced through the SEA of 1986 and accentuated by the 1990s treaties, the EU was considered to have become less consensual and more majoritarian in institutional terms.

A transformation of elite and mass behavioral patterns was thus claimed to correspond to the institutional changes that had already taken place. The EU needed (Magnette and Papadopoulos 2008) to politicize the EP's elections, transforming them into the arena where a popular majority should emerge regarding which governmental program to pursue. Politicization thus came to be seen as a necessary condition for accelerating the EU's parliamentarization. In order to increase the politicization of the EP elections, proposals started to be advanced to transform them into the vehicle for vigorous confrontation between partisan alternatives, in particular through the promotion of different candidatures for the role of Commission president by the main political parties. The parliamentary election of the Commission president has come to be considered a crucial step in transforming the EP into a true parliament and the Union into a parliamentary federation. As Bürgin (N.D.: 10) argued:

an elected Commission president signals a rupture with the old frame of the Commission as a technical agent fulfilling the tasks given by the European Council. Instead it represents the acceptance that the Commission has a political role, which has to be legitimized through election. Therefore the election of a Commission president is a further step towards the parliamentarization of the Union.

If the EP gets the political power to elect its own Commission, then the transformation of the quasi-parliamentary EU into a parliamentary union will be accomplished. To give the EP this power would not even require a change in the Treaties. Hix (2008a: 159) suggested introducing a de facto change in the latter's practice in order "to allow a majority in the European Parliament to nominate, and the European Council to then approve by Qualified Majority Voting" the Commission president. The EU's difficulties were considered to come from political rather than institutional or structural conditions, that is, from the low level of politicization of the EP elections, debate and decision-making process. The EU needed more partisan politics rather than another cycle of treaty reform. For the parliamentary union perspective, the role of political parties has continued to be crucial (Hix 2008b). The democratic nature of the EU depends on their capacity to aggregate citizens' preferences and to transform them into a governmental program. Making the EP the center of the decision-making process would trigger the strengthening of the European parties as both electoral and governmental actors.

For this reason, a panoply of reforms was suggested. The name of European political parties should formally appear on election ballots; the parties should run the EP election on the basis of their pan-European program; after the election the parties should adopt winner-takes-more rules for allocating institutional roles within the EP. But above all, the parties should be required to indicate their candidate for the position of Commission president during the elections for the EP. Having to decide the Commission's political composition and leadership, the EP elections would increase their standing in the eyes of European voters. The candidatures for the Commission president would epitomize and personalize the political battle on the strategies of the Union. The politicization of the EP elections would extend its effects to other institutions, the Council in particular, thus incentivizing the latter to divide along the partisan lines of left vs. right. Implicit in this perspective are the assumptions that parliaments matter if they form (elect) a government (Farrell and Scully 2007) and that executives are legitimated if formed and supported by a popular legislature (Hix, Noury and Roland 2006).

This argument has influenced important aspects of the Lisbon Treaty. The extension, by the Lisbon Treaty, of the ordinary legislative procedure to a large part of single market policies constitutes a striking success for the EP (although this procedure has been excluded in crucial policy areas). Although the power of legislative initiative has remained in the Commission's hands, the EP has learned how to operate to let the Commission know its legislative preferences. The Lisbon Treaty has not only strengthened the legislative role of the EP, but it has also connected the Commission to the latter's formation. According to TEU Article 17.7, the European Council, "taking into account the elections to the European Parliament and after having held the appropriate consultations … acting by qualified majority, shall propose to the European Parliament a candidate for the President of the Commission. This candidate shall be elected by the European Parliament by a majority of its component members." Once the candidate is elected, adds the following paragraph of the same Article, "the Council, by common accord with the President-elect, shall adopt the list of the other persons whom it proposes for appointment as members of the Commission." Thus, "the President, the High Representative of the Union for Foreign Affairs and Security Policy and the other members of the Commission shall be subject as a body to a vote of consent by the European Parliament. On the basis of this consent the Commission shall be appointed by the European Council, acting by a qualified majority." It was the opportunity offered by this Treaty Article that the political parties used in the EP elections of 2014 to indicate their *Spitzenkandidaten* for the Commission president's job; a choice thus sealed by the EP when it communicated that it would have voted as Commission president only the *Spitzenkandidat* (Jean-Claude Juncker) of the party (the EPP) with the plurality of MEPs.

Moreover, the Lisbon Treaty has also codified the power of the EP to vote down the Commission in its collegiality, a power used by the EP during the 1999 crisis of the Santer Commission. According to TEU Article 17.8, "the European Parliament may vote on a motion of censure of the Commission. If such a motion is carried, the members of the Commission shall resign as a body." Thus the Lisbon Treaty has advanced significantly in the direction of making the EP a central institution in voting the Commission both up and down. The political pressure for strengthening this role further has continued. For instance, Viviane Reding (then vice-president of the Commission and commissioner for justice, fundamental rights and citizenship), in a talk given to Deutsche Bank's 13th Women in European Business Conference, Frankfurt, on March 14, 2012, not only supported the

Commission's proposal of parliamentary election of its president, but added that "before the European elections, leaders should agree that the next Commission President would also become the President of the European Council. The current European Treaties allow for this." Interestingly enough, the Commission's memo (Communication IP/13/215) proposes the parliamentary election of its president, but it does not mention the possibility for the EP to introduce European laws (regulations and directives) autonomously. Thus the EP might gain the power "to form" the Commission, but the latter remains formally independent from the former regarding its decision as to whether or not to introduce legislative proposals. In short, the parliamentary Commission would retain its monopoly of legislative initiative.

Contradicting parliamentarization

If it is true that the Lisbon Treaty celebrates a parliamentary idea of the EU, it is also arguable that such celebration has to face an institutional reality that contradicts it. The formula that the European Council shall nominate the president of the Commission "taking into account the elections to the European Parliament" is intentionally ambiguous. Those elections are organized at the member state level by PR systems that cannot generate a parliamentary majority. In PR systems parliamentary majorities emerge after the election, not through the election.[4] Indeed, the plurality party in the 2014 EP elections, the EPP led by Jean-Claude Juncker, conquered only 29.43 percent of the popular vote, that is 221 out of 751 EP seats, only a few more than the seats of the S&D (191). Considering the national divisions within both the EPP and the S&D, even a coalition between them would have been insufficient to grant the absolute parliamentary majority required by the Treaty for election of the Commission president. This is why Jean-Claude Juncker enlarged the majority coalition to ALDE's 67 MEPs, in order to offset the inevitable defections within the three parties. Indeed, he received 422 votes out of the 479 MEPs formally belonging to the three parties of the parliamentary majority. The EP's forcing on the European Council of the candidature of Jean-Claude Juncker introduced a radical change in the practice

---

[4] I refer to the classical analysis of Sartori (1976 now 2005) on the correlation between the electoral system and the party system.

that had been followed by the heads of state and government in the past. Nevertheless, the nomination by the European Council and the election by the EP of Jean-Claude Juncker was part of a complex set of negotiations, also aimed to identify the new president of the EP (the socialist Martin Schulz) and the new commissioners. It was in the European Council that the main negotiations took place. In fact, when division emerged within it, as at the meeting of July 16–17, it was decided to postpone the choice for the new High Representative (HR) to the following meeting of August 29–30, 2014. The 2014 experience shows that the European Council was constrained in the choice of the Commission president, but its role was not that of a collegial head of state simply acknowledging the outcome of the elections (as heads of state, presidents or monarchs generally do in parliamentary systems).

The Commission that emerged from the 2014 EP elections confirms the political role played by the European Council in its formation, not only because the Lisbon Treaty assigns to the European Council, together with the elected Commission president, the task of composing the new Commission, but also because the rule of a commissioner per member state has magnified the role of governmental leaders in selecting candidates expressing national, and not only partisan, preferences. As had never happened in the past, the Juncker Commission (2014–2019), agreed between the president elected and the European Council, is constituted by previous national governmental leaders for two-thirds of its 28 components. In fact, it "includes 5 former Prime Ministers, 4 Deputy Prime Ministers, 19 former Ministers," in addition to "7 returning Commissioners and 8 former Members of the European parliament" (European Commission, Press Release, September 10, 2014). Although the candidates for commissioner had to pass EP scrutiny, positive for all but one, it was the European Council that found the magic formula for balancing partisan and national interests. The very allocation of Commission portfolios was not a business controlled exclusively by the Commission president. Any Commission will have to be multinational and necessarily multi-party. The composition of the Commission must reflect a coalition of parties (especially when, as happened with the elections of 2014, a significant number of anti-EU MEPs entered the EP), but also a balance between member states, according to a magic formula that the European Council should elaborate in the first instance. The EP elections of 2014 served to indicate the candidate for the job of Commission president, but not to decide the composition of the Commission as a whole. Notwithstanding the forcing on the European Council to nominate the most voted-for *Spitzenkandidat*, the EP had to enter into a complex negotiation with the European Council to select a Commission that was the expression of national and not only partisan interests.

At the same time, it is true that the EP may vote down the Commission in its collegiality, but it can do that only on the basis of moral and not political reasons. Indeed, the Santer Commission was called into question in 1999 for the former and not the latter. This power recalls the impeachment prerogatives of the ancient British parliament towards the king during the Tudor constitution (Huntington 1968), a prerogative that then migrated to the US Congress during the Philadelphia Convention of 1787 (Article II Section IV of the US constitution says: "The President, Vice-President and all civil officers ... shall be removed from office on impeachment for and conviction of treason, bribery, or other high crimes and misdemeanours"), although in the EU case it concerns an entire body and not just its head or individual commissioners. This power does not coincide with the parliamentary prerogative to withdraw confidence from the Commission on the basis of political and not legal or moral considerations.

The relationship of political confidence between the EP and the Commission is obstructed by further institutional factors. The EP has a statutory fixed mandate of five years (according to TEU Article 14.3, "the members of the European Parliament shall be elected for a term of five years by direct universal suffrage in a free and secret ballot") and cannot be dissolved at the request of any institution (be it the Commission or the European Council), thus impeding the recourse to the flexibility that is typical of a parliamentary system. If the EP cannot vote down the Commission politically, no institution can dissolve the EP either. This contrasts with a crucial tenet of the parliamentary model, that is, the possibility to dissolve the parliament when there is no longer a political majority supporting the government. At the same time, another crucial tenet of the parliamentary model – that is, the parliamentary status of the executive's members – is contradicted by the Lisbon Treaty. TFEU Article 245 states, in fact, that "the Members of the Commission may not, during their term of office, engage in any other occupation, whether gainful or not," which excludes that members of the Commission could also be MEPs, unlike in parliamentary systems.

Finally, a politicized Commission is at odds with the letter and the spirit of the Lisbon Treaty. According to TEU Article 17.1, the Commission, in ensuring "the application of the Treaties" or in overseeing "the application of Union law under the control of the Court of Justice," should guarantee that "in carrying out its responsibilities … [it] shall be completely independent" and "shall neither seek nor take instructions from any Government or other institution, body, office or entity" (TEU, Article 17.3). Thus, contrary to what Hix and others have argued, a political Commission would require a formal change in the Treaty, not just a de facto adaptation to a practice. The independence of the Commission from both member states' governments and the EP is a constitutive feature of the institutional architecture constructed over decades of integration. A political Commission would not have the legitimacy to carry out its traditional functional duties (Grabbe and Lehne 2013), such as supervising respect for the Union's rules and laws by the member states or requiring member states to enforce anti-trust or balanced budget requirements they do not like. A Commission understood as a "government of the Union," an expression of a clear parliamentary majority, would marginalize the MEPs belonging to minority parties (or at least that might be the fear of the latter), especially if they represent small or medium-sized member states lacking the power to make their voice heard. The Commission's politicization might darken the perception of its technical neutrality in those member state governments or sectors of the population politically unconnected to the EP's majority that supports it.

If it is true that "all the systems that we call parliamentary require governments to be appointed, supported and, as the case may be, discharged by parliamentary vote" (Sartori 1994: 101), then it does not seem plausible to assert that the EU is a parliamentary federation in the making. Probably because parliamentary government represents the most familiar governmental model for the EU political elites (Goetze and Rittberger 2010), and thus for answering the persistent critique of the EU as displaying a democratic deficit, the Lisbon Treaty has done its best to keep alive the parliamentary union perspective. However, institutional constraints have continued to thwart the latter. Indeed, several proposals have been elaborated to overcome those constraints through a new Treaty. I will now discuss one of the main Treaty change proposals in order to show that those institutional constraints are not easy to neutralize.

6.4 Parliamentary union and treaty change

Because of the ambiguities of the Lisbon Treaty towards the parliamentary union perspective, the supporters of the latter (Spinelli Group and Bertelsmann Stiftung 2013) have proposed to resolve those ambiguities through a new treaty, a "Fundamental Law of the European Union," that rationalizes all the main tenets of that perspective. The proposal of a new fundamental law (hereafter called the Proposal) aims to offer a parliamentary way out to the EU stalemate induced by the euro crisis. The Proposal starts from the recognition (Article 8.3) that "The European Parliament and the Council form the two chambers of the Union legislature. The European Commission is the government of the Union and is appointed by and answerable to the legislature." The EP is the first and most important Union institution, exercising legislative and budgetary functions together with "functions of political control" (Article 12.1). The MEPs "shall be elected for a term of five years," although "a certain number of Members of the Parliament shall be elected in a single constituency comprising the whole territory of the Union" (Article 12.3).

In this Proposal, the European Council is brought back to the old role of being a formation of the Council: "the European Council may meet in the formation of the General Affairs Council" (Article 13.3). The European Council still has the power, acting by a qualified majority, to propose a candidate for the Commission president to the EP, as established by the Lisbon Treaty (TEU, Article 17). If the candidate does not obtain the required majority of the EP, the European Council, acting again by a qualified majority, shall propose a new candidate to be elected by the EP following the same procedure. Once elected, the Commission president, "after consulting the Council" (Article 15.8), shall present to the EP the list of the persons proposed for the role of commissioners. The president and the commissioners "shall be subject as a body to a vote of consent by the European Parliament. On the basis of this consent the Commission shall be appointed by the Council, acting by a qualified majority" (Article 15.10). The Commission shall be responsible only to the EP. The EP, acting by a majority of its members, may vote both a loss of confidence in an individual commissioner (Article 15.11) and a censure to the Commission as whole. If the censure vote succeeds (Article 15.12), then the EP has to nominate a successor president of the Commission, adding: "In that case, the European Council *shall accept* that candidate as the nomination for the new President of the Commission" (author's emphasis). Moreover, Article 34 states:

if the motion of censure is carried out by a majority of the component Members of the European Parliament, the members of the Commission shall resign as a body ... In this case, the term of office of the members of the Commission appointed to replace them shall expire on the date on which the term of office of the members of the Commission obliged to resign as a body would have expired.

The Council is recognized to constitute, jointly with the EP, the legislature of the Union, whose deliberations are based on either a simple majority or a qualified majority (Article 14). Under the ordinary legislative procedure, "the qualified majority in the Council shall be defined as at least 55% of the members of the Council representing the participating States comprising at least 65% of the population of these States," whereas under the special legislative procedure "the qualified majority in the Council shall be defined as at least two thirds of the members of the Council representing the States comprising at least 75% of the population of the Union." However, the Council's role in the Commission's formation is purely notarial (appointing a Commission decided by the EP; see above Article 15.10) or even non-existent in case of a crisis with the Commission. Only the EP can vote a loss of confidence and can substitute the Commission president and commissioners. The Commission maintains its monopoly of legislative initiative, but "either the European Parliament or the Council may request the Commission to submit any appropriate proposal ... they consider that a Union act is required." Should the Commission decide not to submit a proposal, both "the European Parliament or the Council may make a proposal for a legislative act" to be deliberated through the ordinary legislative procedure (Article 15.3). It is finally asserted that the Commission, "in carrying out its responsibilities shall be completely independent" (Article 15.4), as established by the Lisbon Treaty (TEU, Article 17).

After defining the parliamentary structure of the Union, the Proposal recognizes to the latter the power to lay out its own financial resources, a power to be shared by the EP and the Council. Both legislative institutions may establish, acting in accordance with the special legislative procedure, "a new category of own resources or abolish an existing

category. That decision shall not enter into force until it is approved
by four fifths of the States in accordance with their respective constitutional requirements." This concerns the possibility to lay down "provisions relating to a system of own resources specific to those States
whose currency is the euro. This revenue shall be assigned to the Union
budget as the fiscal capacity ... specific to those States" (Article 201).
The following Article celebrates the power of the EP and the Council,
acting through the ordinary legislative procedure, to adopt several
measures concerning taxation for the benefit of the Union, whose revenue shall accrue to the Union budget. The euro-area (or EMU) is
thus formalized as enhanced cooperation within the EU. According to
Article 218.2, "the Commission shall be responsible for driving forward the common economic policy and, in particular, through a treas-
ury facility, for the borrowing and lending of funds, the operation and
maintenance of the financial system, the collection of revenues, the
management of accounts, the enforcement of tax laws and the imposition of penalties," while Article 218.3 states "the European Central
Bank shall be responsible for the common monetary policy." Indeed,
Article 222.2 states: "the European Central Bank may purchase government bonds in the primary and secondary markets issued by States
whose currency is the euro and which are subject to a programme of
the European Stability Mechanism." Moreover, Article 224 states: "the
European Parliament and the Council, acting in accordance with the
special legislative procedure, and after having consulted the European
Central Bank, may establish for the States whose currency is the euro
a system for the common management of sovereign debt. Participation
in such a system shall be subject to strict conditionality."

Although the principle of intergovernmental coordination is formally recognized by the Proposal (Article 218.1 affirms that "the Union
shall adopt common fiscal, economic, and monetary policies which are
based on the close coordination of States' economic policies"), that
principle is then undercut by the parliamentary logic. Regarding the
procedure of excessive debt or deficit, it is still the Commission that
has the power to address an opinion to the State concerned "and shall
inform the European Parliament and the Council accordingly" (Article
225.5). And it is still the Council that "shall, on a proposal from the
Commission, after having consulted the European Parliament, and
having considered any observations which the State concerned may
wish to make, decide after an overall assessment whether an excessive

debt or deficit exists" (Article 225.6). However, an important addition is introduced in order to neutralize any intergovernmental drift. In fact, "in the case that the Council opposes the Commission's proposal, the European Parliament, at the request of the Commission, may adopt the decision. The Parliament *shall decide* by a majority of its component Members, acting within four weeks of the Council's decision to oppose the Commission's proposal" (Article 225.8, author's emphasis).

The institutional architecture and the policy powers of the EU emerging from the Proposal constitute an original elaboration of the parliamentary union perspective. Regarding the policy powers, the Commission, under the control of the EP and to a more limited extent of the Council, may take the necessary initiatives to deal with challenges like the financial crisis, having available a fiscal capacity derived from the Union's own taxes and the competences to impose discipline on indebted states. As in Germany, budgetary policy is defined by the executive, but then it should be approved by both the Bundestag and the Bundesrat. Indeed, it is in the Bundesrat that the budgetary laws are negotiated between the federal government and representatives of the *Länder* governments. At the same time, the ECB is not obstructed from acting as the lender of last resort, enjoying room for maneuver as do other central banks of federal unions or states. This policy framework would have certainly been effective in dealing with the euro crisis. However, it is the institutional architecture supporting it that raises compelling doubts about its viability. Although familiar in its shape, the institutional architecture proposed appears to have not a few unrealistic features.

First, the Proposal celebrates a Union institutionally organized around a trilateral decision-making system, represented by the EP, the Council and the Commission. The European Council, notwithstanding its steadfast and formidable decision-making growth and formal recognition by the Lisbon Treaty, is the great loser in this Proposal. If the European Council has come to play a political role in the EU, it does not seem realistic to assume that it would accept a downsizing of its role. It is unrealistic to assume that the heads of state and government of powerful EU member states will come to act like *Ministerpräsident* (minister-president) of the German *Länder* or premiers of Canadian provinces and the European Council as a sort of bureaucratic collegial head of state. Certainly the Proposal preserves the European Council's

prerogative to propose the candidate for Commission president; however, that prerogative has been highly circumscribed by the EP's power
to refuse his/her appointment. The Commission is accountable only to
the EP and only the EP may eventually dismiss it, thus electing a new
Commission. The Proposal confuses federal unions (such as the EU)
and federal states (such as Germany). In the former, the single states
matter in terms of creating and maintaining the union, while the same
cannot be said regarding federal states emerging from the disaggregation of a previously unitary state.

Second, the Proposal introduces a differentiation of roles between
the EP and the Council, with the lower chamber mattering more than
the higher chamber in the Commission's operations, which also seems
unrealistic. The assumption that the Council has to accept the EP's
decisions on the composition of the Commission, merely appointing the latter after a vote of consent of the EP, underestimates the
higher chamber's resources for opposing any attempt to transform it
into a German Bundesrat or Canadian Senate. It seems unlikely that
the Council will accept having important policy competences in specific and important fields but a very limited voice in the Commission's
formation and choices. Historically, the Council was at the origin of
the integration process and has continued to be a crucial stakeholder
in that process. A balance between the two legislative institutions
constitutes a systemic necessity for the EU. The parliamentary union
perspective can hardly accommodate that balance. Parliamentary federations recognize the governmental role only to the lower chamber.
But if the EP is the only legislative institution that matters for defining
the government of the Union, then Maltese voters would have much
less influence than German voters over that government. Owing to
the impossibility of having a homogeneous, trans-member state political competition in the EU, the parliamentary union perspective cannot solve the demographic asymmetry puzzle. Only if decision-making
power is diffused can Maltese voters then make their voice heard in
the Council through their governmental ministers or in the European
Council through their heads of government, also when a qualified
majority is required.

Third, the Proposal contradicts itself when it makes the Commission
accountable to the EP and at the same time preserves the independence of the former. If the Commission were to have the support of
the majority of the EP for pursuing its initiatives, if the Commission

were to be the government of the Union, if the EP were to have the power to fire the incumbent Commission and to substitute it with a new Commission president and members, how is it possible that the Commission can act as an independent institution? The Proposal is unable to solve this ambiguity. On the one hand, it is endeared to the tradition of the Commission as the independent institution representing the European interest and thus legitimated to keep the monopoly of legislative initiative, but on the other it is obliged to recognize that this tradition is incompatible with the parliamentary form of government. If the Commission is the government of the EU, then it cannot be an independent institution. It should express a clear political majority of the EP, as is assumed to emerge from the latter's elections. But if the Commission cannot be an independent executive branch, if the Commission is formed on the basis of partisan cleavages, then how can this be reconciled with its role of supervising respect for the Union's treaties and laws? And how can its decisions be accepted by those member state party governments that are not in tune with the EP coalition supporting the Commission?

The Proposal is a useful contribution to the debate on the future of the EU with regard, in particular, to the latter policy's competences in economic governance. However, its inspiration seems to derive from a previous period of the integration process. Notwithstanding its parliamentary features, the EU that emerged from the institutional transformations that took place between the Maastricht Treaty and the intergovernmental treaties adopted during the euro crisis does not correspond institutionally to parliamentarists' expectations. Even in the supranational constitution of single-market policies, the Lisbon Treaty has formalized a decision-making structure organized around a bicameral legislature (the EP and the Council) and a dual executive (the European Council and Commission). It is a quadrilateral decision-making system constituted by separate institutions unconnected by a vote of reciprocal *political* confidence, representative of different communities of interests, with distinct temporal mandates and bearers of different legitimacy patterns. The Proposal constitutes an attempt to simplify that separate decision-making structure, strengthening the role of the EP through the dethroning of the European Council and the downsizing of the influence of the Council. But simplification is not always the appropriate recipe for solving problems in complex organizations. Moreover, the parliamentary union perspective also has to face structural constraints that would be unaffected by any change in the Treaty.

6.5 The structural conditions of parliamentary federations

Comparative institutional analysis shows that parliamentary federations are structured institutionally on a highly differentiated bicameral legislature. In parliamentary federations only the lower chamber (the popular one) has the prerogative to give or to refuse its support to the government (a prerogative that epitomizes the governmental role of the popular legislature). The higher chamber (the one representing the territorial units) has important legislative prerogatives in particular policies (such as control of the budget and the power to raise taxes and to distribute their costs and benefits in the various components of the federation), but it does not intervene in the formation of the government (although it might influence it once it has been constituted). This legislative differentiation derives from different reasons. It is the outcome of a process of federalization through the disaggregation of a previously unitary state with the popular chamber well enough established to retain its governmental role (as in Belgium). But it is also the outcome of a specific constitutional tradition based on cabinet responsibility to the political majority of the lower chamber (as in Canada or Australia). Alternatively, it has derived from the need to preserve a center of governmental authority in a process of radical decentralization of territorial power (as in post-Second World War Germany)[5] (Burgess and Gagnon 2010). Yet these genetic and constitutional reasons should be seen in a larger structural context. Parliamentary federations require structural conditions that make possible the assignment to only the lower chamber of the governmental role. That is, the demography and culture of their states should not be too asymmetrical and differentiated. Let us consider the cases of Germany and Canada, among the most conspicuous Western parliamentary federations.[6]

---

[5] I do not consider the US and Swiss cases of federalism, because both, at the vertical level, are separation of powers, not parliamentary, systems (see Chapter 7). Indeed, they are federal unions.

[6] Regarding the other established cases of Western parliamentary federations, it is necessary to recall that in Austria (Erk 2004) and Australia (McKay 2001, chapter 5) also, the chamber representing respectively the nine *Länder* and the six states (plus several territories with various degrees of self-government)

After the Second World War, German *Länder* were drawn up by the Allied authorities (Jeffery and Saviger 1991) in order to guarantee a structural equilibrium among them, thus preventing the resurgence of a future territorial hegemonic actor (as happened in the pre-Weimar Republic experience with Prussia dominating the new German confederation: Ziblatt 2006). Only Bavaria, Saxony and the city states of Bremen and Hamburg pre-dated the *Länder* created in 1945 and thus formalized in the 1949 Basic Law. Many of the other *Länder* were created as new entities, as shown by their hyphenated names. In terms of asymmetry, the 1950 demographic ratio between the least populated *Land* (Bremen with 600,000 inhabitants) and the most populated one (North-Rhine Westphalia with 13,200,000 inhabitants) was 1:22. The ratio was inevitably affected by the subsequent demographic development of the country, but not radically altered. Indeed, in 2010 the ratio between Bremen (still the least populated *Land* with 660,706 inhabitants) and North-Rhine Westphalia (still the most populated *Land* with 17,854,154 inhabitants) was 1:26. The representation of relatively balanced relations between *Länder* in the Bundesrat (the legislative chamber representing the *Länder* executives), combined with a political community that has grown homogeneous in political cultural terms (also because of the constitutional ban on neo-Nazi and neo-Communist parties from participating in elections), has thus made it possible to organize a national political competition for the Bundestag (the popular chamber of the legislature) around the two main political parties of the center-right (Christian Democratic Union or CDU) and the center-left (Social Democratic Party or SPD). With the exception of the mainly catholic Bavaria (which has created its own version of Christian democracy – the CSU), the *Länder* have not displayed cultural or linguistic distinctions that could have prevented the development of trans-*Länder* homogeneous partisan competition. The five new *Länder*, which entered into the German Federal Republic with the 1990 reunification (see Appendix, Table A.4), even though they introduced new political issues and actors, have been

plays a minor role in policy-making vis-à-vis the popular chamber. The Belgian crisis seems to confirm that combining vertical decentralization with horizontal centralization is difficult when the territorial or cultural communities are not (or are perceived not to be) symmetrical in terms of capabilities (or demography) (Swender and Brans 2006). All three are federal states.

gradually absorbed into the established pattern of trans-*Länder* political competition.

Although Canada has a much more decentralized federal system than
Germany, the governmental role of the popular chamber (House of
Commons) has been undisputed. According to Fossum and Menéndez
(2011: 183), the founding constitutional act of 1867 "establishes an
institutional structure and a division of competences with a clear centralizing orientation. Indeed, the ensuing Canadian federal model was
a model of parliamentary federalism, based on parliamentary government at both key levels of government." These parliamentary institutions (Fossum and Menéndez 2011: 189) "were ... not simply the
product of imperial UK rule; they were also the products of colonists
struggling to replace oligarchies with elected systems of responsible
government." Notwithstanding the multinational identity of the federation, the centrality of the popular chamber has never been challenged
by the other chamber, a Senate that has remained institutionally weak.
Although Canada is composed of ten provinces and three territories,
the 105 members of the Senate are not only appointed by the governor
general on the advice of the prime minister (expressing the political
majority in the House of Commons), but their seats are assigned on a
regional – and not on a provincial – basis, with each of the four major
regions receiving 24 seats and the remainder of the available seats
being assigned to smaller territories (Smith 2010).

Demography has helped the process of consolidation of the
parliamentary-federal model. In 1951 the ratio between the least populated province (Prince Edward Island with 99,285 inhabitants) and the
most populated one (Ontario with 4,597,542 inhabitants) was 1:46.
The post-Second World War demographic development has increased
the ratio between the two provinces (in 2006, it was 1:89 with Prince
Edward Island still the least populated province with 135,000 inhabitants, and Ontario still the most populated one with 12,600,000 inhabitants), but not to the point of questioning the House of Commons'
political role. Moreover, the process of parliamentarization of the
federation has been eased by the fact that Canadian provinces have
never displayed constitutional distinctiveness vis-à-vis the national
government and each other (Smith 1993),[7] notwithstanding the deep

---

[7] As Smith (1993: 133) reported: "the Canadian situation differs markedly
from that of the United States where, despite the prevalence of common
political norms, the American states display unusual (by Canadian standards)

linguistic division between the French-speaking Quebec and the other English-speaking provinces. The relation between the center and the provinces, rather than through the Senate, has been structured much more by the meetings of the federal prime minister with the prime ministers of the provinces, according to a model defined (Gagnon 2010) as "executive federalism." The recognition of the linguistic distinctiveness of French-speaking Quebec has contributed to triggering a high territorial decentralization in many policies, but this decentralization has not called into question the exclusive role of the House of Commons in the formation of the government. It seems plausible to argue that, in federal states or federations by disaggregation, parliamentarization has been made possible not only by a deep-rooted constitutional tradition, but also by favorable structural conditions (such as relative demographic and economic symmetry and a relatively homogeneous party competition between and within territorial units). The combination of these conditions has legitimated the popular chamber of the legislature to play an exclusive governmental role, consolidating the parliamentary model.

These conditions have been lacking in the EU. If the formation of the "government" is assigned exclusively to the EP, then the least populous member state (i.e. Malta with its 408,000 inhabitants in 2011) will have an evident smaller influence than the most populous member state (i.e. Germany with its 81,471,834 inhabitants in 2011), notwithstanding the criterion of degressive proportionality. The 2011 demographic ratio between the least and the most populous member states was 1:202 (that is six times higher than the 2010 German ratio). Such asymmetry would be necessarily difficult to manage within a single representative institution, unless a trans-member state competition based on parties representing relatively homogeneous supra-state ideological programs and identities could develop. Regional and member state divisions (due not only to their size, but also to their different national language and culture, economic model, regional location and social structure) have, however, weakened partisan attempts to order them into the left vs. right format. The growing party vote registered in the EP (Hix, Noury and Roland 2006) concerned low politics,

constitutional distinctiveness *vis-à-vis* the national government and each other. State constitution-making itself is a venerable activity; in Canada the phrase and concept are empty of meaning."

not high politics. In high politics (such as constitutional or budgetary issues), the parties were unable to neutralize internal national divisions. As shown by the post-2009 euro crisis, divisions between member states have been much more relevant than those between political parties. These economic and political interstate divisions cannot be managed by the EP alone. A German or Canadian model adopted in the EU would be unable to represent these interstate cleavages.

Certainly, the parliamentary federations of Germany and Canada are based on asymmetries between territorial units and both include cultural differentiation between citizens or communities (one has only to think of the religious divide in Germany or the linguistic divide in Canada). That notwithstanding, those asymmetries and differentiations have been manageable by political parties (with necessary adaptation, in Canada in particular). Although it seems implausible to identify the degree of demographic symmetry and cultural compatibility between territorial units and their citizens that would need to be respected in order to have a parliamentary federation, the comparison of the German and Canadian cases has shown that such a degree exists when it can be managed by political parties. Without those favorable structural conditions, it would have been impossible to develop a homogeneous trans-*Länder* or trans-provincial party system underpinning the governmental centrality of the popular legislature. The popular or lower chamber can play its channeling role of the electoral and decision-making processes only if the same political actors run in all the territorial units in order to win the majority of its seats. A parliamentary federation in the EU would thus require the existence of a transnational electorate dividing itself according to partisan rather than national preferences. In this case, the main parties might consequently represent the main division within the EP. In the EU, the degree of demographic asymmetry and cultural/national differentiation is too high to be synthetized in a trans-state partisan cleavage. A change of the Treaty would not affect this structural context.

6.6 Conclusion

This chapter has investigated the rationale of the parliamentary union perspective. It has reconstructed the process of institutionalization of the EP (in single market policies), with regard to both its external role and internal organization. It has then analyzed the institutional features that both support and contradict the parliamentary union perspective on the EU. This chapter has then discussed the most recent and original proposal of setting up a parliamentary union through the substitution of the Lisbon Treaty with a new fundamental law. The analysis has shown that, whereas the policy competences framework of the Union advanced by the new fundamental law is certainly plausible, the same cannot be said for the institutional structure supporting those competences. In particular, this chapter has shown that, from an institutional point of view, the parliamentary perspective continues to consider the EU (also with a change of the Treaty) as organized around a trilateral decision-making system, with the EP, the Council and the Commission.

There is no room, in this perspective, for the European Council, notwithstanding its dramatic decision-making growth since the explosion of the euro crisis. Although the Commission's power of legislative initiative has been formally preserved, the Commission's initiatives have clearly come from European Council's political inputs. As Curtin (2014: 9) observed, "the European Council calls the shots in general terms and largely tells the Commission (and the Council) what to do if formal legislation needs to be adopted." It is certainly valuable to bring the king (the executive power) back to the parliament (the legislative power). But if the king is not only the Commission, to bring the latter under the EP's control does not seem the solution to the question of the democratic accountability of those taking decisions in the EU. If the European Council has come to play an executive role, then the different electoral source and political representativeness of the European Council and the Commission constitute an obstacle to the formation of a unitary parliamentary executive. Certainly, the Lisbon Treaty does not prevent considering, as Vivian Reding did, the possibility of recomposing the two presidencies (of the European Council and the Commission) into one single role, thus approaching a unitary executive. However, it seems highly implausible to assume that the heads of state and government of the European Council would accept being led by an official elected by the EP.

This chapter has finally adopted a comparative perspective on parliamentary federations, considering two of the main cases of the democratic world (Germany and Canada), in order to identify the conditions that make possible, or do not obstruct, the functioning of a parliamentary federation. The comparison has shown that parliamentary federations depend on various specific factors, concerning the genetic origin of the federation, the constitutional culture that has inspired the federation's formation, and the institutional tradition in force when the federation was inaugurated. However, structural factors should also be considered, namely the demographic symmetry between the territorial units constituting the federation, combined with their cultural commonality. Those genetic, institutional and structural conditions have been lacking in the EU.

If the intergovernmental union perspective is based on the necessity of keeping the decision-making power of the Union within the perimeter of relations between the European Council and the Council, the parliamentary union perspective is based on the necessity of keeping the decision-making power of the Union within the perimeter of relations between the EP and the Commission. The former perspective derives from the assumption that only intergovernmental institutions can deal effectively with the crucial issues of integration (as is the case with the EMU); the latter perspective derives from the assumption that only the EP and the Commission can legitimately advance integration also in those crucial areas. Both assumptions are questionable. The intergovernmental assumption has failed because effectiveness cannot be guaranteed by a decision-making process based on voluntary coordination, nor can governments' legitimacy be transferred from the national to the European level. The parliamentary assumption is unpersuasive even in single market policies because of its difficulty in recognizing that effectiveness and legitimacy cannot derive only from citizens' representatives. Although all the perspectives discussed in Part II of this book (the *economic community*, the *intergovernmental union* and the *parliamentary union*) have their justification in one or other component of the Lisbon Treaty, none of them has offered a comprehensive answer to the question of how to promote effectiveness and legitimacy in a union of asymmetrical states and differentiated citizenries. The euro crisis has eventually challenged their coexistence within the same legal and institutional order, raising a dramatic question concerning the very future of the EU. It is time to investigate whether a new perspective on the Union can be identified and a new political order for Europe can be devised.

PART III

Towards the compound union perspective

7 | *Comparing democratic models*

7.1 Introduction

The previous three perspectives have been based on weak analytical grounds because they have not recognized the precise nature of the EU and its democratic functioning. The economic community perspective has unrealistically equated the EU to a regional economic organization. The intergovernmental union perspective has assumed the EU as a *sui generis* union of governments. The parliamentary union perspective has considered the EU as a variant of the federal state, where European citizens matter more than national governments. However, the EU is not a simple economic community; it is more than a union of national governments; it is different from a national federal state. If it is a federal union of states, under which model of democracy does a federal union function? I call it the *compound* democracy model (S. Fabbrini 2010) and its combination with the political division and institutional features of a federal union is at the basis of the *compound union* perspective.

This perspective also has both a descriptive and prescriptive character. In order to meet the first requirement (*analytical description*), it is essential to identify the democratic models of established political systems; that is, the institutional and functional properties that distinguish, first, the different democratic models adopted by nation states and, second, the models of democracy of nation states and the model of democracy of unions of states. Once the model of democracy adopted by unions of states has been identified, then in Chapter 8 I will come back to the EU to compare it with the other unions of states in order to detect similarities and dissimilarities between them. Only on these analytical bases will it then be possible to advance prescriptive proposals for reforming the EU in coherence with the democratic logic of unions of states (as I will do in Chapter 9). A democratic model does not coincide with the specific constitutional form of a political system,

although it is affected by that form, but it conceptualizes the logic
through which a political system takes decisions, combining representation (legitimacy) and governability (effectiveness). Since a democratic model is an empirical concept, it reflects a system of divisions
as it can be interpreted by the main political actors in a given institutional structure. In my CP approach, a democratic model embodies the
modality for reaching political decisions in a given political system.
This modality will institutionalize only if it is congenial with a specific
structure of both political divisions and inter-institutional relations (in
my case, between legislative and executive powers).

In this chapter I will consider twenty-four democratic political systems, corresponding to at least twenty-six relevant empirical cases for
comparative analysis.[1] All of them are established democratic systems.
By established democratic systems, I refer to those democracies that
have been stable for a sufficiently long period of time so as to allow for
a verifiable interpretation of their functioning. Twenty-one countries
have been uninterruptedly democratic for the entire period since the end
of the Second World War, whereas Greece, Spain and Portugal adopted
a democratic system in the mid 1970s (see Appendix, Table A.4). Both
France and Italy have witnessed significant changes in the functioning
of their political systems. In France this took place by means of the
adoption of a new constitution in 1958 that formalized the transition
from the parliamentary Fourth Republic to the semi-presidential Fifth
Republic (see Glossary). On the contrary, no change of the constitution was introduced in Italy with regard to the governmental system
(in the period concerned). Only the electoral system was reformed in
1993, a change that nevertheless modified the functioning of the political system, thus giving rise to the so-called Second Republic as distinct
from the First Republic of the preceding period (the reformed electoral
law of 1993 was changed again in December of 2005, though keeping
the previous majoritarian thrust). Accordingly, by Italy of the Second
Republic I mean the period 1994–2013.

In the context of these twenty-six empirical cases, I will argue that
nation states have adopted (at least) two different democratic models.

---

[1] In order not to complicate the analysis, I will not consider the political systems
of the Eastern European countries that have emerged from the process of
democratization that started in the 1990s. In fact several of those countries are
still in a phase of consolidation, also due to the ongoing transformation in the
organization and identity of their main political actors.

These models, notwithstanding their differences, display common functional and institutional properties, namely a political process based on partisan divisions (expression of a specific *social structure*) and an institutional (or more specifically, a decision-making) structure based on a government as the locus of the last decision (which I conceptualize as *governmental structure*). This is not the case for the democratic model adopted by unions of states. This model differs from those of nation states both functionally and institutionally. In unions of states the political process is based on interstate and not only partisan divisions and the institutional structure is not characterized by a government as a single institution monopolizing the ultimate decision. Once the functional and institutional properties of the model of democracy adopted by unions of states are identified, then it is possible, in the next chapter, to compare the democratic unions of states (the USA and Switzerland among the established democracies) with the EU. Here I will proceed as follows. First, I will discuss the concept of the model of democracy as elaborated by the CP literature, pointing out the functional and institutional properties that are instrumental to my comparison. Second, I will examine the models of democracy adopted by nation states (unitary and federal), distinguishing between competitive and consensus democracies. Although these models differ on several variables and although important variants can be detected within each of them, nevertheless both models presuppose common functional and institutional properties. Those properties make the models of democracy of nation states (unitary and federal) structurally different from the model of democracy that has come to be developed in those federal unions (the USA and Switzerland) emerging from the aggregation of previously independent and separate states. Then this chapter will analyze the latter's model of democracy, identifying its functional and institutional properties. Finally, it will conclude by discussing the model of democracy of unions of states in the context of the models of democracy of nation states. On the basis of this comparative exercise, the EU will then be analyzed in the following chapter.

7.2 Models of democracy: nation states

The analytical approach to comparing different ways of organizing the political process in democratic systems was mainly introduced, and subsequently developed, by Arend Lijphart (1984, 1989, 1999). Lijphart's analysis highlighted how the various national democracies have developed different institutional arrangements in order to guarantee the democratic continuity of their respective political systems. On this basis, Lijphart developed a key typological distinction between consensus democracies and Westminster-type or majoritarian democracies.

Lijphart's two models of democracy differ along several institutional variables which he (Lijphart 1999: 21) subsumes under two separate dimensions: *parties-executive* and *federal-unitary*. Concerning the first dimension, Westminster-type democracies are characterized by the concentration of executive power in single-party majoritarian governments, the dominance of the executive in its relations with the legislature, a two-party system and a majoritarian electoral system. Consensus democracies, instead, are characterized by the management of executive power through multi-party coalitions, a balance of power between the executive and the legislature, a multi-party system and a PR electoral system. Concerning the second dimension, Westminster democracies are characterized by unitary and centralized governments, concentration of legislative power in unicameral parliaments, flexible constitutions and parliaments that have the last word on their legislation. Consensus democracies, instead, are characterized by decentralized (federal or federalized) states, powerful bicameral legislature (although functionally differentiated), rigid constitutions that can be changed only by qualified majorities, and legal systems in which legislation is subject to constitutional review by the supreme or constitutional court.

Lijphart has shown how, after the Second World War, democratic countries have come to be organized according to two different models of democratic politics, respectively consistent with a majoritarian or consensual political logic. The adoption of a specific model of democracy has been conditioned by the particular national historical development of the country concerned. However, one factor, above all, explains that adoption, namely the political culture. According to Lijphart, the political culture of the elites and the political culture of the citizens constitute the independent variables that inform the choice of the model of democracy (Peters 2013). Lijphart has thus constructed his typology of Westminster and consensus democracies precisely by linking the political culture of the elites and the citizens.

By also taking into account research conducted by others (in particular Daalder 1995), Lijphart (2008) has shown how majoritarian or Westminster democracies historically presuppose the existence of a relatively homogeneous society in terms of the political culture of the elites and citizens; a society in which the main cleavage revolves around the diversity of material conditions (according to the left vs. right pattern). In consensus democracies instead, the society is culturally non-homogenous, not only because it is marked by deep and multiple cleavages, but above all because the cultural identities of the various groups have reproduced in distinct ways (due to linguistic, religious, ethnic and, at times, ideological diversity). It follows that the party system representing this multitude of identities has come to evolve in the direction of a set of culturally (and at times ideologically) differentiated actors. In short, the social and territorial pluralism of these societies also corresponds to a pluralism of political cultures, that is to a non-homogenous political culture. As a result, the social cleavages reflect a diversity of cultures, if not of ideologies.

Lijphart's contribution to the understanding of empirical democracies has been monumental (Crepaz, Koelble and Wilsford 2000). I have already followed his lead by employing typologies in order to compare established democracies (Fabbrini and Molutsi 2012). Here, however, I will base my conceptualization of models of democracy on their logic of functioning, rather than on a set of institutional rules and practices. As did Dahl (1989: 5), I will consider as logic of functioning of a specific democratic model the latter's "process of making collective and binding decisions." In this approach, the democratic model is the answer to the question: why do democracies take decisions in a different way? This helps me, first, to redefine the two basic ideal-types of democratic model of nation states and, second, to show their incongruity in terms of conceptualizing the model of democracy of unions of states. Thus, looking to Lijphart's dimension of parties/executives, that is to the relation between representation and decision-making, two assumptions can be made. First, the making of a representative system cannot be explained only through a static description of electoral rules. Indeed, a majoritarian outcome has also emerged in countries adopting PR electoral systems, because the latter's centrifugal effects have been restrained not only by specific technical devices that have reduced

their proportionality,[2] but also by a party system already functioning according to a bipolar logic. Electoral rules and party systems
should thus be considered as relatively independent variables that
dynamically structure the process of formation of the representation system.[3] The differential impact of their dynamic interaction
on the process of forming the representation system cannot be
explained by the mere description of the electoral rules. On this
basis, it is possible to redefine the two Lijphart ideal-types of democracy, distinguishing between democracies functioning on alternation in government of opposite political options (regardless of their
PR electoral systems) and democracies functioning on consociation
in government of those different political options (because of the
cleavages they express).

Second, the structure of what is called the "executive" affects the
very logic of functioning of a democratic system. An "executive" is not
a behavioral construct, but a structured governmental system. There
are two basically different ways of structuring the decision-making
process in established democracies: either fusion or separation of powers. Their institutional differentiation affects the way representation is
translated into collective and binding decisions. Indeed, both Lijphart's
ideal-types of Westminster and consensus democracies presuppose the
existence of a *government as the institution of last decision*, an institution where the decision-making logic of either ideal-types can be
regularized. But the existence of a government as the institution of
last decision implies a *fusion of powers system*, a system where legislative and executive powers are not only interdependent institutions but
also politically connected or *fused* through the "efficient secret" of the
party's or multi-parties' majority (see Glossary). Although the formation of the government is different in the Westminster and consensus
democracies, since it is the immediate outcome of the election in the
former and of post-electoral negotiation in the latter, nevertheless in
both democracies there exists a government that crystallizes the outcome of the political process.

---

[2] In the case of Germany, for instance, one has to think of the 5 percent threshold
of the total vote that a party must overcome to accede to the distribution
of parliamentary seats or to the allocation through uninominal districts of
50 percent of the seats pertaining to the parties according to the PR vote.

[3] On the reciprocal independent correlation between the electoral system and the
party system, it is still necessary to read Sartori (1976).

However, this is not the only institutional model adopted for organizing the governmental decision-making process. In fact, there are democracies where there is not an institution that is the locus of the ultimate decision-making power. Rather the executive and legislative institutions are separated, not only by the constitution but above all by the different institutional interests that each of them represents, and both contribute to the decision-making process. These are *systems of separation of powers* (see Glossary). In both fusion and separation of powers systems, legislative, executive and judiciary powers are *divided* according to Montesquieu's logic, but that division is organized institutionally in different ways in each of them. In the former, institutions are fused and the functions are distinct; in the latter the institutions are separate and the functions are shared. If a democratic model consists of the way in which collective and binding decisions are taken, then the different organization of the governmental system will inevitably have an impact on that process.

Among our twenty-six empirical cases of established democracy, only two have adopted distinct forms of separation of powers, namely the USA and Switzerland. Both are cases of federation by aggregation and both started as federal unions of previously independent states or cantons. In both cases, the political process concerns divisions between states or cantons and not only parties, and in both cases there is not a government as an institution of the ultimate decision. Owing to these logical and institutional features, it seems improper to interpret these democracies (as Lijphart and his followers did, see next chapter) as cases closer to one (Switzerland to the consensus) or the other (the USA to the majoritarian) ideal-type models of democracy. Consensus democracy cannot be confused with an attitude to negotiation between institutions (as in Switzerland). It is certainly true that in Switzerland the search for consensus is the aim of the political actors, but that consensus concerns primarily the relation between cantons more than between parties. Nor can majoritarian democracy be confused with the alternation of different party candidates in the presidency (as in the USA). It is certainly true that in the USA the election for the presidency displays a majoritarian logic, but it is not true that the latter extends to the entire governmental system. If institutions matter, then separation of powers systems are inhospitable to either the majoritarian or consensual logic of taking decisions. In short, the USA and Switzerland have a different political logic and institutional system relative to the other democracies because they are unions of states and not nation states (even if federal or federalized).

7.3 National competitive and consensus democracies

Redefining the typology

Given the above specifications, then Lijphart's typology of democratic models can be translated into a more comprehensive and realistic distinction between consensus democracies[4] and competitive democracies.[5] One might define competitive democracies as those democracies where decisions are taken through alternation in government of opposite parties or political coalitions. Consensus democracies, instead, are those democracies where decisions are taken through consociation in government of different parties and political options. Both democracies have an institutional (governmental) structure that creates incentives, in the former, for competition between the main alternative parties for exclusive control of the government and, in the latter, for agreement between the main parties in order to share control of the government. In competitive democracies the political elites have a cultural predisposition to exclude the minority from the exercise of governmental power, whereas in consensus democracies the political elites have a cultural predisposition to exercise power in a mutually inclusive way. In competitive democracies parties can be mutually adversarial, while this political attitude is considered improper in consensus democracies. In both cases there is a government to be won either through a process that encourages alternation or through a process that encourages consociation. The political logic of competitive democracies is fuelled by the distinction between government and opposition, whereas in consensus democracies it is guided by the reciprocal

---

[4] I use Lijphart's definition of "consensus democracies" because it is now largely accepted in the scientific debate. However, it would be wrong to think that the search for consensus is peculiar to these democracies only. "Consensus" here refers to a way of organizing the political decision-making process.

[5] I prefer the term competitive democracies to majoritarian or Westminster democracies (used by Lijphart) because the latter definitions are connoted by specific institutions (such as the majoritarian electoral system) or by similarity with specific national cases (that of the UK). It goes without saying that democracy and competition do not coincide of necessity, and this is why their coincidence gives rise to a particular democratic model.

accommodation (or consociation) between the various minorities. It follows that competitive democracies have the possibility of replacing the government of one coalition or party with its competitor,[6] whereas consensus democracies are characterized by the necessity of enlarging the support of the governing majority with respect to the parties representing significant minorities.[7]

Although both democracies imply the existence of an institutional structure that channels the political process towards winning the government, they do, however, reflect different social divisions. The former are marked primarily by socio-economic divisions between the citizens and the latter are marked by socio-cultural divisions between the citizens. As Rokkan (1999), Daalder (1995) and Lijphart (1999) have argued, the dynamic of the party system in a given democracy tends to be correlated to the structure of the latter's social divisions or cleavages. A cleavage is a dividing line between groups or units that becomes relevant when it is transformed into the source of a recurrent party representation and action. In consensus democracies the cleavage is between cultural communities, that is, social groups defined by their linguistic, religious or ethnic identities, communities that are generally territorially concentrated. In competitive democracies the cleavage is not based on the differentiation of cultural identities, but on social and economic interests. National societies fractured along identity lines cannot be hospitable to alternation in government: the cultural community excluded from governmental power might be legitimately afraid to be colonized by the cultural community controlling the government. This fear is less plausible in a national society where the divisions concern different economic conditions or professional occupations, not different value systems.

---

[6] At this level of analysis it is irrelevant to consider the forms taken by the alternation in government, whether it is absolute or relative or whether it is between a party and a coalition of parties.

[7] Here, instead, the difference is between an enlargement of the governing coalition that may include all the relevant parties (as in consensus democracies with ethnic-cultural divisions) or an enlargement of the governing coalition that excludes some of the relevant parties (as in consensus democracies with ideological-cultural divisions, because of the presence of parties advocating the overthrow of the democratic system, commonly defined as anti-system parties: Sartori 1976). The ethnic-cultural division and the ideological-cultural division are two species of the genus "socio-cultural divisions."

Table 7.1 *National democracies: competitive vs. consensus*

		Institutional (governmental) structure (fusion of powers)	
		alternation in government	consociation in government
Social structure	socio-economic cleavages	*competitive democracies*	
	socio-cultural cleavages		*consensus democracies*

Combining the institutional structure (constituted by representative and decision-making institutions: Shugart 2006) and the social structure (the structure of divisions or cleavages between citizens: Rokkan 1999), connected through the electoral party process, it is possible to detect why in some democracies decisions are taken by means of the predictable alternation in government of competing political groupings (parties or coalitions) and in other democracies decision-making proceeds by consociation in government of the main political parties. The two different concepts are not the mechanical outcome of the nature of social cleavages: the latter affect political behavior through their shaping of the political culture of the main parties or actors. In both cases we are dealing with the function of democracy in nation states (see Table 7.1).

In competitive democracies, alternation is possible when the party in opposition manages to obtain a majority by associating its own core electorate with a part of the electorate located in the center of the political space (and generally constituted by independent voters). Where alternation is not suitable and the platforms of the political parties are distant, each of them will tend to guard their own position in the electoral space. Thus the formation of the government is not the outcome of the shifting preferences of the electorate at the center of the electoral space, but of top-level post-electoral agreements between the parties' elites. In these democracies no single party succeeds in obtaining a majority, and even if it should do so, it will prefer not to govern alone in order not to arouse suspicion, alarm and distrust on the part of the other parties. After all, the incompatibility between the political parties makes it quite unlikely that the interests of the minority can somehow be represented by the majority. Consensus democracies are characterized by the political difficulty of tolerating a regular alternation in government, not by the constitutional impossibility of doing so. Consensus democracies know no constitutional obstacles to alternation in government, but it is the nature of their society and the incentives of the institutional system that promote the recourse to consociation rather than competition for the control of the government.

Not only should these two models of democracy be interpreted as two poles on a continuum between which the various empirical cases may be located,[8] but the way in which these models function may also change over time or in particular circumstances of crisis or national emergency. Thus competitive democracies may embrace a consensual logic when faced with a particular domestic or external challenge (giving rise to a grand coalition government between the major political parties, as happened in Germany), whereas consensus democracies may be driven to adopt a competitive logic (giving rise to alternation in government of the main political contenders, as happened in the Netherlands). However, barring any structural change in the social divisions and a revision of the rules governing the institutional (governmental) structure, it is implausible that such changes in the political logic will prove to be durable.

National competitive democracies

Because the crucial distinction between the two models of democracies resides in the way the government is formed and then collective and binding decisions are taken, the characteristics of the specific institutional variables must be assessed in terms of their contribution to that outcome, rather than in terms of their strictly formal nature. In this regard, one may discern several empirical variants. Concerning competitive democracies, the first specific variant to be considered is the electoral and party system. In addition to the countries that have adopted a majoritarian electoral system (such as the UK, New Zealand until the early 1990s, Australia, Canada and France during the Fifth Republic), a competitive logic for conquering government has manifested itself also in countries that have adopted PR electoral systems,

[8] Even Lijphart (1999) was forced to locate almost half of the national cases he considered on an intermediate point between the Westminster model and the consensus model.

equipped, however, with technical devices that serve to reduce their degree of proportionality, such as Germany, Sweden, Ireland and Norway, and also Greece and Spain. Similarly, some mixed electoral systems, such as Second Republic Italy during 1994–2013 and Japan after 1994, have also witnessed an alternation between coalitions of the center-left and center-right (see Box 7.1).

Box 7.1 – Alternation in government in competitive democracies

In the UK the Labour Party and the Conservatives have alternated in government, and in New Zealand the Labour Party and the conservative National Party did so too. Both were cases of single-party governments. In New Zealand, Labour and the Conservatives have also remained the main parties after the electoral reform of the 1990s; the same is true in the UK, notwithstanding that the elections of 2010 led to a coalition government of Conservatives and Liberal Democrats, the first time there has been a coalition government in the UK since the end of the Second World War. In Australia, alternation in government has been between the Labour Party and a coalition of the Liberal Party and the National Party. In Canada, the Liberal Party and the Conservatives have alternated in government: here also governments are made up of one party only. In Fifth Republic France, the alternation in government has concerned the conservative-Gaullist bloc and a coalition of socialists and communists. Since the 2000s the alternation has been between two parties and no longer between two groupings (Conservatives and Socialists).

In Germany, alternation at the helm of the government started in 1969, with a coalition of Social Democrats and Liberals, which, after three years of a grand coalition between Christian Democrats and Social Democrats, came to replace the previous coalition of Christian Democrats and Liberals. Starting in the 1990s, alternation involved a coalition of Social Democrats and Greens on the one hand, and Christian Democrats and Liberals on the other. The unification of the country in 1990 has provoked a stalemate of the political system, prompting the birth of a new grand coalition of Christian Democrats and Social Democrats between 2005 and 2009 and then after 2013, while the bipolar logic returned between 2009 and 2013. In Sweden, the government has alternated between the Social Democratic Party and a coalition of parties from the so-called bourgeois bloc. In Ireland, alternation has involved the Republican Party and a coalition of progressives and labourites. In Norway, alternation has involved the Labour Party and a rather varied coalition of parties, among which are usually the Christian Democratic Party and the Center Party.

After the end of the military regime and two governments of national unity headed by Karamanlis between July and November of 1974, Greece has experimented with a regular alternation between the conservative New Democracy Party and the Socialist Party, although the latter formed a grand coalition government in times of crisis, such as during 1989–1993 or after 2012 in the context of the financial bankruptcy of the country. After the end of the Franco regime in 1979, Spain has experimented with alternation in government between the Popular Party and the Socialist Party, from time to time supported by regionalist parties (the Catalan party in particular).

Accordingly the model of competitive democracy can also be adopted when the bipolar dynamics of the party system manages to impose itself on the PR formula of the electoral system (see Appendix, Table A.5). Moreover, in competitive democracies adopting a PR electoral system, the executive is preferably held by a coalition and the legislatures constitute a not insignificant arena of the system of government.

The second specific variant to consider concerns the state system: consolidated competitive countries such as Australia, Canada, Germany and Spain have adopted a decentralized state system (federal in the first three cases and federalized in the last case), even if not all of them are territorially segmented societies. Decentralized (in particular federal) state systems are the outcome of a constitutional process of territorial devolution of powers decided or negotiated at the center between territorial and central elites. In the cases considered here, the level of decentralization is different, but not the genetic logic that led to decentralization. They are all cases of federalization by disaggregation of a previously unitary nation state or dominion. As a result of that, the center has retained crucial competences. The process of federalization has generally led to a re-elaboration of the national identity of the country, but the more radical re-elaboration has also tried to preserve it, through a combination of tradition and convenience. Indeed, these are federal states. The constitutional or quasi-constitutional federal pact promotes a logic of accommodation of the differences between their various territorial units and between them and the center, either within the formal institutions of territorial representation (the Senate of Australia, the German Bundesrat and the Senado de España) or through informal mechanisms of territorial governance (such as, in Canada, the meeting of Canada's provincial premiers with the federal prime minister or, in Spain, the bilateral meeting of the Spanish prime minister with the president of each *comunidad autónoma* and in particular the most prominent, such as Catalonia). The decentralized nature of the state system does not change the overall model of democracy, nor has it called into question the national unity of the country (although periodic attempts have been made, in Spain by separatist movements in Catalonia or the Basque countries, or in Canada by the Mouvement souverainiste du Québec). In these countries, federalism has preserved (or it has aimed to preserve) a pluralist national identity, precisely through the recognition of its internal differentiation. It might be useful to define as competitive centralized those democracies characterized by a competitive logic in the party-executive dimension supported by a unitary or centralized state; and as competitive non-centralized those democracies that display a competitive logic in the functioning of the party-executive dimension, while being characterized by a consensual logic in the state dimension (i.e. in the relations between the center and the territorial units). However, the latter democracies have preserved their competitive logic (in the first dimension) because the legislative chamber representing the territorial units does not play any role in the formation or in the dismissal of the government (it does not have the power of giving confidence to or withdrawing it from the cabinet).

In short, considering the institutional variables in a static way, only very few countries (the UK in particular, after New Zealand moved towards a mitigated PR electoral system in the early 1990s) have a majoritarian electoral system, a one-party government acting in a formal or de facto mono-cameral legislature (although the UK has experienced a coalition government after the elections of 2010) and a centralized state system (although subject to a process of contrasted devolution). If one considers instead the dynamic interaction of the electoral and party systems, then those democracies adopting a (highly mitigated) PR electoral system combined with a party system functioning according to a bipolar logic (such as Germany) can also be classified as competitive. At the same time, the empirical analysis reveals the persistence of a competitive logic in the party-executive dimension also in countries (such as Australia, Canada or Germany) whose state system is organized in a federal way. However, the consensual logic of the federal or federalized state system has been able to coexist with the competitive logic promoted by the characteristics of the electoral and party system on one crucial condition – that only the popular chamber (the one representing the voters), and not the chamber representing the territorial units (the states or the provinces or the *Länder* or the *comunidades autónomas*), has the power to give confidence to or withhold it from the government. This differentiation of functions, between the two chambers of the legislature, is essential for combining parliamentary government with a decentralized (federal or federalized) state system.

National consensus democracies

In the case of consensus democracies, some specific variants also need to be considered. There is no variation at the level of the electoral system, just as there are no empirical cases of consensus democracies with majoritarian electoral systems. The variants that do not alter the overall model concern the composition of the government. The sharing of executive power may exhibit different characteristics depending on the type of predominant cleavage represented by the multi-party system. In countries such as Belgium, the Netherlands, Austria and, to a lesser extent, Luxembourg, where the cultural (i.e. linguistic and religious) cleavage has been predominant, the sharing of governmental power was able to take the form of a coalition open to all the relevant parties. Similar coalitions have also been formed in countries such as Finland, Iceland and Israel where the plurality of cleavages became intertwined (especially during the Cold War period) with a particular geopolitical location that promoted defensive agreements between the main political parties. The influence of the Cold War also made a considerable mark in Austria, a country that emerged defeated from the Second World War. Thus the consensual predisposition favored by the division between Catholics and Socialists was further strengthened by the need to unite a country that had experienced military occupation for a long time after the end of the Second World War.

Where the ideological (communists vs. anti-communists) cleavage was predominant instead, as in Italy during the First Republic (1948–1993) and France during the Fourth Republic (1946–1958), the consociation in the government had to stop at the communist line. Any governmental coalition was not open to the communist parties (despite their electoral strength) as they were allies or supporters of the Soviet Union (i.e. of the rival power of the geopolitical bloc to which those countries belonged). This situation was held in equilibrium by a powerful legislature, where those parties could be associated in varying degrees with the parliamentary majority in contributing to the law-making process[9] (see Box 7.2). This difference between the two consensus democracies can also be detected in the strength of parliamentary support for the government. For example, in Fourth Republic France and in Italy during the First Republic this support never exceeded, on average, 52.5 percent and 55 percent of the seats respectively, whereas in the consensus democracies with coalitions open to all the relevant parties, this percentage was much higher. For example, during the period 1945–1995 (Lane, McKay and Newton 1997), the figure was, on average, 56.2 percent of the seats in Finland, 61 percent in the Netherlands, 61.6 percent in Belgium, 65.5 percent in Israel (1949–1995), 68.2 percent in Luxembourg and an impressive 92.9 percent in Austria.

---

[9] Here I do not enter into the debate about the theory of coalitions. For the sake of my analysis, what matters relative to the consensus democracies is the qualitative difference between coalitions open to all relevant parties and coalitions that are closed to some relevant parties. Concerning the definition of relevant party (or party that matters), suffice it to say, following Sartori (1976), that the parties that do not matter are those that have neither coalition potential nor threat potential. The coalitions of the competitive democracies are a different matter. They generally are of a minimum winning size, i.e. composed of the minimum number of parties necessary to have a governing majority. In some cases minority governments are formed.

Box 7.2 – Consociation in government in consensus democracies

In Belgium the governing coalition was regularly based on the Flemish Christian Peoples Party, the Walloon Christian Social Party, the Walloon Socialist Party and the Flemish Socialist Party. However, between 1999 and 2004 the Christian parties were excluded from government as the result of a coalition between the Socialist parties and the Flemish Liberals. A long crisis developed between 2007–2011. After the election of 2010 it took 541 days to form a coalition government. In the Netherlands, the governing coalition relied on the Christian Democrats and the Socialists from 1946 to 1981. Between 1994 and 2006 the Christian Democrats were excluded from government as the result of a coalition between the Socialists and two smaller parties, the Democrats 66 and the Liberals. However, after the elections of 2007 a grand coalition between Christian Democrats and Socialists was reinstalled. After a minority government, the elections of 2012 led to a new coalition of Liberals and Labour. Austria has generally been governed by a grand coalition of the Social Democrats and the People's Party, interrupted in the second half of the 1960s and 1970s by Social Democrat governments, reinstated between 1987 and 2000, interrupted again between 2000 and 2007, and again reinstated after the elections of January 11, 2007. In Luxembourg the governing coalition has always consisted of the Christian Democrats, generally in alliance with the Socialists and for brief periods with the Democrats. In Finland until the 1990s, the governing coalitions, although of mixed composition, have almost always included the Social Democratic Party, the Center Party and the National Party. Iceland, apart from brief intervals with single-party governments of the Social Democrats, has most frequently known coalition governments consisting of the Social Democrats, the Independence Party, the Progressive Party and the Conservative Party. In Israel, after an initial and long phase (1949–1977) of coalition governments headed by the labourites of the Mapai, followed in 1977–1984 by coalition governments headed by the conservative Likud party, the 1990s and 2000s saw several coalition governments, although composed differently (sometimes skewed towards the right, sometimes towards the left). In First Republic Italy from 1948 to 1993, the governing coalitions had at their core the Christian Democratic Party, allied with parties on the center-right until 1962, and the center-left after 1962. Fourth Republic France, from 1946 to 1958, had several governing coalitions, frequently including the Christian Democrats, the Socialists, the Liberals and the Radicals.

The variant that complicates the model instead concerns the state system. An evidently consensual logic has also manifested itself in countries that have not adopted a decentralized state system. Rather, in empirical terms, centralized consensus democracies constitute the majority of the democracies in question: for example, Israel, Finland, Fourth Republic France, the two small countries of Luxembourg and Iceland, and Italy during the First Republic. Applying the institutional variables in an undifferentiated way would lead to the conclusion that consensus democracy implies the existence of a decentralized state system, as in federal Austria or in Belgium, which became a federation in 1993, or in the Netherlands with its twelve powerful provinces. In these cases, the bicameral legislature has accommodated the representation of both citizens and territorial units. However, the empirical analysis reveals the existence of an evidently consensual logic in countries devoid of a decentralized state system. This is why in this case it is necessary to distinguish between centralized and decentralized consensus democracies. In the latter case it has also been possible to conjugate parliamentary government with federal territorial systems (as in Belgium but also in Austria where the Federal Council, the executive nominated by the directly elected president of the republic, is for all intents and purposes subject to the lower chamber's approval) because only the popular chamber of the bicameral legislature has the power to give confidence to or to withdraw it from the government. In the cases of Austria and Belgium, federalism has emerged by disaggregation of a previously unitary state. Federalism has been utilized for organizing the territorial authority of the nation state, not for calling the latter into question.

7.4 Models of democracy: unions of states

The typology discussed up to now includes neither the USA nor Switzerland. It could not include those cases for structural reasons. Contrary to the decentralized (federal and federalized) countries examined previously, the USA and Switzerland represent the *only cases*, within established democracies, of federalization by aggregation of previously independent states or cantons. The USA started from aggregating thirteen previously independent states in 1781–1787, thus reaching through several enlargements its current fifty states. Switzerland, whose cantons "should be considered true and proper states" (Blondel 1998: 210, author's translation), started from aggregating, as Article 1 of the 1848 constitution stated, "twenty-two sovereign cantons," then becoming twenty cantons and six half-cantons with the constitutional revision of 1999. Both the USA and Switzerland function (i.e. take decisions) according to a logic that does not fit in either of the models of democracy discussed above. The reason for this is their different institutional and social structures vis-à-vis those of national democracies.

The institutional (governmental) structure

The USA and Switzerland are organized according to specific variants of the principle of separation of powers, both vertically (between the institutions of the center and those of the federated states in the US case and cantons in the Swiss case) as well as horizontally (between the executive and legislative institutions of the federal center). If these political systems are comparable vertically to other cases of the decentralized organization of territorial authority, and in particular to federal systems, they differ horizontally from the latter, however, because their governmental system is institutionally at odds with a fusion of powers system. It is the separation of powers that structures their way of taking collective and binding decisions, rather than the specific electoral rules and party systems operating at the level of each of the separate governmental institutions.

The USA and Switzerland are the only empirical cases that combine federalization (which means separation of powers) at the vertical level with separation of powers at the horizontal level. They are *multiple* separation of powers systems. Since all the other federal and federalized systems (such as Germany, Austria, Belgium, Spain and the Netherlands – in Europe[10] – or Australia and Canada – outside of Europe) are cases of *federalization by disaggregation* of a previously unitary state, they can maintain a center of governmental authority (through the fusion of the government with the parliament via the party/parties of the parliamentary majority). In contrast, the USA and Switzerland have passed through a reverse process and this explains why they function without a government as a single institution monopolizing the ultimate decision. Thus, in a separation of powers system, there is not a government but an executive that participates with an internally separate legislature in the decision-making process. The government is a process rather than an institution. These systems have "separate institutions *sharing* powers" (Neustadt 1990: 29, original emphasis), whereas in fusion of powers systems the government is connected to (fused with) its parliamentary majority, but the legislative and executive functions remain distinct. This is why one should use the concept of "executive" for separation of powers systems, and the concept of "government" for fusion of powers systems (see Glossary).

If in fusion of powers systems, whether competitive or consensual, the purpose of the political process is *to form a government*, immediately after the elections (in competitive democracies) or after a post-electoral process of negotiation among elites (in consensus democracies), this does not hold true for the cases discussed here. In the USA and Switzerland, the purpose of the electoral process is to elect or select the members of the various separate institutions. In the USA these institutions are the president (a single-person executive power elected indirectly by the presidential electors for four years, renewable once) and the bicameral Congress, consisting of the Senate (constituted by 100 senators, 2 for each of the 50 states, elected directly by the states' voters for 6 years) and the House of Representatives (with 435 representatives elected for 2 years in districts within each state). Both institutions represent voters, although before Amendment XVII of 1913 the senators were indirectly elected by the legislatures of the

---

[10] Also Italy of the Second Republic may be considered a case of territorial decentralization, in particular after the constitutional reform of 2000 that increased the competences and powers of the regions. However, the post-2009 financial crisis triggered a trend towards a sort of neo-centralization.

states.[11] There is no government (as a single institution) in this system, although the two main political parties have historically played (more or less successfully) the quasi-constitutional role (Riggs 1988) of connecting similar partisan or policy coalitions operating within the three separate governmental institutions (presidency, House and Senate).

In periods of *unified government*, when the same party expresses the president and the majority of the members in the two chambers of Congress, it has been that party that plays a systemic role in coordinating the policy preferences of the members of the congressional majority with those of the president. However, this coordination role must not be confused with party government. It was rather a party *in the* government (Jones 1995). The senators or the representatives of the party of the president are not dependent on the latter to be re-elected, nor are they constrained by the need to support the president. They support him/her only if it is convenient for their political purpose (re-election). Moreover, since the end of the 1960s it has become common for the separate institutions to be controlled by different parties, giving rise to a *divided government*. In this political context, the struggle between parties has been subsumed by a struggle between institutions (Fisher 2007). Thus alternation in the office of the US presidency is not identical to alternation in government as in parliamentary systems (Polsby 2004). Although the president has become pre-eminent with respect to the legislature in the fields of foreign and defense policy, the same does not hold true for domestic policies. Also, in foreign, security and defense policy the president's pre-eminence has regularly been challenged by Congress whenever those policies turned out to be failures (as in the case of the Democratic president Jimmy Carter in 1977–1980), or were electorally counterproductive for the president's supporters in Congress (as in the case of the Republican president George W. Bush during his second mandate of 2005–2008), or became the object of a polarized conflict (as in the case of the Democratic president Barack H. Obama in 2009–2016).

---

[11] The Senate thus represents the state through their two senators. The official site of the Senate still today defines it as "a living symbol of our union of states."

It has been argued, instead, that Switzerland has a "government" (Mazzoleni and Rayner 2008). Lijphart himself (1999: 106) has written that "Switzerland ... for the purpose of classifying the composition of its executive, can be treated as a parliamentary system." The Federal Council (collegial executive power composed of 7 members) is indeed elected by the Federal Assembly, constituted by the Council of States (with 2 councilors for each of the 20 large cantons and 1 councilor for each of the 6 half-cantons, for a total of 46, directly elected in districts of the size of the cantons/half-cantons) and the National Council (with 200 representatives elected through a PR system in districts within the cantons/half-cantons). Moreover, the elections of the Council of States and National Council take place on the same day and the two institutions have the same mandate (four years) (Wolf and Vatter 2001). However, the Federal Council cannot be considered the "government" in the sense of the expression of the parliamentary majority of the Federal Assembly, because once its members are elected, they do not depend on the confidence of the Federal Assembly to operate. The Federal Assembly might decide not to re-elect a member of the Federal Council at the end of the four-year mandate (a power used only on four occasions since 1848, that is, in 1854, 1872, 2003 and 2007), but it cannot vote him/her out of office by a motion of no confidence or even impeach a member of the Federal Council during his/her four-year tenure. This separation of powers has not prevented Swiss political elites from adopting a consensual approach in the election of the seven members of the Federal Council (according to a "magic formula" that has balanced cantonal representation and party representation), thus creating a viable correlation between the composition of the executive and the composition of the majorities in the two chambers of the legislature (Fleiner 2002; Kriesi and Trechsel 2008).[12] There is a difference, however, between consensus democracy (as a model) and consensual politics (as a style).

[12] Ever since the end of the Second World War, the Federal Council has been composed of members representing the Free Democratic Party (FDP), the Christian Democrats (CVP), the People's Party (SVP) and the Social Democrats (SPS), whose members are at the same time an expression of the main cantonal areas. Since 2009 the FDP has joined the Liberal Party.

In short, in the USA and Switzerland the government is a *process* rather than an *institution*. This institutional feature makes them different from national democracies. The USA and Switzerland are organized around the principle of multiple separation of powers. The governmental decisions are the outcome of the interaction between actors operating in separate institutions expressing divergent institutional interests – those of the states and those of the citizens. In both democracies parties matter. In order to function, separation of powers requires political parties that bridge the actors operating in the separate institutions, thus promoting cross-institutional policy coalitions. In different ways, US and Swiss parties have historically played this bridging role. However, when (as in post-1994 USA: Aldrich 1995; S. Fabbrini 2008c) the two parties have become politically polarized (due, in particular, to the radicalization of the Republican party: Mann and Ornstein 2012), then they have been unable to play the bridging role, bringing the governmental system to a decision-making stalemate (or to the "shutdown of the federal government" as occurred in October 2013).[13] Or when (as in Switzerland after the election of 2003) one party calls into question the "magic formula" (Kriesi and Trechsel 2008), then the functioning of the separation of powers system has been hampered. In short, in the USA and Switzerland the governmental process is structured around separate institutions, expressing the different interests of the states or cantons and the union, not only around political parties, expressing the different interests of the citizens. It is difficult to govern without an ultimate decision-making institution, as it is difficult to detect who is, or should be considered, responsible for the outcome of the decision-making process. Indeed, these democracies have been criticized for exhibiting a deficit of both effectiveness and legitimacy (Zweifel 2002), but this criticism is due to the fact that they continue to be wrongly equated to the functioning of (parliamentary or semi-presidential) nation states.

---

[13] From October 1 to 16, 2013, the USA saw a shutdown of most routine federal operations because of the failure of Congress to find an agreement with the President's proposal and thus enact legislation appropriating funds for the fiscal year 2014 or a continuing resolution for the interim authorization of appropriations for the fiscal year 2014. Regular government operations resumed on October 17 after an interim appropriations bill was finally signed into law.

Interstate cleavages

In regard also to the structure of cleavages (what I called, analytically, the *social structure*), the USA and Switzerland differ from both
competitive and consensus democracies. The main cleavages feeding
the political process in the USA and Switzerland have been the divisions between states or cantons, besides the division between the partisan camps of left and right. In particular in the USA, left and right
are politically ambiguous concepts. Historically, left and right have
been within each main party, they have assumed different meanings
in different states, they have created periodical cross-party coalitions,
and they have frequently been the instruments for expressing interstate or sectional divisions (Burnham 1970; Bensel 1987; Reichley
1992). It was the reform of the party selection of presidential candidates through primaries in the 1970s (Polsby 1983) that incentivized the formation of more ideologically coherent political parties.
In the USA, the interstate or sectional division has taken, at times,
the form of an opposition between economic models (as between
export- or import-oriented economies, or between agricultural and
industrial economies) (Sbragia 1996), and at times the form of an
opposition between radically different cultural identities (as between
anti-slavery and pro-slavery states) (Hershey 2012). In Switzerland,
the inter-canton cleavages have taken the form of religious, linguistic,
but also economic divisions. This interstate cleavage structure is at the
origin of unions of states or federal unions by aggregation.

If the cleavages that matter are those that endure over time, as they
are the outcome of structural conditions, interstate cleavage has proven
to be as resistant (in the case of the USA and Switzerland) as the other
two types of cleavage (in the case of national democracies). Indeed,
once a representation system is institutionalized, then the conditions
for its reproduction are preserved (Pierson and Skocpol 2002). Fusion
of powers systems are able to aggregate economic or cultural divisions, not divisions between asymmetrical and differentiated states.
The former division can be synthesized in the confrontation between
parties (along a left vs. right axis) in parliament, whereas the latter
division is unlikely to find political representation in the popular legislature alone. Rather, it has been the confrontation between separate
institutions that has provided a representation to interstate cleavages.
The process of both modernization and nationalization has weakened

the political impact of interstate/canton cleavages. However, the interstate/canton cleavage has continued to condition the decision-making process in these unions. In the USA and Switzerland, the political culture has preserved a state or sectional character, as one would expect given their formation through the aggregation of previously independent states or cantons. That aggregation was not a simple endeavor, as shown by the USA where the contrast between states finally led to the dramatic Civil War of 1861–1865 and where divisions between regional sections of states have structured the various party systems engaged in institutionalizing and integrating them (Bensel 1987). That aggregation was also disputed in Switzerland, where the divisions between cantons have continued to matter more than the divisions between parties (Elazar 1998).

The genetic origins of the two democratic unions of states/cantons and the structure of their interstate/inter-canton cleavage help to explain the historically weak institutionalization of their federal center. Since they represent cases of federalization by aggregation of previously independent states or cantons, the powers and competences retained by the constituent states (from their sovereign experience) have been significant vis-à-vis the powers and the competences allocated to the center. In the USA and Switzerland, for instance, for a long time the federated states and cantons tried successfully to limit the size of the financial resources at the disposal of the federal center. In particular in the USA, it has been the processes of internal economic modernization (started after the Civil War: Lowi 1985) and the country's formidable projection in the external world (initiated after the First World War and which exploded with the Second World War: Hendrickson 2009) that have broken states' resistance to an increase in the resources and powers of the federal institutions. At the same time, the country's neutrality and the limited size of its economy have constrained similar processes in Switzerland.

7.5 Compound democracy for unions of states

The USA and Switzerland have created a highly complex institutional (governmental) structure with multiple separation of powers, in order to encourage a decision-making process including actors operating within reciprocally independent institutions and expressing interests that the parties cannot easily aggregate. Any governmental decision has thus to gain the support of actors representing different institutional interests, other than different party interests. Although significant differences exist between the USA and Switzerland (in terms of size, economic capability and international power), their governmental structure and the structure of their cleavages encourage a decision-making outcome based neither on competition nor on consociation between political parties in order to gain control of the government, but on confrontation between separate institutions, each one expressing a combination of different state or sectional and party interests and views. This is why these cases should be subsumed under a different democratic model, which I defined (S. Fabbrini 2010) as *compound democracy* (see Box 7.3).

In a compound democracy, the confrontation for reaching collective and binding decisions generally takes the form of a negotiation (at times also of a conflict) between separate institutions (representing either territorial or political interests, or a combination of both). Since the states constituting the union have a different population, culture, economy, even language, and given that they historically aggregated for instrumental reasons (to guarantee their external security and internal peace), they set up a system of multiple separation of powers in order to prevent internal domination by one state/canton or a group of them over the others. Vertically, the institutions of the center and the states/cantons were initially based on distinct competences (although they have gradually evolved in a cooperative direction); horizontally, the center's institutions represent different interests and do not require a reciprocal confidence vote to operate. Here lies a crucial difference with national democracies of a federal state. In the latter, power is separated vertically, but not horizontally. In the former, power is separated in both dimensions. The majoritarian electoral rules adopted for the elections of the members of the US Congress and the president have fostered competitive politics in each specific electoral arena, whereas the PR electoral rules adopted for the election of the members (in particular) of the Swiss popular legislature have incentivized consensual politics in their respective electoral arena. However, this difference does not alter the decision-making logic of the two systems, which is based on the necessity to find a compromise between institutions rather or more than between parties.

Box 7.3 – The concept of compoundness

The concept of compoundness derives from the US debate. James Madison talked of a compound republic in the 1787 Philadelphia constitutional convention (Kernell 2003). Robert A. Dahl investigated in 1956 (now Dahl 2006) the anti-majoritarian nature of the compound republic that he defined as Madisonian democracy. Vincent Ostrom (1987) normatively magnified the political theory of a compound republic as the theory of a radically anti-centralized federal system. Martha Derthick (2001) critically discussed the challenge brought to the compound republic by the centralizing policies promoted by the Progressives, the New Dealers and the Civil Rights activists from 1900 to the 1960s. David C. Hendrickson (2003) discussed the unionist paradigm of "a republic of many republics," which inspired (with the republican and liberal paradigms) the US founding fathers. In relation to Europe, only recently has the concept of compoundness started to be used. Vivien Schmidt (2006) used it to address polities characterized by a low degree of institutional centralization (such as Germany and Italy) other than the EU. In my approach (S. Fabbrini 2010, 2011), compoundness is more than a political/cultural property of non-centralized political systems. It is the systemic property of unions of states (or *federal unions by aggregation*). Although Bickerton (2010) critically reviewed this literature under the heading of a neo-Madisonian Europe, my interpretation of "Madison in Brussels" (S. Fabbrini 2005b) is more parsimonious, because it is strictly institutional. A compound polity becomes a *compound democracy* when its institutional features correspond to multiple (vertical and horizontal) separations of powers and its political logic is mainly motivated by divisions between states or regions of the union. Compound democracy is thus an ideal-type comparable to the ideal-types of competitive or consensus democracy, but distinguishable from them because of the lack of a government as a single institution and the existence of a cleavage between territorial units. I define as *compound union* a federal union functioning according to the logic of a compound democracy. For a discussion on the EU–US comparative literature, see Martinelli (2008) and Tortola (2014).

Trans-state/canton party coalitions may emerge within the legislative chamber representing voters (the US House of Representatives and the Swiss National Council), giving rise to a left–right logic on specific socio-economic issues, but rarely do they emerge in the legislative chamber representing the states or the cantons (the US Senate and the Swiss Council of States). At the same time, executive institutions such as the Swiss Federal Council may reflect partisan interests, but they mainly operate as an aggregation of the cultures and interests of the states/cantons. Partisan majorities have emerged in the US presidential elections, although historically any ticket for the presidency and the vice-presidency has generally had to include a northern and a southern candidate to be legitimate, before being successful. If in Switzerland the synchronized election of the two legislative chambers and the consensual attitude of the political elites have made it possible to identify a formula for a cross-institutional governmental majority, this has been much more difficult in the USA. In the USA, the differentiated schedule of the elections of the two chambers of Congress and the president has hindered the stable formation of a partisan majority, unless dramatic circumstances (as was the case of the terrorist attack of September 11, 2001) have pushed all the institutions to coalesce around the president in his capacity as Commander-in Chief (so defined by Article II, Section II.1 of the constitution) (Schwarz and Huq 2008).

Established political systems thus function according to different democratic logics. These differences are due to the different nature of their social cleavages. The dividing lines may be of an economic nature (socio-economic cleavage), may concern identity (socio-cultural cleavage), may be based on linguistic or religious as well as ideological divisions, or may have a national/statist/cantonal or sectional nature (interstate cleavage) (S. Fabbrini 2001). In competitive democracies, the social divisions have evolved into a homogenous configuration, in the sense that the divisions or social cleavages have grouped around a basic socio-economic axis of political conflict, whereas in consensual countries the social divisions have come to display a non-homogenous configuration, in the sense that the divisions or social cleavages have given rise to several axes of political conflict of a socio-cultural type in addition

Table 7.2 *Models of democracy: nation states vs. unions of states*

		Institutional (governmental) structure		
		alternation in government as single institution	consociation in government as single institution	separate institutions sharing governmental power
Social structure	socio-economic cleavages	*competitive democracies*		
	socio-cultural cleavages		*consensus democracies*	
	interstate cleavages			*compound democracies*

to a socio-economic axis. In compound democracies the cleavage structure has been motivated by different (national or material) interests of states or cantons (or sections of them), although political divisions matter as well. At the same time, established political systems differ in terms of the institutional organization of relations between the executive and the legislature, which are fused in both competitive and consensus democracies and separate in compound democracies. Table 7.2 summarizes the effects of the interaction, on the democratic model, of the variables representing the institutional (governmental) and social structures.

Thus, the USA and Switzerland represent different species of the same genus – the compound democracy model – because they have had to compound divisions between states or cantons of different demographic size, cultural identity, political economy structures, religious predisposition and or even national language. This is why unions of states are not in a continuum with nation states, nor are they hybrid regimes located midway between competitive and consensus democracies. They are different democracies that cannot be evaluated with same criteria that are utilized for the democracies of nation states. Summarizing the discussion up to now, we arrive at the following classification of contemporary democracies (see Table 7.3).

Table 7.3 *Democracies: competitive, consensual, compound*

	Competitive democracies (nation states)	Consensus democracies (nation states)	Compound democracies (unions of states)

Territorial centraliza-tion	New Zealand
	Sweden
	Greece
	Ireland
	Norway
	Denmark
	Portugal
	United Kingdom
	France Fifth Republic
		Israel
		France Fourth
		  Republic
		Iceland
		Finland
		Luxembourg
		Italy First
		  Republic	

Territorial decentraliza-tion	Italy Second Republic Japan Spain Germany Australia Canada	The Netherlands Belgium Austria	United States Switzerland

7.6 Conclusion

This chapter has shown that the democratic models of national democracies fall into two empirical categories: the competitive model and the consensus model, with some countries oscillating between the two. These two models reflect the different nature of the existing cleavages in national societies and the different functioning of their institutional system. Competitive democracies function on the basis of a plausible alternation in government between alternative political groupings, whereas consensus democracies function on the basis of consociation in government of distinct political views. In the first case, alternation at the helm of the government is plausible because the main parties share basic democratic values, being divided only on the policies for dealing with the main issues of the country; whereas, in the second case, because the parties represent distinct cultural communities that mistrust each other, alternation in government is considered undesirable. In this case, it is preferable for the main parties to consociate in the government in order to check each other directly.

Although different, both models imply the possibility of representing the cleavages through political parties and the availability of a government as a single institution, whose political control is entrusted to the majority of the parliament. Both models function via a government, regardless of whether it is formed through a bipolar electoral competition or through the post-electoral aggregation of the main actors of a multi-party system. Both models are typical of nation states based on the popular legislature as the pre-eminent institution to represent democratic sovereignty.

This chapter has thus argued that both democratic models differ from the way the USA and Switzerland function, a difference that is explained by the fact that both are unions of states, that is, federal unions formed through the aggregation of previously independent states or cantons. Their genetic foundation, plus the demographic asymmetry and the cultural and material differentiation between the constituting states or cantons of the union, have made the interstate/inter-canton cleavages the main division of the system – a division that could not be represented through parties alone. In order to prevent a majority of states controlling the governmental process, federal unions have set up an institutional structure where governmental power has been diffused among several separate institutions. The decision-making power is shared by separate institutions of government, not entrusted to only one of them (the popular legislature). Their model of democracy is thus different from both the competitive and consensual models because it is based on interstate/inter-canton cleavages (rather than partisan ones) and reaches decisions in an institutional system where representation and decision-making power is dispersed among several and separate institutions. Having assumed the nation state perspective as the natural one, CP scholars have apparently neglected to conceptualize unions of states regarding both their interstate division and institutional (governmental) structure. Even the most sophisticated scholars have tried to assimilate our cases of unions of states (such as the USA and Switzerland, but also the EU as we will see) to one or the other type of democracy for nation states. Certainly, processes of modernization and nationalization have pushed both the USA and Switzerland to strengthen the federal center, a pressure that, in the case of the USA, has been triggered by the country's role in the international system since the Second World War. However, that external pressure has not changed their internal (social and institutional) structures.

Given the comparative analytical framework elaborated here, it is thus possible to investigate the democratic model of the EU. If the EU is a union of previously independent states, then it will be necessary to compare it more in depth with the two democratic unions of states considered above (the USA and Switzerland), in order to identify similarities and dissimilarities between them.

8 | *Compound unions and the EU*

8.1 Introduction

Having identified the model of democracy of unions of states, it is then possible to investigate whether that model fits the democratic functioning of the EU. Certainly, it might be questioned whether the EU can even be considered a democracy (Majone 2009). However, as shown in Part I, there are good arguments for considering the EU as a democracy. A polity may be considered *democratic* (Dahl 1989: Part 3 and Part 4) when it is regulated by a higher legal order, it protects the fundamental rights of its citizens and the decision-making system meets basic criteria of representation and accountability (Mény and Surel 2002). The EU is a constitutionalized polity, although contrasted and contested, based on treaties interpreted as a quasi-constitution (or as a material constitution) and on a Charter of Fundamental Rights finally recognized by the Lisbon Treaty. Moreover, those who take decisions in the supranational EU are elected by citizens either in national elections (governmental leaders of the European Council and ministers of the Council) or in European elections (MEPs), or (as is the case for the president and commissioners of the Commission) nominated through an interlocking decision-making process started by politicians elected in national elections (leaders of the European Council) and concluded by politicians elected in European elections (MEPs). Finally, the supranational EU satisfies both inter-institutional and electoral accountability (Morlino 2012). EU decision-makers are compelled to act within a complex system of inter-institutional controls and, at the same time, all of them are subject to the control of national constitutional courts and the ECJ, thus satisfying inter-institutional accountability. At the same time, EU decision-makers have to face the periodical evaluation of the voters, at both national and European level, thus satisfying electoral accountability as well. Of course, the existence of a growing intergovernmental side of the EU, with its confusion of powers, has made the democratic functioning of the EU much more problematic.

Defining the EU as a democratic polity does not mean shielding it from criticism. However, criticisms, albeit of a different nature, might also be addressed to each and every national democracy. At the same time, the EU has acquired a consolidated character, having passed through a process of constant, albeit uneven, institutionalization since the 1957 Rome Treaty. Starting from aggregating six European states in 1957, it has then periodically enlarged, reaching the current number of twenty-eight with the accession of Croatia in 2013. This development has created an extremely complex but also quite stable set of institutions at the Union level, a set of institutions that have acquired increasing responsibilities in a growing number of policy areas. With the end of the Cold War, the EU extended its competences also to policy realms traditionally at the core of national sovereignty. Foreign and security policies, justice and home affairs, monetary and financial policies finally entered the sphere of competence of the Union. But as we have seen, since the 1992 Maastricht Treaty, two unions, one supranational and one intergovernmental, have come to be institutionalized. The 2009 Lisbon Treaty has not overcome that distinction, although it has crystallized it within a single legal framework. Their contradictory logics have, however, shadowed the democratic functioning of the EU.

If it is plausible to assume the EU as a sufficiently established democracy, it is, however, much less so to equate the democratic model of the EU with the one adopted by nation states. Indeed, that has continued to be a common approach to the EU by both politicians and scholars. According to several politicians and public officials (Cohn-Bendit and Verhofstadt 2012; Padoa-Schioppa 2001; Prodi 2008; Verhofstadt 2006), the EU is a supranational democracy that should be similar to the federal democracy of a nation state. The interpretation of the EU as a variant of the democratic model adopted at the nation state level has also been supported by influential scholarly literature. Lijphart (1999: 34, author's emphasis) wrote that:

the European Union is a supranational organization – more than just an international organization – but it is not, *or not yet* – a sovereign state. Because of the EU's intermediate status, analysts … disagree on whether to study it as an international organization or an *incipient federal state*, but the latter approach is increasingly common … This is also my approach: if the EU is regarded as a federal state, its institutions are remarkably close to the consensus model of democracy.

Magnette and Papadopoulos (2008), and earlier Costa and Magnette (2003), Gabel (1998) and Hottinger (1997), following Lijphart's approach, have all argued that the EU is a case of a consociational democracy, consociationalism being the democratic model of deeply divided or segmented national societies (such as Belgium and Switzerland, the latter considered equivalent to a federal state).

Indeed, the EU is not a state, nor a federal state. It is a federal union that has emerged from the aggregation of previously independent states and reflects the subsequent institutionalization and constitutionalization of that aggregation. If it is a compound polity, can it also be considered a compound union (a federal union functioning according to a compound democracy model)? In order to answer this question, this chapter will compare the EU with the two other empirical cases of democratic unions of states and citizens, the USA and Switzerland. If the larger framework of the previous chapter has been useful for understanding the differences between the democratic model of nation states and unions of states, it is now necessary to go deeper into the comparison of the latter. The comparison of unions of states will be developed at three levels of analysis: their *systemic foundations*, their *constitutional framework* and their *institutional structure*, in order to show similarities and dissimilarities between them. The comparison aims to analyze the institutional structure of the EU (which is the focus of my investigation) from a broader perspective. Through this comparison I will try to delineate the logical connections developed in the USA and Switzerland between the basic features of their foundation, the constitutional framework built on that foundation and the decision-making structure supported by the constitutional framework. These connections are much less coherent in the EU case. Finally, this chapter will identify dilemmas of inter-institutional relations that should be dealt with if one wishes to lead the EU towards the model of compound democracy.

8.2 Systemic foundation of compound unions

The systemic foundation of unions of states such as the USA and Switzerland derives from their being experiments in the aggregation of previously independent states or in *federations by aggregation* (on the USA, see Ostrom 1987 and on Switzerland, see Blondel 1998 and Zweifel 2002). This historical genesis affected their systemic

Table 8.1 *Compound unions: systemic foundation*

	United States/ Switzerland	European Union
aim	external and internal security	common market
purpose	federal union	undefined ("ever-closer") union
source	states and their citizens	states and their governments
authority	general but delimited	specific but expanding

foundation. Considering their experience, I dissect the concept of systemic foundation into four empirical categories: the reason or aim of the aggregation process; the purpose of the union's creation; the source of the latter; and the nature of the authority embodying the union project. The EU is also the outcome of a process of aggregation of previously independent states; nevertheless its systemic foundation displays different features from the US and Swiss experiences (see Table 8.1).

The USA started as a peaceful and defensive *pact* among republican (or democratic, we would say today) states of different demographic size, material capabilities and cultural values (e.g. regarding slavery) aimed at guaranteeing both internal and external security to the contracting states. As Hendrickson (2003: 7) has written, "it seems fair to denominate the federal Constitution as a peace pact, the most unusual specimen of this kind yet known to history." It was an interstate or intersectional pact with the purpose of creating a federal union, that is, a union of states combining confederal and federal principles and institutions (although, interestingly enough, the constitution never uses the word "federalism" or "confederation"), with the authority and the resources for preserving the union from external attack, without, however, replicating the centralized model of the European states. It originated from a decision taken by the states, later legitimized by their convention or legislatures on behalf of the citizens of each of them. It was a pact between states aware of their deep divisions. Indeed, it tried to anticipate possible conflicts among them or groups (sections) of them (in particular, between those located in the North and the South of the same union territory). Had a conflict broken out, the independence of all states and sections would have been jeopardized, because of the interests of the great European powers of the period to play off one state or group of states against the other (Deudney 2007: chapter 6). In satisfying that aim, the USA represents the first attempt to go beyond Westphalia. In order to avoid a reiteration of the experience already familiar in Europe at the end of the eighteenth century, namely the inability of the Westphalian system of states to guarantee a stable balance of powers between them in order to prevent war (Onuf and Onuf 1994), the USA pursued a different perspective. It developed as "a Republic of different republics and a nation of many nations [and] the resulting system was *sui generis* in establishing a continental order that partook of the character of both a state and a state system" (Hendrickson 2003: 258). The USA inaugurated a Philadelphia system as a practical and conceptual alternative to the Westphalian one. As Deudney and Meiser (2012: 31–2) wrote:

The founding of the United States took place through a process of confederation and federation among thirteen separate states. The organization of the British colonial activity in the New World was highly decentralized and colonies had a significant measure of local autonomy. After banding together to reach their common goal of independence, the thirteen states then formed a more substantial union with a weak central government. This negotiated union was a "peace pact" that created the "Philadelphia System" as an explicit antithesis to the Westphalian system of hierarchies in anarchy that marked European politics … The small professional army, minuscule national bureaucracy, and substantial state militias prevented the resolution of state and sectional conflicts through coercion.

Switzerland is also to be considered the outcome of a peace pact between jealously independent cantons. The Treaty on the basis of which the last confederation of 1815–1847 was set up, then substituted by the new federal constitution of 1848 (which preserved the title of Confederation), reported in Article 1 that its aim is "to defend the freedoms and independence [of the cantons] from any foreign attack as well as preserving internal order and peace." After the Napoleonic conquest, "Switzerland … re-emerged as a modern confederation in 1815 … for defensive purposes" (Elazar 1998: 47). Article 4 of the Treaty made it explicit that the Confederation was a mutual defense guarantee, based on cantonal contingents (and not on a central permanent army) directed in time of war by a general chosen consensually by the cantons. However, "within a generation ... [the Swiss] found that the whole idea of confederation did not serve them well in the modern world of that time ... Matters were brought to a head by the brief *Sonderbund* conflict of the mid-1840s. The result was the establishment of the Swiss federation in 1848" (Elazar 1998: 47–8). After a conflict with the Southern cantons, the 1848 constitution established a federal union (a formal confederation with substantial federal traits) whose internal security was considered the pre-eminent need. As Chapter I, Article 2 of the 1848 constitution reads, "The aim of the Confederation is to preserve the outward independence of the fatherland, to maintain internal peace and order, to protect the freedom and the rights of the confederates and to promote their common prosperity."

Both unions thus have their source of foundation and legitimacy in the states' or cantons' willingness to set up a pact between them. The citizens arrived after the pact was decided by the states' or cantons' elites, in order to legitimize it. They gave their legitimation as citizens of the states or cantons, not as citizens of the union. The constitutions of both unions recognize the source of their legitimacy in the *people/s*, but the latter have a plural and not a unitary connotation. This is why both constitutions promise to promote a common bond between the states' peoples. In both unions of states, there was not one demos at the founding moment, but several *demoi*. The formation of a union's demos was considered, by the founding fathers of the two unions, the possible historical outcome and not the prerequisite of the integration process. That same outcome (a homogeneous demos) was probably believed to be undesirable, at least by the more liberal founders (Kernell 2003). Article 1 of the 1848 Swiss constitution states "the peoples of the twenty-two sovereign cantons" are to be considered the source of legitimacy of the union, although the Preamble refers to a "Swiss nation."

In the USA it is legitimately assumed that the constitution celebrates a covenant among citizens ("in America ... it is the People who are the source of rights": Ackerman 1991: 15), but for a long time the covenant was understood to be between citizens organized into distinct states (Elazar 1988). The celebrated introduction of the constitutional Preamble "We the People of the United States, in Order to form a more perfect Union ..." has triggered a two-century debate about

"whether ... [it] refers to the whole people of the United States acting as a national democratic majority or to the peoples of the united
states acting both independently and collectively as dispersed democratic majorities. Although the Constitution provides no way for a
majority of American as a whole to elect anyone or decide anything"
(Kincaid 2010: 124), a dilemma that is typical of a union emerged
from the uniting of previously separate and distinct states and peoples
(Glencross 2012). As Forsyth (1981: 65) explained, "neither the preamble, nor Madison's successful endeavour to provide the constitution
with a deeper foundation than that of a normal treaty between governments, prevented it from being considered from the start as a species of
contract or compact. Ratification was unequivocally a matter for each
state individually; none could be bound without their assent." The dispute was only apparently settled by the 1863 Gettysburg address given
by President Abraham Lincoln.

Because of the aim of preventing internal territorial conflicts but
also the need to reciprocally guarantee the constituent states, both federal unions decided to move in the direction of embedding the constituent states or cantons in an authority system based on the empirical
fragmentation of decision-making power. The federal authority had
to have a general scope, but at the same time had to be limited in its
competences and powers. This was the condition for creating mutual
trust between the states or cantons of the union, given each state or
canton's fear of slipping under the control of other states or cantons,
let alone under the control of the federal center.[1] This is why the USA
and Switzerland were founded as *federal unions*, not *federal states*.
A federal union does not imply a concentration of public authority and
institutional power at the center of the polity. If both federal unions
and federal states combine the principles of self-rule and shared rule
(Elazar 1987), it might be arguable that federal unions stress the former
principle and federal states the latter one. The light concentration of
powers at the center was considered a condition, as Deudney and
Meiser (2012) argued, for relying solely on negotiation and compromise to resolve disputes between states, sections and cantons. A crucial
device for preventing concentration of powers at the center consisted
in the institutionalization of confederal alongside federal institutions.

---

[1] For a discussion of the federal method, see Burgess and Gagnon (2010: Part 1).

In the USA the confederal institution par excellence was the Senate, constituted by two senators for each state regardless of the latter's demographic size. But confederal elements also affect the electoral college for the election of the president (see Glossary). The confederal nature of the US Senate has implied the over-representation of small states vs. the larger states. For instance, after the 2010 census, the 22 smallest states (represented by 44 senators) had a total population of 38 million inhabitants, the same as California, represented by its 2 senators. The Swiss Council of States reflects the same confederal logic of the US Senate, that is, to give representation to territorial units, not to the population living within them. Nevertheless, in the USA the Philadelphia system was insufficient to prevent the explosion of a sectional war in 1861–65. That war constitutes a dramatic reminder of the persistence of interstate or intersectional divisions within a federal union. Indeed, the memory of the war has contributed to making post-war US politics a successful exercise in political compromise between opposing sectional views and interests (Greenstone 1993), at least until polarization exploded in the 1990s and 2000s (S. Fabbrini 2008c). Cantonal divisions were and have continued to be at the basis of the Swiss federal union as well. Those divisions have concerned different languages, different religious faiths, different cultural predispositions and different national references outside of the union. In the USA and Switzerland, the structure of political cleavages has continued to be characterized by contrasts between territorial units, motivated by a panoply of reasons, many of them connected to diverse identities and interests.

These systemic foundations have been challenged by later processes. In the USA, it was the quasi century-long economic and political development between the end of the 1880s and the 1940s that led the federal union to increase the power of the federal center. First to regulate the gigantic economic transformation of its continental market and then to deal with an unprecedented international role, an accumulation of organizational resources and decision-making prerogatives took place at the center of the union. The economic and technological transformation of the internal market, and (above all) the growing role the country came to play in the international arena after the Second World War, required increased federal centralization of powers to support both regulation of the market system (Jacobs and King 2009) and military and commercial intervention in the global system (Katznelson and Shefter 2002). Nevertheless, the confederal institutions, and the interstate logic epitomized by them, have continued to constrain and weaken the process of building an "American state," which is in fact still considered to be unsustainable (Jacobs and King 2009). In Switzerland, the 1848 federal constitution, although it altered significantly the confederal nature of the previous Treaty, nevertheless preserved most of the previous cantonal powers. Indeed, the small size of the country and its historical decision to remain neutral in international affairs[2] have significantly prevented Switzerland from building a powerful federal center.

The EU also started as a peace pact between the main European Continental states, aimed at closing a long era of European civil wars through the taming of national sovereignties. It was a pact signed by the political elites governing the states that were responsible for those internecine massacres. After the 1954 refusal by the French Assemblée Nationale of the project to set up the EDC, European governmental elites had, however, to downsize their federal expectations. They decided to move integration in an economic direction, leaving to NATO the task of providing military security. The project of the common market was an adaptation to reality. Removing the federal union from the purpose of the interstate aggregation has had ambiguous consequences in terms of setting up a supranational authority. The political purpose of the Treaties remained undefined, but the commitment to create an ever-closer union foresaw a dynamic view of the integration process. The supranational authority (constituted by an intergovernmental Council of ministers and the supranational Commission and ECJ) instituted to promote economic integration inevitably had specific competences; however, these were open to expansion. Integration has indeed proceeded on the basis of the neo-functional logic of creating a common and then single market, moving from solving a policy problem to other policy problems created by the solution of the previous policy problem. This neo-functional logic, driven by the Commission and supported by the ECJ, had to operate within the boundaries defined by member state governments (through their intergovernmental institutions or IGC grand bargains).

---

[2] Switzerland is not party to several international organizations. In fact, only after a prolonged debate did it decide, through a popular referendum, to join the United Nations in 2002.

In the EU, the states and their governments were (and have continued to be for long time) the source of the pact (or the masters of the treaties, as they were later called by legal sentences). From the beginning they introduced confederal institutions to preserve their role as states in the new union, such as the Council, the informal European Council and the regular IGCs for rationalizing the institutional system. The later institutionalization of the Union and the increase in its policy competences have raised the need to also involve European citizens in order to legitimize the process of integration. With the post-Maastricht deepening of the integration process, citizens' consent has become a crucial factor in the politics of integration. However, notwithstanding the attempt to create a "European citizenship," citizens have made their voice heard as members of national communities. The EU was and continues to be based on several *demoi* and not on a single demos (Nicolaidis 2013).

In short, the EU has the systemic properties of the other two compound unions, although it has implemented them differently. The EU was created through the aggregation of previously independent states with the aim of closing a long era of military conflicts in Europe, although through economic means because the security side of the aggregation was guaranteed by a different organization (NATO). The political purpose of creating a union was thus undeclared, although the necessity to move towards an ever-closer union was recognized. The source of the integration process derived mainly from the governments of the constituent states, although the treaties they set up had to be legitimized by their national parliaments and in a few cases by the citizens through national referenda. As in the other two compound unions, the supranational authority set up for managing the integration process in the EU was also weak, because the structure of interstate or inter-regional cleavages could not allow centralizing projects, although its specific competences have been subject to regular expansion. It is the lack of a clear federal union purpose, and the method derivable from it for dealing with the union of states' dilemmas, that most explains the differences between the EU and the other two compound unions.

8.3 Constitutional framework of compound unions

The constitutional framework of compound unions such as the USA and Switzerland can be conceptualized by considering four aspects: the

Table 8.2 *Compound unions: constitutional framework*

	United States/Switzerland	European Union
basis	formal constitution	material constitution
goal	to divide sovereignty	to embed sovereignties
principle	multiple separation of powers	horizontally mixed (sharing and pooling of powers) and vertically uneven
change	double super-majority	unanimity

constitutional basis of the union; the constitutional principle inspiring the union's formation; the translation of the constitutional principle into a specific organization; and the criteria utilized for amending the constitution. If one correlates the EU to those aspects as they have been implemented in the USA and Switzerland, then it seems plausible to assert that the EU also has dissimilarities and similarities with those unions in this regard (see Table 8.2).

Both the USA and Switzerland are based on formal/written constitutions. In both cases, the constitutional text is constituted by the formal founding documents and their amendments or revisions, whereas the EU has no formal constitution but has been based on successive interstate treaties interpreted as a material constitution. Although the EU is a constitutionalized regime, constitutionalization based on a material constitution, aimed at creating an ever closer union through the formation of a common/single market, is significantly different from constitutionalization based on a formal constitution giving birth to a federal union (Ziller 2009). In both the USA and Switzerland, the goal of the interstate constitutional project is the division of sovereignty between the center and the units, that is, the dissection of competences at both the federal and state/canton levels according to the policy in question. If sovereignty coincides, empirically, with the power to take the final decision on a specific course of action (or policy), then both constitutions reflect the strategy of allocating that power to different institutional levels in relation to different policies. The splitting of the few competences pertaining to the federal center and the many pertaining to the federated states or cantons was the condition not only for making possible the process of aggregation, but for reaching its constitutional goal.

The principle of divided sovereignty has thus been institutionalized, at the supra-state level, through the organization of a representative and decision-making structure based on specific adaptation of
the principle of the separation of powers, both vertically and horizontally. Separation of powers was conceived by the constitution's makers as a political strategy, not only as an abstract principle, to use
for reaching practical targets – in the USA, to hamper the formation
of (permanent) state and popular majorities (Kernell 2003). As Citrin
(2008: 179) stressed, "the Constitution created a fragmented and
decentralized government with the intention of making rapid positive
action difficult"; in Switzerland, to foster the search for consensual
relations between cantons (and the political parties operating within
them) (Kriesi and Trechsel 2008). In both cases, majorities can emerge
only when there is an overwhelming consensus in the union, something
that historically has occurred only in the wake of major domestic or
international crises or traumas or threats. In both cases, the constitutional language has historically helped to frame disputes between
federated states (in the USA particularly after the Civil War: Schutze
2012). In both cases it was, and continues to be, an inclusive language
based on accepted normative premises. In the USA it has even acquired
the status of the language of a "civil religion," in particular after the
1861–65 massacre (see Bellah 1967 for the original elaboration of the
latter concept, but also Slaughter 2007 for its sophisticated updating).
In both cases, the formal constitution has been the basis for creating
an emotional bond between the citizens and the institutions it created. In the USA, "the making of the constitution is the act of founding the nation" (Preuss 1996: 21). In Switzerland, the *"raison d'être*
as *Willensnation* – or nation by will – is entirely based on its political institutions and political culture, centered on the peculiarly Swiss
forms of federalism and democracy" (Dardanelli 2010: 157).

At the same time, both US and Swiss constitutional texts have
allowed for the use of a super-majority to emend them, although both
have introduced procedural hurdles to prevent the routine changing of
their basic structure. In national democracies it is possible to change
the constitutional rules through a parliamentary majority, although
in some countries the change needs to be confirmed by a subsequent
electoral majority expressed through a popular referendum. In the USA
and Switzerland, instead, any such change has to enjoy a broader basis
of consensus. In the USA, the translation of a political or territorial

majority into a constitutional majority is constrained by the double super-majority requirement to pass a constitutional amendment. Article V stipulates that "whenever two thirds of both Houses shall … propose amendments to this Constitution (the proposal) will be valid to all intents and purposes as part of this Constitution, when ratified by the legislatures of three-fourths of the several States, or by conventions in three-fourths thereof, as one or the other mode of ratification may be proposed by the Congress." The principle of a double majority, although highly constrictive, has not proven insurmountable, as shown by the twenty-seven amendments approved so far at the federal level. Yet, while twenty-seven amendments have been approved, thousands were proposed. Moreover, when the process for amending the constitution has become politically rigid, owing either to the formation of conservative majorities able to control both chambers of Congress, or to the formation of veto minorities in one of the two federal chambers or in the state legislatures, major constitutional changes have been introduced via other channels, such as rulings by the Supreme Court, the latter now considered by many (Ackerman 1991: chapter 5) as an integral part of the constitution.

If the US constitution excludes amendments being subject to examination by state referenda, popular referenda at the level of single cantons are instead required by the Swiss constitution for any change of the latter. Article 195 of the Swiss constitution states that "the totally or partly revised Federal Constitution shall come into force when it is approved by the People and the Cantons." In Switzerland, any constitutional amendment, whether introduced by popular or legislative initiative, in order to be approved needs the support of both the majority of the cantons and the citizens (voting in cantonal popular referenda). Thus the principle of double majority is implemented differently in the USA and Switzerland, but the logic is the same: hindering the process of constitutional change, but not making it impossible. Indeed, the 1787 US and the 1848 Swiss constitutions came into force through super-majorities (and not unanimity). In Switzerland, "in June 1848, the new constitution was endorsed by the [legislative] Diet, with 13 votes in favour and 9 against or abstaining. Subsequently, the new constitution was ratified by popular referendum in all but one of the cantons, with 13 and a half votes in favour and 6 and a half against" (Church and Dardanelli 2005: 167). The US constitution came into effect on March 4, 1789, ratified by eleven of the thirteen states. In short, the amendment procedure, although stringent, furnishes the "safety valve" allowing the constitution to be adapted to a changing environment, if considered necessary by a large (super) majority of federal and state representatives. Constitutional conflicts are inevitable in unions of asymmetrical and differentiated states, as has been the case in both the USA and Switzerland. However, in both cases the constitution has not only furnished a common (or accepted) constitutional discourse for managing those conflicts, but also the procedural modality for regulating them.

In the EU, the interstate treaties, even if they have been constitutionalized by the interpretation of the ECJ, have never acquired the status of a formal constitution. Consequently, the constitutional goal of the union has never been declared, although the founders of the EU shared a common understanding of the need to embed national sovereignties into a larger supranational framework. The concept of national sovereignty, as we have seen in Chapter 3, has continued to be hotly contested in the European experience. The elites promoting the 1957 Rome Treaties tried to deal with that concept pragmatically. National sovereignties were unpacked in single market policies through the sharing of decision-making power between the center and the states, but a different approach was then adopted in those policies traditionally at the core of member states' sovereignty. The Maastricht Treaty decision to pool member states' power within the Union's intergovernmental institutions has ended up stressing, rather than embedding, the national sovereignty of the stronger member states. Although the original aim of the EU was to restrain the national sovereignty of European states, this aim has been insufficiently satisfied. In crucial policies, national sovereignties have been redefined but not unpacked. Their intergovernmental redefinition has ended up in creating, under the impact of the euro crisis, a hierarchy among member states.

As with the other two unions, the supranational EU has also organized its decision-making process through a separation of powers principle. But this principle was never formally enshrined in the Treaties and, after the Maastricht Treaty, that framework has been no longer inclusive of all the Union's policies. The EU has come to pursue two different decision-making strategies, one based on the sharing of powers in common/single market policies and one based on the pooling of powers in other crucial policies. Thus regarding the organization of the supra-state level, it is true that within the various interstate treaties, and finally in the 2009 Lisbon Treaty, the separation of powers has emerged empirically as the organizational criterion for setting relations between the Union's institutions, and between the latter and the member states. However, not only has the separation of powers emerged with significant ambiguities, but it has also been constrained by the *confusion* of powers institutionalized in the intergovernmental side of the Treaty (where a legislative institution, such as the Council, performs also an executive role). The institutionalization of these two different decision-making regimes has had unexpected implications with regard to the principle of self-rule concerning member states' autonomy.

Moreover, the EU has continued to adopt the unanimity criterion for changing its treaties, thus bringing the argument over the future of the EU to a regular stalemate. It was for this reason that the most important new intergovernmental treaty adopted under the impact of the euro crisis, the Fiscal Compact Treaty, abolished that criterion (for the first time in European integration history). However, this intergovernmental treaty is outside of the EU legal framework. In the latter context, *all* the member state parliaments or electors have to agree on the change to the Lisbon Treaty. At the same time, interstate treaties and thus the Lisbon Treaty itself cannot provide the homogeneous and accepted language for framing the normative discourse on the basis of which to manage constitutional disputes (Halberstam 2008).

In short, regarding the constitutional framework, the EU reveals significant differences with the other two compound unions. It is not based on a formal constitutional text, although it has been constitutionalized through the ECJ's interpretation of the Treaties as a material constitution; it has not agreed on a univocal constitutional goal, although it has empirically practiced a fragmentation of decision-making power between the Union and its member states within a supranational framework for embedding national sovereignties; it has not adopted the separation of powers in all policy realms, but a form of it only in those related to the common/single market; it has not formalized an amendment procedure of the Lisbon Treaty characterized by some criterion of super-majority, although it has adopted the latter with regard to the intergovernmental treaty instituted outside of its legal framework.

8.4 Institutional structure of compound unions

By institutional structure I mean the architecture that connects both the representative and decision-making institutions at the center and the center and states' institutions under the supervision of the judicial institutions (in other words the larger structure of inter-institutional relations, not only the inter-institutional relations concerning the governmental process as we saw in the previous chapter). Considering federal unions, the latter can be conceptualized with reference to four basic institutional components, that is, the organization of the legislature, the nature of the executive, their relations vis-à-vis the federated states or cantons, and the role of judiciary. The overall logic of the US and Swiss institutional structure consists in the dispersion of decision-making power both horizontally and vertically. The architecture of those compound unions is shaped by the necessity to keep the legislature separate from the executive, the center separate from the states or cantons, and the governmental institutions separate from the judiciary. In 1787 Philadelphia, constitution makers, who wanted to construct a union that would combine interstate (confederal) and supra-state (federal) features, decided to experiment with the formation of a system of multiple separation of powers. The experiment seemed to work reasonably well so that the 1848 Swiss constitution imitated it, although with specific adaptation to the historical legacy of the previous confederation. In both cases, the project was the setting up of an institutional structure where each component enjoys operational independence from the others and at the same time has to share governmental functions with all of them. The same cannot be said for the EU, although its institutional structure on the supranational side reflects many aspects of the institutional structure of the USA and Switzerland (see Table 8.3).

In the USA and Switzerland, the dispersed decision-making structure at the center is protected not only by the constitution, but also by a diffusion of veto positions. Each member state/canton or institutional actor may hinder or postpone an undesired decision, unless it is partially changed in accordance with the request of that member state or institutional actor. This veto power epitomizes the confederal logic that has been used within the federal union since its foundation. In the USA, for instance, the right is still recognized to 40 senators (within the 100-member Senate) to *filibuster* during the discussion on

Table 8.3 *Compound unions: institutional structure*

	United States/Switzerland	European Union
legislature	separated bicameralism (USA) differentiated bicameralism (Switzerland)	imperfect bicameralism
executive	independent president (USA) independent directory (Switzerland)	undefined two-head structure
center/ territorial units	dual federalism evolved towards cooperative practices reciprocal financial independence	quasi-cooperative federalism formalized as subsidiarity center's financial dependence on the states
judiciary	judicial review (USA) popular review (Switzerland)	judicial review by intermediation

an undesired piece of legislation or on presidential nominees.[3] Thus a number of senators representing a small minority of the population can stop any legislation or presidential nominee proposal supported by a majority of senators representing the large majority of the population. From a normative point of view, this is certainly a case of tyranny of minorities. In order to reduce the paralyzing impact of the filibuster, in November 2013 the Democratic majority of the Senate decided finally to break this deeply rooted convention, approving a rule prohibiting the minority party from filibustering presidential nominees for the federal judiciary and the executive branch. Presidential nominees can now be approved by a simple majority of senators. However, filibustering remains in place for legislation and for nominees to the Supreme Court. Let us dissect the institutional structure.

[3] The Senate, in fact, has the power to approve (formally "to give advice and consent" on) presidential nominees, besides its legislative power to approve federal laws with the House of Representatives.

US and Swiss horizontal separation of powers

First consider the horizontal level. In the USA, the separate institutions at the center (president, House of Representatives; and Senate), but also those of the states (governors and bicameral legislatures[4]), have been endowed with independent legitimacy: direct legitimacy in the case of the House of Representatives, indirect (as we have seen) in the case of the Senate until 1913 and direct after that; indirect in the case of the president as he or she is elected through the states' electoral colleges (see Glossary). However, the latter has acquired the status of a popular legitimacy with the direct election of the members of the states' electoral colleges, a practice that had only been adopted by a few states in the nineteenth century and then later formalized by all the states (before that, the members of the states' electoral colleges were nominated by the states' legislature: see S. Fabbrini 2008c, chapter 2). The bicameral legislature is institutionally separate (see Chapter 7), because the members of each chamber are elected by different constituencies (the representatives are elected in districts within states, whereas the two state senators are both elected in colleges coinciding with their state) and their mandates have a different time span (two years for the representatives and six years for the senators, with one-third of the latter's mandate expiring in coincidence with the two-year mandate of the representatives) (Cain and Jones 1989). Once elected, the senators vote individually as representatives of the state's electors.

Regarding the president (whose mandate is four years, renewable once, after Amendment XXII of 1951), his/her separation from the legislature is guaranteed by several barriers. The first is the constitution, which not only does not make the president dependent on the confidence of the legislature, but also does not allow the president and the legislators to mingle. Article I, Section VI.2 of the constitution (which reads: "No Senator or Representative shall, during the time for which he was elected, be appointed to any civil office under the authority of the United States ... and no person holding any office under the United States shall be a member of either House during his continuance in office"), introducing the reciprocal incompatibility

---

[4] With the sole exception of Nebraska, which adopted a unicameral system in 1934.

between the office of legislator and that of member of the executive, has further protected the separation between the two institutions. The second barrier is the electoral college, which creates a distinct body of electors and which dissolves after having elected the president. The third is the winner-takes-all criterion adopted gradually (in the course of the nineteenth century) by the states to allocate the presidential elector votes to the various candidates (S. Fabbrini 2008c: chapter 2). In fact, the original 1787 text of the constitution requires the House of Representatives to elect the president, choosing between the five candidates with the most votes,[5] if no candidate receives the majority of the electoral votes. Amendment XII of 1804 reduced the power of the House of Representatives to select the president from among the three candidates with the most votes, thus leaving open the possibility of a popular legislature role in the presidential election. Indeed, during the founding period of the union, with the two-party system not yet formed and the electoral votes assigned to the candidates on a proportional representation basis, it happened (in 1796, 1800, 1824) that no candidate won the majority of the electoral college votes, thus leaving the choice to the House (which, in 1824, chose the candidate with the second highest number of votes, John Quincy Adams, and not Andrew Jackson, who had received the most votes, thus triggering a strong reaction that led to the gradual adoption by the states of the *winner-takes-all* criterion in the allocation of the electoral votes in the states, with the exception of two states[6]).

With the diffusion of that criterion and the consolidation of a two-party system in all the states, the possibility of congressional control of the presidential election was neutralized. The new electoral-party system was able to guarantee a winner with an absolute majority of the electoral votes, thus removing the choice of the president from the House of Representatives (and thus preventing any claim by the latter that the president should depend on its political will). The new

---

[5] Article II, Section I.3, stated that "if no Person have a Majority, then from the five highest on the List the … House shall in like Manner *choose* the President. But in choosing the President, the Votes shall be taken by States, the Representation from each State having one Vote; a quorum for this Purpose shall consist of a Member or Members from two-thirds of the States, and a Majority of all the States shall be necessary to a Choice," author's emphasis.

[6] Nebraska and Maine give two electoral votes to the popular-vote winner and apportion the rest to the popular-vote winner in each House of Representatives' district.

rule has had, however, a not unimportant side effect, namely that the majority of the electoral votes might not correspond to the majority of the popular votes (as happened in 1876, 1888 and 2000). In short, through the introduction of and experimentation with various devices, the US separation of powers system has been fully institutionalized. In this system, no institution depends on the others in order to function and none of them requires the confidence of the others in order to perform its tasks. Nevertheless, in order to make the system function, all of them should cooperate, under the incentives of the checks and balances that connect those institutions.

In Switzerland, the model of the separation of powers has been implemented in a different form. The bicameral legislature is institutionally separate (between the Council of States and the National Council constituting the Federal Assembly, see Chapter 7). Their members are elected concurrently. The Council of States' members are elected in their cantons according to rules established autonomously by the cantons themselves, on the condition that they respect democratic criteria. Today they are elected through forms of a PR system with a majority's logic in cantons electing only one councilor. The councilors are expected to represent their cantons through their electorates. The National Council's members, representing the voters of the Swiss confederacy, are elected through a PR system in constituencies designed within the boundaries of each canton. Nevertheless, they are separate in terms of the roles and functions exercised in the legislative process. Although the executive, the Federal Council, is elected by the Federal Assembly (the two chambers meeting together), "following each general election to the National Council" (Title 5, Article 175.2), it is independent from the legislature.

Once elected, the members of the Federal Council are not responsible to the Federal Assembly that elected them. Federal Council members can participate in the debates of the Federal Assembly, but only as observers (without any right to vote). Moreover, the internal organization of the Federal Council is collegial and anti-hierarchical. Article 176.13 of the constitution, states that:

The President of the Confederation shall chair the Federal Council ... The President and the Vice-President of the Federal Council shall be elected by the Federal Assembly from the members of the Federal Council for a term of office of one year ... Re-election for the following year is not permitted. The President may not be elected Vice-President for the following year.

Thus the Federal Council is a collegial executive, whose presidency is held on rotation for one year by one of the seven members. The seven members of the Federal Council "shall be elected for a term of office of four years from all the Swiss citizens who are eligible for election to the National Council" (Title 5, Article 175.3), they cannot be members of either chamber of the Federal Assembly and each of them is elected individually, through a secret ballot, by the absolute majority of the votes of the Federal Assembly. The Swiss executive has been defined as a directorial executive, whose role is to be head of the Swiss union as a *council in corpore*. Once instituted, the Federal Assembly and the Federal Council are reciprocally independent, in the sense that the latter does not need the formal confidence of the former for operating. Thus, although through different institutional devices, in both Switzerland and the USA none of the governmental institutions depends on the confidence of the others to operate, thus fulfilling the basic criterion of horizontal separation of powers.

The mechanism of checks and balances operates across policies. For instance, regarding budgetary policy, in the USA the president has pre-eminence in delineating the yearly budget for the federal government, but then has to deal with an independent Congress. It has become customary since the 1920s that the president uses his February State of the Union Address to inform Congress of his budgetary strategies (Wildavsky 1988). However, the president's prerogatives have continued to be constitutionally constrained by Congress' powers (Jones 1995): without the agreement of the two legislative chambers (the House of Representatives and the Senate), the president's budgetary proposal will remain a proposal. As Polsby (2004) argued, what characterizes the US system is the persistence of Congress' power, more than the growth of the president's power.

US and Swiss vertical separation of powers

Consider now the vertical separation of powers. Since the USA and Switzerland aggregate previously independent states, it is not surprising that their constitutions establish few competences for the federal center, leaving broad autonomy to the federated states or the cantons. Both initially started from a model of dual federalism, setting up reciprocal independent institutions at the center and in the states/cantons, although both have later moved on to experiment with practices typical of a model of cooperative federalism (for the USA, see Schutze

2010; for Switzerland, see Sciarini and Bochsler 2006). Each level of the union, in governing the specific policies allocated to it by the constitution, has its own autonomous legislative, executive and judiciary organs. Both have their own administrative structure in order to fulfill their own specific functions. Each has finally acquired its own fiscal and regulatory autonomy,[7] but within severe constraints presided over by the states or cantons.

Institutionally, dual federalism has an anti-hierarchical bias. In both unions, the constitution has never resolved the question of the proper balance between the federal center and the federated states or cantons, as became evident in the USA with the outbreak of the Civil War in 1861 (Glencross 2009) and the continuous swing of powers to and from the federal center and the federated states; or in Switzerland with the permanent tensions between the various cantons that finally led to the constitutional revision of 1999 (Vatter 2008). In particular in the USA, because of the effects of the magnitude of its economy and its international role, the competition between the federal center and the federated states has had powerful effects on the competition between the president (claiming to represent a national view) and Congress (necessarily representing state and local views). For the first century of the new republic, Congress played a much more important role than the president and the federated states were much more influential than the federal center (this was the era of *congressional government*: Wilson 1956). However, with the nationalization of the USA, which has developed since the 1930s and especially since the end of the Second World War, the president has become pre-eminent vis-à-vis the legislature as the federal center has become more influential than the states (characterizing the era of *presidential government*) (Lowi 1985). If, as we have seen, the increasing role of the president has not diminished the power of Congress, the increasing role of the center has not diminished the policy-making influence of the states. Indeed, in the 1970s a powerful wind in favor of transferring powers back to the states started to blow again (Conlan 1998). The power pendulum has thus continued to swing back and forth (Beer 1993).

---

[7] For the US case, see Super (2005) for a detailed reconstruction of the logic and structure of fiscal federalism and its historical evolution, and Rodden (2006) for a more theoretical discussion.

In all federal political systems, in order to understand the power relations between the center and the territorial units, it is necessary to consider which level controls fiscal resources. In the USA, with Amendment XVI of 1913, "The Congress shall have the power to lay and collect taxes on incomes, from whatever source derived, without apportionment among the several States, and without regard to any census or enumeration".[8] Article I, Section 8 of the constitution already empowered Congress to "lay and collect Taxes, Duties, Imposts and Excises, to pay the Debts and provide for the common Defense and general Welfare of the United States; but all Duties, Imposts and Excises shall be uniform throughout the United States." Article I, Section 2.3 also states that "Representatives and direct Taxes shall be apportioned among the several States." However, before the approval of Amendment XVI, the federal government had to share money from direct taxes with the states. There was an income tax before Amendment XVI. It was in effect during the Civil War, but it ended in 1866. Indeed, the federal government had the power to collect taxes on houses or other properties, but both these types of taxes, which were considered direct taxes, would have to be divided back among the states. The power to levy income taxes was rendered impotent because all income taxes were apportioned among the states according to their populations. By specifically affixing the language "from whatever source derived," Amendment XVI removed the direct tax dilemma.

In Switzerland, the financial support for federal activities was, for the first century of its existence (1848–1941), extremely limited, coming mainly from internal custom duties. Only with the 1941 National Defence Tax was the federal center allowed to levy direct taxes. However, Article 128.1, paragraph 4 of the constitution clarifies that "the tax shall be assessed and collected by the Cantons. A minimum of 17 percent of the gross revenue from taxation shall be allocated to the Cantons." The historically limited fiscal basis of the center might help to explain why the US Senate and the Swiss Council of States are constituted by senators or councilors representing the voters and not the corporate bodies of the states or cantons. Only where the federal center is powerful (as in Germany) do the territorial units

---

[8] For an analysis of the federal budgetary policy made possible by that constitutional amendment, see Wildavsky (1988).

need to participate as corporate bodies in the decision-making process (in particular regarding budgetary policy) (Filippov, Ordeshook and Shvetsova 2004). Indeed, as we have seen, the German Bundesrat represents the governments, not the voters, of the *Länder*. In the USA and Switzerland, dual federalism, which started as a territorial system favoring competition between jurisdictions whose frictions have to be regulated by their judicial procedures and institutions, later included forms of intergovernmental cooperation (Bolleyer 2009) because of the necessity to manage the growing complexity of multilevel policies.

In multiple separation of powers systems, the role of the higher court is necessary for resolving disputes. However, a significant distinction is detectable between the USA and Switzerland in this regard. In the USA, it is the Supreme Court and in Switzerland the people empowered by popular referendum that function as the guardian of the structure of multiple separation. In the USA, the power of judicial review implies that every decision taken by the federal legislature and countersigned by the president can be annulled by federal courts if considered to be unconstitutional (Shapiro 2002: 136–48). This has never been the case in the European fusion of powers systems.[9] In Switzerland, on the other hand, the power of judicial review is not recognized to the Federal Supreme Court. Article 189.4 of the constitution states that "acts of the Federal Assembly or the Federal Council may not be challenged in the Federal Supreme Court. Exceptions may be provided for by law." This is because that power is recognized to the citizens. Article 141.1 states that:

if within 100 days of the official publication of the enactment any 50,000 persons eligible to vote or any eight Cantons request it, the following shall be submitted to a vote of the People: a. federal acts; b. emergency federal acts whose term of validity exceeds one year; c. federal decrees, provided

---

[9] Of course, in fusion of powers (parliamentary or semi-presidential) systems the legislature is also obliged to respect constitutional principles and procedures in approving a law. Laws may be subject to a *constitutional review* exercised by an ad hoc constitutional court (constituted by judges but also members elected by the parliament and the head of state) and initiated by another public institution. Nevertheless, those laws are not subject to a judicial review exercised by ordinary courts as in the USA (on the crucial difference between constitutional review and judicial review, see Stone Sweet 2000: chapters 2 and 5). It might be added that, to date, most constitutional courts are open to individual claims, as has historically been the case for the US Supreme Court.

the Constitution or an act so requires; d. international treaties that: 1. are of unlimited duration and may not be terminated; 2. provide for accession to an international organization; 3. contain important legislative provisions or whose implementation requires the enactment of federal legislation.

Multiple separation of powers in the EU

The EU as institutionalized by the 2009 Lisbon Treaty has many similarities with the institutional structure of the other two compound unions, but also significant differences. The Lisbon Treaty has institutionalized a bicameral legislature, organized around a double principle of representation (individual voters and member states), which has proper federal features (Kelemen 2004). The EP and the Council have been recognized as the two chambers of the EU legislature, thanks to the institutionalization of the co-decision procedure as the "ordinary legislative procedure" for most EU deliberations (TFEU, Article 289). In this regard, the Council, in its differentiated ministerial configurations, is a legislative institution more similar to the German Bundesrat, which consists of the representatives of the *Länder* executives, than to the US Senate or Swiss Council of States. However, two crucial Council configurations, the Foreign Affairs Council and the ECOFIN Council, are not only legislative but also executive institutions. And, above all, in both the CFSP and the EMU, because in those policies many deliberations do not take legal form, the EP has been located at their margins. This is why EU bicameralism should be considered imperfect.

At the same time, the Lisbon Treaty, recognizing the European Council as an executive institution, has also institutionalized a dual executive consisting of the European Council and the Commission, apparently as in semi-presidential systems (Fifth Republic France being the most coherent example, see Glossary) (Colomer 2010), with the crucial difference that, unlike the French executive, the Commission is not formed within the parliament as is the case for the French Council of Ministers (Elgie 1999), although its president and commissioners, nominated by the European Council, should then receive approval by the majority of the EP. The Commission is a technocratic body, unlike the French Council of Ministers which is a political institution. The president of the European Council (elected by the majority of the latter's members) is the chairman of a collegial body, unlike the French president elected personally by the voters. The relation between the president of the European Council and the president of the Commission (and between their respective institutions) is not clearly defined in the Lisbon Treaty. At the same time, however, the European Council and its president are supported in their activities by the General Secretariat of the Council, a legislative institution, rather than by the Commission structure. Confusion, rather than separation of powers between executive and legislative institutions, is formalized on the intergovernmental side of the Treaty.

In the supranational EU there is not a government as such, but a quadrilateral system of institutions contributing to the decision-making process. Decision-making power is shared by distinct separate institutions. Notwithstanding (or because of) the possibility of deciding through QMV in the Council or absolute majority in the EP (Egenhofer, Kurpas and Van Schaik 2009), many legal acts are approved after elaborate negotiations between those institutions in order to balance member state and partisan interests. The electoral differentiation between the two legislative chambers and the nature of the dual executive have made the identification of a homogeneous policy majority across them unlikely. This makes the EU decision-making process particularly complex. The formation of the EU bicameral legislature is not synchronized, thus making impossible the elaboration between the two chambers of a stable "magic formula" for composing an executive that balances state and partisan interests. The composition of the Council varies with the differentiated schedule of domestic elections, thus introducing a factor of uncertainty into the process; nor do the Council and the EP have the same temporal mandate. The EU does not even have an executive structure that might express, as in Switzerland, the practice of consensual politics. The EU executive is dual; it is not a single institution as is the Swiss Federal Council (with its rotating president). Thus there is not even an institution where a "magic formula" for recomposing the state and the party divisions could be tested. The EU has used its way of sharing powers between member states and the Union's institutions in common/single market policies, but not in the policies that were traditionally reserved to national sovereignty. Here legislative and executive roles overlap. Although organized differently, in both the USA and Switzerland the system of separation of powers does not allow for such a confusion of roles and institutions.

There are similarities and differences between the EU and the other two compound unions regarding the vertical separation of powers (Menon and Schain 2006; Stein 2000). The relation between the member states and the Union has passed through different definitions. It was initially based on the empirical concept of assigning limited competences to the Union's institutions, leaving the rest to the member states, as in other unions. With the Maastricht Treaty, the EU formally introduced the principle of subsidiarity for organizing cooperation between the member states and the Union (Cartabia, Lupo and Simoncini 2013). That principle thus formed part of the Lisbon Treaty that declares the resolution of the member states to promote a decision-making logic where decisions are taken "as closely as possible to the citizen in accordance with the principle of subsidiarity." That principle would allow the EU institutions to perform only those tasks that cannot be performed more effectively at a national or local level (see Chapter 2).

In order to strengthen respect of this principle two important Protocols were added to the Lisbon Treaty. Protocol No. 1 recognizes national parliaments' power (Article 3) "to send to the Presidents of the European Parliament, the Council and the Commission a reasoned opinion on whether a draft legislative act complies with the principle of subsidiarity." Protocol No. 2 introduces the so-called "yellow card" that national parliaments can use to block a Commission legislative proposal considered to infringe on national prerogatives. In this case (Article 7.1), "each national Parliament shall have two votes, shared out on the basis of the national Parliamentary system. In the case of a bicameral Parliamentary system, each of the two chambers shall have one vote," then adding (Article 7.2), "where reasoned opinions on a draft legislative act's non-compliance with the principle of subsidiarity represent at least one third of all the votes allocated to the national Parliaments ... [then] the draft must be reviewed."

The concept of subsidiarity has been highly contested due to the difficulty of measuring or testing effectiveness at the various levels in which policies are managed (F. Fabbrini 2014b). Its implementation has led the EU de facto to practice a form of cooperative federalism. Contrary to the model of dual federalism (Borzel and Hosli 2003; Kelemen 2007), in the cooperative federalism model few competences are exclusively controlled either by the Union or member state. In cooperative federalism, the majority of competences are

shared between the two levels, coherently with the model of cooperation tried out foremost by Germany. Since many competences are
shared, then it is understandable that in both the EU and Germany
the member states are represented at the center by their governments
(the Council or the Bundesrat). However, in the EU the recognition of
the principle of subsidiarity has not prevented the growth of forms of
decision-making centralization in policies based on voluntary coordination and not legislative action. Indeed, as at the end of 2014 the subsidiarity yellow card had been used with regard to two Commission
proposals (Fabbrini and Granat 2013): (1) in spring 2012, with regard
to a Commission proposal for a Council regulation "on the exercise
of the right to take collective action within the context of the freedom
of establishment and the freedom to provide services"; (2) in summer
2013, with regard to a Commission proposal for a Council regulation
"on the establishment of the European Public Prosecutor's Office."
The principle of subsidiarity does not apply where integration does
not proceed through law.

Thus, in the intergovernmental policies of EMU it has been difficult to counter a process of centralization that has subtracted substantial discretion from member state parliaments and governments
in budgetary or fiscal policy. Although intergovernmental institutions
have intruded into member states' budgetary discretion, the reaction
to such intrusion has been uncertain. The member states can use the
principle of subsidiarity to reclaim their decision-making power from
the supranational institutions, but such claims seem implausible in a
context where the decision-making power has moved to the institutions of national governments, not to supranational institutions. This
is a significant difference from the other two unions. In the latter,
notwithstanding recent practices of cooperation between the center
and the territorial units, a federal boundary has continued to preside
over the relations between the two levels of governments. The center
and the states/cantons are reciprocally independent in their spheres
of competence and on these bases they have developed practices of
cooperation for dealing (in particular) with new issues. In the EU, on
the contrary, this distinction appears opaque in the intergovernmental
union, whereas the subsidiarity principle cannot be easily applied.

Finally, regarding the role and power recognized to the judiciary, the
ECJ looks more like the US Supreme Court than the Swiss Supreme
Federal Court. The ECJ has come to play a role of judicial, rather

than constitutional, review, although through the intermediation of member state judiciaries. Thanks to the preliminary reference mechanism, member state judiciaries, without passing through their respective constitutional courts, have made recourse to the ECJ for an opinion on the congruence of a national law with EU primary or secondary legislation. In the EU, control over the constitutionality of domestic parliamentary acts has become widespread, decentralized and horizontal, a process that has strengthened, within the EU member states, low-level judiciaries in relation to their national constitutional courts. The ECJ has been legitimized by this cooperation and increasingly accepted as the authoritative interpreter of EU law. With the recognition of the Charter of Fundamental Rights as the third fundamental Treaty of the EU legal order, the powers of judicial review of the ECJ have been strengthened even more.

Thus the institutional structure of the EU has similarities with the institutional structure of the USA and Switzerland, but it also displays significant differences due to the institutionalization of its intergovernmental side and the lack of an effective criterion for organizing the multiple separation of powers. As an undeclared federal union, the EU has stressed the role of states to the exclusion of that of the citizens in its foundation. The interstate treaties have affected its constitutional framework, leaving its goal ambiguous, preventing the formalization of a clear constitutional principle for organizing its decision-making system and introducing amending criteria constrained by unanimity. Its constitutional uncertainty, which is an expression of the divisions between member states, has allowed the formation of an intergovernmental union distinct from the supranational one. Combining the three levels of analysis, it is thus possible to assert that the EU is a union of states whose political logic is conditioned by its interstate cleavages, but obstructed in its functioning as a coherent compound democracy because of the political ambiguities of its foundation, the lack of an agreed constitutional framework and the institutionalization of an intergovernmental decision-making regime.

8.5 The institutional dilemmas of the EU

Given these systemic and constitutional limitations, the perspective of the compound union would require the EU at least to deal with basic dilemmas of inter-institutional relations. Here my focus will be on the identification of the institutional structure that might better bring the EU close to a compound union. Institutional change proceeds through adaptation and rationalization of existing arrangements, rarely through abrupt substitution of an existing arrangement with a new one. Critical junctures can open up a new direction for innovation, as happened with the post-1954 decision to build a common market, with the post-1990 decision to set up two constitutional regimes within the same legal order, with the post-2009 decision to create new intergovernmental treaties for organizing the euro-area member states; however, innovation frequently consists in framing existing institutions within a new ideational paradigm. It is highly implausible that an institutional change can start from scratch. Thus it is true that in order to make the EU a compound union, a reform of its institutional structure according to the criterion of separation of powers is necessary; but it is also true that such a reform should be based on the institutional developments that have emerged from the various critical junctures, and the euro crisis in particular. This means recognizing the existence of a quadrilateral system of representative and decision-making institutions. The reform strategy would necessarily have to deal with three basic dilemmas of inter-institutional relations. The first dilemma concerns relations between the supranational and the intergovernmental unions. The second dilemma concerns relations between the European Council and the Commission. The third dilemma concerns relations between the EP and the executive power of the Union.

Supranational vs. intergovernmental institutions

It seems certain that the institutional development of the intergovernmental union has represented the most significant challenge to the separation of powers at the Union level. While integration through law has supported the structuring of a system of separation of powers, organized around a quadrilateral system of institutions, integration through policy coordination among member state governments has squeezed, or severely constrained, that system. Integration through voluntary policy coordination has emphasized the (executive and legislative) role of the European Council and the Council to the detriment of the EP, the Commission and the ECJ. National governments have recognized the need to have the cooperation of the Commission, but with the deepening of the euro crisis the latter's contribution has acquired mainly a technical or implementing role. In the intergovernmental policies of the EMU or CFSP, there is no significant place for the EP in the policy-making process. It is inevitable that certain crucial decisions (in foreign and security or economic policies, for instance) have pre-eminently a political, rather than legal nature; it is also inevitable that those decisions are taken by executive institutions such as the European Council. Nevertheless, it is not inevitable that an executive-centered decision-making process must operate outside of any political (let alone legal) control.

The intergovernmental union has been inhospitable to the separation of powers, or even to a basic distinction of institutional roles and policy functions. In foreign policy, the double hat of the HR has created contradictory relations between the Foreign Affairs Council and the Commission. The confusion between the legislative role of the latter and the executive role of the former is unlikely to bring effectiveness and legitimacy to foreign policy decisions. Without distancing the HR from the Foreign Affairs Council, thus making the former a full member of the executive and the latter an independent checking institution, the need to guarantee a reasonable degree of effectiveness and legitimacy to the Union's foreign policy will remain unmet. A similar confusion affects the relations between the ECOFIN Council (and Euro Group) and the commissioner for economic and monetary affairs and the euro (who has also been a vice-president of the Commission since October 2011). Their intermingling obscures the respective responsibility for the decisions taken. If the ECOFIN (or Euro Group) decides a policy and then implements it, it is unclear where to locate the line dividing executive action and legislative control. At the same time, the intergovernmental union has also subverted the dividing line between Brussels and the member states, triggering a process of centralization that has called into question the balance between the two levels of government.

It seems however certain that it would not be sufficient to bring the intergovernmental arrangements back to the supranational framework, if the supranational framework is interpreted according to the "Community method" approach. The challenge is to recompose the two constitutions in a new supranational framework characterized by the full recognition of the European Council's role. Contrary to the US states and Swiss cantons, the EU member states are the expression of historical and deeply rooted configurations of institutional power. Their political salience cannot be equated to that of thirteen young independent states that started the process of integration in 1776–1787 in the USA or twenty-two relatively small cantons that did the same in 1815–1848 in Switzerland. Any attempt to downsize the influence of member state governments in the EU is unrealistic. The EU cannot prosper without developing an institutional structure that emphasizes the role of intergovernmental institutions much more than has been recognized by the other two compound unions (and by the same "Community method").

This would also require a strengthening of the resources and powers of a supranational institution such as the EP. The EP with the Council should benefit from autonomous fiscal capacity in order to achieve democratically decided targets and, correspondingly, each member state should be considered responsible for any financial default (although this has not happened notwithstanding the Lisbon Treaty). The dividing line between member states and the Union's institutions has to be better protected through democratic politics that should become part of the economic constitution of the Union. The EP should have a comparable voice to the Council in all the policies of the Union, not only in single market policies. This requires a new and original institutional architecture able to recompose intergovernmental and supranational institutions. The USA and Switzerland have adopted different species of the separation of powers' genus. The EU should find its own solution to the need for recognizing the role of the intergovernmental institutions in the Union's decision-making process, without jeopardizing the separation of powers' logic that guarantees the viability of a union of asymmetrical and differentiated states.

The European Council vs. the executive power

A second inter-institutional dilemma concerns the structure and functioning of the executive. There is no questioning the fact that the EU has a dual executive consisting of the European Council and the Commission, with the two respective presidents representing a two-faced Janus. The institutionalization, with the Lisbon Treaty, of the European Council has been a key condition in the advancement of the integration process in sensitive policy areas. With the election of the permanent president of the European Council, the latter has been transformed into a stable executive institution of the EU. The euro crisis has thus accelerated the transformation of the European Council into an executive institution. Indeed, it would be appropriate for the European Council to be renamed the *European Presidency*, thus avoiding any misunderstanding with the Council (legislative body) and at the same time underlining its institutional function (executive body). Furthermore, if the European Council is an executive institution, why are its activities supported by the General Affairs Council (the configuration of the legislative Council coordinating all the latter's other ministerial configurations)? The Lisbon Treaty affirms that the General Affairs Council (TEU, Article 16.6) is in charge of preparing the work and ensuring "the follow-up to the meetings of the European Council, in liaison with the president of the European Council and the Commission." However, if the President of the European Council is an executive officer, then his/her activity should be supported by the Commission and not by that of a legislative committee (such as the General Affairs Council). The General Affairs Council might support the various Council configurations, in order to let them perform their co-decisional role with the EP effectively. The General Secretary of the Council should also support the activities of the member state holding the rotating presidency of the various Council configurations.

There is also no question that the president of the European Council, Herman van Rompuy, under the impact of the euro crisis in particular, has become the mouthpiece of the heads of state and governments of the larger or stronger member states (who indeed contributed to his election). The creation of the office of the permanent president of the European Council has not been sufficient to prevent the formation of hierarchical relations within the latter. Under the state of exception caused by the crisis, within the European Council political decisions have been affected by the power of the stronger and larger member state governments to the detriment of the others. The president of the European Council, limiting himself to playing the role of chairman, has not guaranteed the necessary equilibrium between governments. The nomination of Donald Tusk as the new European Council president in 2014 is a further confirmation of the will of the main national governments to have control of the institution. As long as the national governments nominate the European Council president, their choice will favor an official who will not question the role of the stronger members among them. This is why it would be necessary to move from a nomination to an election of the European Council president, although the latter should have an indirect nature.[10] If it is true that the effectiveness of the European Council's president would be stronger if he/she could benefit from greater decision-making autonomy than the majority of the European Council's members, then this outcome might be ensured only through a larger basis of legitimacy for his/her election. One might also assume the possibility of downsizing the executive role of the European Council, strengthening the executive role of the Commission and recomposing the two presidencies into a single office. But this assumption, as argued in Chapter 6, seems unrealistic. In any case, what is crucial from a compound union perspective is the separation of the executive from the legislature, not the monocentric or dual nature of the executive. The two roles might be recomposed, but that would not represent the solution to our puzzle, unless one assumes that the single head of the executive should be formed separately from the EP. By remaining in the dual executive, the Commission will continue to guarantee the proper and necessary execution of EU laws and the respect for EU treaties, whereas the European Council and its presidency should become the focus of the politicization process. The EU as an original compound union needs to find a solution to the dilemma of recognizing the political role of the intergovernmental European Council and, at the same time, increasing the supranational characterization of its presidency.

Parliamentary vs. congressional EP

A third institutional dilemma concerns the relations between the EP and a European Council-based executive system. The EP has increased its legislative powers with the recognition of its role in the ordinary legislative procedure. However, the EP has a limited budget to control, its fiscal capacity is dependent on intergovernmental decisions and it has been excluded from or downsized in crucial policy fields such as the CFSP and EMU. There is, thus, the necessity to increase the role of the EP, without at the same time bringing the EU to the dead end

---

[10] Indirect because unions of asymmetrical and differentiated states cannot easily accommodate direct election of their executive officers, if they do not want to call into question the fragile equilibrium between their constituent states. As I argued with regard to the USA, this explains the persistence in the latter of the electoral college method for electing the president. In the case of the EU, I advanced a first proposal in S. Fabbrini (2012).

of parliamentary government. The logic of the separation of powers would require the EP to play a congressional, rather than parliamentary role. While the latter role consists in forming or electing a government, the congressional role requires the EP to balance the other legislative chamber and to check the executive branch. Parliaments dissolve when they are not able to form a government, but congresses operate according to a fixed temporal mandate because they do not depend on the existence of the government. Parliaments are flexible; congresses are rigid (Kreppel 2011). Since the seminal article by Polsby (1968), there has been a general acceptance of the basic distinction between the *policy-making legislature* in separation of power systems and the *arena legislature* in fusion of powers systems, where the former is a law-making institution and the latter an institution for adversarial confrontation between the government and the opposition (in competitive parliamentary systems) or for the negotiation between the main political parties (in consensual parliamentary systems) (Loewenberg and Patterson 1988; Norton 1998).

Although the EP does not have the power to introduce autonomous legislation, its role is, however, closer to the *working* legislature of the separation of power systems (such as the US House of Representatives) than to the *debating* legislature of the parliamentary systems of nation states (Shackleton 2005). It has indeed been considered a variant of the former, definable as a *controlling* legislature (Dann 2003). The EP should thus be given the necessary resources to develop its congressional role. This requires the power to initiate legislation, a fiscal capacity to support the latter and resources to play its role of controlling the executive and balancing the Council. If the EP cannot have control of autonomous fiscal resources, then its congressional role would be severely constrained. The congressional role of the EP is vital in the context of an EU that has become European Council-based (De Scoutheete 2011). The EP should balance the legislative institution representing EU member states' ministers (the Council) and check the operation of the two faces of the EU executive, the Commission and the European Council. If, relative to the Commission, this role has been successfully played and probably will become more effective after the 2014 election of Jean-Claude Juncker, the same cannot be said with regard to the European Council. The EP should recognize that certain decisions in the field of foreign policy and economic policy have an inevitable executive bias. Because of their political sensitivity, it is understandable that those decisions originate from the institution that most represents the national governments, namely the European Council. However, those decisions should be checked by an independent legislature, that is, the EP, backed by sanctioning powers. The solution to the dilemma on how to make the decision-making power of the European Council accountable can be found in strengthening the congressional role of the EP, whose powers should be constituted by legal (law-making) but also extra-legal resources (such as overseeing the European Council's behavior and to investigate its choices based on some form of sanctioning power) (van de Steeg 2009). As shown by the EP's vote on March 13, 2013 against the Multiannual Financial Framework (MFF) for 2014–2021 agreed by the member state governments (politically in the European Council and formally in the Council), this congressional role can magnify the political power of the EP.[11]

In conclusion, a separation of powers system is not the recipe for easily meeting the goals of effectiveness and legitimacy. However, empirically it is the only system that might reasonably approach those goals in the context of asymmetrical and differentiated unions of states, as shown by the comparative analysis of the USA and Switzerland. Because the comparison has also shown that separation of powers can take different forms, it might also be argued that the EU can pursue its own form, given its specific experience of aggregating historically rooted states. A system with an executive structured organizationally by the Commission and directed politically by the president of the European Council and a bicameral legislature with the powers and the resources to control the executive might promote a sufficient degree of both effectiveness and legitimacy. Certainly, it might also end up in institutional in-fighting whose outcome is policy stalemate, if not decision-making gridlock, a situation that, in the USA, has at times generated what Polsby (1997: 177) called "the tyranny of the status quo." This is not so different from what already

---

[11] It should also be noted that although TFEU Article 312.1 points out that the framework "shall be established for a period of at least five years," the multiannual financial framework has acquired a time span of 7 years. It was an intergovernmental decision symbolically aimed to loosen the relation between the EP (whose mandate lasts 5 years) and the Union's budget. In this case, too, a "congressional" EP should reclaim respect of the Treaty clause, something that the EP has not dared to do.

happens in the EU, where an existing rule "is protected against changes by exactly the same high consensus requirements that had impeded its earlier adoption" (Scharpf 2009b: 182). Separation of powers encourages the affirmation of (and in any case requires) a political elite (at both national and supranational levels) that is able to generate positive-sum solutions to interstate and partisan divisions – political or party elite specialized in mediating between the interests expressed by the separate institutions, in promoting the necessary compromises between states and political factions in order to reach a shared decision, in constructing contingent and ad hoc coalitions in favor of given courses of action. Separation of powers encourages (and at the same time presupposes) a politics of moderation. This system also offers several avenues for ventilating citizens' and member states' concerns. The politicization of the role of the European Council president and the EP elections might furnish a window of opportunity to citizens seeking a change in the overall direction of the Union's policies, as important avenues for affecting the latter will continue to be the national elections.

Comparative analysis has shown that unions of states, given their structural and political constraints, have no other choice in organizing their decision-making process than to rely on whichever form of separate institutions sharing power but enshrined in a constitutional document. In the case of the EU, however, that constitutional choice has been prevented by its internal divisions. Although I considered the EU as such a union here, the latter's transformation into a coherent compound union would require its simultaneous deconstruction and the reassembling of its parts within a new institutional order.

8.6 Conclusion

This chapter has investigated the EU from the perspective of the established compound unions of the USA and Switzerland. Like the latter, the EU is a union of states structurally different from nation states. The comparative analysis has shown that the EU is a compound polity prevented from operating fully as a compound union by contradictory features. If the EU shares the compound union's property of a political dynamic based on interstate cleavages, it has, however, not institutionalized a coherent system of separation of powers in all policy realms. Owing to the compromises underpinning the Lisbon Treaty and the contradictory effects of a euro crisis managed through the intergovernmental framework, this chapter has identified basic dilemmas in inter-institutional relations that would require resolution in order to move the EU in the direction of a compound union. The EU should find an original way of constitutionalizing the separation of powers as the criterion for setting up and preserving a new institutional architecture.

The new institutional architecture should be based on the necessary recognition of the role of the European Council in the executive process of the Union. But this would not be sufficient. In order to prevent the formation, within the European Council, of *directoires*, the decision-making role of its president should be strengthened and made less dependent on the other members of the institution through an enlargement of his/her legitimacy and representativeness. The decision-making role of the European Council should be recognized as a systemic condition for promoting integration, but it should also be adequately balanced, both from within and from outside. The larger legitimacy of its president and the stricter cooperation with the Commission would help to achieve the former aim, whereas an EP with the powers and resources to play a congressional role, in cooperation with the Council, would help to achieve the latter aim. If the EU has to be a democratic union of states, then it has to find its own way to make its decision-making powers checked and balanced. The executive role recognized to the European Council and its president and the implementing role exercised by the Commission and its president have to be kept under the control of a strengthened and internally differentiated bicameral legislature, thus setting up a system of separate institutions sharing decision-making power.

Governing a union of states democratically is a much more difficult endeavor than governing a nation state democratically. If it acquires the institutional features of an original compound union, the EU might reasonably get close to the necessary requirements of effectiveness and legitimacy for its decisions, its complexity notwithstanding. But can the EU of the multiple and diverse perspectives become a coherent compound union? This question will be addressed in the following and final chapter.

9 | *A new political order in Europe*

La fédération des États-nations [est une] philosophic institutionnelle pour finir par plaider … pour un bon compromise entre la méthode communautaire et la méthode intergouvernementale.

Jacques Delors, past president of the European
Commission, July 6, 2012

9.1 Introduction

The process of European integration has been accompanied by alternative competing visions regarding its finality. Those competing visions were not coherently articulated during the first decades of the process. Indeed, they were often kept implicit. Nevertheless, different perspectives on the EU have accompanied the integration process. Although the EU started as an international organization in the first years of its life, since the rulings of the ECJ in the 1960s and the decisions taken at the IGCs in the 1970s and 1980s, it has silently acquired the features of a supranational polity presiding over an increasingly large common and then single continental market. The different waves of enlargement in the 1970s and 1980s increased the pluralism of perspectives on the finality of the process of integration, with the formation of an economic community vision of the integration process competing with the political union vision that was still in the majority. The end of the Cold War and the implosion of the Soviet Union between 1989 and 1991 led the EU to face dramatic new challenges. Two in particular became crucial: first, the EU had to assume an international role, developing an autonomous foreign and security policy, given that it could no longer justify the traditional protection from the USA once the Soviet Union had disappeared; second, the EU had to find a supranational counterweight to the unification of Germany made inevitable by the crumbling of the Berlin Wall.

The 1992 Maastricht Treaty was the answer to those challenges. For this reason it represents a qualitative leap in the process of integration. The preparation and then approval of the Treaty made clear that the EU had to Europeanize new policies that were traditionally at the core of national sovereignty, such as (inter alia) foreign, security, economic and monetary policies. However, in that Treaty it was also decided that the new policies should not be managed within the supranational framework, but in a new framework controlled mainly by the intergovernmental institutions and through the voluntary coordination of national governments. The formation of different institutional pillars in the Maastricht Treaty enshrined the compromise between an intergovernmental and a supranational perspective on the EU. Both perspectives recognized the necessity to deepen the process of integration, but they differed regarding the power structure that was needed to drive that process. Articulated for the first time in that critical juncture, the two visions have come to represent alternative perspectives on the EU as a political union.

The expectation of a further widening of the integration process to the East and South of Europe led to the need, in the 2000s, to better define the constitutional framework of the EU. The constitutional debate brought to the surface three main divisions, the first based on a different interpretation of the place of national sovereignty within the Union, the second on different views of the democratic legitimacy of the Union's institutions and the third on how to balance the different sizes and national/linguistic identities of the Union's member states. The cleavage based on size reflected the demographic asymmetry and differentiation of a Union that has to keep small and large states on board, with the former fearing they will be colonized or controlled by the latter and the latter fearing they will become a modern-day Gulliver in Lilliput. The cleavage based on democracy reflected the political non-homogeneous nature of a Union where some member states have developed a strong attachment to the practices and institutions of their domestic democracy, while other member states perceive their domestic democracy as more secure if enmeshed into a supranational framework. The cleavage based on nationalism reflected the historical, non-homogeneous nature of a Union where some member states have a national identity that served their freedom well in the past and other member states have a national identity that was historically the cause of many of their problems. The debate in the 2000s triggered by these cleavages was sharpened by the past memories of the hot and cold wars experienced by Europeans in the twentieth century and by the awareness of a changing world that threatens to make Europe irrelevant economically and politically.

The euro crisis has further and dramatically exacerbated those cleavages, highlighting the difficulty of keeping the different views of the Union within the same project. Indeed, those visions have coexisted uneasily, offering radically different interpretations on the rationale of the integration process and advancing alternative perspectives on its future. Within the EU, there has emerged *more than one union,* each one obstructing the coherent development of the others. The euro crisis has finally called into question the ambiguity surrounding the relations between those perspectives. This final chapter will critically discuss each of the three main perspectives on the EU in order to synthesize their ambiguities and deficiencies. On these bases, it will then identify the contours of an alternative political union, the compound union perspective, and then set out the political and constitutional conditions for the promotion of latter. The euro crisis has opened a new critical juncture for organizing the components that have constituted and made possible the integration process in a different way.

9.2 The ambiguity of the economic community

The 1992 Maastricht Treaty is important because it made clear that the EU could not be a purely regional economic organization. Recognizing the need to move in the direction of coordinated foreign and financial policies, the EU also distanced itself symbolically from the vision of an economic regional organization. Nevertheless, this leap did not displace the interpretation of the EU as exclusively a common market, an interpretation that has become significant since the 1973 entrance of Denmark, Ireland and the UK into the Union. Although the EU had gradually developed a supranational structure built around distinct legislative, executive and judiciary institutions regarding the organization of the common and then single market, the idea of the EU as a project to rationalize and maximize the functioning of a continental market not only survived, but came to be strengthened by the new waves of enlargement involving Eastern and Southern European states. This vision has continued to assert that the EU should be no more than the organization of a common market, an economic community as it was called by the Rome 1957 Treaty, a commercial republic whose rationale should be the promotion and backing of economic growth, without affecting the core sovereignty of its members. Indeed, the EU as an economic community has been interpreted (by the UK in particular) as a project fully controlled by national governments whose leaders go to Brussels to negotiate among themselves and whose ministers go to Brussels to control the Union's bureaucracy. The economic community view has emphasized the role of every single national government, rather than the role of the intergovernmental institutions aggregating the national governments, in the decision-making process of the Union. This view has come to despise supranational institutions (such as the Commission) and has consisted in an attitude of making claims for national prerogatives (the "red line" to protect) and national resources (the budget to negotiate). Margaret Thatcher's expression of "I want my money back" has become the battle cry of the supporters of this view.

The post-Maastricht Treaty development of the EU has empirically refuted this vision, but it has not made it redundant. Indeed, the UK, undoubtedly the leader of the coalition supporting this interpretation – a coalition strongly influenced by those ex-EFTA countries (such as Sweden and Denmark) that decided not to adopt the euro although they could have – has pursued an effective strategy of limiting the alternative political visions of integration. During the 2002–2003 Brussels constitutional convention, the UK effectively maneuvered to achieve the lowest common denominator for the CT, then distancing itself from (parts of) the latter when the agreement nevertheless went beyond the UK's red line (Geddes 2013). This strategy of the consistent undercutting of the more integrationist proposals was accepted by the other members of the Brussels constitutional convention on the basis of the unquestioned principle of the unitary and expanding character of the integration process. This has been made possible by flexible implementation of parts of the statutory and ordinary laws of the Union with regard to the supporters of the economic community perspective, that is through the use of the opt-out clause. Although primary and secondary legislation is generally valid in all the EU member states, some member states have been allowed certain opt-outs from legislation or treaties, meaning they have not had to participate in certain policy areas or be subjected to general jurisdictions. As we know, Denmark and the UK, and de facto also Sweden, have opted out from adopting the euro, although their macroeconomic parameters would have allowed them to enter the euro-area. Through this compromise, it was possible to create the EMU in the first place and then institutionalize it within the legal order of the EU.

It might be argued that the opt-out clause has been the counterweight to the provision on enhanced cooperation. Enhanced cooperation is a measure introduced in the 1997 Treaty of Amsterdam and then embraced by the Lisbon Treaty (TEU, Article 20 and TFEU, Article 329), whereby a minimum of nine member states are allowed to cooperate within the structure of the EU without involving other member states, after the Commission and a qualified majority of the Council have approved the measure (and the EP has given its consent). According to TEU Article 20.1, member states "within the framework of the Union's non-exclusive competences may make use of its institutions and exercise those competences ... to further the objectives of the Union." If the opt-out clause has protected the less integrationist member states, the enhanced cooperation clause aimed to do the same with the more integrationist member states (F. Fabbrini 2012). Both clauses have represented the main instruments for accommodating the needs of member states that fear too much integration and those of member states eager for further integration, thus providing the EU with the necessary flexibility (and ambiguity).

It goes without saying that, although the opt-out clause has been necessary in terms of preventing the obstruction of the integration process, it has nevertheless contributed to making it uncertain and contradictory. The opt-out member states have responded to the cleavages that emerged in the constitutional decade of the 2000s with unmistakable clarity: national sovereignty is not only a value in itself, because it allows the preservation of specific national customs and traditions, but it is the condition for making democracy possible. What characterizes the opt-out coalition is a common cultural predisposition, regardless of size or other ecological factors. Indeed, it includes large (the UK) and small (Czech Republic, Sweden, Denmark, Ireland) member states, one of them (Ireland) even participating in the euro-area. These member states come from national experiences that have developed largely in the Northern islands or peninsulas of Europe or are the expression of the pride of small Eastern European communities that have finally regained their independence from the political domination of a superpower (the Soviet Union). The supporters of the economic community interpretation have converged towards the idea that the preservation of national sovereignty is compatible with the functioning of a single market. Through the opt-outs and the blockage or postponement of proposals for deeper integration, it has been possible for the supporters of the economic community perspective to remain within the common market framework, even though it has become highly integrated and supranational.

The opting out from adoption of the euro has, however, been strategically important. It has allowed the formation of different monetary and economic regimes within the same Union. This coexistence has been called into question by the post-2009 euro crisis. More specifically, the euro crisis has shown how fragile the coexistence within the same legal framework of a single market shared by all the member states and a single currency not shared by all of them might become. Indeed, in order to respond to the financial crisis, the euro-area member states have introduced policy measures and approved intergovernmental treaties that have further distanced their economic fate from that of the non-euro-area member states. At the same time, growing public malaise in the opt-out member states towards the very process of integration (as shown by the electoral success in the 2014 EP elections of UKIP and the anti-European Danish People's Party, both becoming the first party in their country) has increased intolerance even towards some regulations of the single market, pressuring their governments to ask for a renegotiation of some of them. The position expressed by the British Prime Minister David Cameron, in his speech on Europe in January 2013, formalized that malaise. However, the roots of the malaise are in the post-Maastricht Treaty transformation of the EU rather than in the post-2009 financial crisis.

The euro crisis has thus led to a distancing, if not to a conflict of interests, between non-euro-area and euro-area economic and monetary regimes. The crisis has created tremendous pressure for the further Europeanization of the economic and financial policies of the euro-area, further separating the latter's functioning from the non-euro-area member states (McTernan 2012). A deep legal and policy divide has emerged between the two areas, with unexpected implications. The new intergovernmental Treaties (the ESM, Fiscal Compact and SRF) were established outside the legal order of the Lisbon Treaty, although the objectives that were set out under those Treaties could have been attained through either an amendment to the Lisbon Treaty or recourse to enhanced cooperation, if not to secondary EU law. The governments of the larger euro-area member states chose to resort to international treaties to neutralize the veto threatened by the UK government, but also to keep the EP and Commission at bay (which would not have been possible by resorting to enhanced cooperation or Union laws). In any case, in order to prevent future veto threats, those treaties set up new organizations where unanimity is no longer necessary for taking decisions.

The formation of new legal orders outside the Lisbon Treaty, although not incompatible with the latter (De Witte 2012), has necessarily called into question the constitutional compromise between the EMU and the opt-out member states, the UK in particular. With the Fiscal Compact Treaty, most member states will come to coordinate their economic, fiscal and budgetary policies, leaving only the UK on the margins (the Czech Republic, which refused to sign the Treaty in 2011, approved it in March 2014). Moreover, the UK is also outside of the Euro Plus Pact, a political commitment between the euro-area member states and several non-euro-area states (such as Denmark, Poland, Latvia, Lithuania, Bulgaria and Romania) aimed at fostering stronger economic policy coordination among them. De facto, the UK and the EMU member states have come to acknowledge that their economic and monetary interests diverge. The economic community perspective has shown itself to be incompatible with the need to govern the euro (as emerged from the crisis). The new organization set up by the Fiscal Compact has made this reality evident. The most crucial decisions have been taken at meetings of the governmental leaders or ministers of the member states that have adopted the euro (the Euro Summit and Euro Group), with the pre-in and opt-out member states only informed about their content. As Taverne (2012: 28, original emphasis) reported during the height of the financial crisis: "The Eurogroup of the 17 eurozone finance ministers already meet separately *before* the full EcoFin Council, which has effectively turned this into a rubber stamp. If Euro Summits now precede European Council meetings, as Sarkozy wants, something very similar is likely to happen." Indeed, it has happened, leaving the UK in particular further isolated. To counter this process, non-euro-area member states pressured in 2014 to elect Donald Tusk, a previous prime minister coming from a member state – Poland – not participating in the euro-area, as the new president of the European Council *and* the Euro Summit, after the expiration of Herman van Rompuy's mandate.

In short, the compromise between the sovereignist coalition supporting the economic community perspective and the EMU member states involved in deeper integration has been upset by the euro crisis. A new structure of institutions and a new set of procedures have been formalized around the Fiscal Compact, the ESM and the SRF Treaties, making evident the distinction of interests between the euro-area member states and the others. The euro-area member states have come to constitute a permanent distinct union, whose logic has a systemic and not a sectoral nature. The magnitude of the euro crisis has required the introduction of institutional and policy measures that have deeply divided the two member state areas. The euro crisis has dissolved the ambiguity of an EU including member states interested only in an economic community controlled by national governments and member states moving (or obliged to move) "towards a genuine economic and monetary union" (as per the title of the Report submitted by the four presidents on December 5, 2012: see Chapter 2) as a step for achieving a more effective and legitimate economic governance of the Union.

9.3 Beyond intergovernmental and parliamentary unions

Since its founding in the Treaties of Paris and Rome, the EU has been predominantly interpreted as a political project, a political federation in the making, whose institutional development would have to restrain (if not to substitute in the most radical interpretations) the sovereignty of each of its member states. This interpretation has been fed by a meta-cultural narrative, based on the assumption that nationalism is the inevitable grave of democracy, although it was historically its natural cradle. If the economic community view of the EU assumed that democracy is safe only if wrapped in national institutions, the view of the EU as a federation in the making has assumed that democracy is at risk if wrapped only in national institutions. The economic community view has interpreted the nation state as the bulwark of democracy, whereas the alternative view has interpreted the nation state as a limit on the further development of democracy. Meta-narratives are useful for representing aspirations, but much less so for reflecting institutional realities and defining feasible projects (Della Sala 2010). Indeed, the economic community view has come to contrast with the reality of the EU, which has become much more than the institutional setting of a regional free trade area or the institutional organization of a customs union. That view has shown intrinsic difficulties in recognizing the supranational achievements of the Union and the extension of its policy competences to realms traditionally managed at the domestic level, an extension that has dramatically enlarged the scope of the process of integration.

At the same time, the political union narrative has also been wrong-footed by institutional development, which has been different from the linear view of a federal state gradually substituting nation states through the functional spillover of the policy-making process. True, the 1992 Maastricht Treaty enlarged the scope of the integration process, but the new policies were framed within an intergovernmental setting, distinct and separate from the supranational one. Processes of cross-pillarization certainly took place after the Maastricht Treaty, but the decision-making distinction between policy areas remained and emigrated to the Lisbon Treaty. Indeed, with the Maastricht Compromise, the political union narrative had to recognize the existence of at least two different *political* perspectives on the integration process, one supranational and the other intergovernmental. Both represented political projects, but their institutional implications were and are significantly different. If after the Maastricht Compromise it has become unrealistic to imagine the rolling back of the institutionalization of the EU to return it to the status of the international organization of its founding years, it has also become unrealistic to imagine the institutional development of the EU in the direction of its linear transformation into a parliamentary federation similar to those of nation states. The EU has gone too far to be led back to the state of an economic community, but it has not developed according to the logic of a parliamentary-federal state either. Since the Maastricht Compromise, the institutional complexity of the EU has become much greater than expected from the economic community perspective, but at the same time that complexity has not matched the expectation of the federal parliamentary union perspective. The 1992 Maastricht Treaty thus institutionalized two different unions, one supranational dealing with single market policies and the other intergovernmental dealing with policies previously at the core of national sovereignty. The two unions coexisted alongside each other in the 1990s; they were formalized in the CT, to finally become constitutionalized in the Lisbon Treaty. Both unions assumed integration as a necessary process, but pursued different institutional perspectives to make this possible.

The intergovernmental union perspective assumes that size or demographic asymmetry can be regulated through the reciprocal control of national governments within intergovernmental institutions; the divisions on nationalism can be restrained through the decision-making centrality of domestic governments; the different views on democracy can be mitigated through the preservation of domestic democracies as the primary legitimate basis of the Union. In this perspective, it is considered necessary to keep the supranational institutions (such as the Commission and the EP) under the strict control of the intergovernmental institutions. Contrary to the sovereignists, here the decision-making barycenter of the EU should be located in the formal institutions aggregating national governments in Brussels, rather than in each of the governments themselves. The euro crisis has shown that the intergovernmental union has not worked as predicted. It has been unable to generate effective and legitimate decisions as the management of the crisis required. Moreover, constrained by its very logic, it has shown an intrinsic inability to solve the basic dilemmas of collective action, thus being obliged to set up a crisis prevention system outside the same Lisbon Treaty. The intergovernmental union has increased the integration of the euro-area member states, but not in a supranational direction. It has concentrated the decision-making power in the European Council and the Council, with a growing implementation role for the Commission. This centralization has provided incentives for the formation of hierarchies between member state governments within those intergovernmental institutions. Free from any significant check by the supranational legislature (EP), the European Council's and Council's decisions have come to reflect the preferences of the stronger and larger member states. Since that centralization has impacted strongly on member states' prerogatives, the net outcome has been the perception in the weaker states of being dominated by the stronger ones. The 2014 election of Donald Tusk as European Council president has further weakened the check on the governmental leaders of the stronger member states within the European Council – and the Euro Summit in particular. Indeed, the paradox of having a Euro Summit presided over by a non-euro-area politician plays in favor of the stronger member states' leaders who can now directly negotiate between themselves without constraints coming from the presidency of that institution.

The supranational union understood as a parliamentary federation in the making has been based on different assumptions. For the parliamentary union perspective, size or demographic asymmetry can be regulated through the formation of cross-national party coalitions, actively politicizing the elections to the EP; the national identity cleavage can be managed through a territorial distribution of competences that encourages cooperation between the national and the supranational institutions; the democracy cleavage can be overcome by increasing the decision-making power of the EP. The Lisbon Treaty has formalized a supranational union with some parliamentary features, as evidenced by the role recognized to the EP in electing the Commission president and in approving the Commission or voting it down, although for collective misconduct and not for political reasons. In this perspective, the parties should organize a transnational competition for the EP elections that should prioritize political, rather than territorial or interstate, divisions. This would increase the parliamentarization of the EU, making the EP elections the crucial arena for deciding the government and policies of the Union. The 2014 EP election of Jean-Claude Juncker as Commission president epitomized the logic of this perspective. Although the supranational union has played a subordinate role, relative to national governmental leaders, in dealing with the euro crisis, the crisis has, however, tested the weak political basis of the parliamentary union perspective. Instead of an increase in transnational politicization of the political party contest, the euro crisis has reversed the trend towards the parliamentarization of the EU, bringing to the surface a division between (Northern and Southern) euro-area member states rather than between (left and right) political parties, thus obfuscating the project of making the EP the crucial institution for deciding the Union's government and its policies. During the euro crisis the EU has shown itself to be a resilient union of states, and not only of citizens, whose representation and decision-making needs cannot be answered by only one institution (the EP).

The euro crisis has thus dramatically challenged the coexistence of the two unions that emerged from the Maastricht Compromise. In fact, throughout the constitutional process of the 2000s it was generally assumed by supranationalists that the further development of integration would lead to a weakening of the intergovernmental framework and to the transfer of intergovernmental policies to the supranational setting. In the 2002–2003 Brussels constitutional convention there was the expectation that the EU could be recomposed through the approval of a single legal framework, thus converging towards a supranational/ parliamentary perspective. The abolition of the pillar structure, finally formalized in the Lisbon Treaty, was considered the utmost expression of the plausibility of that expectation. It reinvigorated the idea of a unitary and expanding Union, although sufficiently flexible to accommodate (through the opt-out clause and the provision on enhanced cooperation) its internal differentiation, moving ultimately towards political supranationalism of a parliamentary-federal type.

Exploding shortly before the coming into force of the Lisbon Treaty, the euro crisis not only halted the supranationalists' expectation of the gradual convergence of the intergovernmental union into the supranational union, but it also complicated the coexistence of the two unions. Indeed, the new intergovernmental treaties introduced a legal divide between them, with the stronger and larger member states (Germany in particular) relying more and more on intergovernmental institutions and practices set up outside of the legal order of the EU to organize crucial programs (such as fiscal consolidation or resolution of bank failures). At the same time, that crisis has also deepened the institutional distinction between the two unions, forcing the intergovernmental union to increase its institutional complexity and integration along a path that overlaps only partially with the supranational union. The euro crisis has ended the Maastricht Compromise between the two unions, putting a tremendous strain on the coexistence of a supranational union unable to become a *parliamentary federation* and the intergovernmental union that has become a post-democratic (Habermas 2012b) *federation of governments*. How should the set of institutional strains induced by the crisis be dealt with?

9.4 A pluralist institutional order and the compound union

Policy differentiation

Two strategies might be considered for dealing with the institutional tensions of the EU. I would call the first the *policy differentiation* strategy. It would consist in the reconstruction of the unitary order of the Lisbon Treaty, albeit internally differentiated on the basis of different policy regimes (see Leuffen, Rittberger and Schimmelfennig 2013). The action of the EP during the elaboration of the Fiscal Compact Treaty, which aimed to formalize a clear deadline for bringing it back to the Lisbon Treaty (European Parliament 2012; Kreilinger 2012), constitutes the epitome of this strategy. In fact, as we have seen (Chapter 5), the Fiscal Compact Treaty declares (Article 16) that "within five years at most following the entry into force of this Treaty, on the basis of an assessment of the experience with its implementation, the necessary steps shall be taken ... with the aim of incorporating the substance of this Treaty into the legal framework of the European Union," as had already happened with the Schengen Agreement. This strategy became the official position of the second Barroso Commission (2009–2014) and was supported by the main European political parties during the EP elections of May 22–25, 2014. The 2014 election of the Polish nominee Donald Tusk as president of both the European Council and the Euro Summit and the assignment of crucial portfolios of the Juncker Commission to commissioners coming from non-euro-area member states (as the British nominee Jonathan Hill become commissioner for "Financial stability, financial services and capital markets union") are further examples of the attempt to reduce the centrifugal trends induced by the euro crisis. Rather than a multi-speed Europe, this strategy would lead to the institutionalization of an EU based on concentric policy circles, with different clusters of member states participating permanently in different policy regimes with different degrees of integration. It would not be a Union à la carte, but a unitary, internally differentiated, organization. The teleological expectation of a multi-speed EU, with all the member states moving towards the same end but at different speeds, is substituted by an EU based on structural or permanent differentiations. What matters is the reconstruction of a legally unitary union whose internal policy differentiations will be sewn up by the main political actor. As Leuffen (2013: 5) stated, "differentiated integration [is] a political program."

If the strength of this strategy lies in the effort to reconstitute a unified legal order for the EU, it has nevertheless significant weaknesses. The Fiscal Compact Treaty certainly calls for its reincorporation into the Lisbon Treaty. However, for the latter to take place, the consent of the UK will once again be required – an unlikely outcome, given that the rules of the Fiscal Compact would continue to affect London's financial district negatively, as it would have done at the point of the UK opposition to the Lisbon Treaty amendment. The alternative would be to transform the Fiscal Compact Treaty into an enhanced cooperation within the Lisbon Treaty, but this would require the initiative of the Commission and the approval of the EP, conditions opposed by those euro-area member state governments that fear going back to the old "Community method." More generally, the conflict of interests between the non-euro-area and the euro-area member states could not easily be kept within a unitary legal order. The need for deeper integration into EMU policies would continue to strain the common legal and institutional order, as is happening with banking union. As the House of Lords (2014: 6) recognized, "eurozone Members are politically committed to deeper integration. The UK has made clear that it will not participate." As we have seen, the outcome of the EP elections of May 22–25, 2014 in the UK and in Denmark shows that any step towards more integration within the legal framework of the Lisbon Treaty might trigger a definitive rift against the EU in the opt-out member states. In that case, a British referendum on whether the country should remain within or exit from the EU would have a predictable outcome.

At the same time, a concentric circles differentiation would leave untouched the intergovernmental logic of the EMU, whose decisions have lacked the necessary democratic legitimacy to be accepted by the affected citizens of the Southern and debtor euro-area member states. The dissatisfaction at the management of financial policy in the latter member states cannot be silenced by confirmation of their intergovernmental source. Again, as the EP elections of May 22–25, 2014 show, the dissatisfaction towards intergovernmentalism and its policies has grown dramatically. Increasing the role of national parliaments in the differentiated regime of economic governance (Chalmers 2013), although desirable (Glencross 2014b), will not solve the structural legitimacy deficit of the intergovernmental regime. Legitimacy of decisions taken at the supranational level should come from supranational institutions, in our case the EP. However, not only has the EP been excluded from the EMU's main decisions, but its inclusion in those policies would be constitutionally constrained by the Lisbon Treaty. The parliamentarist hubris that imposed, first in the CT and then in the Lisbon Treaty, the legal celebration of the EP as the institution representing the European citizenry has fallen prisoner to its own rhetoric. Pragmatic solutions might be tried out (Curtin and Fasone 2014) to distinguish (in its internal deliberative process) representatives from non-euro-area and euro-area member states, thus allowing only the latter to have a say on the decisions taken by euro-area institutions (Euro Summit and Euro Group). But these solutions will fall short of activating effective mechanisms of accountability over the intergovernmental institutions. Nor does multilevel parliamentarism, combining the EP and national parliaments of euro-area member states, seem to represent an effective check on the intergovernmental institutions. Finally, a concentric circles EU would also leave intact the technocratic (ordo-liberal) order of the EMU with its institutionalized bias in favor of the economic interests and cultural values of the Northern and creditor euro-area member states.

Institutional differentiation

If one assumes instead that the euro crisis has irreversibly altered the constitutional compromises that structured the EU from Maastricht to Lisbon, then an alternative strategy should be considered. I would call it the *institutional differentiation* strategy. It would consist in the formation of a new institutional order in Europe, through the structural redefinition of the relations between euro-area and non-euro-area member states. A comprehensive treaty reform would be necessary to define, on one side, the constitutional frame of an exclusive euro-area and, on the other side, the regulatory frame of an inclusive single market. In this case, the issue is no longer whether the UK or other opt-out member states will leave the EU or not. There is no EU to leave. The EU is an intersection of several treaties, with their multiple opportunities and obligations, not a club to enlist in or to leave. Any econometric assessment of an exit shows the highly negative economic implications on the UK economy (CER 2014). As Ottaviano *et al.* (2014: 5) asserted, "the dream of splendid isolation may turn out to be a very costly one indeed." A new grand bargain would rather be necessary to establish a larger framework within which to define new relations between the two areas of member states (and other European states interested in the project). If the assumption that non-euro-area and euro-area member states would respectively pay dramatic costs from a reciprocal stalemate is agreed, then the institutional and legal differentiation between the two areas should be necessarily formalized in two different organizations, with the authority and the resources to pursue their specific aims coherently.

Institutional differentiation should not be interpreted as external differentiation. The EU has already implemented forms of external differentiation (through the European Economic Area, with non-member states such as Norway, Iceland and Lichtenstein, or through bilateral agreements with a non-member state, such as Switzerland) that allow those states to participate in the single market without, however, contributing to deliberations on its policies. This solution would be unacceptable for restructuring the relations between the euro-area and non-euro-area member states. The single market belongs to all EU member states, not only to the former or the latter. It would be unjustifiable to have the UK and other non-euro-area member states outside of the Lisbon Treaty and at the same time participating in the single market without affecting the latter's policies. A negotiation should be opened in order to agree on a revised and simplified version of the Lisbon Treaty as the legal framework of the single market open to all the European states, currently in or outside the EU, on the condition that they have to meet specific requirements. At the same time, the euro-area member states should have the possibility to define the constitutional bases of their political union. The Lisbon Treaty would continue to provide the legal basis for the single market, although deprived of those parts concerned with the policies (such as monetary, financial, economic, fiscal, budgetary, foreign, security, defense, employment, welfare, inter alia) unconnected to it. The Lisbon Treaty should be simplified to relieve it from unnecessary regulatory constraints, as requested by the opt-out member states (the UK in particular).

However, as shown by the comparative analysis of regional economic organizations (Chapter 4), a common market (and more so a single market) requires a supranational structure and regulation to function properly. A single market is more than an economic community. The organization of the single market should be based on lighter decision-making and judicial institutions, but it has to have a supranational reach, although its scope should be strictly connected to its economic aims. A revised version of the Lisbon Treaty should no longer celebrate the aim of promoting "an ever closer union," while the latter should be insufficient to delineate the aim of the euro-political union. The current institutional structure will have to be redefined, starting from the EP, which should again become the institution representing the citizens of the states, and not the European citizenry, and the Commission, a significant part of which should be redirected towards the activities of the euro-political union. Nevertheless, the current quadrilateral system of institutions, with its judicial supervision, can constitute the bases around which to negotiate the features of the organization of the single market. The latter might also decide to have a different name than the EU, but in any case it cannot consist in a project of purely economic cooperation. Finally, precise decision-making rules should be institutionalized in order to prevent the euro-bloc imposing its majoritarian will on the other single market participants,[1] rules that should be presided over by the ECJ. The redefinition of the legal and institutional bases of the organization of the single market and the setting up of the organization of the euro-area should be concomitant. This concurrence constitutes a reciprocal assurance between the leaders of the two groups of states that they are both engaged in a positive sum game.

A political compact

The necessity of strengthening the EMU and moving it towards a political end has been repeatedly raised by several governments or national ministers of the euro-area. For instance, the Westerwelle Groups of twelve foreign ministers[2] assessed, in a Final Report made public on September 17, 2012, that in order to give EMU "full democratic legitimacy and accountability," "the possibility of treaty reform" cannot be excluded. The Report of the four presidents submitted to the European

---

[1] In a speech given to the Nordic-Baltic Ambassadors, Lord Owen (2011) proposed to set up a Non Euro Group (NEG) whose members, chaired by the president of the European Council, "would be able to adjust their currency exchange rates ... to establish their own corporation tax levels, their own fiscal regimes and their own monetary policy governed by their own central bank." This would reflect "an existing reality that there are at present two groupings in relation to currency management within the EU – an informal Euro Group and informal Non Euro Group ... The EU is a mixture of the intergovernmental and the supranational. The mix will probably evolve in both directions."

[2] The Future of Europe Group, known as the Westerwelle Group because it was promoted by the then German foreign minister, was constituted by the foreign ministers of Austria, Belgium, Denmark, France, Italy, Germany, Luxembourg, the Netherlands, Poland, Portugal and Spain.

Council on December 5, 2012 ended with the claim that a new architecture would be necessary to promote "democratic legitimacy and accountability" in a genuine economic and monetary union. The proposal of a euro-political union has been advanced by several think tanks (CEPS 2014; Group Eiffel Europe 2014; Lamond 2013; Spinelli Group and Bertelsmann Stiftung 2013), but it has also been discussed by scholars (more recently, Kelemen 2014; Somek 2013) and observers of the EU (De Schoutheete and Micossi 2013). In this debate the possibility has been considered of using the Fiscal Compact and the other intergovernmental treaties as the bases of a future euro-political union. The Fiscal Treaty has created a distinct institution of the euro-area (the Euro Summit) and formalized a previously informal one (the Euro Group), besides the introduction of a legal order for the euro-area separate from the Lisbon Treaty. As Calliess (2014: 21) noted: "The Fiscal Compact made interesting steps into a special governance of the Eurozone outside the EU-Treaty. It is a first step into a new institutional arrangement between a possible Euro-Treaty and the EU … [Yet] its institutional design is not up to the tasks that need to be done in a Fiscal and Economic Union." Indeed, a group of German economists, lawyers and political scientists (Glienicker Gruppe 2013) stated that "the euro area needs a new contractual basis of its own. What is called for now is a Euro-treaty to replace previous piecemeal reforms."

The comparative analysis developed in the previous chapter has shown that a democratic union of states should first rely on a constitutional commitment, not on the interpretation of interstate agreements as a quasi-constitution. In particular, the new intergovernmental treaties have too many democratic deficiencies to be transformed into the bases of a euro-political union. The euro-area member states should agree on signing a political compact treaty to set up a new organization – a political compact that should have (as the comparison with the other two compound unions has indicated) the features of a basic treaty specifying the values and aims of the compact instituting the union, the rights and duties of the member states and the citizens, the competences and resources allocated to the supranational and national levels of the union, the separation-of-powers architecture to organize its functioning at the former level, and the power of the judiciary in protecting citizens' rights and member states' prerogatives. The political compact treaty might also decide a new name and select new symbols for the euro-political union.

A new Compact would be necessary for recomposing the two competing political perspectives of supranationalism and intergovernmentalism in the direction of a compound union. Each of the two perspectives on the political union has proven unilateral and unrealistic. In fact, a union of historically established and powerful states cannot prosper without institutionalizing an important decision-making role for their governments. At the same time, established supranational institutions independent from those states are necessary not only to make intergovernmental negotiation possible, but also to guarantee the effectiveness and legitimacy of the Union's democratic process. The perspective of the compound union assumes that intergovernmentalism (*as the logic expressing the interests and views of the member state governments*) is, and should remain, an essential feature of a union of states. But it also requires that intergovernmental institutions operate within a framework binding them to interact with supranationalism (*as the logic expressing the interests and views of the supra-state institutions*). The compound union is the institutionalized combination of the two logics. It is aimed at setting up a balance between intergovernmental and supranational institutions, a balance that only a form of separation of powers, both vertically and horizontally, may guarantee, in particular if integrated by mechanisms of checks and balances that encourage actors operating within intergovernmental and supranational institutions to keep each other under reciprocal control. It might be argued that, by using the compound union perspective, it would also be possible to reconcile the opposite views on political union traditionally advanced by French (intergovernmental) and German (supranational) elites. It is the institutional answer to the idea of a federation of nation states evoked by Jacques Delors, for instance in his speech in July 2012, when he proposed creating a union through "un bon compromis entre la méthode communautaire et la méthode intergouvernementale."

Our CP approach has shown that, in established democratic experiences, only the institutional logic of the *separation of powers* has been able to consolidate federal unions. That logic has found, and might find, different institutional applications because it has to reflect current empirical processes, not just abstract normative principles. It is likely that, at least for a transitional period, the euro-political union will have to share institutions and resources with the organization of the single market, although the latter is expected to decrease and the former to increase their specific institutional density. If the EP returns to its role of representing citizens of member states and the Commission continues to be composed of one commissioner per member state, then the quadrilateral structure of the euro-political union might be gradually carved out from the existing institutional structure. This means:

(a) recognizing the executive role of the Euro-Summit and at the same time strengthening the office of its president, extending the latter's legitimacy, although maintaining the collegial nature of the institution;

(b) preserving the necessary functional role of the Euro-Commission and at the same time strengthening the coordination between the president of the Euro-Summit and the Euro Commission and its president, setting up a dual executive system;

(c) consolidating the existing rules for the Euro-Commission's formation, maintaining or reinvigorating its special relation with the Euro-EP, and at the same time keeping politicization outside of the Euro-Commission but inside the Euro-Summit's presidency;

(d) extending the co-decisional role of the Euro-EP and the Euro-Councils to all policy fields of the euro-political union, but also strengthening their congressional role of checking the dual executive through various forms of supervision and monitoring;

(e) granting to the Euro-ECJ the constitutional function of judicial review of all the legal decisions taken by the euro-political union;

(f) reconstituting the vertical boundary between the member states and the center.

For instance, in order to prevent interstate relations of domination, each member state of the euro-political union should be univocally responsible for its public budget, although the euro legislative institutions should have the resources and the authority to promote policies in support of economic growth in indebted member states, if that is required by democratic majorities that have emerged through separate electoral processes. Indeed, proposals of endowing the EU with independent fiscal capacity have already been advanced during the euro crisis by several scholars (see Maduro 2012) and the same Report of the four presidents stressed the necessity of giving the EMU its fiscal independence. The point, in fact, is to disrupt the pattern of financial transfer of resources from the states to the union's center. Thus, although elected by different constituencies or through inter-institutional negotiation (as in the case of the Commission), each of the institutions in the decision-making quadrangle can increase its effectiveness without subtracting anything from the others. At the same time, those capabilities would be supported by a multiplicity of legitimacies

The organization of the single market, not the compound union, should be open to those European states in the Balkans or semi-European states (such as Turkey or other countries on the fringe of Europe), provided that they meet precise macroeconomic and micro-institutional conditions, but also to those European states (such as Norway or Switzerland) that have distanced themselves from the legal order of the EU, but not from its single market. Both the single market and the compound union should be open to new members, although the threshold for entering the former will be necessarily lower than that for becoming part of the latter. The necessity to close the various eras of bleak European interstate and infrastate wars has transformed the enlargement into a project that has dramatically increased divergences within the EU (Majone 2014). Distinguishing between the organizations of the single market and the compound union constitutes an answer to that complexity. It might also help to deal with expectations for further enlargement, although the euro crisis has silenced them for now. The ending of the unitary institutional order should not mean the end of structured collaboration among European states.

This strategy will also have to face powerful constraints. The complexity of the concurrent renegotiations of an inclusive single market and exclusive euro-political union might prove too great to be handled successfully. The inertia of the status quo would suggest to national and supranational actors to adopt short-run muddling-through devices to keep the system working. National electorates (as in Germany) may not have the appetite for reopening a constitutional process, while other national electorates (as in France) might oppose it. In addition, in the main supranational institutions, such as the EP and the Commission, sections or groups might fear any structural change because they do not know the benefits they will receive at the end of the process, but they certainly know the costs they have to pay at the beginning of it. Moreover, this strategy would have to deal with the natural predisposition of any political elite in any established context, namely that continuity

is safer than discontinuity. Finally, this strategy would require political leadership of the highest quality in both member state areas, a
common good that cannot be artificially generated.

9.5 The act of forming a political union

Forming a euro-political union would necessarily be an act of will,
not the outcome of an evolutionary process, as the comparison with
the other two compound unions has indicated. Although reduced in
size, that political union would continue to be constituted by demographically asymmetrical states, with different experiences regarding
nationalism and democracy, an institutionalized expression of different national languages and cultures. The formation of such a political
union cannot rely on the established patterns of polity-formation traditionally used in Continental Europe (Greenfeld 1992). Both the civic
and ethnic conceptions of citizenship and democracy that developed
historically in Europe are of no use in terms of prescribing an analytical path to the formation of a democratic union of states (S. Fabbrini
2010: chapter 2).

According to the civic conception (epitomized by the French experience), democracy should be the outcome of a state-building process
that creates a civic nation, then transforming it in a democratic community. The historical sequence in France was clear: first, build the territorial state, then invent the nation, finally democratize the latter. On
the basis of this paradigm, the existence of a state is a condition for the
formation of a democratic citizenship. As France was a state before it
was a people, according to this paradigm it seems unthinkable to have
a European people (or *peuple* as a singular entity) not preceded by the
formation of a European state. A constitution without the backing of
a European state (as was argued during the 2005 French campaign
against the CT) would expose the citizens to the domination of market
forces. They would risk losing their historical rights now enshrined in
the democratic state. It follows that the absence of a European state
makes democracy in a supranational Europe implausible. As Lacroix
(2010: 108) put it, there is "a ... fundamental feature of French political imaginary: the incapacity to accept that there might be politics
beyond the nation-state. This 'mimetic obsession' ... boils down to the
notion that politics could only happen at the European level if there
were a European federal state."

At the same time, according to the ethnic conception (epitomized by the German experience), democracy can develop only if it expresses the common culture of a pre-existing homogeneous people (again, in the singular). Thus the pre-existence of a European demos is the existential condition for developing a democracy at the European level. Since Germany started from a demos, it follows that any political experiment should presuppose the pre-existence of a culturally homogeneous people. This paradigm has inspired the German Constitutional Court from the *Maastricht-Urteil* sentence of 1993 (concerning the constitutionality of the Maastricht Treaty) to the 2012 decision concerning the constitutionality of the Fiscal Compact and the ESM Treaties. For the Court (Muller 2010: 95), "further transfers of sovereignty were inadmissible as long as there existed no democratic structures at the European level – which in turn depended on a homogeneous European people." The EU can claim superior legitimacy over its member states only if its decisions are the democratic expression of the will of a European demos, a condition that it is not yet (and it is probably assumed will never be)[3] fulfilled. As we know, the Court has even questioned the democratic nature of the EP, given its formation through the disproportional criterion of degressive proportionality. For this polity-building paradigm, too, people is a singular entity (*Volk*) endowed with common cultural qualities that may justify its transformation into the source of legitimacy for a democracy. Thus the *Volk* is not a construction but a natural fact; it is not the outcome of ad hoc policies adopted by ad hoc elites trying to answer ad hoc contingencies but an existential condition with ontological implications. The German lawyers influenced by this paradigm seem to have forgotten that, historically, German elites engaged in the project of formation of the German demos for political reasons. Unable to build a territorial state (because of the Holy Roman Empire, which precluded the development of a Westphalian state in the German territories), German elites had to foster the cultural (rather than civic)

---

[3] Regarding the German Constitutional Court, Nicolaidis (2011: 990) writes: "the Court is wrong to see the lack of a European people as an explanation as to why European democracy is not only limited today but unlikely to develop in the future." This is due to the Court's failure "to imagine or perceive ... the EU as a demoi-cracy, a space where states and citizens are inventing a form of democracy ... which does not rest on the existence – potential or actual – of a single people."

identification of the ruled in order to protect themselves from outside challenges (Spruyt 1994). They asserted the existence of a linguistic and ethnic *pre-political community* exactly because of the lack of territorial boundaries delimiting and defining their German political community. They created a sentiment of national identity that anticipated the subsequent process of state-building and that was *independent* from it. Indeed, Germany is a late state-builder, whereas France is an early one. Can this specific experience be employed to order (or rather to conceptualize) the process of European integration? To transform a particular experience into a normative paradigm is the property of parochialism.

Both historical experiences are thus equally worthless in terms of thinking about the formation of a federal union with democratic features (a compound union). We cannot have a European demos based on ethnic homogeneity. On the contrary, we have many European demoi with different national identities, languages, memories, cultures, faiths – and much else besides that (Nicolaidis 2013). This does not imply their unbridgeable separation. Indeed, those demoi can be connected, as already happens, through transnational public spheres supporting and structuring a European community of communication, as well argued by Risse (2010). Indeed, this is not only a European asset, but also a guarantee for the freedom of Europeans. A homogeneous people at the level of a continent might reveal itself to be a danger to, not a resource for, freedom. At the same time, not only is it intellectually arduous to think of a European (super)state that will create a European nation and thus support a European democracy, but it is also politically advisable not to look for it (for a different opinion, see Morgan 2005). The institutionalization of centralized authority at the level of a continent would represent a challenge to the democratic nature of a union of states. Is there an alternative way of thinking about the building of a political project for a union of states, without relying either on the ethnic or the civic paradigms of nationhood and democracy? The comparison with the other two established compound unions, Switzerland and the USA, has furnished the answer.

Switzerland and the USA represent unusual cases (from a European nation state perspective) of political unions constructed and developed without either a pre-existing demos or the support of a pre-existing state. Both unions were created out of a *political compact* between independent states/cantons enshrined in a formal constitution (in 1789 in the USA, in 1848 in Switzerland). The founding role of the constitution was particularly significant in the USA, which served as a model for Switzerland. Apart from the propaganda written by John Jay in the Federalist No. 2 to convince New York voters to support the new Philadelphia constitution,[4] Americans became peoples (plural), that is members of a union, through a sequence of political acts, from the Declaration of Independence in 1776 to the Federal Constitution of 1789 with its first ten constitutional amendments (or Bill of Rights) of 1789 (Wills 1978). The constitution aggregated the various independent states and ethnic and religious groups through a political compact. This multifarious USA has come to be held together not by a common language or by common habits, nor through a (prior central) state that indeed came to be formed only one century after the formation of the union (Skowroneck 1982), but by the political values and institutional practices enshrined in the constitution. Democracy and constitutional government supported not only the formation of the federal union, but structured the conterminous identification of citizens with the latter (Wiebe 1995). In both Switzerland and the USA (in particular after the end of the Civil War), the constitution not only created the legal order of the union, but it defined the political space for democratizing it. As Kincaid (2010: 138) observed, in the USA the "democratic reformers [have worked] through the institutions established by the federal Constitution to achieve their objectives."

In the USA and Switzerland, the compound union was thus formed without relying on either a pre-existing state structure or a pre-existing set of ethnically based values and attitudes. Both compound unions (and the USA in particular) have been built upon a political choice enshrined in a written constitution – a political choice made by elites who became aware of the existential need for a federal union after a realistic reading of the insufficiency of the previous confederal project (the 1781 Articles of Confederation in the USA and the 1815 Confederal Treaty in Switzerland). Certainly, in both compound unions the constitution has been regularly challenged, as the political pact justifying the federal union has been regularly contested. Unions of states are intimately fragile projects because they are based on the

---

[4] That is that Americans were "one united people – a people descended from the same ancestors, speaking the same language, professing the same religion, attached to the same principles of government," now in Beard (1964: 39).

aggregation of asymmetrical and differentiated states that were previously independent and that aggregate for instrumental more than for sentimental reasons. Both the USA and Switzerland emerged on the basis of a defensive rationale, more than out of a prospective aspiration. They were created with the aim of promoting peace in a given regional area, although in the US case the constitutional pact was then dramatically called into question with the Civil War of 1861–65. In both the USA and Switzerland, nevertheless, the antidote to the systemic fragility of the project has come from the constitution (as the celebration of the political compact). Through the constitution it has been possible to create both a new layer of collective identity (to add to and not to substitute the previous identities, around shared political values, rules and procedures) and to set up a new institutional structure to keep on board states of different sizes, history, language and political tradition. Unions of states do not evolve naturally towards a democratic organization. The aggregation of separate states and culturally distinct citizens, and the transformation of that aggregation into a functioning democracy, imply a political act by political elites able to win over the political consent of the citizens of their states. This is why the political formation of a European compound union should be conceptualized in radically different terms than the formation of both the French and German democratic nation states.

Comparative analysis shows that, if a common market does not need to rely on a formal constitution to function properly, the same cannot be said for a compound union. A compound union requires a political compact treaty, equivalent to a formal constitutional document or basic law (see Box 9.1), as we have seen from the experience of both the USA and Switzerland. This treaty should be the source of legitimacy of the union (Harbo 2007). For this reason it should have those symbolic properties (starting from a preamble expressing the justification of the states' aggregation) able to connect the states and their citizens with the political union. The political compact treaty should not only be part of a European multilevel constitutionalism that is already in action (Pernice 2008–2009), but it should also synthesize that multilevel constitutionalism in an explicit set of values, rules and institutions. The political compact treaty should be elaborated by a special convention, preceded by a public pre-constitutional agreement, signed only by the national elites participating in the project, defining the treaty's aims and the procedures for approving it.

Box 9.1 – Basic law vs. political compact treaty

The term *basic law* is used in some nation states (as in Germany or Israel) as an alternative to the term constitution, implying that it is a *temporary but necessary measure* for ordering the political system, without the enactment of a formal constitution (see Chapter 7). A basic law is either a codified set of constitutional rules or an organic law given to have constitutional powers and effects. The name is usually used to imply an interim or transitory nature, but also (as in the case of Israel) to avoid claiming to be "the highest law" for religious reasons. A basic law is entrenched if it overrides ordinary law passed by the legislature. In the case of a European compound union, a political compact treaty should function as the equivalent of both the constitution of the union of states and of the basic law of nation states. To keep the word "treaty" in the title (rather than "law") helps to clarify that the document symbolizes a pact between states and not only between citizens.

In fact, before starting the specific elaboration of the political compact treaty, the convened representatives should first agree on adopting a super-majority (but not unanimous) criterion for approval of the final text by the citizens or parliaments of the constituent states involved. The persistence of this criterion has in fact been the source of a recurrent stalemate in the EU. If the Lisbon Treaty has differentiated (Article 48) between an ordinary and a simplified revision procedure, nevertheless it has kept the principle that any agreement (Article 49) "shall be submitted for ratification by all contracting States in accordance with their respective constitutional requirements." In the past, the constitutional requirement of some EU member states to hold a popular referendum before ratifying any new treaty introduced a further hurdle to this procedural context, with the paradoxical effect that one member state alone could obstruct the coming into force of a treaty approved by all the other member states (as was the case of Ireland, in 2008 and 2009, regarding the approval of Lisbon Treaty: see Chapter 2). Only by escaping from the trap of unanimity is it possible to recognize the democratic virtues of the popular referendum. The popular referendum should be an instrument for promoting domestic participation, not for jeopardizing external agreements (Hobolt 2009). It should also be added that a popular referendum expressing a negative majority against the political compact treaty would have to be followed by another popular referendum on the existential issue of whether to remain in the union or not.

Since stalemate, if not a backlash, was the outcome of the EU constitutional debate of the 2000s, agreement on overcoming the unanimity criterion for approving a basic treaty or political compact treaty should precede any discussion on the features of the latter. Indeed, the euro crisis has already called into question this remnant of an EU that started formally as an international organization set up by a limited number of states. Facing the urgent needs of crisis management and prevention, a new treaty (the Fiscal Compact) has been set up outside of the EU, the coming into force of which no longer requires the unanimity of the contracting parties (but two-thirds of the then 17 euro-area member states and even less if the signatories to the Treaty are considered: 12 out of 25). It has become evident that the unanimity criterion has been gradually transformed into a device for imposing a tyranny of minorities, a no less pernicious principle (for democracy) than the opposite one of the tyranny of the majority. The experience of the USA and Switzerland also shows that an amendable constitutional document is a necessity for a compound union, both to adapt the latter to changes but also to provide a common language for those arguing about change. The comparative experience of the USA and Switzerland shows that compound unions consolidate themselves *only* when they are able to keep disputes on the nature of the polity within a shared constitutional document and when they have available a procedure for solving such disputes unconstrained by the unanimity criterion. An agreed constitutional document and a not-unanimous amendment procedure are the necessary conditions for neutralizing the centrifugal impetus of the divisions between states and between citizens. If the compound union requires a political compact treaty (considered equivalent to a constitutional document), the single market, instead, needs a functional text (a simplified Lisbon Treaty) specifying the rules, organs and procedures for deciding common policies and resolving the inevitable disputes.

The euro crisis has led the EU into a constitutional conundrum. The different perspectives on the EU have ended up contrasting, if not obstructing, each other. The EU cannot go back, but it cannot also go forward. Here resides the conundrum with which the euro crisis has suffocated the EU. In order to escape from it, three steps should be taken. First, it is necessary to *separate* the member states interested only in a single market (the non-euro-area member states) and the member states involved in a process of deeper integration. Second, it is necessary to *recompose* the two perspectives, the supranational and the intergovernmental, on the EU as a political project within an original framework whose constitutional logic and institutional structure are coherent with a compound union model – a model able to neutralize the intrusive, hierarchical and technocratic effects of the intergovernmental euro-area, but also the unilateralism of a supranationalism unable to acknowledge the necessary decision-making role of national governments. Third, it is necessary to *connect* the various member states participating in a single market community and the compound union through a flexible agreement aimed at preserving and regulating their economic cooperation. In short: separate, recompose, connect.

Escaping from the EU conundrum requires recognition of the *multiple unions* that have accompanied and constrained the development of the integration process. It requires the creation of a plural institutional framework to connect the different unions without impeding each of them from pursuing its specific project. The future political order of Europe (Olsen 2007) will be based on multiple unions. The debate on multiple unions should finally begin. The deep divisions on the *finalité* of the process of integration can no longer be masked by the deception of a unitary and expanding Union. After the euro crisis, it is no longer plausible to assume that deeper integration will emerge through the functional spillovers of a growing number of common policies, nor through a renewed intergovernmentalism. But it is also risky to assume that the single market can be guaranteed by obstructing a more coherent integration of the euro-area. The potential incapability of the euro-area member states to deal with the systemic challenges of economic and financial instability would impact negatively on the very viability of the single market itself (with negative consequences also for the non-euro-area member states). At the same time, a compound union unable to recognize a proper role in the decision-making system to both member state governments and their citizens, thus combining them in a separation of powers architecture, will not have a real chance of overcoming the paralyzing contrast between supranational and intergovernmental views and interests. The euro crisis has created the need to look for a new perspective on the institutional future of Europe.

9.6 Conclusion

This chapter has discussed the political implications of multiple unions. In order to free the EU from the conundrum where it has ended up as a result of the euro crisis, the chapter has offered arguments for recognizing the institutional and legal separation that has already taken place between the non-euro-area and the euro-area member states. Among the former, the opt-out member states have continued to claim their interest only in the economic community perspective of integration, whereas the latter are engaged in more (although convoluted) integration, under the impact of the euro crisis and in order to prevent future financial instability. To recognize this separation of perspectives and interests is the prerequisite for their re-elaboration in order to create a pluralist institutional order in Europe. The supporters of the economic community perspective should admit that the preservation and functioning of a single market is incompatible with a loose form of economic cooperation. As the comparative analysis has shown, a common (and even more so a single) market requires a supranational structure in charge of its regulation, although lighter than the one envisioned in the Lisbon Treaty. In short, it needs a simplified version of the latter, relieved of all the parts unconnected to single market policies (i.e. the strategic policies Europeanized with the Maastricht Treaty), without any reference to the promotion of "an ever closer union" and celebrating exclusively its economic aims. This redefinition of the Lisbon Treaty, as the legal basis of the single market, should take place with the concomitant formation of a distinct organization of the euro-area based on a proper political compact among its members.

Once the separation between the two areas of member states is recognized, then the negative implications of the dual constitution set up by the 1992 Maastricht Treaty for organizing the euro-area should also be recognized, thus adopting a new perspective for organizing the euro-area member states into a comprehensive and original model of compound union. The European compound union should recompose supranational and intergovernmental institutions and interests in a new architecture able to keep them in balance through a system of separation of powers. This chapter has also demonstrated that such a compound union would be unlikely to derive from an internal evolution of the EU or from the pressure of external events. The experience of the USA and Switzerland shows that compound unions are created by a political act consciously made by national political leaders who are engaged in mobilizing and involving citizens in support of their choice. Leaders lead; they do not follow. Their legitimacy derives from winning the minds and the hearts of the citizens towards their project. A compound union requires a leaders-driven contest if it is to succeed. Compound unions are political compacts, not organic polities. Their formation requires the exercise of political leadership at the highest level as constitution-makers are expected to do. The European compound union should be founded on a political compact treaty, with constitutional significance, declaring the federal union purpose of the aggregation. Finally, the compound union should be part of the single market, through some form of agreement regulating the participation of its members in such a way as to prevent their domination of the latter. Because the single market would need a supranational structure to function, with its four-sided decision-making system, at least for the transition period, the compound union might carve out its institutional structure from the one organizing the single market. Once the EP's nature has been revised, the two institutional structures can be distinguished, without being duplicated.

The experience of the USA and Switzerland shows that compound unions, once constituted, consolidate themselves *only* when they are able to keep disputes on the nature of the polity within the shared language of an agreed founding text, when they are organized according to the principle of a separation of powers and when they can call on a procedure for resolving their disputes without being paralyzed by the unanimity criterion. Given the fragility of their systemic foundation, federal unions as federations by aggregation also require, for their consolidation, responsible and self-restrained (national and supranational) political elites, political leaders willing to make the necessary compromises to neutralize the centrifugal impetus of interstate cleavages. Separation of powers not only prevents centralization but makes the central authority of the federal union necessarily weak. The center's weakness is the condition for preserving relations of mutual trust between states and institutional actors and thus for compelling them to specialize in politics of inter-institutional negotiation and not inter-partisan combat. The future of Europe is a pluralistic institutional order, wherein different projects should find their distinct institutional form. This future is in the hands of those European political leaders who attempt to answer the question Hamilton (now in Beard 1964: 34) raised some time ago: "whether societies of men are really capable or not of establishing good government from reflection and choice, or whether they are forever destined to depend for their political constitutions on accident and force," then adding, "the crisis at which we are arrived may with propriety be regarded as the era in which that decision is to be made."

Appendix

(Basic information referred to in the text)

Table A.1 *The Treaties of the European Union*

Treaties	Member States	Aims
European Coal and Steel Community ECSC (Paris, 1951)	Belgium, France, Germany, Italy, Luxembourg, the Netherlands	To guarantee equal access of all the member states to the market for coal and steel.
European Atomic Energy Community EURATOM (Rome, 1957)	Belgium, France, Germany, Italy, Luxembourg, the Netherlands	To promote nuclear research and technology in the member states.
European Economic Community EEC (Rome, 1957)	Belgium, France, Germany, Italy, Luxembourg, the Netherlands	To create a common market between the member states.
Single European Act (Luxembourg, The Hague, 1986)	Denmark, Belgium, France, Germany, United Kingdom, Ireland, Italy, Luxembourg, the Netherlands	To establish a single market between the member states.
European Union (Maastricht, 1992)	Denmark, Belgium, France, Germany, United Kingdom, Ireland, Italy, Luxembourg, the Netherlands	To create a pillar structure: A supranational pillar for the single market (EEC to become European Community or EC); Intergovernmental pillars for Common Foreign and Security Policies (CFSP) and Justice and Home Affairs (JHA);

Table A.1 (*cont.*)

Treaties	Member States	Aims
		Setting up of the criteria for activating an Economic and Monetary Union (EMU).
European Community EC (Amsterdam, 1997)	Austria, Denmark, Belgium, Finland, Greece, Germany, United Kingdom, Ireland, Italy, Luxembourg, the Netherlands, Sweden	To reorganize the EC Treaty.
Nice (2001)	Austria, Denmark, Belgium, Finland, Greece, Germany, United Kingdom, Ireland, Italy, Luxembourg, the Netherlands, Sweden	To proclaim the Charter of Fundamental Rights. To rationalize the institutional system.
Lisbon (2009)	Austria, Belgium, Bulgaria, Croatia (2013), Czech Republic, Denmark, Cyprus, Estonia, Finland, France, Germany, Greece, Hungary, Ireland, Italy, Latvia, Lithuania, Luxembourg, Malta, the Netherlands, Poland, Portugal, Romania, Slovakia, Slovenia, Spain, Sweden, United Kingdom	To define the powers and competences of the Union and the member states. To adopt the Charter of Fundamental Rights. To attribute legal personality to the Union.

Note: The intergovernmental treaties adopted during the euro crisis are not considered because they constitute different organizations than the EU.

Table A.2 *The enlargement of the European Union*

Year of accession	Member States
1952	Belgium, France, Germany, Italy, Luxembourg, the Netherlands
1957	
1973	Denmark, United Kingdom, Ireland
1986	Spain, Portugal, Greece
1995	Austria, Finland, Sweden
2004	Cyprus, Estonia, Latvia, Lithuania, Malta, Poland, Czech Republic, Slovakia, Slovenia, Hungary
2007	Bulgaria, Romania
2013	Croatia

Table A.3 *Council formations*

General Affairs; Foreign Affairs; Economic and Financial Affairs; Justice and Home Affairs (JHA), Employment, Social Policy, Health and Consumer Affairs; Competitiveness (Internal Market, Industry, Research and Space); Transport, Telecommunications and Energy; Agriculture and Fisheries; Environment; Education, Youth, Culture and Sport

Published in the Official Journal of the European Union (OJEU), 2122009, L. 315/46.

Table A.4 *Established democracies: constitutional developments*

Country	Adoption of the current constitution (with major developments)
Australia	1901
Austria	1920 (1955)
Belgium	1831
Canada	1867 (1982)
Denmark	1849 (1953)
Finland	1919 (2000)
France	1958
Germany	1949*

Table A.4 (*cont.*)

Country	Adoption of the current constitution (with major developments)
Greece	1975
Ireland	1937 (1949)
Iceland	1944
Israel	1948**
Italy	1948
Japan	1947
Luxembourg	1868 (1919)
Norway	1814
New Zealand	1986
Netherlands	1815 (1983)
Portugal	1976
Spain	1978
Sweden	1974
Switzerland	1848
United Kingdom	[1688]***
United States	1789

* In West Germany the constitution of 1949 was labeled as *Grundgesetz* or Basic Law to underline its provisional character as long as Germany was divided. Germany was officially reunited on October 3, 1990. The Deutsche Demokratische Republik (DDR or East Germany) joined the Bundesrepublik Deutschland (BRD or West Federal Republic of Germany) as the five *Länder* (states) of Brandenburg, Mecklenburg-Vorpommern, Saxony, Saxony-Anhalt and Thuringia. These states had been the five original states of East Germany, but had been abolished in 1952 in favor of a centralized system. At the same time, East and West Berlin reunited into one city, which became a city-state along the lines of the existing city-states of Bremen and Hamburg. Therefore, reunification did not witness any institutional discontinuity.

** Between 1958 and 1984 the Israeli Parliament (Knesset) passed a series of Basic Laws that served as placeholders for the formal constitution. In 1992 another Basic Law was passed concerning the direct election of the prime minister, but was then abolished in 2001. Also in the case of Israel, the term Basic Law is used, instead of constitution, for symbolic reasons. Only the reunification of the Jewish people will legitimize the latter term.

*** We know from the Introduction that the UK does not have a written constitution. Nevertheless, a series of parliamentary Acts, starting with those passed during the Glorious Revolution of 1688, are considered the functional equivalent of a constitution, that is, those Acts instituted constitutional conventions.

Table A.5 *Competitive democracies: years of alternation in government (1945–2013)*[1]

Predominantly single-party governments	Period 1945–2012	Predominantly coalition governments	Period 1945–2013
United Kingdom	1945, 1951, 1964, 1970, 1974, 1979, 1997, 2010 (coalition)	Australia	1945, 1949, 1972, 1975, 1983, 1996
New Zealand	1946, 1949, 1957, 1960, 1972, 1975, 1984, 1990, 1999, 2008	France Fifth Republic[2]	1965, 1981, 1995, 2012
Canada	1945, 1957, 1963, 1979, 1980, 1984, 1993, 2006	Ireland	1944, 1948, 1951, 1954, 1957, 1973, 1977, 1981, 1982, 1987, 1994, 1997, 2011
Greece (post 1974)[4]	1974, 1981, 1989, (1989),[3] 1990, 1993, 2004, 2009 (2012 coalition)	Sweden	1945, 1976, 1982, 1991, 1994, 2006
Spain[4]	1976, 1982, 1996, 2004, 2011	Norway	1945, 1963, 1965, 1971, 1972, 1973, 1981, 1986, 1989, 1990, 1997, 2000, 2001, 2005
Portugal[5]	1985, 1995, 2002, 2005, 2011	Denmark[6]	1990, 1993, 1994, 1996, 2001, 2011
Japan[7]	1993, 1994, 2001, 2009	Germany	1949, (1966),[3] 1969, 1982, 1998, (2005), 2009, (2013)
		Italy Second Republic	1996, 2001, 2006, 2008, (2011 – 2013 technocratic government), (2013 – left/right coalition)

[1] During the Second World War, almost all countries had governments of national unity. Accordingly, all the cases considered here start from the first post-war election.

2 Alternating control of the presidency of the Republic, starting from the first direct election. Due to its semi-presidential system France during the Fifth Republic belongs in this column as the president must govern together with a parliamentary executive (which had always been a coalition until 2007). Moreover, the presidential majority does not always coincide with the parliamentary majority (as was the case in 1986–1988, 1993–1995 and 1997–2002).

3 Figure in brackets: formation of a grand coalition government between the two main parties (plus a junior partner).

4 Starting from the first post-authoritarian elections.

5 After an initial phase of single-party governments, Portugal was governed by coalition governments headed by the PSD (the Social Democratic Party, but of a center-right orientation) until the mid 1980s. Subsequently it was governed for a short period by a coalition of the PSD and the main center-left party PS (Socialist Party). Since 1985 there has been an alternation between single-party governments of the center-right PSD (in coalition with the People's Party between 2002 and 2005) and the center-left PS.

6 Denmark has frequently had (minority) coalition governments. After the long dominance of the Social Democratic Party (center-left), in the 1990s, the country has seen several governments headed by the main center-right party, the Liberal Party, in coalition with the Conservative People's Party. It is worth noting that between September 1994 and December 1996, the country was governed by a coalition of centrist parties, thus excluding both the Social Democratic Party and the Liberal Party.

7 Until 1993 Japan had single-party governments of the Liberal Democratic Party (LDP). Between July 1993 and June 1994, the LDP was replaced by a coalition of parties, among which were the Socialist Party and the Social Democratic Party. As of June 1994, the LDP returned to government, in coalitions with different parties (among which was the Socialist Party). Starting with the elections of September 1999, the LDP has headed more consistently center-right coalitions.

Glossary

(Basic concepts of comparative politics used in the text)

Electoral college in the United States

The US president is indirectly elected by the so-called presidential electors who constitute the electoral college of each state. The electoral college of each state is composed of a number of ad hoc presidential electors equal to the number of representatives of that state in the House of Representatives plus the two senators each state has in the Senate. In this way, thanks to the Senate clause, the small states have a number of presidential electors superior to what they would have according to the sole criterion of representation proportional to the population adopted for the House of Representatives. The candidate elected president is thus the one who receives the majority of votes from the presidential electors of the various state electoral colleges, gathering in the capital of their states 40 days after the elections. Thus there is no national electoral college, although the winning candidate should get the absolute majority (today) of the total of the 538 presidential electors (equivalent to the 435 members of the House of Representatives, 100 members of the Senate plus three representatives of Washington DC, which is deprived of representation in both chambers of Congress). Amendment XII of the constitution (ratified in 1804) states that, in the event that no candidate wins the absolute majority of the votes of the presidential electors, "then from the persons having the highest numbers not exceeding three on the list of those voted for as President, the House of Representatives shall choose immediately, by ballot, the President. But in choosing the President the votes shall be taken by States, the representation from each state having one vote." In order to avoid the parliamentarization of the presidential election, implicit in the constitution and experienced in the first decades of the Union, the states quickly introduced the criterion of *winner-takes-all* for the allocation of the votes of the presidential electors. This criterion, combined with the submission of candidates representing the two main parties in all the states, neutralized the possibility of a presidential election without a candidate winning the absolute majority of the votes of the presidential electors (S. Fabbrini 2008c; Polsby, Wildavsky and Hopkins 2007).

Fusion of powers system (parliamentary and semi-presidential democracies)

The fusion of powers system is characterized by a political connection between the (majority) of the legislature and the executive. The latter may govern as long as the legislature supports it. The parliamentary system epitomizes historically the fusion of powers logic. Any parliamentary government requires the confidence (direct or indirect) of the legislature to operate. The "efficient secret" for keeping the connection between the legislature and the executive is the party (or the multiparty coalition) representing the majority of the popular chamber of the parliament. "The efficient secret of the English Constitution may be described as the close union, the nearly complete fusion, of the executive and legislative powers" (Bagehot 1867: 12). Thus the British Parliament has inherited the unitary nature of sovereignty previously embodied in the office and the body of the king (Kantorowics 1957). Semi-presidential systems also belong to the family of fusion of powers systems, as long as the dual executive cannot govern without the legislature's confidence (see below). In fusion of powers (parliamentary and semi-presidential) systems only the legislature controls the law-making process, under the supervision of a constitutional court or council. In decentralized or federal fusion of powers systems, the law-making power pertains to the popular chamber of the parliament, for matters that are the competence of the federal center. The institutional feature of the fusion of powers system is the centralization of decision-making power in the popular chamber of the parliament (or better in the government that enjoys the latter's support).

Government vs. executive

Although "government" and "executive" are frequently considered as synonymous, they in fact reflect two structurally different institutional systems. The "government" is typical of the fusion of powers system, where it constitutes the institution holding the ultimate decision-making power. The "executive" is typical of the separation of powers system, where it constitutes one of the institutions sharing the decision-making power. In a separation of powers system there is no government as the ultimate decision-making institution, whereas the formation of a government as the ultimate decision-making institution is the basis of the functioning of a fusion of powers system. In the former, but not the latter, the government is a process that is the decision-making outcome of the political process taking place between the separate institutions (Neustadt 1990; Polsby 1986; Rockman 1984).

Semi-presidential France of the Fifth Republic

In the French semi-presidential government sovereignty remains in the popular chamber of the legislature (the Assemblée Nationale) and the government is structured around two heads: the president of the republic elected directly by voters in a national college and a prime minister enjoying the direct or indirect support of the Assemblée Nationale. This government is called a *dual executive* or Janus-faced government. Both the election of the president of the republic and the election of the parliament are organized by a run-off majoritarian electoral system (according to which, if no candidate gets an absolute majority of votes in the first round, a second ballot will be run between the two candidates receiving the most votes – in the case of the presidential elections – or between those candidates who overcome the threshold of 12.5 percent of votes in the uninominal colleges – in the case of parliamentary elections). The direct election of the president was introduced in 1965 after the successful 1962 referendum. Previously (in 1958) the president was elected by an electoral college. After the referendum on the "Reduction of the Mandate of the President of the French Republic" held in 2000, the length of the term of office was reduced from 7 to 5 years; the first election to a shorter term was held in 2002. President Chirac was first elected in 1995 and again in 2002. At that time there was no limit on the number of terms that could be served, so Chirac could have run again, but chose not to. He was succeeded by Nicolas Sarkozy in 2007, in his turn succeeded by Francois Hollande in 2012. Following a further change (the constitutional law on the "Modernization of the Institutions of the Fifth Republic" of 2008), a president cannot serve for more than two consecutive terms. Thus, since 2002 the terms of the presidential and parliamentary tenure have been synchronized in order that both last 5 years, although each election is held on different days/months of the same year (with the parliamentary elections following the presidential one). This is done to promote a political majority in the parliament coherent with the one already expressed in the election of the president. In the past, the separate election of the 7-year president of the republic and the 5-year parliament generated (in 1986–1988 and 1993–1995) situations of *cohabitation* between a president of one party/coalition and a parliament controlled by a different party/coalition. Cohabitation also occurred in the period 1997–2002 ((Elgie 2004, 2010).

Separation of powers system (USA and Swiss democracies)

The separation of powers system implies that no institution can claim the ultimate decision-making power. The legislature is organized into two separate chambers and both are separate from the executive. The reciprocal separation between the various institutions is guaranteed not only by the constitution, but also by the fact that none of them requires the (direct or indirect) confidence of the others to perform its functions. All of the separate institutions are equal before the constitution, whether they are directly elected or indirectly formed. In the two historical cases of separation of powers systems (the USA and Switzerland), sovereignty is fragmented vertically and horizontally. Specific institutional devices (generally called *checks and balances*) encourage each separate institution to take into consideration the preferences of the other institutions. The government is not an institution but a process through which those institutions reach an agreed decision. The principle of checks and balances should thus be kept distinct from the principle of the separation of powers. The former makes possible the functioning of the latter. The law-making process is not controlled exclusively by one or other branch of the legislature, because a bill will be transformed into a law only with approval of both chambers. In the USA, contrary to the situation in Switzerland, a bill will become a law only after the signature of the president. The president can refuse to sign the bill for political reasons, sending it back to the legislature, which might approve it again but through a qualified majority of two-thirds of the members in each chamber. This (relative) veto power corresponds to a legislative power of the president (Vile 1967; Polsby 2008).

Bibliography

Ackermann, B. (1991). *We The People: Foundations*, Cambridge, MA: Harvard University Press.

Adams, M., F. Fabbrini and P. Larouche (eds.) (2014). *The Constitutionalization of European Budgetary Constraints*, Oxford: Hart Publishing.

Aggarwal, V. (1994). 'Comparing Regional Cooperation Efforts in the Asia-Pacific and North America', in A. Mack and J. Ravenhill (eds.), *Pacific Cooperation: Building Economic and Security Regimes in the Asia-Pacific Region*, St. Leonard, New South Wales: Allen and Unwin, pp. 40–65.

Aldrich, J. H. (1995). *Why Parties? The Origin and Transformation of Political Parties in America*, University of Chicago Press.

Alesina, A. and F. Giavazzi (eds.) (2010). *Europe and the Euro*, University of Chicago Press.

Allen, D. (2012). 'The Common Foreign and Security Policy', in E. Jones, A. Menon and S. Weatherill (eds.), *The Oxford Handbook of the European Union*, Oxford University Press, pp. 643–60.

Allerkamp, D. K. (2009). 'Intergovernmentalism Reloaded: The Transformative Power of "Intergovernmental" Council Policy-Making', *mimeo*.

Amato, G. and J. Ziller (2007). *The European Constitution: Cases and Materials in EU and Member States' Law*, Cheltenham: Edward Elgar.

Avbij, M. and J. Komàrek (eds.), (2012). *Constitutional Pluralism in the European Union and Beyond*, Oxford: Hart Publishing.

Bagehot, W. (1867). *The English Constitution*, London: Chapman and Hall.

Balassa, B. (1961). *The Theory of Economic Integration*, London: Allen and Unwin.

Bartolini, S. (2008). 'Should the Union be "Politicised"? Prospects and Risks', in 'Politics: The Right or the Wrong Sort of Medicine for the EU? Two Papers by Simon Hix and Stefano Bartolini', *Notre Europe* Policy Paper no. 19, www.notre-europe.eu/uploads/txpublication/Policypaper19-en.pdf.

Barucci, E., F. Bassanini and M. Messori (eds.) (2014). *Achievements and Open Problems of the Banking Union*, Rome: Astrid.

Bastasin, C. (2014). *Saving Europe: How National Politics Nearly Destroyed the Euro*, Washington, DC: Brookings Institution Press.

Baun, M. J. (1995). 'The Maastricht Treaty as High Politics: Germany, France and European Integration', *Political Science Quarterly* 110/4: 605–24.

Beard, C. A. (ed.) (1964). *The Enduring Federalist*, New York: Ungar, 2nd edn.

Beer, S. H. (1993). *To Make a Nation: The Rediscovery of American Federalism*, Cambridge, MA: Harvard University Press.

Bellah, R. N. (1967). 'Civil Religion in America', *Journal of the American Academy of Arts and Sciences* 96/1: 1–21.

Bellamy, R. (2007). *Political Constitutionalism: A Republican Defense of the Constitutionality of Democracy*, Cambridge University Press.

 (2013). '"An Ever Closer Union among the Peoples of Europe": Republican Intergovernmentalism and *Demoi*cratic Representation within the EU', *Journal of European Integration* 35/5: 499–516.

Bensel R. F. (1987) *Sectionalism and American Political Development: 1880–1980*, Madison: The University of Wisconsin Press.

Berrington, H. and R. Hague (2001). 'The Further Off From England: British Public Opinion and Europe', in A. Menon and V. Wright (eds.), *From the Nation State to Europe?*, Oxford University Press, pp. 66–94.

Best, E., T. Christiansen and P. Settembri (eds.) (2008). *The Governance of the Wider Europe: EU Enlargement and Institutional Change*, Cheltenham: Edward Elgar Publishing.

Bickerton, C. J. (2010). 'Une Europe Neo-Madisonienne? Pouvoir Limité et Légitimité Democratique', *Revue Française de Science Politique* 60/6: 1077–90.

Blondel, J. (1998). 'Il modello svizzero: un futuro per l'Europa?', *Rivista Italiana di Scienza politica* XXVIII/2: 203–27.

Bogdandy, A. von (2000). 'The European Union as a Supranational Federation: A Conceptual Attempt in the Light of the Amsterdam Treaty', *Columbia Journal of European Law* 6/1: 27–54.

Bogdanor, V. (1986). 'The Future of the European Community: Two Models of Democracy', *Government and Opposition* 21/2: 161–76.

 (2007). 'Legitimacy, Accountability and Democracy in the European Union', A Federal Trust Report, London.

Bolleyer, N. (2009). *Intergovernmental Cooperation: Rational Choices in Federal Systems and Beyond*, Oxford University Press.

Borzel, T. (ed.) (2006). *The Disparity of European Integration: Revisiting Neofunctionalism in Honour of Ernst B Haas*, London: Routledge.

 (2010). 'European Governance: Negotiation and Competition in the Shadow of Hierarchy', *Journal of Common Market Studies* 48/2: 191–219.

Borzel, T. and M. O. Hosli (2003). 'Brussels between Bern and Berlin: Comparative Federalism Meets the European Union', *Governance* 16/2: 179–202.

Bouzas, R. and H. Soltz (2001). 'Institutions and Regional Integration', in V. Bulmer-Thomas (ed.), *Regional Integration in Latin America and the Caribbean: The Political Economy of Open Regionalism*, London: Institute of Latin American Studies.

Bowler, S. and D. M. Farrell (1995). 'The Organizing of the European Parliament: Committees, Specialization and Co-ordination', *British Journal of Political Science* 25/2: 219–43.

Bressanelli, E. (2012). 'National Parties and Group Membership in the European Parliament: Ideology or Pragmatism', *Journal of European Public Policy* 19/5: 737–54.

Bulmer, S., C. Jefferey and S. Padgett (eds.) (2010). *Rethinking Germany and Europe: Democracy and Diplomacy in a Semi-Sovereign State*, New York: Palgrave.

Bulmer-Thomas, V. (ed.) (2001). *Regional Integration in Latin America and the Caribbean: The Political Economy of Open Regionalism*, London: Institute of Latin American Studies.

Bunse, S. and K. A. Nicolaidis (2012). 'Large Versus Small States: Anti-Hegemony and the Politics of Shared Leadership', in E. Jones, A. Menon and S. Weatherill (eds.), *The Oxford Handbook of the European Union*, Oxford University Press, pp. 249–66.

Burgess, M. (2014). 'Federal Imperatives in the Institutional Evolution of the European Union: Political Architects and Democratic Builders of the European Union', in S. Piattoni, *The European Union: Democratic Principles and Institutional Architectures in Times of Crisis*, Oxford University Press, forthcoming.

Burgess, M. and A.-G. Gagnon (eds.) (2010). *Federal Democracies*, London: Routledge.

Bürgin, A. (N.D.). 'The Parliamentarization of the EU From Nice to the Constitution: Shared Norms in Argumentative Processes', www.uni-koeln.de/wiso-fak/powi/wessels/DE/ARCHIV/IGC_Net/Buergin_EU%20parliamentarization_arguing.pdf.

Burnham, W. D. (1970). *Critical Elections and the Mainsprings of American Politics*, New York: W. W. Norton.

Cain, B. E. and W. T. Jones (1989). 'Madison's Theory of Representation', in B. Grofman and D. Wittman (eds.), *The Federalist Papers and the New Institutionalism*, New York: Agathon Press, pp. 11–30.

Calleo, D. P. (2001). *Rethinking Europe's Future*, Princeton University Press.
(2011). 'De Gaulle's Vision for Europe', in B. M. Rowland (ed.), *Charles De Gaulle's Legacy of Ideas*, Lanham: Lexington Books, pp. 1–10.

Calliess, C. (2014). 'The Governance Framework of the Eurozone and the Need for a Treaty Reform', Paper presented at conference on 'What Form of Government for the European Union and the Eurozone?' Tilburg University Law School, Tilburg, the Netherlands, June 5–6.

Capoccia, G. and D. Kelemen (2007). 'The Study of Critical Junctures: Theory, Narrative, and Counterfactuals in Historical Institutionalism', *World Politics* 59/3: 341–69.

Caporaso, J. A. and S. Tarrow (2009). 'Polanyi in Brussels: Supranational Institutions and the Transnational Embedding of Markets', *International Organization* 63/4: 593–620.

Caporaso, J. A. and J. Wittenbrinck (2006). 'The New Modes of Governance and Political Authority in Europe', *Journal of European Public Policy* 13/4: 471–80.

Cappelletti, M., M. Seccombe and J. Weiler (eds.) (1986). *Integration through Law: Europe and the American Federal Experience*, Berlin: De Gruyter.

Carta, C. (2012). *The European Union Diplomatic Service: Ideas, Preferences and Identities*, London: Routledge.

Cartabia, M., N. Lupo and A. Simoncini (2013). *Democracy and Subsidiarity in the EU: National Parliaments, Regions and Civil Society in the Decision-making Process*, Boulogne: Il Mulino.

CEPS (2014). *Shifting EU Institutional Reform into High Gear*, Report of the CEPS High Level Group, chaired by D. Hubner, Brussels.

CER (2014). *The Economic Consequences of Leaving the EU*, The Final Report of the CER Commission on the UK and the EU Single Market, London, www.cer.org.uk.

Chalmers, D. (2013). 'Democratic Self-Government in Europe: Domestic Solutions to the EU Legitimacy Crisis', Policy Network Paper, May.

Charlemagne (2012). '1789 and All That', *The Economist*, www.economist.com/node/21547253.

Christiansen, T. and C. Reh (2009). *Constitutionalizing the European Union*, New York: Palgrave Macmillan.

Church, C. and P. Dardanelli (2005). 'The Dynamic of Confederalism and Federalism: Comparing Switzerland and the EU', *Regional and Federal Studies* 15/2: 163–85.

Citrin, J. (2008). 'Political Culture', in P. H. Schuck and J. Q. Wilson (eds.), *Understanding America: The Anatomy of an Exceptional Nation*, New York: Public Affairs, pp. 147–80.

Closa, C. (2012). 'Institutional Innovation in the EU: The "Permanent" Presidency of the European Council', in F. Laursen (ed.), *The EU's Lisbon Treaty*, Burlington, VA: Ashgate, pp. 119–40.

(2013). *The Politics of Ratification of EU Treaties*, London: Routledge.

Cohn-Bendit, D. and G. Verhofstadt (2012). *For Europe*, Online, CreateSpace Independent Publishing Platform.

Cole, A. (2010). 'Franco-German Europe', in K. Dyson and A. Sepos (eds.), *Which Europe? The Politics of Differentiated Integration*, New York: Palgrave Macmillan, pp. 156–69.

Colomer, J. M. (2010). 'The new semipresidential Europe', *Joseph Colomer's Weekly Blog*, April 25, http://jcolomer.blogspot.it/.

Conlan, T. (1998). *From New Federalism to Devolution: Twenty-Five Years of Intergovernmental Reform*, Washington DC: Brookings Institution Press.

Corbett, R., F. Jacobs and M. Shackleton (2005). *The European Parliament*, London: John Harper, 6th edn.

Costa, O. and P. Magnette (2003). 'The European Union as a Consociation? A Methodological Assessment', *West European Politics*, 26/3: 1–18.

Costa, O., R. Dehousse and A. Trakalova (2011). 'Codecision and "early agreement": An improvement or a subversion of the legislative procedure?', *Notre Europe*, Studies and Research, Report n. 84.

Craig, P. (2010). *The Lisbon Treaty: Law, Politics and Treaty Reform*, Oxford University Press.

(2011). 'The European Union Act 2011: Locks, Limits and Legality', *Common Market Law Review* 48/6: 1915–44.

(2014). 'Economic Governance and the Euro Crisis: Constitutional Architecture and Constitutional Implications', in M. Adams, F. Fabbrini and P. Larouche (eds.), *The Constitutionalization of European Budgetary Constraints*, Oxford: Hart Publishing, pp. 19–40.

Craig, P. and G. De Bursa (eds.) (1999). *The Evolution of EU Law*, Oxford University Press.

Crepaz, M. M. L., T. A. Koelble and D. Wilsford (eds.) (2000). *Democracy and Institutions: The Life Work of Arend Lijphart*, Ann Arbor: The University of Michigan Press.

Crum, B. (2010). *Learning the EU Constitutional Treaty*, London: Routledge.

(2012). 'The Democratic Dilemma of Monetary Union', Paper submitted at the EUDO Dissemination Conference on 'The Euro Crisis and the State of European Democracy', EUI, Florence, November 22–23.

Curtin, D. (2009). *Executive Power of the European Union: Law, Practices, and the Living Constitution*, Oxford University Press.

(2014). 'Challenging Executive Dominance in European Democracy', *Modern Law Review* 77/1: 1–32.

Curtin, D. and C. Fasone (2014). 'Differentiated Representation: Is a Flexible European Parliament Desirable?', *mimeo*, July 15.

Curtin, D. and A. E. Kellerman (2006). *The EU Constitution: The Best Way Forward?*, The Hague: Asser Press.

Daalder, H. (1995). 'Paths Toward State Formation in Europe: Democratization, Bureaucratization, and Politicization', in H. E. Chehabi and A. Stepan (eds.), *Politics, Society and Democracy*, Boulder, Westview Press, 113–30.

Dahl, R. A. (1989). *Democracy and Its Critics*, New Haven: Yale University Press.

(2001). *How Democratic Is the American Constitution*, New Haven: Yale University Press.

(2006). *A Preface to Democratic Theory. Expanded Edition*, University of Chicago Press, original edn 1956.

Dann, P. (2003). 'European Parliament and Executive Federalism: Approaching a Parliament in a Semi-Parliamentary Democracy', *European Law Journal* 9/5: 549–74.

Dardanelli, P. (2010). 'Federal Democracy in Switzerland', in M. Burgess and A. G. Gagnon (eds.), *Federal Democracies*, London: Routledge, pp. 142–59.

Dawson, M. and F. De Witte (2013). 'Constitutional Balance in the EU after the Euro-Crisis', *The Modern Law Review* 76/5: 817–44.

Decker, F. and J. Sonnicksen (2009). 'The Direct Election of the Commission President. A Presidential Approach to Democratising the European Union', ZEI Discussion Paper C 192, Bonn: Center for European Integration Studies.

(2011). 'An Alternative Approach to European Union Democratization: Re-Examining the Direct Election of the Commission President', *Government and Opposition* 46/2: 168–91.

Dehousse, R. (2005). 'We the States: Why the Anti-Federalists Have Won', in C. Parsons and N. Jabko (eds.), *With US or Against US? The State of the European Union*, vol. VII, Oxford University Press, pp. 103–21.

(ed.) (2011). *The 'Community Method': Obstinate or Obsolete?*, New York: Palgrave Macmillan.

Della Sala, V. (2010). 'Political Myth, Mythology and the European Union', *Journal of Common Market Studies* 48/1: 1–19.

De Lombaerde, P. and M. Schulz (eds.) (2009). *The EU and World Regionalism: The Makability of Regions in the 21st Century*, Burlington, VT: Ashgate.

Delors, J. (2012). 'Visions d'Europe: Perspectives et priorités pour l'Union Européenne', Conférence Mouvement Européen France, Palais du Luxembourg, July 6.

Derthick, M. (2001). *Keeping the Compound Republic: Essays on American Federalism*, Washington DC: Brookings Institution Press.

De Scoutheete, P. (2011). 'Decision-making in the Union', *Notre Europe* Policy Brief n. 24, April.

(2012). 'The European Council and the Community Method', *Notre Europe* Policy Paper n. 56.

De Schoutheete, P. and S. Micossi (2013). 'On Political Union in Europe: The Changing Landscape of Decision-Making and Political Accountability', CEPS Policy Brief, February.

Deudney, D. H. (1995). 'The Philadelphian System: Sovereignty, Arms Control, and Balance of Power in the American States-Union, circa 1787–1861', *International Organization* 49/2: 191–228.

(2007). *Bounding Power: Republican Security Theory from the Polis to the Global Village*, Princeton University Press.

Deudney, D. H. and J. Meiser (2012). 'American Exceptionalism', in M. Cox and D. Stokes (eds.), *US Foreign Policy*, Oxford University Press, pp. 21–39.

Devuyst, Y. (2012). 'The Constitutional and Lisbon Treaties', in E. Jones, A. Menon and S. Weatherill (eds.), *The Oxford Handbook of the European Union*, Oxford University Press, pp. 163–80.

De Witte, B. (1999). 'Direct Effect, Supremacy and the Nature of Legal Order', in P. Craig and G. De Bursa (eds.), *The Evolution of EU Law*, Oxford University Press, pp. 177–213.

(ed.) (2003). *Ten Reflections on the Constitutional Treaty for Europe*, Fiesole (Florence): EUI, Robert Schuman Centre.

(2012). 'International Treaty on the Euro and the EU Legal Order', Paper delivered at the international conference on 'The Euro Crisis and the State of European Democracy', Florence, EUI, November 22–23.

Dinan, D. (ed.) (2006). *Origins and Evolution of the European Union*, Oxford University Press.

(2011). 'Governance and Institutions: Implementing the Lisbon Treaty in the Shadow of the Euro Crisis', *Journal of Common Market Studies* 49 (Annual Review): 103–21.

Dri, C. (2009). 'At What Point Does a Legislature Become Institutionalized? The Mercosur Parliament's Path', *Brazilian Political Science Review* 3/2: 60–97.

Duchene, F. (1994). *Jean Monnet: The First Statesman of Interdependence*, New York: W. W. Norton and Company.

Dullien, S. and J. J. Torreblanca (2012). 'What Is a Political Union', European Council on Foreign Relations Policy Brief n. 70, December, pp. 1–8.

Dyson, K. and L. Quaglia (2010). *European Economic Governance and Policies*, 2 vols. Oxford University Press.

Dyson, K. and A. Sepos (eds.) (2010). *Which Europe? The Politics of Differentiated Integration*, New York: Palgrave Macmillan.

Easton, D. (1971). *The Political System: An Inquiry into the State of Political Science*, New York: Knopf, 2nd edn.

Egenhofer, C., S. Kurpas and L. Van Schaik (2009). 'The Ever-Changing Union: An Introduction to the History, Institutions and Decision-Making Processes of the European Union', CEPS Paperback.

Eggermont, F. (2012). *The Changing Role of the European Council and the Institutional Framework of the European Union: Consequences for the European Integration Process*, Cambridge, MA: Intersentia.

Elazar, D. J. (1985). 'Constitution-making: The Pre-eminently Political Act', in K. G. Banting and R. Simon (eds.), *Redesigning the State: The Politics of Constitutional Change in Industrial Nations*, University of Toronto Press, pp. 232–48.

 (1987). *Exploring Federalism*, Tuscaloosa: University of Alabama Press.

 (1988). *The American Constitutional Tradition*, Lincoln, NE: University of Nebraska Press.

 (1998). *Constitutionalizing Globalization: The Postmodern Revival of Confederal Arrangements*, Lanham: Rowman and Littlefield.

Elgie, R. (1999). *Semi-presidentialism in Europe*, Oxford University Press.

 (2004). 'Semi-Presidentialism: Concepts, Consequences and Contesting Explanations', *Political Studies Review* 2/3: 314–30.

 (2010). 'Semi-Presidentialism, Cohabitation and the Collapse of Electoral Democracies 1990–2008', *Government And Opposition* 45/1: 29–45.

Elster, J. (1997). 'Ways of Constitution-Making', in A. Hadenius (ed.), *Democracy's Victory and Crisis*, Cambridge University Press, pp. 123–42.

Eriksen, E. O. (2014). *The Normativity of the European Union*, New York: Palgrave Macmillan.

Erk, J. (2004). 'Austria: A Federation Without Federalism', *Publius* 34/1: 1–26.

Estella, A. (2009). 'A Proposal for Electing the European Government', Fundacion Ideas n.1.

EUCO (European Council) (2011). *Conclusions. Annex II*.

EUCO (European Council) (2012). *Towards a Genuine Economic and Monetary Union*, December 5.

EUCO (European Council) (2013). 'The European Council decides on the number of members of the European Commission', Brussels, EUCO 119/13, Presse 210.

European Parliament (2012). 'New Institutional Solutions for Multi-Tier Governance', Directorate General for Internal Policies, Constitutional Affairs, October 29.

Everson, M. and J. Eisner (2007). *The Making of a European Constitution. Judges and Law Beyond Constitutive Power*, London: Routledge.

Fabbrini, F. (2012). 'The Enhanced Cooperation Procedure: A Study in Multispeed Integration'. Research Paper, Turin, Centro Studi sul Federalismo.

(2013). 'The Fiscal Compact, the "Golden Rule" and the Paradox of European Federalism', *Boston College International and Comparative Law Review* 36/1: 1–38.

(2014a). 'On Banks, Courts and International Law', *Maastricht Journal of European and Comparative Constitutional Law* 21/3, forthcoming.

(2014b). 'The Principle of Subsidiarity', in T. Tridimas and R. Schütze (eds.), *Oxford Principles of EU Law*, Oxford University Press, forthcoming.

Fabbrini, F. and K. Granat (2013). 'Yellow Card, but No Foul: The Role of the National Parliaments under the Subsidiarity Protocol and the Commission Proposal for an EU Regulation on the Right to Strike', *Common Market Law Review* 50/1: 115–44.

Fabbrini, S. (2001). 'Cleavages: Political', in N. J. Smelser and P. A. Baltes (eds.), *International Encyclopedia of the Social and Behavioral Sciences*, vol. III, Amsterdam: Elsevier, pp. 1987–90.

(2004). 'Transatlantic Constitutionalism: Comparing the United States and the European Union', *European Journal of Political Research* 43/4: 547–69.

(2005a). 'To Build a Market without a State: The EU in American Perspective', in S. Fabbrini (ed.), *Democracy and Federalism in the European Union and the United States: Exploring Post-national Governance*, London: Routledge, pp. 119–32.

(2005b). 'Madison in Brussels: The EU and the US as Compound Democracies', *European Political Science* 4/2: 188–98.

(2008a). 'Contesting the Lisbon Treaty: Structure and Implications of the Constitutional Divisions within the European Union', *European Journal of Law Reform* X/4: 457–76.

(2008b). 'The Constitutionalisation of a Compound Democracy: Comparing the European Union with the American Experience', ConWEB-Webpapers on Constitutionalism & Governance beyond the State, no. 3, ISSN: 1756–7556, www.wiso.unihamburg.de/fileadmin/sowi/politik/governance/ConWeb_Papers/conweb3-2008.pdf.

(2008c). *America and Its Critics: Virtues and Vices of the Democratic Hyperpower*, Cambridge: Polity Press.

(2010). *Compound Democracies: Why the United States and Europe Are Becoming Similar*, Oxford University Press, updated edition.

(2011). 'Compound Democracy', in M. Bevir (ed.), *Encyclopedia of Political Theory*, vol. I, London: Sage, pp. 261–6.

(2012), 'After the Euro Crisis: The President of Europe. A New Paradigm for Increasing Legitimacy and Effectiveness in the EU', CEPS and EuropEos Commentary no. 12, June 1, pp. 1–8.

(2013). 'Intergovernmentalism and Its Limits: The Implications of the Euro Crisis on the European Union', *Comparative Political Studies*, 46/9: 1003–29.

(2014). 'The European Union and the Libyan Crisis', *International Politics*, 51/2: 177–95.

Fabbrini, S. and P. D. Molutsi (2012). 'Comparative Politics', in B. Badie, D. Berg-Schlosser and L. Morlino (eds.), *Encyclopedia of Political Science*, vol. II, London: Sage, pp. 342–59.

Farrell, M. (2007). 'From EU Model to External Policy? Promoting Regional Integration in the Rest of the World', in S. Meunier and K. R. McNamara (eds.), *The State of the European Union Volume 8: European Integration and Institutional Change at Fifty*, Oxford University Press, pp. 299–315.

Farrell, M. D. and R. Scully (2007). *Representing Europe's Citizens? Electoral Institutions and the Failure of Parliamentary Democracy*, Oxford University Press.

Ferrera, M. (2005). *The Boundaries of Welfare: European Integration and the New Spatial Politics of Social Protection*, Oxford University Press.

Filippov, M., P. Ordeshook and O. Shvetsova (2004). *Designing Federalism: A Theory of Self-Sustainable Federal Institutions*, Cambridge University Press.

Finer, S. E., V. Bogdanor and B. Rudden (1995). *Comparing Constitutions*, Oxford: Clarendon Press.

Fisher, L. (2007). *Constitutional Conflicts between Congress and the President*, Lawrence: University Press of Kansas, 5th edn.

Fleiner, T. (2002). 'Recent Developments of Swiss Federalism', *Publius*, 32/2: 97–124.

Fligstein, N. (2010). *Euro-Clash: The EU, European Identity, and the Future of Europe*, Oxford University Press, 2nd edn.

Follesdal, A. and S. Hix (2005). 'Why There Is a Democratic Deficit in the EU: A Response to Majone and Moravcsik', European Governance Papers no. C0502, pp. 1–27.

Forsyth, M. (1981). *Unions of States: The Theory and Practice of Confederation*, New York: Leicester University Press.

Fossum, J. E. and A. J. Menéndez (2011). *The Constitution's Gift: A Constitutional Theory for a Democratic European Union*, Lanham: Rowman and Littlefield.

Foster, N. (2010). *EU Treaties and Legislation 2010–2011*, Oxford University Press.

Gabel, M. J. (1998). 'The Endurance of Supranational Governance: A Consociational Interpretation of the European Union', *Comparative Politics* 30/4: 463–75.

Gagnon, A.G. 2010. 'Executive Federalism and the Exercise of Democracy in Canada', in M. Burgess and A.G. Gagnon (eds.), *Federal Democracies*, London: Routledge, pp. 232–50.

Gamble, A. (2007). 'Regional Blocs, World Order and the New Medievalism', in M. Telò (ed.), *European Union and the New Regionalism. Regional Actors and Global Governance in a Post-Hegemonic Era*, Aldershot: Ashgate, 2nd edn, pp. 21–32.

Garton Ash, T. (2001). 'Is Britain European?', *International Affairs* 77/1: 1–13.

(2004). *Free World: America, Europe, and the Surprising Future of the West*, New York: Random House.

(2006). 'Why Britain Is in Europe', *Twentieth Century British History* 17/4: 451–63.

Geddes, A. (2013). *The European Union and British Politics*, New York: Palgrave Macmillan, 2nd edn.

Gifford, C. (2008). *The Making of Eurosceptic Britain: Identity and Economy in a Post-Imperial State*, Aldershot: Ashgate.

Gilbert, M. (2003). *Surpassing Realism: The Politics of European Integration since 1945*, Lanham: Rowman and Littlefield.

Ginter, C. and R. Narits (2013). 'The Perspective of a Small Member State to the Democratic Deficiency of the ESM', *Review of Central and East European Law* 38: 54–76.

Glencross, A. R. (2009). *What Makes the EU Viable? European Integration in the Light of the Antebellum US Experience*, Basingstoke: Palgrave Macmillan.

(2012). 'The Uses of Ambiguity: Representing the "People" and the Stability of States Unions', *International Theory* 4/1: 107–32.

(2014a). *The Politics of European Integration*, Oxford: Wiley Blackwell.

(2014b) 'The Absence of Political Constitutionalism in the EU: Three Models for Enhancing Constitutional Agency', *Journal of European Public Policy* 21/8: 1163–80.

Glienicker Gruppe (2013). 'Towards a Euro Union', originally published in *Die Zeit* on October 17.

Goetz, K. H. and J.-H. Meyer-Sahling (2009). 'Political Time in the EU: Dimensions, Perspectives, Theories', *Journal of European Public Policy*, 16/2: 180–201.

Goetze, S. and B. Rittberger (2010). 'A Matter of Habit? The Sociological Foundations of Empowering the European Parliament', *Comparative European Politics* 8/1: 37–54.

Goulard, S. and M. Monti (2012). *De la démocratie en Europe*, Paris: Flammarion.

Grabbe, H. and S. Lehne (2013). 'The 2014 European Elections: Why a Partisan Commission President Would Be Bad for the EU', Centre for European Reform, www.cer.org.uk.

Grant, C. (2008). 'Why Is Britain Eurosceptic?, Center for European Reform Essays, December.

Greenfeld, L. (1992). *Nationalism: Five Roads to Modernity*, Harvard University Press.

Greenstone, J. D. (1993). *The Lincoln Persuasion: Remaking American Liberalism*, Princeton University Press.

Griller, S. and J. Ziller (eds.) (2008). *The Lisbon Treaty: EU Constitutionalism without a Constitutional Treaty?*, Vienna: Springer.

Grossman, E. (ed.) (2008). *France and the European Union: After the Referendum on the European Constitution*, London: Routledge.

Group Eiffel Europe (2014). *Pour une Communauté politique de l'euro*, Paris, February 14.

Growland, D., A. Turner and A. Wright (2010). *Britain and European Integration since 1945*, London: Routledge.

Guyomarch, A., H. Machin and E. Ritchie (1998). *France in the European Union*, New York: Palgrave Macmillan.

Haas, E. B. (1958). *The Uniting of Europe*, Stanford University Press.

Habermas, J. (2009). *Europe: The Faltering Project*, Cambridge: Polity.
  (2012a). *The Crisis of the European Union: A Response*, Oxford: Polity Press.
  (2012b). 'The Crisis of the European Union in the Light of a Constitutionalization of International Law', *The European Journal of International Law* 23/2: 335–48.

Haggard, S. (1997). 'Regionalism in Asia and the Americas', in E. D. Mansfield and H. V. Milner (eds.), *The Political Economy of Regionalism*, New York: Columbia University Press, pp. 20-49.

Halberstam, D. (2008). 'Constitutional Heterarchy: The Centrality of Conflict in the European Union and the United States', Public Law and Legal Theory Working Paper Series, Working Paper No. 111, University of Michigan Law School, June.

Hall, P. A. and D. Soskice (eds.) (2001). *Varieties of Capitalism: The Institutional Foundations of Comparative Advantage*, Oxford University Press.

Haller, M. (2011). *European Integration as an Elite Process: The Failure of a Dream?*, London: Routledge, 2nd edn.

Hallerberg, M., B. Marzinotto and G. B. Wolff (2012), 'An Assessment of the European Semester', European Parliament, Directorate General for Internal Policies, September.

Harbo, T.I. (2007). 'The Function of a European Basic Law: A Question of Legitimacy', ConWEB, Webpapers on Constitutionalism & Governance beyond the State No. 2.

Hayes-Renshaw, F. and H. S. Wallace (2006). *The Council of Ministers*, New York: Palgrave, 2nd edn.

Hefftler, C. and W. Wessels (2013). 'The Democratic Legitimacy of the EU's Economic Governance and National Parliaments', IAI Working Papers, No. 13, Rome, April 13.

Heipertz, M. and A. Verdun (2010). *Ruling Europe: The Politics of the Stability and Growth Pact*, Cambridge University Press.

Hemmer, C. and P. J. Katzenstein (2002). 'Why Is there No NATO in Asia? Collective Identity, Regionalism, and the Origins of Multilateralism', *International Organization* 53/3: 575–607.

Hendriks, G. and A. Morgan (2001). *The Franco-German Axis in European Integration*, Northampton, MA: Edward Elgar.

Hendrickson, D. C. (2003). *Peace Pact: The Lost World of the American Founding*, Lawrence: University Press of Kansas.

(2009). *Union, Nation, or Empire: The American Debate Over International Relations, 1789–1941*, Lawrence: University Press of Kansas.

Henning, C. R. and M. Kessler (2012). *Fiscal Federalism: US History for Architects of Europe's Fiscal Union*, Brussels: Bruegel Essay and Lectures Series.

Heritier, A. (2007). *Explaining Institutional Change in Europe*, Oxford University Press.

Heritier, A. and M. Rhodes (eds.) (2010). *New Modes of Governance in Europe: Governing in the Shadow of Hierarchy*, London: Palgrave Macmillan.

Hershey, M. R. (2012). *Party Politics in America*, Upper Saddle River: Pearson, Longman Classics, 15th edn.

Hettne, B., A. Inotai and O. Sunkel (eds.) (2002). *Globalism and the New Regionalism*, New York: Palgrave Macmillan.

Heywood, A. (2004). *Politics*, New York: Palgrave Macmillan.

Hierlemann, D. (2008). 'Lessons from the Treaty Fatigue', *Spotlight Europe*, no. 13, December.

Higgott, R. (1998). 'The Asian Economic Crisis: A Study in the Politics of Resentment', *New Political Economy* 3/3: 333–6.

(2007). 'Alternative Models of Regional Cooperation? The Limits of Regional Institutionalization in East Asia', in M. Telò (ed.), *European Union and the New Regionalism: Regional Actors and Global Governance in a Post-Hegemonic Era*, Aldershot: Ashgate, 2nd edn, pp. 75–106.

Hix, S. (2005). *The Political System of the European Union*, New York: Palgrave Macmillan, 2nd edn.

(2008a). *What's Wrong with the European Union and How to Fix It*, Cambridge: Polity.

(2008b). 'Why the EU needs (Left–Right) Politics? Policy Reform and Accountability are Impossible without it', in 'Politics: The Right or the Wrong Sort of Medicine for the EU? Two Papers by Simon Hix

and Stefano Bartolini', *Notre Europe* Policy Paper no. 19, www
.notre-europe.eu/uploads/txpublication/Policypaper19-en.pdf.

(2011). 'The EU as a New Political System', in D. Caramani
(ed.), *Comparative Politics*, Oxford University Press, 2nd edn,
pp. 429–50.

(2013). 'Why the 2014 European Elections Matter: Ten Key Votes in the
2009–2013 European Parliament', European Policy Analysis, Swedish
Institute for European Policy Studies (SIEPS).

Hix, S. and B. Hoyland (2011). *The Political System of the European Union*,
New York: Palgrave.

Hix, S. and C. Lord (1996). 'The Making of a President: The European
Parliament and the Confirmation of Jacques Santer as President of the
Commission', *Government and Opposition* 31/1: 62–76.

Hix, S., A. Noury and G. Roland (2006). *Democratic Politics in the European
Parliament*, Cambridge University Press.

Hobolt, S. B. (2009). *Europe in Question: Referendums on European
Integration*, Oxford University Press.

Hoffman, L. (2003). 'Leading the Union: An Argument in Favour of a Dual
EU Presidency', *The Federal Trust*, paper no. 15/03, April (pp. 1–6),
www.fedtrust.co.uk/filepool/15_03.pdf.

Hoffmann, S. (1966). 'Obstinate or Obsolete? The Fate of the Nation-State
and the Case of Western Europe', *Daedalus* 95/3: 862–915.

Hollande, F. (2013). 'François Hollande contre le monstre fédéral', interview
with *Sauvons l'Europe*, September 5.

Hottinger, J. T. (1997). 'La Suisse, une démocratie consociative ou de con-
cordance?', *Revue internationale de politique comparée* 4/3: 625–38.

House of Lords (2014). *'Genuine Economic and Monetary Union' and the
Implications for the UK*, European Union Committee, 8th Report of
Session 2013–14, HL Paper 134, published by the Authority of House
of Lords.

Howorth, J. (2007) *Security and Defence Policy in the European Union*,
London: Palgrave.

Huntington S. P. (1968) *Political Order in Changing Societies*, New
Haven: Yale University Press.

Hurrell, A. (1995). 'Explaining the Resurgence of Regionalism in World
Politics', *Review of International Studies* 21: 331–58.

(2001). 'The Politics of Regional Integration in Mercosur', in
V. Bulmer-Thomas (ed.), *Regional Integration in Latin America
and the Caribbean: The Political Economy of Open Regionalism*,
London: Institute of Latin American Studies.

Idema, T. and D. Kelemen (2006). 'New Modes of Governance, the Open
Method of Coordination and Other Fashionable Red Herring',
Perspectives on European Politics and Society 7/1: 108–23.

Ikenberry, J. (2001). *After Victory: Institutions, Strategic Restraints, and the Rebuilding of Order after Major Wars*, Princeton University Press.

Issing, O. (2008). *The Birth of the Euro*, Cambridge University Press.

Jabko, N. (2006). *Playing the Market: A Political Strategy for Uniting Europe, 1985–2005*, Ithaca: Cornell University Press.

Jacobs, L. and D. King (eds.) (2009). *The Unsustainable American State*, Oxford University Press.

Jeffery, C. and P. Saviger (eds.) (1991). *German Federalism Today*, Leicester University Press.

Joerges, C. (2012). 'The European Economic Constitution in Crisis: Between "State of Exception" and "Constitutional Moment"', in M. Poiares Maduro, B. de Witte and M. Kumm (eds.), *The Democratic Governance of the Euro*, RSCAS Global Governance Programme, RSCAS Policy Paper 2012/8, Florence, San Domenico di Fiesole: European University Institute, pp. 39–44.

  (forthcoming 2015). 'The European Economic Constitution and Its Transformation through the Financial Crisis', in D. Patterson and A. Sodersen (eds.), *Companion to European Union Law and International Law*, Oxford: Wiley-Blackwell.

Jones, C. O. (1995). *Separate but Equal Branches: Congress and the Presidency*, Chatham, NJ: Chatham House.

Judt, T. (2005) *Postwar: A History of Europe Since 1945*, London: Penguin Books.

Kantorowics, E. H. (1957). *The King's Two Bodies*, Princeton University Press.

Katzenstein, P. J. (2005). *A World of Regions: Asia and Europe in the American Imperium*, Ithaca, NY: Cornell University Press.

Katznelson, I. and M. Shefter (eds.) (2002). *Shaped by War and Trade: International Influences on American Political Development*, Princeton University Press.

Kelemen, R. D. (2004). *The Rules of Federalism: Institutions and Regulatory Politics in the EU and Beyond*, Cambridge, MA: Harvard University Press.

  (2007). 'Built to Last? The Durability of EU Federalism', in S. Meunier and K. McNamara (eds.), *The State of the European Union Volume 8: European Integration and Institutional Change at Fifty*, Oxford University Press, pp. 51–66.

  (2014). 'Une gouvernance fédérale: mort et résurrection', *Pouvoir* 149: 135–49.

Kernell, S. (ed.) (2003). *James Madison: The Theory and Practice of Republican Government*, Stanford University Press.

Kincaid, J. (2010). 'Democracy versus Federalism in the United States of America', in M. Burgess, and A.G. Gagnon (eds.), *Federal Democracies*, London: Routledge, pp. 121–41.

Klom, A. (2003). 'Mercosur and Brazil: A European Perspective', *International Affairs* 79/2: 351–68.

Kocharov, A. (ed.) (2012). *Another Legal Monster? An EUI Debate on the Fiscal Compact Treaty*, EUI Working Paper, Law 2012/9, Fiesole (Florence), EUI, Department of Law.

Kohler-Koch, B. and B. Rittberger (2006). 'The "Governance Turn" in EU Studies', *Journal of Common Market Studies* 44: 27–49.

(eds.) (2007). *Debating the Democratic Legitimacy of the European Union*, Lanham: Rowman and Littlefield.

Kreilinger, V. (2012). 'The Making of a New Treaty: Six Rounds of Political Bargaining', *Notre Europe* Policy Brief, no. 32, February.

(2014). 'Inter-parliamentary control in the EMU', Paper submitted at the Conference on 'What Form of Government for the European Union and the Eurozone?', Tilbur University, June 5–6.

Kreppel, A. (2002). *The European Parliament and Supranational Party System: A Study in Institutional Development*, Cambridge University Press.

(2003). 'Necessary but Not Sufficient: Understanding the Impact of Treaty Reform on the Internal Development of the European Parliament', *Journal of European Public Policy* 10/6: 884–911.

(2006). 'Understanding the European Parliament from a Federalist Perspective: The Legislatures of the United States and the European Union Compared', in A. Menon and M. Schain (eds.), *Comparative Federalism: The European Union and the United States in Comparative Perspective*, Oxford University Press, pp. 245–71.

(2011) 'Legislatures', in D. Caramani (ed.), *Comparative Politics*, Oxford University Press, 2nd edn, pp. 121–40.

Kriesi, H. and E. Grande (2012). 'The Euro-crisis: A Boost to Politicization of European Integration?', Paper delivered at the EUDO 2012 Dissemination Conference on 'The Euro Crisis and the State of European Democracy', EUI, Florence, November 22–23.

Kriesi, H. and A. H. Trechsel (2008). *The Politics of Switzerland: Continuity and Change in a Consensus Democracy*, Cambridge University Press.

Lacroix, J. (2010). 'Borderline Europe: French Visions of the European Union', in J. Lacroix and K. Nicolaidis (eds.). *European Stories: Intellectual Debates on Europe in National Context*, Oxford University Press, pp. 105–21.

Lacroix, J. and K. Nicolaidis (eds.) (2010). *European Stories: Intellectual Debates on Europe in National Context*, Oxford University Press.

Laffan, B., R. O'Donnell and M. Smith (2000). *Europe's Experimental Union: Rethinking Integration*, London: Routledge.

Lamond, A. (2013). 'The Eurozone's Path to a Federalist Future', The Federal Trust for Education and Research, September.

Lane, J., D. McKay and K. Newton (1997). *Political Data Handbook: OECD Countries*, Oxford University Press.

Lassalle, D. and N. Levrat (2004). 'Un triangle à quatre cotés: L'équilibre institutionnel et le Conseil Européen', *Journal of European Integration* 26/4: 431–50.

Laursen, F. (ed.) (2010). *Comparative Regional Integration: Europe and Beyond*, Burlington: Ashgate.

(2012). 'The Treaty of Maastricht', in E. Jones, A. Menon and S. Weatherill (eds.), *The Oxford Handbook of the European Union*, Oxford University Press, pp. 121–34.

Laursen, F. and S. Vanhoonacker (eds.) (1992). *The Intergovernmental Conference on Political Union: Institutional Reforms, New Policies and International Identity of the European Community*, Maastricht: European Institute of Public Administration.

Laver, M. *et al.* (1995). *Electing the President of the European Commission*, Trinity Blue Papers in Public Policy: 1, Trinity College, Dublin.

Lawson, F. H. (ed.) (2009). *Comparative Regionalism*, Burlington: Ashgate.

Legrain, P. (2014). 'Euro-Zone Fiscal Colonialism', *The New York Times*, op-ed page, April 21.

Lehmann, W. and S. Schunz (2005). 'Anticipating the European Constitution: Parliamentarization or Renationalization?' Online, Archive of European Integration.

Leino, P. and J. Salminen (2012). 'Should the Economic and Monetary Union Be Democratic after All? Some Reflections on the Current Crisis', *German Law Journal* 14/7: 844–68.

Leonardi, R. (2005). *Cohesion Policy in the European Union: The Building of Europe*, New York: Palgrave Macmillan.

Leonardy, U. (2010). 'Is the European Federation a "Mission Impossible"? A Critical Analysis of the German Constitutional Court's Judgment on the Lisbon Treaty', Discussion Paper C201, Center for European Integration Studies, University of Bonn.

Lequesne, C. (2012). 'Old Versus New', in E. Jones, A. Menon and S. Weatherill (eds.), *The Oxford Handbook of the European Union*, Oxford University Press, pp. 267–77.

Leuffen, D. (2013) 'European Union as a Blueprint? Nine Hypotheses on Differentiated Integration in a Comparative Perspective', University of Bonn, WAI-ZEI Paper No. 8.

Leuffen, D., B. Rittberger and F. Schimmelfennig (2013). *Differentiated Integration: Explaining Variation in the European Union*, New York: Palgrave Macmillan.

Lijphart, A. (1984). *Democracies: Patterns of Majoritarian and Consensus Government in Twenty-One Countries*, New Haven: Yale University Press.

(1992). 'Introduction', in A. Lijphart (ed.), *Parliamentary Versus Presidential Government*, Oxford University Press, pp. 1–27.

(1989). 'Democratic Political Systems: Types, Causes and Consequences', *Journal of Theoretical Politics* 1/1: 33–48.

(1999). *Patterns of Democracy*, New Haven: Yale University Press.

(2008). *Thinking about Democracy: Power-Sharing and Majority Rule in Theory and Practice*. London: Routledge.

Lindberg, L. N. (1963). *The Political Dynamics of European Economic Integration*, Stanford University Press.

Lindseth, P. (2014), 'Reconciling Europe and National Parliaments: Reflections on Technocracy, Democracy, and Post-Crisis Integration', University of Connecticut School of Law Working Papers.

Loewenberg, G. and S. C. Patterson (1988). *Comparing Legislatures*, New York: University Press of America, 2nd edition.

Longo, M. (2006). *Constitutionalizing Europe: Processes and Practices*, Aldershot: Ashgate.

Lord, C. (2003). 'The European Parliament: Not a Very European Parliament?', *Politique Européenne* 9: 30–48.

(2011a). 'The Political Theory and Practice of Parliamentary Participation in the Common Security and Defence Policy', *Journal of European Public Policy* 18/8: 1133–50.

(2011b). 'Polecats, Lions, and Foxes: Coasian Bargaining Theory and Attempts to Legitimize the Union as a Constrained Form of Political Power', *European Political Science Review* 3/1: 83–102.

Lord, C. and J. Pollack (2013). 'Unequal but Democratic? Equality According to Karlsruhe', *Journal of European Public Policy* 20/2: 190–205.

Lowi T. J. (1985). *The Personal President: Power Invested, Promise Unfulfilled*, Ithaca, NY: Cornell University Press.

Ludlow, P. (2011a) 'The European Council and the Media: Some Preliminary Reflections Prompted by the March European Council', *EuroComment*, April 5.

(2011b) 'The Meeting of the Euro Area Heads of State and Government on 21 July: Preliminary Evaluation', *EuroComment*, July 26.

Ludlow, N. P. (2012). 'Problematic Partners: de Gaulle, Thatcher and their Impact', in E. Jones, A. Menon and S. Weatherill (eds.), *The Oxford Handbook of the European Union*, Oxford University Press, pp. 206–18.

Lyons, G. M. and M. Mastanduno (1995). 'Introduction: International Intervention, State Sovereignty, and the Future of International Society', in G. M. Lyons and M. Mastanduno (eds.), *Beyond Westphalia? State Sovereignty and International Intervention*, Baltimore: The Johns Hopkins University Press, pp. 1–18.

McCormick, J. (1999). *The European Union*, Boulder: Westview Press.

MacCormick, N. D. (1996). 'Liberalism, Nationalism and Post-Sovereign State', in R. Bellamy and D. Castiglione (eds.), *Constitutionalism in Transformation: European and Theoretical Perspective*, Oxford: Blackwell, pp. 141–55.

McKay, D. (2001). *Designing Europe: Comparative Lessons from the Federal Experience*, Oxford University Press.

McTernan, M. (ed.) (2012). 'The Future of Economic Governance in the EU: Where Does This Leave Britain?', *Policy Network*, March.

Madeira, M. A. and J. A. Caporaso (2011). 'Regional Integration (Supranational)', in B. Badie, D. Berg-Schlosser and L. Morlino (eds.), *Encyclopedia of Political Science*, London: Sage, pp. 2239–44.

Maduro, M. P. (2003). 'Europe and the Constitution: What If this Is as Good as It Gets?', in M. Wind and J. H. H. Weiler (eds.), *Constitutionalism Beyond the State*, Cambridge University Press, pp. 74–102.

(2012). 'A New Governance for the European Union and the Euro: Democracy and Justice', Report, European Parliament, Directorate General for Internal Policies.

Magnette, P. and K. Nicolaidis (2004). 'Coping with the Lilliput Syndrom: Large vs. Small Member States in the European Convention', *Politique Européenne* 14: 1–25.

Magnette, P. and Y. Papadopoulos (2008). 'On the Politicization of the European Consociation: A Middle Way between Hix and Bartolini', European Governance Papers No. C–08–01.

Mahoney, J. and C. M. Villegas (2007). 'Historical Enquiry and Comparative Politics', in C. Box and S. C. Stokes (eds.), *The Oxford Handbook of Comparative Politics*, Oxford University Press, pp. 73–88.

Majone, G. (2009). *Europe as the Would-Be World Power*, Cambridge University Press.

(2014).*Rethinking the Union of Europe Post-Crisis: Has Integration Gone Too Far?*, Cambridge University Press.

Malamud, A. (2003). 'Presidentialism and Mercosur: A Hidden Cause for a Successful Experience', in F. Laursen (ed.), *Comparative Regional Integration: Theoretical Perspectives*, London: Ashgate, pp. 53–73.

(2005). 'Presidential Diplomacy and the Institutional Underpinnings of Mercosur. An Empirical Examination', *Latin American Research Review* 40/1: 138–64.

(2013). 'Overlapping Regionalism, No Integration: Conceptual Issues and the Latin American Experiences', EUI Working Papers, Fiesole (Florence), European University Institute, Robert Schuman Center for Advanced Studies, RSCAS 2013/20.

Malamud, A. and P. C. Schmitter (2010), 'The Experience of European Integration and the Potential for Integration in South America', in

N. Robinson, B. Rosamand and A. Warleigh-Lack (eds.), *New Regionalism and the European Union*, London: Routledge.

Mancini, G. F. (1998). 'Europe: The Case for Statehood', *European Law Journal* 4/1: 29–43.

Mann, T. E. and N. J. Ornstein (2012). *It's Even Worse than It Looks: How the American Constitutional System Collided with the New Politics of Extremism*, New York: Basic Books.

Manners, J. (2002). 'Normative Power Europe: A Contradiction in Terms?', *Journal of Common Market Studies* 40/2: 235–58.

Mansfield, E. and H. Milner (2000). 'The New Wave of Regionalism', *International Organization* 53/3: 589–627.

Marquand, D. (1979). *A Parliament for Europe*, London: Jonathan Cape.

Martin, A. and G. Ross (eds.) (2004). *Euro and Europeans: Monetary Integration and the European Model of Society*, Cambridge University Press.

Martinelli, A. (2008). *Transatlantic Divide: Comparing American and European Society*, Oxford University Press.

Mazzoleni, O. and H. Rayner (2008). 'Une coalition gouvernementale durable. Emergence, institutionalization et crise de la "formule magique" en Suisse (1959–2003)', Political Science Working Papers, Centre de Recherche sur l'Action Politique de l'Université de Lausanne, No. 39.

Mechan, M. (2003). 'Mercosur: A Failing Development Project?', *International Affairs* 79/2: 369–87.

Menéndez, A. J. (2004). 'Three Conceptions of the European Constitution', in E. O. Eriksen, J. E. Fossum and A. J. Menéndez (eds.), *Developing a Constitution for Europe*, London: Routledge, pp. 109–28.

    (2013). 'The Existential Crisis of the European Union', *German Law Journal* 14/5: 453–526.

A. Menon and M. Schain (eds.) (2006), *Comparative Federalism: The European Union and the United States in Comparative Perspective*, Oxford University Press.

Mény, Y. and Y. Surel (2002). *Democracies and the Populist Challenge*, London: Palgrave.

Milner, H. (1998). 'Regional Economic Co-operation, Global Markets and Domestic Politics: A Comparison of NAFTA and the Maastricht Treaty', in W. Coleman and G. Underhill (eds.), *Regionalism and Global Economic Integration*, London: Routledge.

Milward A. S. (2000). *The European Rescue of the Nation-State*, London: Routledge, 2nd edn.

Missiroli, A. (2010). 'The New EU "Foreign Policy" System after Lisbon: A Work in Progress', *European Foreign Affairs Review* 15/4: 427–52.

Monnet, J. (1978). *Memoirs: The Architect and Master Builder of the European Economic Community*, New York: Doubleday and Company.

Moravcsik, A. (1998). *The Choice for Europe: Social Purpose and State Power from Messina to Maastricht*, Ithaca, NY: Cornell University Press.

(ed.) (2005). *Europe without Illusion*, Lanham: University Press of America.

Moravcsik, A. and F. Schimmelfennig (2009). 'Liberal Intergovernmentalism', in A. Weiner, and T. Diez (eds.), *European Integration Theory*, Oxford University Press, 2nd edn.

Morgan, G. (2005). *The Idea of a European Superstate: Public Justification and European Integration*, Princeton University Press.

Morlino, L. (2012). *Changes for Democracy: Actors, Structures, Processes*, Oxford University Press.

Moury, C. (2007). 'Explaining the European Parliament's Right to Appoint and Invest the Commission', *West European Politics* 30/2: 367–91.

Muhlbok, M. (2013). 'Linking Council and European Parliament? Voting Unity of National Parties in Bicameral EU Decision-making', *Journal of European Public Policy* 20/4: 571–88.

Muller, J.-W. (2010). 'In the Shadow of Statism: Peculiarities of the German Debate on European Integration', in J. Lacroix and K. Nicolaidis (eds.), *European Stories: Intellectual Debates on Europe in National Context*, Oxford University Press, pp. 87–104.

Nanto, D. (2002). *Asia Pacific Economic Cooperation (APEC), Free Trade and the 2002 Summit in Mexico*, Report for Congress, Congressional Research Service, Washington DC: The Library of Congress, pp. 1–20.

Naurin, D. and H. Wallace (eds.) (2008). *Unveiling the Council of the European Union: Games Governments Play in Brussels*, New York: Palgrave Macmillan.

Neustadt, R. E. (1990). *Presidential Power and the Modern President: The Politics of Leadership from Roosevelt to Reagan*, New York: The Free Press, 3rd edn.

Nicolaidis, K. (2003). 'The New Constitution as European Demoi-cracy?', *The Federal Trust*, December.

(2011). 'Germany as Europe: How the Constitutional Court Unwittingly Embraced EU Demoi-cracy', *International Journal of Constitutional Law* 9/3–4: 986–92.

(2013). 'European Demoicracy and Its Crisis', *Journal of Common Market Studies* 51/2: 351–69.

Nicolaidis, K. and R. Howse (eds.) (2001). *The Federal Vision: Legitimacy and Levels of Governance in the United States and the European Union*, Oxford University Press.

Norman, P. (2003). *The Accidental Constitution: The Story of the European Convention*, Brussels: Eurocomment.

Norton, P. (ed.) (1998). *Parliaments in Contemporary Western Europe*, London: Routledge.

Offe, C. and U. K. Preuss (2006). 'The Problem of Legitimacy in the European Polity: Is Democratization the Answer?', ConWEB, Webpapers on Constitutionalism & Governance beyond the State, No. 6.

Olsen, J. P. (2007). *Europe in Search of Political Order*, Oxford University Press.

O'Neil, M. (2008). *The Struggle for the European Constitution: A Past and Future History*, London: Routledge.

Onuf, P. and N. Onuf (1994). *Federal Union, Modern World: The Law of Nation in an Age of Revolution, 1776–1814*, Madison: Madison House Publishers.

Orbie, J. (2009). 'A Civilian Power in the World? Instruments and Objectives in European Union External Policies', in J. Orbie (ed.), *Europe's Global Role: External Policies of the European Union*, London: Ashgate.

Ostrom, V. (1987). *The Political Theory of a Compound Republic: Designing the American Experiment*, Lincoln, NE: University of Nebraska Press, 2nd revised edn.

Ottaviano, G. *et al.* (2014). '*Brexit or Fixit? The Trade and Welfare Effects of Leaving the European Union*', Centre for Economic Performance, London School of Economics (LSE), London, May.

Owen, D. (2011). 'Working Together: A Euro Group and a Non-Euro Group', proposal presented at the Nordic-Baltic Ambassadors Lunch, November 16.

Padoa-Schioppa, T. (2001). *Europa forza gentile: Cosa ci ha insegnato l'avventura europea*, Bologna, Il Mulino.

Page, E. C. (1997). *People Who Run Europe*, Oxford University Press.

Parent, J. M. (2011). *Uniting States: Voluntary Unions in World Politics*, Oxford University Press.

Parsons, C. (2003). *A Certain Idea of Europe*, Ithaca, NY: Cornell University Press.

Pederson, T. (1998). *Germany, France and the Integration of Europe: A Realist Interpretation*, London: Pinter.

Pennock, J. R. and J. W. Chapman (eds.) (1979). *Constitutionalism: Nomos XX*, New York University Press.

Pernice, I. (2008–2009). 'The Treaty of Lisbon: Multilevel Constitutionalism in Action', *Columbia Journal of European Law* 15/3: 349–408.

Peters, B. G. (2013). *Strategies for Comparative Research in Political Science: Theory and Methods*, New York: Palgrave Macmillan.

Piattoni, S. (2010). *The Theory of Multi-Level Governance: Conceptual, Empirical, and Normative Challenges*, Oxford University Press.

Pierson, P. (2004). *Politics in Time: History, Institutions and Social Analysis*, Princeton University Press.

Pierson, P. and S. Skocpol (2002). 'Historical Institutionalism in Contemporary Political Science', in I. Katznelson and H. V. Milner (eds.), *Political Science: State of the Discipline*, New York: W. W. Norton, pp. 693–721.

Piris, J.C. (2010). *The Lisbon Treaty: A Legal and Political Analysis*, Cambridge University Press.

  (2012). *The Future of Europe: Towards a Two-Speed EU?*, Cambridge University Press.

Pitkin, H. (1972). *The Concept of Representation*, Berkeley: University of California Press.

Polsby N. W. (1968). 'The Institutionalization of the U.S. House of Representatives', *American Political Science Review* 62/1: 144–68.

  (1983). *The Consequences of Party Reform*, Oxford University Press.

  (1986). *Congress and the Presidency*, Upper Saddle, NJ: Prentice Hall, 4th edition.

  (1997). 'Constitutional Angst: Does American Democracy Work?', in A. Brinkley, N. W. Polsby and K. M. Sullivan, *New Federalist Papers: Essays in Defense of the Constitution*, New York: W. W. Norton & Company, pp. 159–79.

  (2004). *How Congress Evolves: Social Basis of Institutional Change*, Oxford University Press.

  (2008). 'The Political System', in P. H. Schuck and J. Q. Wilson (eds.), *Understanding America: The Anatomy of an Exceptional Nation*, New York: Public Affairs, pp. 3–26.

Polsby, N. W., A. Wildavsky and D. A. Hopkins (2007). *Presidential Elections: Strategies and Structures of American Politics*, New York: Seven Bridge Press, 12th edn.

Ponzano, P., C. Hermanin and D. Corona (2012). 'The Power of Initiative of the European Commission: A Progressive Erosion?', *Notre Europe Studies and Research no. 89*.

Preuss, U. K. (1996). 'The Political Meaning of Constitutionalism', in R. Bellamy (ed.), *Constitutionalism, Democracy and Sovereignty: American and European Perspectives*, Aldershot: Avebury, pp. 11–27.

Prodi, R. (2008). *La mia versione dei fatti. Cinque anni di governo in Europa*, Bologna: Il Mulino.

Puetter, U. (2006). *The Eurogroup: How a Secretive Circle of Finance Ministers Shape European Economic Governance*, Manchester University Press.

  (2012). 'Europe's Deliberative Intergovernmentalism: The Role of the Council and European Council in EU Economic Governance', *Journal of European Public Policy* 19/2: 161–78.

(2013) 'The European Council: The New Centre of EU Politics', European Policy Analysis Paper, SIEPS, issue 2013:16 epa, October.

Ravenhill, J. (2001). *APEC and the Construction of Asia-Pacific Regionalism*, Cambridge University Press.

Reichley, A. J. (1992). *The Life of the Parties: A History of American Political Parties*, New York: Free Press.

Ricard-Nihoul, G. (2012). 'For a European Federation of Nation States: Jacques Delors's Vision Revisited, *Notre Europe*, April 17.

Riggs, F. W. (1988). 'The Survival of Presidentialism in America: Para-Constitutional Practices', *International Political Science Review* 9/4: 247–78.

Risse, T. (2010). *A Community of Europeans? Transnational Identities and Public Spheres*, Ithaca, NY: Cornell University Press.

Rittberger, B. (2003). 'The Creation and Empowerment of the European Parliament', *Journal of Common Market Studies* 41/2: 203–26.

(2005). *Building Europe's Parliament: Democratic Representation beyond the Nation-State*, Oxford University Press.

Rittberger, B. and F. Schimmelfennig (eds.) (2007). *The Constitutionalization of the European Union*, London: Routledge.

Rockman, B. A. (1984). *The Leadership Question: The Presidency and the American System*, New York: Palgrave.

Rodden, J. A. (2006). *Hamilton's Paradox: The Promise and Peril of Fiscal Federalism*, Cambridge University Press.

Rokkan, S. (1999). *State Formation, Nation-Building and Mass Politics in Europe: The Theory of Stein Rokkan*, edited by P. Flora, S. Kuhnle and D. Urwin, Oxford University Press.

Roy, J. and R. Dominguez (eds.) (2005). *The European Union and Regional Integration: A Comparative Perspective and Lessons for the Americas*, University of Miami, Jean Monnet Center.

Sandholtz, W. and A. Stone Sweet (eds.) (1998). *European Integration and Supranational Governance*, Oxford University Press.

Sartori, G. (1976). *Parties and Party Systems: A Framework for Analysis*, Cambridge University Press, new edition in 2005.

(1994). *Comparative Constitutional Engineering: An Inquiry into Structure, Incentives and Outcomes*, New York University Press.

Sbragia, A. M. (1992). 'Thinking About the European Future: The Uses of Comparison', in A. M. Sbragia (ed.), *Euro-Politics: Institutions and Policy-Making in the new 'European' Community*, Washington DC: Brookings Institution Press, pp. 257–91.

(1994). 'From "Nation-State" to "Member State": The Evolution of the European Community', in P. M. Lutzeler (ed.), *Europe after Maastricht: American and European Perspectives*, Oxford: Berghahn Books, pp. 69–87.

(1996). *Debt Wish: Entrepreneurial Cities, U.S. Federalism, and Economic Development*, University of Pittsburgh Press.

(2007). 'European Union and NAFTA', in M. Telò (ed.), *European Union and the New Regionalism: Regional Actors and Global Governance in a Post-Hegemonic Era*, Aldershot: Ashgate, 2nd edn, pp. 153–64.

et al. (2006). 'Symposium: The EU and Its "Constitution"', *PS: Political Science and Politics* 39/2: 237–72.

Scharpf, F. (2009a). 'The Asymmetry of European Integration or Why the EU Cannot Be a "Social Market Economy"', KFG Working Paper Series, Freie Universität Berlin.

(2009b). 'Legitimacy in the Multilevel European Polity', *European Political Science Review* 1/2: 173–204.

(2013). 'Monetary Union, Fiscal Crisis and the Disabling of Democratic Accountability', in A. Schäfer and W. Streeck (eds.), *Politics in the Age of Austerity*, Cambridge: Polity Press, pp. 108–42.

Schelkle, W. (2012). 'Rich Versus Poor', in E. Jones, A. Menon and S. Weatherill (eds.), *The Oxford Handbook of the European Union*, Oxford University Press, pp. 278–91.

Schild, J. (2010). 'Mission Impossible? The Potential for Franco-German Leadership in the Enlarged EU', *Journal of Common Market Studies* 48/5: 1367–90.

Schmidt, M. (2003). *Political Institutions in the Federal Republic of Germany*, Oxford University Press.

Schmidt, V. A. (2002). *The Futures of European Capitalism*, Oxford University Press.

(2006). *Democracy in Europe: The EU and National Polities*, Oxford University Press.

(2008). 'Trapped by Their Ideas: French Elites' Discourses of European Integration and Globalization', in E. Grossman (ed.), *France and the European Union: After the Referendum on the European Constitution*, London: Routledge, pp. 1–18.

(2010). 'The European Union's Eurozone Crisis and What (Not) To Do about It', *Brown Journal of World Affairs* 10/1: 199–214.

(2012). 'Democracy and Legitimacy in the European Union', in E. Jones, A. Menon and S. Weatherill (eds.), *The Oxford Handbook of the European Union*, Oxford University Press, pp. 661–75.

Schmitt, H. (2010). *European Parliament Elections after Eastern Enlargement*, London: Routledge.

Schnapper, P. (2012). 'Quel avenir pour le Royaume-Uni dans l'Union européenne?', Policy Paper No. 254, Fondation Robert Schuman, October 8.

Schutze, R. (2010). *From Dual to Cooperative Federalism*, Oxford University Press.

(2012). 'Federalism as Constitutional Pluralism: "Letter from America"', in M. Avbeij and J. Komareck (eds.), *Constitutional Pluralism in the European Union and Beyond*, Oxford: Hart Publishing, pp. 185–212.

Schwarz, A. O. and A. Z. Huq (2008). *Unchecked and Unbalanced: Presidential Power in a Time of Terror*, New York: The New Press, 2nd edn.

Sciarini, P. and D. Bochsler (2006). 'Reform du Federalisme Suisse: contribution, promesses et limites de la collaboration intercantonale', in J. Chappelet (ed.), *Contributions à l'action publique*, Lausanne: Presses Polytechniques et Universitaries Romandes, pp. 267–85.

Settembri, P. and C. Neuhold (2009). 'Achieving Consensus through Committees: Does the European Parliament Manage?', *Journal of Common Market Studies* 47/1: 127–51.

Shaw, J. (2005). 'What Happens If the Constitutional Treaty Is Not Ratified?', in I. Pernice and J. Zemaneck (ed.), *The Treaty on a Constitution for Europe: Perspective after the IGC*, Baden-Baden: NOMOS.

Shackleton, M. (2005). 'Parliamentary Government or Division of Powers: Is the Destination Still Unknown', in N. Jabko and C. Parsons (eds.), *The State of the European Union: Volume 7: With US or Against US? European Trends in American Perspective*, Oxford University Press, pp. 123–41.

Shapiro, M. (2002). 'The Success of Judicial Review and Democracy', in M. Shapiro and A. Stone Sweet, *On Law, Politics and Judicialization*, Oxford University Press, pp. 149–83.

Shugart, M. S. (2006). 'Comparing Executive-Legislative Relations', in R.A.W. Rhodes, S.A. Binder and B.A. Rockman (eds.), *The Oxford Handbook of Political Institutions*, Oxford University Press, pp. 344–65.

Sjursen, H. (2011). 'The EU's Common Foreign and Security Policy: The Quest for Democracy', *Journal of European Public Policy* 18/8: 1069–77.

Skowroneck, S. (1982). *Building a New American State: The Expansion of National Administration Capacities, 1877–1920*, Cambridge University Press.

Slaughter, A.M. (2004). *A New World Order*, Princeton University Press.
  (2007). *The Idea that Is America: Keeping Faith with Our Values in a Dangerous World*, New York: Basic Books.

Sloam, J. (2005). *The European Policy of the German Social Democrats* (New York: Palgrave Macmillan).

Smith, A. D. (1991). *National Identity*, Reno: University of Nevada Press.

Smith, D. E. (1993). 'Representation and Policy Formation: The Canadian Provinces', in D. M. Olson and C. E. S. Franks (eds.), *Canada and the United States: Representation and Policy Formation in Federal*

Systems, Berkeley: Institute of Governmental Studies Press, University of California, pp. 131–75.

(2010). *Federalism and the Constitution of Canada*, Toronto University Press.

Snyder, F. (2003). 'The Unfinished Constitution of the European Union: Principles, Processes and Culture', in J. H. H. Weiler and M. Wind (eds.), *European Constitutionalism Beyond the State*, Cambridge University Press, pp. 55–73.

Somek, A. (2013) 'What Is a Political Union?', *German Law Journal* 14(5): 561–80.

Spinelli Group and Bertelsmann Stiftung (2013). *A Fundamental Law of the European Union*, Bielefeld: Verlag Bertelsmann Stiftung.

Spruyt, H. (1994). *The Sovereign State and Its Competitors*, Princeton University Press.

Stein, R. (2000). *Thoughts from a Bridge: A Retrospective of Writings on New Europe and American Federalism*, Ann Arbor: The University of Michigan Press.

Stetter, S. (2007). *EU Foreign and Interior Policies: Cross-pillar Politics and the Social Construction of Sovereignty*, London: Routledge.

Steuenberg, B. and J. Thomassen (2002). *The European Parliament: Moving Towards Democracy in the EU*, Lanham: Rowman and Littlefield.

Stone Sweet, A. (2000). *Governing with Judges: Constitutional Politics in Europe*, Oxford University Press.

(2005). 'The Constitutionalization of the EU: Steps Towards a Supranational Polity', in S. Fabbrini (ed.), *Democracy and Federalism in the European Union and the United States: Exploring Post-National Governance*, London: Routledge, pp. 44–56.

Stone Sweet A., W. Sandholtz and N. Fligstein (eds.) (2001). *The Institutionalization of Europe*, Oxford University Press.

Super, D. A. (2005). 'Rethinking Fiscal Federalism', *Harvard Law Review* 118: 2544–652.

Swender, W. and M. Brans (2006). 'The Hyphenated State, Multi-level Governance and the Communities in Belgium: The Case of Brussels', in M. Burgess and H. Vollard (eds.), *State Territoriality and European Integration*, London: Routledge, pp. 120–44.

Taggart, P. (2006). 'The Domestic Politics of the 2005 French and Dutch Referendums and Their Challenge for the Study of European Integration', *Journal of Common Market Studies* 44: 7–25, Annual Review.

Tallberg, J. (2006). *Leadership and Negotiation in the European Union*, Cambridge University Press.

Taverne, D. (2012). 'The mechanics of Britain's marginalisation', in *The Future of Economic Governance in the EU and Where Does This Leave Britain?*, Report of the Policy Network, pp. 28–9.

Telò, M. (ed.). (2007). *European Union and the New Regionalism: Regional Actors and Global Governance in a Post-Hegemonic Era*, Aldershot: Ashgate.

  (ed.). (2009), *The European Union and Global Governance*, London: Routledge.

Thym, D. (2011). 'The Intergovernmental Constitution of the EU's Foreign, Security and Defence Executive', *European Constitutional Law Review* 7: 453–80.

Tilly, C. (ed.) (1975). *The Formation of National States in Western Europe*, Princeton University Press.

Torfing, J., B. G. Peters, J. Pierre and E. Sorensen (2012). *Interactive Governance: Advancing the Paradigm*, Oxford University Press.

Tortola, P. D. (2014). 'The Limits of Normalization: Tacking Stock of the EU–US Comparative Literature', *Journal of Common Market Studies* forthcoming.

Tosato, G. (2014). 'The Governance of the Banking Sector in the EU: A Dual System', *Rassegna Astrid* 13 (July).

Trondal, J. (2010). *An Emergent European Executive Order*, Oxford University Press.

Trubek, D. M. and L. G. Trubek (2007). 'New Governance and Legal Regulation: Complementarity, Rivalry, and Transformation', *Columbia Journal of European Law* 13/3: 539–64.

Tsebelis, G. and G. Garrett (2001). 'The Institutional Determinants of Intergovernmentalism and Supranationalism in the European Union', *International Organization* 55/2: 357–90.

Tuori, K. and K. Tuori (2014). *The Eurozone Crisis: A Constitutional Analysis*, Cambridge University Press.

Umbach, M. (ed.) (2002). *German Federalism: Past, Present, Future*, New York: Palgrave Macmillan.

Van de Steeg, M. (2009). 'Public Accountability in the European Union: Is the European Parliament Able to Hold the European Council Accountable?', European Integration online Papers, 13/3.

Van Middelaar, L. (2013). *The Passage to Europe: How a Continent Became a Union*, New Haven: Yale University Press.

Vanke, J. (2006). 'Charles de Gaulle's Uncertain Idea of Europe', in D. Dinan (ed.), *Origins and Evolution of the European Union*, Oxford University Press, pp. 141–65.

Vasconcelos, A. (2007). 'European Union and Mercosur', in M. Telò (ed.), *European Union and the New Regionalism: Regional Actors and*

Global Governance in a Post-Hegemonic Era, Aldershot: Ashgate, 2nd edn, pp. 165–83.

Vatter, A. (2008). 'Swiss Consensus Democracy in Transition: A Re-analysis of Lijphart's Concept of Democracy for Switzerland from 1997 to 2007', *World Political Science Review* 4/2 (online).

Verhofstadt, G. (2006). *The United States of Europe*, London: Federal Trust.

Vile, M. J. C. (1967). *Constitutionalism and Separation of Powers*, Oxford: Clarendon Press.

Von Hagen, J. and B. Eichengreen (1996). 'Federalism, Fiscal Restraints, and European Monetary Union', *The American Economic Review* 86/2: 134–8.

Walker, N. (2004). 'The EU as a Constitutional Project', *The Federal Trust*, paper, 19/04, www.sv.uio.no/arena/english/research/projects/cidel/old/WorkshopLondon/Walker.pdf.

  (2007). 'After finalité? The Future of the European Constitutional Idea', Fiesole (Florence), EUI, Department of Law, *mimeo*.

Wallace, H. and W. Wallace (2007). 'Overview: The European Union, Politics and Policy-Making', in E. J. Knud, M. A. Pollack and B. Rosamond (eds.), *Handbook of European Union Politics*, London: Sage, pp. 339–58.

Warlouzet, L. (2011). 'De Gaulle as a Father of Europe: The Unpredictability of the FTA's Failure and the EEC's Success (1956–58)', *Contemporary European History* 20/4: 419–34.

Watts, R. L. (1998). 'Federalism, Federal Political Systems, and Federations', *Annual Review of Political Science* 1: 117–37.

Webber, D. (ed.) (1999). *The Franco-German Relationship in the European Union*, London: Routledge.

Weiler, J. H. H. (1999). *The Constitution of Europe*, Cambridge University Press.

  (2000). 'Federalism and Constitutionalism: Europe's Sonderweg', Harvard Law School, Jean Monnet Chair Working Papers, http://ftp.infoeuropa.eurocid.pt/files/database/000036001-000037000/000036583.pdf.

Westlake, M. (1998). 'The European Parliament's Emerging Powers of Appointment', *Journal of Common Market Studies* 36/3: 431–44.

Wiebe, R. H (1995). *Self-Rule: A Cultural History of American Democracy*, The University of Chicago Press.

Wiener, A. (2008). *The Invisible Constitution of Politics: Contested Norms and International Encounters*, Cambridge University Press.

Wildavsky, A. (1988). *The New Politics of the Budgetary Process*, Glenview: Scott, Foresman and Company.

Wills, G. (1978). *Inventing America: Jefferson Declaration of Independence*, New York: Vintage Books.

Wilson, W. (1956). *Congressional Government: A Study in American Politics*, Baltimore: Johns Hopkins University Press (original edition 1885).

Wolf, L. and A. Vatter (2001). 'Institutions and Outcomes of Swiss Federalism: The Role of the Cantons in Swiss Politics', *West European Politics* 24/2: 95–122.

Yamazawa, I. and A. Hirata (eds.) (1996). *APEC: Cooperation From Diversity*, Tokyo: Institute of Developing Economies.

Young, B. (2012). 'The German Debates on European Austerity Programs: The Ideas of Ordoliberalism Against the Rest of the World', *mimeo*.

Ziblatt, D. (2006) *Structuring the State: The Formation of Italy and Germany and the Puzzle of Federalism*, Princeton University Press.

Zielonka, J. (2006). *Europe as Empire: The Nature of the Enlarged European Union*, Oxford University Press.

Ziller, J. (2009). 'The Constitutionalization of the European Union: A Comparative Perspective', *Loyola Law Review* 45: 413–47.

Zweifel T. D. (2002). *Democratic Deficit? Institutions and Regulation in the European Union, Switzerland and the United States*, Lanham: Lexington Books.

Index

Lightning Source UK Ltd
Milton Keynes UK
UKOW06f2238081215

9 781107 503977